Pearson Edexcel GCSE (9–1)

Mathematics

Purposeful Practice Book

Higher

◆ **Skills practice** ◆ **Problem-solving practice** ◆ **Exam practice**

Series Editors:

Dr Naomi Norman

Katherine Pate

PEARSON

Published by Pearson Education Limited, 80 Strand, London, WC2R 0RL.

www.pearsonschoolsandfecolleges.co.uk

Text © Pearson Education Limited 2019
Edited by Haremi Ltd.
Typeset by York Publishing Solutions Pvt. Ltd., India
Cover design by Pearson Education Limited 2018
Cover photo/illustration © Sahua D/Shutterstock and Ozz Design/Shutterstock

The rights of Peter Hall, Mark Heslop, Caroline Locke, Martin Noon, Diane Oliver, Dr Naomi Norman and Katherine Pate to be identified as authors of this work has been asserted by them in accordance with the Copyright, Designs and Patents Act 1988.

First published 2019

22 21 20
10 9 8 7 6 5 4 3

British Library Cataloguing in Publication Data
A catalogue record for this book is available from the British Library

ISBN 978 1 292 27370 9

Printed in Italy by LEGO S.p.A

Acknowledgements
Pearson Education: Adapted from 1MA1/2H, June 2018, November 2017, Specimen Papers, June 2017, May 2018, November 2016, Spring 2017, Autumn 2017, 2, 3, 4, 5, 6, 7, 8, 9, 10, 12, 13, 15, 16, 17, 18, 19, 20, 22, 23, 25, 26, 27, 28, 30, 35, 40, Mixed exercises A, Mixed exercises B, Mixed exercises C, Mixed exercises D, Mixed exercises E; Pearson Education: Adapted from 1MA1/1H, Specimen Papers, November 2017, June 2018, June 2017, May 2018, May 2017, 3, 4, 5, 6, 7, 8, 9, 11, 12, 13, 15, 16, 18, 19, 22, 23, 26, 30, 166,263, Mixed exercises A, Mixed exercises C, Mixed exercises D, Mixed exercises E; Pearson Education: Adapted from 1MA1/3H, May 2018, June 2018, Specimen Papers, June 2017, November 2017, Autumn 2017, 3, 4, 5, 6, 7, 8, 9, 10, 11, 12, 13, 14, 15, 16, 17, 18, 21, 22, 23, 31, Mixed exercises A, Mixed exercises B, Mixed exercises C, Mixed exercises D, Mixed exercises E; Pearson Education: Adapted from 1MA0/1H,June 2016, May 2016, November 2015, 12, 15, 28, 31; Pearson Education: Adapted from 1MA0/2H June 2015, June 2014, Specimen Papers, November 2013, 3, 4, 19; Pearson Education: Adapted from MA1/1H, Specimen Papers, 10; Pearson Education: Edexcel GCSE (9-1) Mathematics: Foundation Student Book, Pearson Education Limited (February 3, 2015), 1, 2, 3, 4, 5, 6, 7, 10, 11, 14, 15, 17, 18, 19, 23, 24, 25, 26, 29, 30, 31, 32, 36, 37, 39; Pearson Education: Edexcel GCSE (9-1) Mathematics Higher Student Book, 5, 9.

Note from the publisher
Pearson has robust editorial processes, including answer and fact checks, to ensure the accuracy of the content in this publication, and every effort is made to ensure this publication is free of errors. We are, however, only human, and occasionally errors do occur. Pearson is not liable for any misunderstandings that arise as a result of errors in this publication, but it is our priority to ensure that the content is accurate. If you spot an error, please do contact us at resourcescorrections@pearson.com so we can make sure it is corrected.

Contents

Pearson Edexcel GCSE (9–1) Mathematics Purposeful Practice Book:
Higher

8 key messages from Series Editors Dr Naomi Norman and Katherine Pate

These GCSE Mathematics Purposeful Practice books offer:

1 Lots of practice – you can never have too much!

2 Practice that develops mathematical confidence.

3 Purposeful practice questions that lead students on a path to understanding. These questions:
   - cannot be answered mechanically, by rote
   - make connections to prior knowledge
   - develop thinking skills
   - target specific concepts

4 Reflect and reason questions to:
   - make students aware of their understanding
   - show teachers what students do (or don't yet!) understand
   - encourage students to think about the underlying mathematical patterns

5 Problem-solving practice to:
   - allow students to apply their understanding to problem-solving questions and contexts
   - practise problem-solving strategies
   - prepare for GCSE exams

6 GCSE exam-style questions with:
   - real exam feedback
   - evidence-informed grade indicators, informed by **ResultsPlus**

7 Designed with the help of UK teachers so you can use it flexibly alongside your current resources, in class or for independent study.

8 Purposeful practice, problem-solving practice and exam practice all in one book – the first of its kind.

Key Features of this Purposeful Practice Book:

△ **Purposeful practice** has been embedded in 3 different ways:

1. **Variation**

   Carefully crafted questions that are minimally varied throughout an exercise.
   As students work out the answers, they are exposed to what stays the same and what changes, from question to question. In doing so, by the end of the exercise, students deepen their understanding of the mathematical patterns, structures and relationships that underlie concepts.

2. **Variation and progression**

   A mixture of minimally varied questions, along with small-stepped questions that get incrementally harder. These exercises are designed to both deepen understanding and move students on.

3. **Progression**

   Questions where the skills required become incrementally harder. These small-stepped questions mean there are no uncomfortable jumps, and help to build students' confidence.

Reflect and reason

Metacognition (reflection) is a powerful tool that is used to help students become aware of their own understanding. Reasoning is a key part of the GCSE (9–1), so we've included lots of opportunities for students to show what they do (or don't yet!) understand.

⊠ **Problem-solving practice** is where the skill(s) from each sub-unit can be demonstrated and applied. These problem-solving activities will be a mixture of contextualised problems, 'working backwards' problems, and synoptic problems, ensuring that the skills practised in each sub-unit are fully embedded in new and interesting ways to build confidence.

✦ **Exam practice** is the final part of the sub-unit. Here the students will work with modified versions of real exam questions. These will follow a similar level, structure and concept to the *Purposeful practice* and *Problem-solving practice* sections, giving students the opportunity to answer exam questions with confidence.

Exam feedback   **ResultsPlus**

We've used ResultsPlus live data to provide grade indicators for each exam-style question, where possible. Using the full cohort for each exam sitting, we've looked at the average score of students from across the grade range. If it is more than 65% of the available marks, we've identified it as 'answered well' by that cohort at that grade range.

Note: For some exam paper questions (e.g. November sittings) the cohort is too small to provide an indication of grade. In this case, we have provided meaningful examiner report information.

Get to know your Purposeful Practice Book

10.2 Mutually exclusive events

Key points

- When events are mutually exclusive, you can add their probabilities.
  For mutually exclusive events, P(A or B) = P(A) + P(B)
- The probabilities of an exhaustive set of mutually exclusive events sum to 1.
- For mutually exclusive events A and not A, P(not A) = 1 − P(A)

△ **Purposeful practice 1**

For this set of counters, write down these probabilities

1 P(R)	2 P(B)	3 P(Y)	4 P(W)
5 P(R or Y)	6 P(R or W)	7 P(R or B or Y)	8 P(R or B or W)
9 P(B or Y or W)	10 P(not B)	11 P(not Y)	12 P(not W)
13 P(not B or R)	14 P(not B or W)	15 P(not W or Y)	

Reflect and reason

Use your answers to **Q1–15** to show that
P(R or W) = P(R) + P(W)
P(B or Y or W) = P(B) + P(Y) + P(W)
P(not W) = 1 − P(W)

△ **Purposeful practice 2**

In each question, there are only blue (B), yellow (Y), red (R) and green (G) counters in a bag.

1 The table shows the probabilities of getting a blue or yellow or green counter.
Work out the probability of getting a red counter.

Colour	B	Y	R	G
Probability	0.1	0.2		0.3

2 The table shows the probabilities of getting a blue or yellow or red counter.
Work out the probability of getting a green counter.

Colour	B	Y	R	G
Probability	0.1	0.25	0.6	

3 The table shows the probabilities of getting a blue or red or green counter.
Work out the probability of getting a yellow counter.

Colour	B	Y	R	G
Probability	$\frac{3}{8}$		$\frac{1}{4}$	$\frac{1}{4}$

4 The table shows the probabilities of getting a blue or yellow or red counter.
Work out the probability of getting a green counter.

Colour	B	Y	R	G
Probability	15%	15%	25%	

Reflect and reason

For **Q2** Karl writes,
0.1 + 0.25 + 0.6 = 0.95, so P(green) = 0.5
Explain what Karl has done wrong.

135

⊠ **Problem-solving practice**

1 The probability that a train is late is 0.03.
What is the probability that the train is not late?

2 The weather forecast says the probability of rain is <10%.
What is the probability that it does not rain?

3 A counter is picked at random from a bag.
The table shows the probabilities of getting a blue or yellow counter.
The probability of getting a red counter is the same as the probability of getting a green counter.
Work out the probability of getting a green counter.

Colour	blue	yellow	red	green
Probability	0.15	0.25		

4 The table shows the probabilities of getting a blue or yellow counter.
The probability of getting a red counter is twice the probability of getting a green counter.
Work out the probability of getting a red counter.

Colour	blue	yellow	red	green
Probability	0.3	0.4		

5 The probability of picking a black counter from a bag of counters is $\frac{1}{12}$.
Alex says there are 6 counters in the bag.
Explain why there cannot be only 6 counters in the bag.

6 The table shows the probabilities of getting different colours of counters.

Colour	pink	black	white	green
Probability	0.3	0.15	0.45	0.1

There are 12 pink counters in the bag.
a Which colour counter is half as likely as pink?
b Work out the numbers of black, white and green counters in the bag.

⭐ **Exam practice**

1 There are some cubes in a bag.
The cubes are red or blue or green or white.
Sam is going to take a cube at random from the bag.
The table shows each of the probabilities that the cube will be red or will be white.

Colour	red	blue	green	white
Probability	0.4			0.45

There are 8 red cubes in the bag.
The probability that the cube Sam takes will be blue is twice the probability that the cube will be green.
Work out the number of green cubes in the bag. **(4 marks)**

Adapted from 1MA1/3H, June 2018, Q6a

Exam feedback ResultsPlus

Most students who achieved a **Grade 5** or above answered a similar question well.

Unit 10 Mutually exclusive events 136

Mixed exercise A

Mixed problem-solving practice A

1 Helen is going to choose a main course and a dessert from a menu.
She can choose from 7 main courses and 5 desserts.
Helen says that to work out the number of different ways of choosing a main course and a dessert you add 7 and 5.
Is Helen correct? You must give a reason for your answer.

2 20 teams play in a competition.
Each team plays each other team exactly once.
Work out the total number of games played.

3 Buses to Cardiff leave a bus station every 30 minutes.
Buses to Bristol leave the bus station every 18 minutes.
A bus to Cardiff and a bus to Bristol both leave the bus station at 7 am.
When will buses to Cardiff and to Bristol next leave the bus station at the same time?

4 Can you use the pie charts to determine which team won the greater number of matches? If so, which team was it?
Explain your answer.

5 PQR is a triangle.

VII

1 Number

1.1 Number problems and reasoning

Key point

- When there are m ways of doing one task and n ways of doing a second task, the total number of ways of doing the first task then the second task is $m \times n$.

 △ **Purposeful practice 1**

How many **different** ways are there of arranging these letters?

Start listing them systematically to help you find the pattern.

1 A, B

2 A, B, C

3 A, B, C, D

4 A, B, C, D, E

5 A, B, C, D, D

6 A, B, C, C, C

7 A, B, B, B, B

8 A, A, A, A, A

Reflect and reason

Q1 and **Q7** both contain only the letters A and B.

Explain why their answers are not the same.

 △ **Purposeful practice 2**

Without listing, work out how many **different** ways there are of arranging

1 the first 5 letters of the alphabet

2 the first 6 letters of the alphabet

3 the first 7 letters of the alphabet.

Reflect and reason

What can you do to the answer to **Q2** to get the answer to **Q3**?

 △ **Purposeful practice 3**

1 a How many positive 3-digit numbers are there?

  b How many positive 3-digit even numbers are there?

2 Malcolm wants to set up a 3-digit passcode for his smartphone.
  He cannot use any digit more than once.
  The code can start with a zero.
  How many possible passcodes are there?

Reflect and reason

Malcolm can use three letters rather than three numbers to create his passcode. Explain why this might be more secure than using numbers.

⊠ **Problem-solving practice**

1 A company makes cars in 5 different colours.
   Customers can choose from 3 different seat fabrics.
   How many different combinations of car colour and seat fabric are there?

2 Ali is selecting her GCSE options.
   She must choose 2 languages, 1 humanity and 1 science.
       Language 1: French, Chinese, Arabic
       Language 2: German, Spanish, Italian
       Humanities: Geography, History, Sociology
       Sciences: Chemistry, Biology, Physics
   How many different combinations are there?

3 A restaurant offers 5 different starters and 7 different main courses.
   The owner wants to offer over 150 combinations of starter, main course and dessert.
   How many different desserts should he offer?

4 180 Year 10 students enter a cross country race.
   Prizes are awarded for 1st, 2nd and 3rd places.
   How many different combinations are there for 1st, 2nd and 3rd places?

5 A red 6-sided dice and a blue 6-sided dice are rolled.
   a How many possible combinations are there?
   b How many possible combinations only contain prime numbers?

6 Three 6-sided dice are rolled together.
   Each dice is a different colour.
   a How many combinations are there in total?
   b How many more dice are needed for there to be more than 5000 combinations in total, if each new dice added is a different colour?

 ⬦ **Exam practice**

1 There are 90 15-year-olds and 83 16-year-olds in Year 11 at a school.
   Four will be chosen to go on an exchange trip.
   One 15-year-old will be chosen for the first place.
   A different 15-year-old is going to be chosen for the second place.
   One 16-year-old is going to be chosen for the third place.
   A different 16-year-old is going to be chosen for the fourth place.
   Work out how many different ways this can be done, assuming the order in which they are chosen matters. **(3 marks)**

   Adapted from 1MA1/2H, Specimen Papers, Set 2, Q12b

2 There are 12 tennis players in a tournament.
   Each player must play two matches against each of the other players.
   Work out the total number of matches played in the tournament. **(2 marks)**

   Adapted from 1MA1/3H, June 2018, Q14

Exam feedback   ResultsPlus

Q2: Most students who achieved a **Grade 9** answered a similar question well.

1.2 Place value and estimating

Key points

- You can use place value to work out calculations with decimals.
- To work out an estimate, round the numbers before doing the calculation.

⚠ Purposeful practice 1

1 Without using your calculator, work out

    a 126×1000 **b** 126×100 **c** 126×10 **d** 126×0.1

    e 126×0.01 **f** 126×0.001 **g** $54.83 \div 1000$ **h** $54.83 \div 100$

    i $54.83 \div 10$ **j** $54.83 \div 0.1$ **k** $54.83 \div 0.01$ **l** $54.83 \div 0.001$

2 $126 \times 3.68 = 463.68$. Use this fact to work out the calculations below.

    a 12.6×36.8 **b** 0.126×3680 **c** 1260×0.368

3 $256 \div 12.5 = 20.48$. Use this fact to work out the calculations below.

    a $25.6 \div 1.25$ **b** $2560 \div 125$ **c** $2.56 \div 0.125$

Reflect and reason

How could you write a multiplication with the same answer as 45×1.2?

How could you write a division with the same answer as $45 \div 1.2$?

⚠ Purposeful practice 2

Work out whole-number estimates.

1 $\sqrt{37}$ **2** $\sqrt{48}$ **3** $\sqrt{4.2 \times 10.3}$ **4** $\sqrt{8.6 \times 5.5}$ **5** $\sqrt{19.7 + 15.9}$

Reflect and reason

How do you round a number to work out a whole-number estimate for its square root?

⚠ Purposeful practice 3

1 Estimate the answers to these calculations.

    a 10.6×9.4 **b** 109×1032 **c** 81.9×0.48 **d** 14.4×9.8

    e 22.1×4.9 **f** $55.4 \div 4.8$ **g** $96.3 \div 9.1$ **h** $0.502 \div 2.03$

2 Say whether each calculation will give an overestimate / underestimate / difficult to tell, when trying to estimate the answer to

    a 96.4×106.3 **i** Estimate 96×106 **ii** Estimate 100×110 **iii** Estimate 100×100

    b $\dfrac{106.3}{96.4}$ **i** Estimate $\dfrac{106}{100}$ **ii** Estimate $\dfrac{110}{96}$ **iii** Estimate $\dfrac{110}{100}$

Reflect and reason

When two numbers are multiplied, say whether each of these situations will lead to an overestimate, an underestimate, or whether more information is needed.

If both numbers are rounded up.

If both numbers are rounded down.

If one is rounded up and the other is rounded down.

1   Jon estimates that $\dfrac{\sqrt{10\,024}}{x}$ is 200.
    Find one possible value of x.

2   A bookshop sells 208 books at an average price of £4.99.
    The bookshop pays the publisher, on average, £3.53 per book it sells.
    Estimate the bookshop's profit.

3   Kim is covering a wall with rectangular tiles.
    The wall measures 3.9 m by 2.45 m.
    The tiles measure 0.41 m by 0.49 m.
    Each tile costs £1.49.
    Estimate the cost of covering the wall.

4   The volume of a cube is 8073 cm^3.
    Work out an estimate for its surface area.

5   Car A's fuel tank holds 62 litres.
    Car A can travel 34 miles per gallon of fuel.
    Car B's fuel tank holds 49 litres.
    Car B can travel 50 miles per gallon of fuel.
    A gallon is 4.54 litres.
    By estimating, work out which car can travel furthest on a tank of petrol.

6   A rectangle measures 35.2 cm by 54.8 cm.
    An estimate of the area is 1925 cm^2.
    Use this fact to estimate the area of these rectangles.
    All measurements are in cm.
    a 352×54.8
    b 0.352×0.548
    c 3.52×0.548

7   a   Write three more calculations that have the same answer as
        $179 \times 2.45 = 438.55$

    b   Write three more calculations that have the same answer as
        $497 \div 28.4 = 17.5$

8   A birthday card weighs 21 grams.
    a   Work out an estimate for the total weight of 1024 of these cards in kg.

    b   Is your estimate likely to be an underestimate or an overestimate?
        Justify your answer.

Exam practice

1   Work out an estimate for
    $\sqrt{9.7} + 3.88 \times 6.21$

(3 marks)

Adapted from 1MA1/1H, Specimen Papers, Set 2, Q8

1.3 HCF and LCM

Key point

• To work out the highest common factor (HCF) and lowest common multiple (LCM) of two or more numbers, you can start by writing each number as a product of its prime factors.

△ Purposeful practice 1

Write each number as a product of its prime factors in index form.

1 15   **2** 30   **3** 60   **4** 420   **5** 1260

Reflect and reason

Jonathan says, '1 is a prime number because it can be divided by itself.' Explain why he is wrong.

△ Purposeful practice 2

1 Use your answer to Purposeful practice 1 **Q5** to find two other factors of 1260 that are between 100 and 200.

2 Copy and complete.

15, 30 and 60 are _____ of 1260

1260 is a _____ of 15, 30 and 60

Reflect and reason

Explain how you would use the prime factors of 1260 to find a non-prime factor.

△ Purposeful practice 3

Use a Venn diagram to help you find the HCF and LCM of each pair of numbers.

1 8 and 6   **2** 8 and 12   **3** 40 and 12   **4** 40 and 60

5 40 and 120   **6** 4 and 12   **7** 15 and 8

Reflect and reason

Look at your Venn diagram for **Q6**. What does the empty region of the Venn diagram show you?

Look at your Venn diagram **Q7**. What does the empty region of the Venn diagram show you?

△ Purposeful practice 4

Find the HCF and LCM of each pair of numbers.

1 15 and 14   **2** 6 and 12   **3** 15 and 22   **4** 100 and 150

5 24 and 72   **6** 25 and 24   **7** 15 and 9   **8** 14 and 8

Reflect and reason

Explain how to find the LCM of two numbers that do not have any common factors.

Explain how to find the LCM of two numbers where one number is a factor of the other.

⊠ Problem-solving practice

1 $1320 = 2^3 \times 3 \times 5 \times 11$

   a Is 6 a factor of 1320? Explain how you know.

   b Is 21 a factor of 1320? Explain how you know.

2 Camille says, 'The highest common factor of my two numbers is 6. Their lowest common multiple is less than 150. Both the numbers are between 20 and 40.'
What are Camille's numbers?

3 Jordan says, 'The lowest common multiple of two numbers will be their product if their only common factor is 1.'
Find an example of two, 2-digit, non-prime numbers for which this is true.

4 Wall tiles are arranged in a pattern.
The top row only contains 30 cm tiles.
The middle row only contains 50 cm tiles.
The bottom row only contains 40 cm tiles.
Cameron continues each row until the tiles make a rectangle.
What is the width of the smallest rectangle he could make?

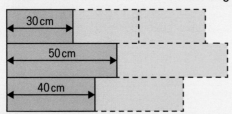

5 $1800 = 2^3 \times 3^2 \times 5^2$ and $a = 2^2 \times 33 \times 5^b$
The HCF of 1800 and a is 180.
Work out the value of a and b.

⚛ Exam practice

1 Trains to Penrith leave a station every 18 minutes.
Trains to Carlisle leave the same station every 24 minutes.
A train to Penrith and a train to Carlisle both leave the station at 8.30 am.
When will a train to Penrith and a train to Carlisle next leave the station at the same time? **(3 marks)**

Adapted from 1MA1/3H, June 2018, Q10

2 **a** Find the lowest common multiple (LCM) of 30 and 26. **(2 marks)**

   b $A = 2 \times 3^2 \times 5 \qquad B = 3^3 \times 5^2$

   Write down the highest common factor (HCF) of A and B. **(3 marks)**

Adapted from 1MA1/2H, June 2018, Q2

Exam feedback **ResultsPlus**

Q1: Most students who achieved a **Grade 8** or above answered a similar question well.

Q2a: Most students who achieved a **Grade 5** or above answered a similar question well.

Key points

- To multiply, add the indices: $x^m \times x^n = x^{m+n}$
- You can only add the indices when multiplying powers of the same number.
- To divide powers, subtract the indices: $x^m \div x^n = x^{m-n}$
- To work out a power to another power, multiply the powers together: $(x^m)^n = x^{mn}$

△ Purposeful practice 1

Write as a single power.

1 $3^2 \times 3^2$

2 $3^2 \times 3^2 \times 3^2$

3 $3^2 \times 3^2 \times 3^2 \times 3^2$

4 $3^2 \times 3^2 \times 3^2 \times 3^2 \times 3^2$

5 $\dfrac{3^2 \times 3^2 \times 3^2 \times 3^2 \times 3^2}{3^2}$

6 $\dfrac{3^2 \times 3^2 \times 3^2 \times 3^2 \times 3^2}{3^2 \times 3^2}$

7 $\dfrac{3^2 \times 3^2 \times 3^2 \times 3^2 \times 3^2}{3^2 \times 3^2 \times 3^2}$

8 $\dfrac{3^2 \times 3^2 \times 3^2 \times 3^2 \times 3^2}{3^2 \times 3^2 \times 3^2 \times 3^2 \times 3^2}$

Reflect and reason

For **Q5** Caitlin writes

$$\frac{3^{10}}{3^2} = \frac{1^{10}}{1^2} = 1^8 = 1$$

Explain her error.

△ Purposeful practice 2

1 Write as a single power.

    a $(3^2)^2$

    b $(3^2)^3$

    c $(3^4)^2$

    d $(3^2)^4$

    e $\dfrac{(3^2)^4}{(3^2)^2}$

2 Work out

    a $\dfrac{7^2 \times 7^5}{7^3} = 7^{\square}$

    b $\dfrac{7^5 \times 7^5}{7^4} = 7^{\square}$

    c $\dfrac{3^4 \times 7^5}{7^4} = 3^{\square} \times 7^{\square}$

    d $\dfrac{7^5 \times 7^5}{7^3} = 7^{\square}$

    e $\dfrac{(7^5)^2}{7^3} = 7^{\square}$

    f $\dfrac{(7^5)^4}{7^3} = 7^{\square}$

    g $\dfrac{7^5 \times (7^5)^2}{7^3} = 7^{\square}$

    h $\dfrac{7^5 \times (7^5)^4}{(7^5)^2} = 7^{\square}$

    i $\dfrac{7^5 \times (7^5)^4}{7^5 \times (7^4)^2} = 7^{\square}$

    j $\dfrac{7^5 \times (7^5)^4}{7^5 \times (7^4)^3} = 7^{\square}$

    k $\dfrac{7^5 \times 6^6}{7^3 \times (6^2)^2} = 6^{\square} \times 7^{\square}$

    l $\dfrac{(7^5)^2 \times (6^6)^4}{7^3 \times (6^2)^2} = 6^{\square} \times 7^{\square}$

Reflect and reason

Explain why the answer to $7^5 \times 6^4$ is not 42^9.

⊠ Problem-solving practice

1 Write 9^3 in the form 3^x.

2 Copy and complete.

   a $8^\square \times 8^2 = 8^7$ **b** $8^\square \div 8^2 = 8^7$

3 Copy and complete.

   $3^6 \times 2^\square \times (3^2)^\square \times (2^2)^4 = 3^{12} \times 2^{11}$

4 Work out

   a $4^2 \times 2^3 = 2^\square$ **b** $\dfrac{16^2 \times 2^3}{4} = 2^\square$ **c** $25^4 \div 5^2 = 5^\square$

5 Find the value of n.

   a $4^3 \times 2^4 = 2^n$

   b $\dfrac{3^n \div 3^4}{3^6 \div 3^2} = 3^2$

6 Work out the area of each shape.
Give your answers in the form 3^x.

   a 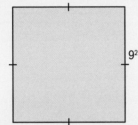   **b**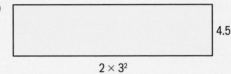

7 Work out the area of the triangle.
Give your answer in the form 2^x.

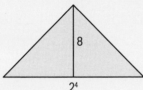

✾ Exam practice

1 Write $\dfrac{3^7 \times 3^9}{(3^2)^2}$ as a power of 3.   **(2 marks)**

2 **a** $p^7 \times p^x = p^{12}$
     Find the value of x.   **(1 mark)**
   b $(6^2)^y = 6^{10}$
     Find the value of y.   **(1 mark)**

Adapted from 1MA1/2H, November 2017, Q6a and Q6b

Exam feedback   ResultsPlus

Q2b: In a similar question, a common incorrect response was $y = 8$.
Students incorrectly added the powers instead of multiplying them.

1.5 Zero, negative and fractional indices

Key points

- $x^{-n} = \dfrac{1}{x^n}$ for any number n, $x \neq 0$.
- $x^{\frac{1}{n}} = \sqrt[n]{x}$
- $x^0 = 1$, where x is any non-zero number.
- $x^{\frac{n}{m}} = \left(\sqrt[m]{x}\right)^n$

△ Purposeful practice 1

Write answers to these calculations as a power of 5. Write your answers to **Q6** and **Q7** as fractions.

1   $5^7 \div 5^3$ 2 $5^7 \div 5^4$ 3 $5^7 \div 5^5$ 4 $5^7 \div 5^6$

5   $5^7 \div 5^7$ 6 $5^7 \div 5^8$ 7 $5^7 \div 5^9$

Reflect and reason

Look at the pattern of your answers. How do you get from each answer to the next? What logically is the alternative answer to **Q5**?

△ Purposeful practice 2

1   Write these in the form $\sqrt[b]{7}$ or $\dfrac{1}{\sqrt[b]{7}}$

   a $7^{\frac{1}{2}}$ **b** $7^{\frac{1}{3}}$ **c** $7^{\frac{1}{4}}$ **d** $7^{\frac{1}{5}}$ **e** $7^{-\frac{1}{2}}$ **f** $7^{-\frac{1}{3}}$

2   Write these in index form.

   a $\sqrt{6}$ **b** $\sqrt[3]{6}$ **c** $\sqrt[4]{6}$ **d** $\dfrac{1}{\sqrt{6}}$ **e** $\dfrac{1}{\sqrt[3]{6}}$ **f** $\dfrac{1}{\sqrt[4]{6}}$

Reflect and reason

Alfie writes

$$16^{-\frac{1}{2}} = -\sqrt{16} = 4$$

Explain his error.

△ Purposeful practice 3

Write these in the form 6^n and in the form $\left(\sqrt{6}\right)^b$ or $\dfrac{1}{\left(\sqrt{6}\right)^b}$

1   $6^3 \times 6^{\frac{3}{2}}$ 2 $6^{-3} \times 6^{\frac{3}{2}}$ 3 $6^3 \times 6^{-\frac{3}{2}}$ 4 $6^{-3} \times 6^{-\frac{3}{2}}$

5   $6^3 \div 6^{\frac{3}{2}}$ 6 $6^{-3} \div 6^{\frac{3}{2}}$ 7 $6^3 \div 6^{-\frac{3}{2}}$ 8 $6^{-3} \div 6^{-\frac{3}{2}}$

9   $6^3 \times \left(\sqrt{6}\right)^3$ 10 $\dfrac{1}{6^3} \times \left(\sqrt{6}\right)^3$ 11 $6^3 \times \dfrac{1}{\left(\sqrt{6}\right)^3}$ 12 $6^3 \div \dfrac{1}{\left(\sqrt{6}\right)^3}$

Reflect and reason

For **Q10**, explain why the cubes do not simply cancel each other out to leave $\frac{1}{6} \times \sqrt{6}$.

1 Work out

    a $8^{-\frac{1}{3}}$

    b $25^{\frac{3}{2}}$

    c $9^{-1.5}$

    d $\left(\dfrac{8}{27}\right)^{-\frac{2}{3}}$

2 Work out

    a $\sqrt{\dfrac{25}{4}}$

    b $12.25^{\frac{1}{2}}$

3 Write $\dfrac{\left(\sqrt[3]{6}\right)^2}{\sqrt{6}}$ as a power of 6.

4 Work out $\left(\left(\left(7^3\right)^2\right)^0\right)^5$

5 Fill in the missing values.

    a $\left(\dfrac{1}{3}\right)^{\square} = 27$

    b $2^{\square} \times 3^2 = 9$

    c $2^4 \div 2^{\square} = 8^2$

    d $\left(\dfrac{4}{5}\right)^{\square} = \dfrac{\sqrt{5}}{2}$

    e $8^{\square} \times 4^{\frac{3}{2}} = 8$

    f $\left(\dfrac{2}{3}\right)^{-2} \times 7^{\square} = \dfrac{9}{4}$

6 Work out the values of x.

    a $3^{2x} = \dfrac{1}{27}$

    b $5^x = 0.04$

7 $5^n = 0.3$

    Work out $(5^n)^{-2}$

    Give your answer as a fraction.

8 Mia writes

    $16^{-\frac{3}{4}} \times 27^{\frac{2}{3}} = -72$

    a Show that Mia is wrong.

    b What mistake has Mia made?

1 Work out the exact value of x.

    $16^{\frac{1}{2}} \times 2^x = 8^{\frac{3}{4}}$ **(2 marks)**

Key points

- A number is in standard form when it is in the form $A \times 10^n$, where $1 \leqslant A < 10$ and n is an integer. For example, 6.3×10^4 is written in standard form because 6.3 is between 1 and 10.
- 63×10^4 is **not** in standard form because 63 does not lie between 1 and 10.

△ Purposeful practice 1

Write these numbers as a power of 10.

1 10 000	**2** 1000	**3** 100	**4** 10	**5** 1	**6** 0.1
7 0.01	**8** 0.001	**9** 0.0001	**10** 0.000 01	**11** 0.000 001	

Reflect and reason

Kate wants to know how to write 10 000 and 0.0001 as powers of 10. What advice would you give her?

△ Purposeful practice 2

1 Write these as ordinary numbers.

a 6.3×10^6	**b** 6.3×10^5	**c** 6.3×10^4	**d** 6.3×10
e 6.3×10^2	**f** 6.3×10^1	**g** 6.3×10^0	**h** 6.3×10^{-1}
i 6.3×10^{-2}	**j** 6.3×10^{-3}	**k** 6.3×10^{-4}	**l** 6.3×10^{-5}

2 Write these numbers in standard form.

a 3 425 000	**b** 342 500	**c** 34 250	**d** 3425	**e** 342.5
f 34.25	**g** 3.425	**h** 0.345	**i** 0.0345	**j** 0.003 45
k 34.25×10^3	**l** 34.25×10^4	**m** 34.25×10^5	**n** 34.25×10^{-3}	
o 34.25×10^{-4}	**p** 34.25×10^{-5}	**q** $0.034\,25 \times 10^4$	**r** $0.034\,25 \times 10^3$	
s $0.034\,25 \times 10^2$	**t** $0.034\,25 \times 10^5$	**u** $0.034\,25 \times 10^{-3}$		

Reflect and reason

Explain how you know that **Q2k** is not in standard form? How did you change it into standard form?

△ Purposeful practice 3

Work out

1 $(2 \times 10^3) \times (3 \times 10^5)$	**2** $(2 \times 10^3) \times (3 \times 10^7)$	**3** $(2 \times 10^{-2}) \times (3 \times 10^7)$
4 $(2 \times 10^{-5}) \times (3 \times 10^7)$	**5** $(2 \times 10^{-5}) \times (3 \times 10^5)$	**6** $(2 \times 10^{-5}) \times (3 \times 10^{-7})$
7 $(4 \times 10^3) \times (3 \times 10^5)$	**8** $(4 \times 10^3) \times (3 \times 10^{-7})$	**9** $(4 \times 10^{-7}) \times (3 \times 10^{-5})$
10 $(9 \times 10^5) \div (3 \times 10^3)$	**11** $(9 \times 10^5) \div (3 \times 10^7)$	**12** $(9 \times 10^{-7}) \div (3 \times 10^5)$

Reflect and reason

Look at **Q1–9**. How can you tell if the answer to a multiplication will not be in standard form when you first work it out?

⊠ Problem-solving practice

1. Give two other ways of writing $\frac{1}{100}$

2. Write these numbers in order of size.
   Start with the smallest.
   2.6×10^6
   28×10^5
   -6.9×10^{-5}
   8×10^3
   0.0016×10^8
   -2×10^3

3. Work out
   $$\frac{3 \times 10^5 + 6 \times 10^4}{2 \times 10^7}$$
   Give your answer in standard form.

4. Find the value of
   a $\sqrt[3]{27 \times 10^6}$
   b $\sqrt[4]{8 \times 2 \times 10^8}$

5. The Moon is 3×10^5 km from Earth.
   A rocket travels at 7×10^2 km per hour.
   How many hours will it take the rocket to travel from Earth to the Moon?
   Give your answer in standard form to 3 significant figures.

6. Copy and complete.
   $(2 \times 10^3) \;\square\; (5 \times 10^5) = \square \times 10^{-3}$

7. One gram of hydrogen contains 6×10^{23} atoms.
   How many atoms are there in 1 kg of hydrogen?

8. Work out
   $8 \times 10^6 + 8 \times 10^4 + 8 \times 10^2$

9. Fill in the missing indices.
   $2.02 \times 10^{\square} + 2.02 \times 10^{\square} + 2.02 \times 10^{\square} = 2\,042\,220$

✾ Exam practice

1. Write 0.000 708 in standard form. **(1 mark)**

   Adapted from 1MA1/3H, Specimen Papers, Set 1, Q19a

2. One uranium atom has a mass of 4×10^{-22} grams.
   Work out an estimate for the number of uranium atoms in 10 kg of uranium. **(3 marks)**

   Adapted from 1MA1/1H, Specimen Papers, Set 1, Q8a

Key points

- A surd is a number written exactly using square or cube roots.
- $\sqrt{mn} = \sqrt{m}\sqrt{n}$
- $\sqrt{\frac{m}{n}} = \frac{\sqrt{m}}{\sqrt{n}}$
- To rationalise the denominator of $\frac{a}{\sqrt{b}}$, multiply by $\frac{\sqrt{b}}{\sqrt{b}}$

  Then the fraction will have an integer as the denominator.

△ Purposeful practice 1

Simplify these roots where possible.

1 $\sqrt{8}$	**2** $\sqrt{18}$	**3** $\sqrt{32}$	**4** $\sqrt{50}$	**5** $\sqrt{72}$
6 $\sqrt{98}$	**7** $\sqrt{12}$	**8** $\sqrt{27}$	**9** $\sqrt{48}$	**10** $\sqrt{75}$
11 $\sqrt{108}$	**12** $\sqrt{147}$	**13** $\sqrt{15}$	**14** $\sqrt{21}$	**15** $\sqrt{35}$

Reflect and reason

Which of **Q1–15** cannot be simplified? Explain why not.

△ Purposeful practice 2

Simplify

1 $\sqrt{\frac{1}{4}}$	**2** $\sqrt{\frac{3}{4}}$	**3** $\sqrt{\frac{3}{16}}$
4 $\sqrt{\frac{64}{16}}$	**5** $\sqrt{\frac{12}{9}}$	**6** $\sqrt{\frac{72}{9}}$

Reflect and reason

Judy's answer to **Q6** is $\frac{\sqrt{72}}{3}$. Explain how she could have simplified this further.

△ Purposeful practice 3

Rationalise

1 $\frac{1}{\sqrt{2}}$	**2** $\frac{1}{\sqrt{3}}$	**3** $\frac{1}{\sqrt{5}}$
4 $\frac{2}{\sqrt{2}}$	**5** $\frac{3}{\sqrt{2}}$	**6** $\frac{2}{\sqrt{12}}$

Reflect and reason

In **Q6**, does it matter whether you simplify $\sqrt{12}$ before or after rationalising the denominator?

Problem-solving practice

1 Simplify as far as possible.

$$3\sqrt{2} + \sqrt{15} - \frac{4}{\sqrt{2}} + 7 + \frac{6}{\sqrt{5}}$$

2 Work out the value of k.

$$3\sqrt{7} = \sqrt{k}$$

3 Fill in the missing values.

   a $\sqrt{\dfrac{\square}{2}} = \dfrac{3}{\sqrt{2}}$

   b $\sqrt{\dfrac{16}{18}} = \dfrac{\square}{\square\sqrt{2}}$

4 Fill in the missing values.

   a $\dfrac{\square}{\sqrt{2}} = 2\sqrt{2}$

   b $\dfrac{\sqrt{\square}}{2} = 3\sqrt{3}$

5 The perimeter of a square is $\sqrt{128}$.
Work out the area of the square.

6 A square has an area of $\frac{9}{2}\,\text{m}^2$.
What is the perimeter?

7 Work out the missing values. Give your answers as surds in their simplest form.

a

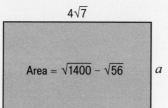

b

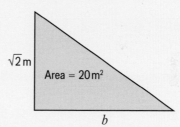

Exam practice

1 Rationalise the denominator and simplify if possible.

   a $\dfrac{3}{\sqrt{5}}$ **(1 mark)**

   b $\dfrac{4}{\sqrt{20}}$ **(2 marks)**

2 Simplify

   $\dfrac{3}{\sqrt{3}} + \dfrac{7}{\sqrt{12}}$ **(2 marks)**

2 Algebra

2.1 Algebraic indices

Key points

- $x^0 = 1$ and $x^{-m} = \dfrac{1}{x^m}$
- $x^{\frac{1}{n}} = \sqrt[n]{x}$
- $x^m \times x^n = x^{m+n}$
- $x^m \div x^n = x^{m-n}$

△ Purposeful practice 1

1 Write as fractions.

a x^{-1} **b** x^{-2} **c** x^{-3} **d** $2x^{-3}$ **e** $7x^{-3}$ **f** $\dfrac{7}{2}x^{-3}$ **g** $\dfrac{7}{2}x^{-2}$

2 Write in the form of roots.

a $x^{\frac{1}{2}}$ **b** $x^{-\frac{1}{2}}$ **c** $x^{\frac{1}{3}}$ **d** $x^{-\frac{1}{3}}$ **e** $x^{-\frac{1}{4}}$

f $x^{0.5}$ **g** $x^{-0.5}$ **h** $4x^{\frac{1}{2}}$ **i** $4x^{-\frac{1}{2}}$

Reflect and reason

Sam writes $4x^{\frac{1}{2}} = 2\sqrt{x}$

Sam is wrong. Explain the mistake he has made.

△ Purposeful practice 2

Simplify

1 $x^2 \times x^2$ **2** $x^2 \times x^4$ **3** $3x^2 \times 7x^4$ **4** $\dfrac{x^2}{3} \times \dfrac{x^4}{7}$ **5** $x^5 \times x^{-1}$

6 $x^{-5} \times x^{-1}$ **7** $x^5 \times x^{-7}$ **8** $2x^5 \times 9x^{-7}$ **9** $x^{\frac{1}{2}} \times x^{\frac{1}{2}}$ **10** $x^2 \times x^{\frac{1}{2}}$

11 $\dfrac{x^6}{x^4}$ **12** $\dfrac{x^6}{x^5}$ **13** $\dfrac{x^6}{x^6}$ **14** $\dfrac{6x^6}{2x^6}$ **15** $\dfrac{6x^9}{2x^6}$

Reflect and reason

Use $\dfrac{a^b}{a^b}$ to help you explain why $a^0 = 1$

△ Purposeful practice 3

Simplify

1 $(x^3)^4$ **2** $(x^3)^7$ **3** $(3x^3)^{-4}$ **4** $\left(\dfrac{x^{-3}}{2}\right)^4$ **5** $\left(3x^{\frac{1}{2}}\right)^4$

6 $(9x^4)^{\frac{1}{2}}$ **7** $(9x^4y^6)^{\frac{1}{2}}$

Reflect and reason

Deepa's answer to **Q7** is $9x^2y^3$. Explain her error.

1   Find the pair of matching expressions.

   A $\left(\dfrac{9}{x^4}\right)^{-1}$ **B** $\sqrt{81x^6}$ **C** $3^{-2}x^2$ **D** $\left(\dfrac{x^2}{3}\right)^2$ **E** $9x^{-4}$

2   Copy and complete.

   a $\left(\dfrac{2a^2\square}{\square}\right)^3 = \dfrac{\square a^6 s^{12}}{27}$

   b $\sqrt{9\square t^4} = \square p\square$

   c $(\square c^3 k^2)^\square = 16c^6 k^\square$

3   Copy and write in the missing mathematical operations.

   $9x^4 \square\ 3xy \square\ 2y^3 = 6x^3 y^2$

4   Aidan thinks of a number, x.

   a He squares that number and then quadruples it. Write an expression for the new number.

   b He cubes his last expression. What is his expression now?

   c He divides his new expression by x^2. What is his expression now?

   d He square roots his new expression. What is his expression now?

5   $p = 3^a$ and $q = 3^b$
   Write in terms of p and q

   a 3^{a+b} **b** 3^{b-a}

   c 3^{2a} **d** 3^{b-2}

6   Four of the small squares fit together to make a new larger square.
   The area of the smaller square is $4x$.
   Work out an expression for the perimeter of the larger square.
   Leave your answer in the form $2^a x^b$.

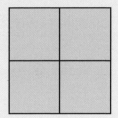

7   Write as a power of x.

   $\dfrac{3x^2 \times 2x^4}{\sqrt{x}}$

1   **a** Simplify $a^4 \times a^2$ **(1 mark)**

   b Simplify $(2b^2 c^3)^2$ **(2 marks)**

   c Simplify $\dfrac{15d^4 e^2}{6d^3 e}$ **(2 marks)**

   Adapted from 1MA1/2H, June 2018, Q1

Exam feedback   Results**Plus**

Q1a: Most students who achieved a Grade 3 or above answered a similar question well.

Q1b: Most students who achieved a Grade 8 or above answered a similar question well.

Q1c: Most students who achieved a Grade 5 or above answered a similar question well.

Key point

- To expand a bracket, multiply each term inside the brackets by the term outside the brackets.

△ Purposeful practice 1

Expand

1 $x(x + 2)$ **2** $5x(x + 2)$ **3** $5x(x - 2)$

4 $x(5x - 2)$ **5** $x(2 - 5x)$ **6** $-x(2 - 5x)$

7 $y(2 - 5x)$ **8** $y(5x + 2)$ **9** $y(5x - 2)$

10 $y(5x - 2y)$ **11** $y(2y - 5x)$ **12** $x(2y - 5x)$

13 $-x(2y - 5x)$ **14** $x(2y + 5x)$ **15** $y(2y + 5x)$

Reflect and reason

Arvin expands $-3x(2x - 6)$

He writes

$-6x^2 - 18x$

Arvin has made a mistake.

Explain his error.

△ Purposeful practice 2

1 Expand and simplify

    a $3(x - 4) + 2x$ **b** $3(x - 4) + 2(x + 6)$

    c $3(x - 4) - 2x$ **d** $3(x - 4) - 2(x - 5)$

    e $3(x - 4y) - 2(2x - 5y)$ **f** $3x(x - 4y) - 2x(2x - 5y)$

2 Factorise completely

    a $3x + 6$ **b** $6x + 15$ **c** $12a + 6c$

    d $3bd + d$ **e** $6ghk - 12k$ **f** $x^2y + 2x^2$

    g $2xy^2 + 2y^2a$ **h** $6x^2y^2 - 9xy^3$ **i** $5b + 50ab$

3 Factorise completely, simplifying where possible

    a $(f + 2)^2 + 3(f + 2)$ **b** $(f + 2)^2 - 3(f + 2)$

    c $2(p + 2)^2 + 3(p + 2)$ **d** $2(p + 2)^2 + 6(p + 2)$

    e $2(r + 2)^2 - 6(r + 2)$ **f** $2(r + 2s)^2 - 6(r + 2s)$

    g $(t + 2)^2 + (t + 2)$ **h** $(t + 2)^2 - (t + 2)$

Reflect and reason

Beth fully factorises $3x^2y - 12x^3y^2$ as

$3xy(x - 4x^2y)$

What has Beth done wrong?

1   Write an expression for the total area of these two shapes.
    Factorise your answer completely.

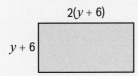

2   Write an expression for the blue shaded area.

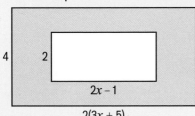

3   Copy and complete.
    $3(2x - 4) - 2(\square x - \square) = -4x - 6$

4   Find the highest common factor.
    $16(x + 3)^2 - (x + 3)^3$

5   2 is a factor of
    $2cd^2 + 12c^2d^2 - 16c^3d^5$

    a   List all the other possible factors of this expression.
        There are ten others.

    b   Which would be considered the highest common factor of this expression?

    c   Factorise $8c^3d^2 + 12c^2d^4 - 16c^3d^5$ completely.

1   Factorise
    $12m - 9m^2$ **(1 mark)**

    Adapted from 1MA1/1H, Specimen Papers, Set 2, Q1a

2   Expand and simplify
    $3a(b - 6g) + 2b(a - 4g)$ **(2 marks)**

    Adapted from 1MA1/3H, June 2018, Q2

Exam feedback   Results**Plus**

Q2: Most students who achieved a Grade 4 or above answered a similar question well.

Key points

- Unless a question asks for a decimal answer, give non-integer solutions to an equation as exact fractions.
- To solve an equation involving fractions, multiply each term on both sides by the LCM of the denominators.

△ Purposeful practice 1

Solve

1 $4x - 3 = 5$

2 $4x - 3 = 3x$

3 $4x - 3 = 2x$

4 $4x - 3 = 5x$

5 $4x - 3 = 5x + 5$

6 $6x - 3 = 5x + 5$

7 $6x - 3 = 5 - 2x$

8 $7 - 6x = 5 - 2x$

Reflect and reason

Larry says, 'When solving the equation in **Q8**, it is easier to collect all the xs on the right-hand side.'
What do you think Larry means?

△ Purposeful practice 2

Solve

1 $2(x + 3) = 12$

2 $3(x + 4) = 12$

3 $2(x + 3) = 3(x + 4)$

4 $2(x + 3) + 3(x + 4) = -12$

5 $2(x + 3) - 3(x + 4) = -12$

6 $2(x + 3) - 3(x - 4) = -12$

7 $2(x + 3) - 3(2x - 4) = -12$

Reflect and reason

$3(x + 4) = 12$
Explain why 4 cannot be subtracted from both sides as the first step.

△ Purposeful practice 3

Solve

1 $x + 4 = \dfrac{2x - 6}{3}$

2 $3(x + 4) = \dfrac{2x - 6}{2}$

3 $3(x - 4) = 0.5(2x + 4)$

4 $\dfrac{x - 4}{3} = \dfrac{2x + 4}{2}$

5 $\dfrac{4x - 4}{3} = \dfrac{8x + 3}{5}$

6 $\dfrac{4 - 4x}{3} = \dfrac{3 - 8x}{5}$

7 $\dfrac{x - 2}{4} = \dfrac{x + 2}{12}$

8 $\dfrac{6x - 2}{3} = \dfrac{4 - 8x}{8}$

Reflect and reason

Adam is solving **Q7**.
He says, 'I multiply both sides by 48 to eliminate the denominators of the fractions.'
Give the smallest number that he could multiply by.
Explain why you have chosen this number.

⊠ Problem-solving practice

1 Work out the value of x in this isosceles triangle.

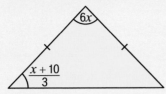

2 Work out the value of x.

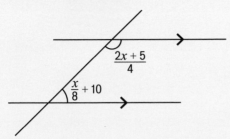

3 Solve, giving your answer as a fraction.

$$\frac{x}{2} + \frac{x}{3} + \frac{x}{4} = \frac{3}{4}$$

4 Five times a man's age 23 years ago is the same as twice the man's age in 7 years' time.

   a Form an equation to represent this problem.

   b Solve this equation to work out the man's age.

5 The area of the larger rectangle is twice the area of the smaller rectangle.
Work out the area of the smaller rectangle.

$$\frac{x}{4} + 8$$

3

2

$$\frac{x}{3} - 1$$

✦ Exam practice

1 Solve

$$\frac{10 - x}{4} = 5x - 14$$

(3 marks)

Adapted from 1MA1/3H, June 2018, Q7

Exam feedback

ResultsPlus

Most students who achieved a **Grade 6** or above answered a similar question well.

Key points

- A formula has an equals sign and letters to represent different quantities, for example, $A = \pi r^2$
  The letters are variables as their values can vary.
- The subject of a formula is the letter on its own, on one side of the equals sign.

⚠ Purposeful practice 1

Make b the subject of the formulae.

1 $a = 2b$

2 $a = 3bd$

3 $a = \dfrac{b}{3}$

4 $a = \dfrac{2b}{3}$

5 $a = b - 3$

6 $a = 2b - 3$

7 $a = \dfrac{b}{2} - 3$

8 $a = \dfrac{3b}{2} - 3$

9 $2a = 2b - 3$

10 $2a = 2(b - 3)$

11 $a = \dfrac{3cd(b - 3)}{2}$

12 $a = b^2$

13 $a = b^2 + 6$

14 $a = 3b^2 + 6$

15 $a^2 = b^2 + 9$

Reflect and reason

Louis is rearranging a formula to make r the subject.

$$\dfrac{p + q}{2} = fr$$

He says, 'I now divide both sides by f to give the following.'

$$\dfrac{\frac{p + q}{2}}{f} = r$$

Explain what Louis has done wrong.

⚠ Purposeful practice 2

The formula $s = ut + \frac{1}{2}at^2$ connects speed (u), time (t), acceleration (a) and distance (s).

1 Find u when

    a $s = 119$, $t = 7$ and $a = 4$

    b $s = 8.75$, $t = 3.5$ and $a = -2$

    c $s = 3$, $t = \frac{1}{6}$ and $a = 72$

2 Find a when

    a $s = 24$, $u = 4$ and $t = 6$

    b $s = -8$, $u = 6$ and $t = 2$

    c $s = 50$, $u = 5$ and $t = 0.5$

Reflect and reason

Look at **Q2**. Explain why it is easier to rearrange the formula to make a the subject before answering parts **a**, **b** and **c**.

1 Euler's formula for polyhedra is

Number of Faces − Number of Edges + Number of Vertices = 2

A regular polyhedron has 6 edges and 4 vertices.

a Work out the number of faces.

b What is the name of this polyhedron?

2 The formula for the volume of a sphere is

Volume $= \frac{4}{3}\pi r^3$

Work out the volume when the radius is $\frac{1}{3}$ m.

Give your answer to 3 s.f.

3 The formula for the area of a trapezium is

Area $= \frac{(a + b)h}{2}$

a Find the area when $a = 6$ m, $b = 3$ m and $h = 7$ m.

b Find the height when Area $= 26$ m^2, $a = 2.5$ m and $b = 4$ m.

c Johnny says, 'I can draw a trapezium with an area of 50 cm^2, $a = 10$ cm and $h = 25$ cm.'

  i Work out the value of b based on these values.

  ii Explain why this value of b is impossible.

4 Sophie correctly rearranges a formula to make t the subject.

This is her answer

$t = \frac{u - v}{10}$

Write three different possible formulas Sophie may have started with.

At least one must include a bracket.

5 The force, F (newtons), needed to make a car turn a corner is given by $F = \frac{mv^2}{r}$

The mass of the car is m (kg).

The velocity of the car is v (ms^{-1}).

The radius of the corner is r (m).

Calculate the velocity of the car when the force is 1000 newtons, the mass is 1500 kg and the radius is 15 m.

Give your answer rounded to 3 s.f.

6 The volume of a cone is one third of π, multiplied by the square of the radius, multiplied by the height.

a Write a formula for the volume of a cone.

b Rearrange the formula to make the height the subject.

c Work out the height of a cone with a volume of 250 cm^3 and a radius of 5 cm.

Give your answer rounded to 3 s.f.

✧ **Exam practice**

1 $S = \frac{a^2 - 6}{b}$

$S = 25, a = 9$

Calculate the value of b.

(3 marks)

2.5 Linear sequences

Key points

- u_n denotes the nth term of a sequence. u_1 is the first term, u_2 is the second term and so on.
- In an arithmetic sequence, the terms increase (or decrease) by a fixed number called the common difference.
- The nth term of an arithmetic sequence = common difference $\times n$ + zero term.
- When an arithmetic sequence with common difference d is input into this function machine, the output sequence has common difference $p \times d$.

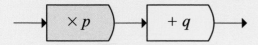

△ Purposeful practice 1

1 Copy and complete these linear sequences.

    a 10, 12, 14, 16, ☐, ☐, ...   **b** $2\frac{5}{7}, 3\frac{1}{7}, 3\frac{4}{7}, 4,$ ☐, ☐, ...

    c 2.14, 2.42, 2.7, 2.98, ☐, ☐, ...   **d** 16, 12, 8, 4, ☐, ☐, ...

    e $2\frac{1}{4}, 1\frac{7}{8}, 1\frac{1}{2}, 1\frac{1}{8},$ ☐, ☐, ...   **f** $-19, -15, -11, -7,$ ☐, ☐, ...

    g $-7, -6.5, -6, -5.5,$ ☐, ☐, ...   **h** ☐, ☐, 11.5, 13, 14.5, 16, ...

    i 3, ☐, 11, ☐, 19, ☐, 27, ...

2 Work out the first five terms of the sequence with nth term

    a $2n + 1$ **b** $2n + 3$ **c** $2n - 1$ **d** $3n + 1$ **e** $3n + 3$ **f** $3n - 1$

    g $5n + 1$ **h** $5n + 3$ **i** $n - 1$ **j** $7n + 1$ **k** $7n + 3$ **l** $7n - 1$

Reflect

Look at **Q2**. What do you notice about the number before the n and the sequences that are generated?

Look at your sequence for **Q2k**, $7n + 3$. Which times table is it similar to? How is each term different from the corresponding term in that times table?

△ Purposeful practice 2

Write, in terms of n, expressions for the nth term of these arithmetic sequences.

    1 1, 2, 3, 4, 5, ...   **2** 2, 4, 6, 8, 10, ...   **3** 5, 7, 9, 11, 13, ...

    4 6, 8, 10, 12, 14, ...   **5** 7, 9, 11, 13, 15, ...   **6** 0, 2, 4, 6, 8, ...

    7 1.5, 3.5, 5.5, 7.5, 9.5, ...   **8** 4, 8, 12, 16, 20, ...   **9** 7, 11, 15, 19, 23, ...

    10 8, 12, 16, 20, 24, ...   **11** 9, 13, 17, 21, 25, ...   **12** 2, 6, 10, 14, 18, ...

    13 3.5, 7.5, 11.5, 15.5, 19.5, ...   **14** 7, 14, 21, 28, 35, ...   **15** 10, 17, 24, 31, 38, ...

    16 11, 18, 25, 32, 39, ...   **17** 12, 19, 26, 33, 40, ...   **18** 5, 12, 19, 26, 33, ...

    19 6.5, 13.5, 20.5, 27.5, 34.5, ... **20** $-3, -6, -9, -12, -15,$ ... **21** $0, -3, -6, -9, -12,$ ...

    22 $1, -2, -5, -8, -11,$ ...   **23** $2, -1, -4, -7, -10,$ ...   **24** $-5, -8, -11, -14, -17,$ ...

    25 $-3.5, -6.5, -9.5, -12.5, -15.5,$ ...

Reflect and reason

Look at the questions in this section. Explain the steps you used to work out the nth term.

1 $u_n = \dfrac{n}{2} + 6$

    a Work out the 1st, 2nd, 3rd and 10th terms.

    b Jamie says, 'Only even number positions give an integer term in this sequence.'
       Is Jamie correct? Explain.

2 A sequence starts 10, 14, 18, 22, 26.
   Without working out the nth term, explain why 81 is not a term in the sequence.

3 Show that 81 is not a term in a sequence that starts 10, 13, 16, 19, 22.

4 A sequence has nth term $6n - 4$
   Find the 1st term in the sequence that exceeds 1000.

5 A sequence has nth term $10 - 7n$
   Find the term in the sequence that is closest to -500.

6

      1st   2nd   3rd   4th

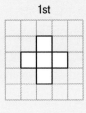 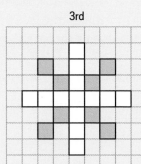 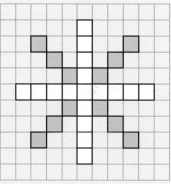

   Work out

    a the nth term for the number of white squares

    b the nth term for the number of green squares

    c the nth term for the total number of squares

⬙ **Exam practice**

1 Here are the first five terms of an arithmetic sequence.
     3   6   9   12   15

    a Write an expression, in terms of n, for the nth term of this sequence. **(1 mark)**

    b Is 299 a term of this sequence?
       You must give a reason for your answer. **(2 marks)**

    c Write an expression, in terms of n, for the $(n + 1)$th term of this sequence. **(1 mark)**

      Adapted from 1MA1/2H, June 2017, Q22 and 1MA10/1H, June 2017, Q10a and Q10b

---

Exam feedback   Results**Plus**

Q1a: Most students who achieved **Grade 7** or above answered a similar question well.

2.6 Non-linear sequences

Key points

- A quadratic sequence has n^2 and no higher power of n in its nth term
- The second differences of a quadratic sequence, $u_n = an^2 + bn + c$, are constant and equal to $2a$.
- The nth term of a quadratic sequence can be worked out in three steps.
  Step 1 Work out the second differences.
  Step 2 Halve the second difference to get the coefficient, a, of the n^2 term.
  Step 3 Subtract the sequence an^2 from the given sequence. You may need to add a constant, or find the nth term of the remaining linear sequence.

△ Purposeful practice 1

1 Work out the second difference of each of these sequences and write the value of a in an^2.

    a 2, 6, 12, 20, 30, ...
    b 3, 7, 13, 21, 31, ...
    c 4, 8, 14, 22, 32, ...

    d 3, 10, 21, 36, 55, ...
    e 4, 11, 22, 37, 56, ...
    f 5, 12, 23, 38, 57, ...

    g 4, 14, 30, 52, 80, ...
    h 5, 15, 31, 53, 81, ...
    i 6, 16, 32, 54, 82, ...

    j 5, 18, 39, 68, 105, ...
    k 6, 19, 40, 69, 106, ...
    l 13, 44, 95, 166, 257, ...

2 Find a formula for the nth term of each sequence. You are given the first 5 terms of each sequence and the n^2 term in brackets.

    a (n^2) 2, 6, 12, 20, 30
    b (n^2) 4, 9, 16, 25, 36
    c (n^2) 4, 12, 22, 34, 48

    d $(2n^2)$ 9, 18, 31, 48, 69
    e $(2n^2)$ 3, 10, 21, 36, 55
    f $(2n^2)$ 6, 14, 26, 42, 62

    g $(3n^2)$ 15, 26, 43, 66, 95
    h $(3n^2)$ 10, 21, 38, 61, 90
    i $(3n^2)$ 3, 14, 31, 54, 83

    j $(4n^2)$ 13, 32, 59, 94, 137
    k $(4n^2)$ 0, 13, 34, 63, 100
    l $(4n^2)$ 7, 19, 39, 67, 103

Reflect and reason

Finding the nth term of a quadratic sequence involves lots of steps.
Look back at your answers to **Q1** and **Q2**.
Could someone else easily determine the steps you have taken, from your working?
If not, rewrite one or two answers so that the steps are clear.

△ Purposeful practice 2

Work out u_n

1 6, 12, 20, 30, 42, ...
2 0, 10, 26, 48, 76, ...
3 6, 15, 28, 45, 66, ...

4 16, 36, 66, 106, 156, ...
5 17, 26, 37, 50, 65, ...
6 8, 16, 28, 44, 64, ...

Reflect and reason

Aisha is working with the sequence 6, 10, 15, 21, 28.
She says, 'The first part of the nth term of the sequence is n^2.'
She subtracts n^2 from the sequence to give 5, 6, 6, 5, 3.
She says, 'This is not a linear sequence so I must have been wrong about the sequence being quadratic.'
Find her error.
Find the nth term of the quadratic.

1 Work out the nth term for the number of squares in this sequence.

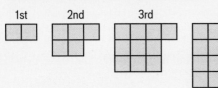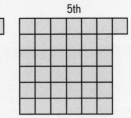

2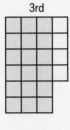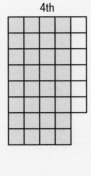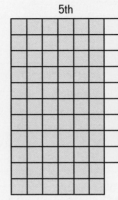

Work out

a the nth term for the number of blue squares

b the nth term for the number of yellow squares

c the nth term for the total number of squares

3 Ben is working out the nth term for the sequence
3, 11, 21, 33, 47.
He subtracts the terms of n^2 from the sequence to leave
$-2, -7, -12, -17, -22$.
He says that the nth term of the original sequence is $n^2 - 5n + 3$.
He is incorrect.
Explain his error.

4 A sequence is given as 1, 3, 6, 10, 15, …
a Work out the nth term of the sequence.
b Write the term-to-term rule for the sequence.
c What is the name of this sequence?

✦ **Exam practice**

1 Here are the first four terms of a quadratic sequence.
5, 15, 29, 47
Find an expression, in terms of n, for the nth term of this sequence.

Adapted from 1MA1/2H, June 2017, Q22

Exam feedback   Results Plus

Most students who achieved a Grade 7 or above answered a similar question well.

Key points

- To expand double brackets, multiply each term in one bracket by each term in the other bracket.
- To square a single bracket, multiply it by itself, and then expand and simplify.
  $(x + 1)^2 = (x + 1)(x + 1) = x^2 + 2x + 1$

△ Purposeful practice 1

Expand and simplify

1 $(x + 1)(x + 1)$ **2** $(x + 2)(x + 1)$ **3** $(x + 1)(x + 2)$

4 $(x + 1)(x - 3)$ **5** $(x - 1)(x + 3)$ **6** $(x - 2)(x + 5)$

7 $(x - 2)(x - 2)$ **8** $(x - 3)(x - 6)$ **9** $(x - 4)(x - 4)$

10 $(x + 3)^2$ **11** $(x - 1)^2$ **12** $(x - 2)^2$

Reflect and reason

Michael says, 'The expansion of $(x + 2)(x + 2)$ is $x^2 + 4x + 4$. Therefore, the expansion of $(x + 6)(x + 6)$ is $x^2 + 12x + 12$.'
Explain his error.

△ Purposeful practice 2

1 Factorise

  a $x^2 + 2x + 1$ **b** $x^2 + 5x + 6$ **c** $x^2 - x - 2$

  d $x^2 + 7x + 12$ **e** $x^2 - 7x + 12$ **f** $x^2 - x - 12$

  g $x^2 - x - 20$ **h** $x^2 + 17x + 70$ **i** $x^2 - 2x + 1$

  j $x^2 + 9x + 14$ **k** $x^2 - 6x + 9$ **l** $x^2 - 10x + 25$

2 Factorise

  a $x^2 - 1$ **b** $p^2 - 4$ **c** $c^2 - 9$

  d $x^2 - 100$ **e** $a^2 - 36$ **f** $k^2 - 169$

  g $100 - x^2$ **h** $25 - y^2$ **i** $2^2 - k^2$

  j $4x^2 - 4$ **k** $9x^2 - 16$ **l** $16 - 9x^2$

Reflect and reason

Copy and complete these factorisations.

$x^2 - 6x - 16 = (x \square 8)(x \square 2)$

$x^2 - 36 = (x \square 6) (x \square 6)$

Explain how you decided on the missing operations.

1   The areas of two rectangles are added to make the area of a square.
    Work out an expression for the length of the side of the square.

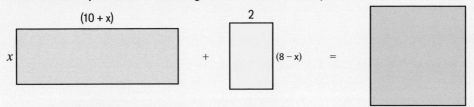

2   $y^2 + ay + 8$ can be factorised as $(y + b)(y + 2b)$.
    Find the values of a and b.

3   I think of a number and then add 3.
    I multiply that answer by my original number.
    It is now the same as my original number squared, plus 6.

    a   Write an equation to represent the problem.

    b   Solve the equation.

4   Aidan is trying to expand and simplify $(h - 6)^2$.
    Here is his working
    $$(h - 6)^2 = (h - 6)(h - 6)$$
    $$= h^2 - 6h - 6h - 36$$
    $$= h^2 - 12h - 36$$
    Aidan's answer is wrong.
    Find the error in his working.

5   Find an expression for the blue shaded area.

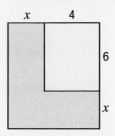

6   The difference between the area of the two rectangles is 30.
    Find x.

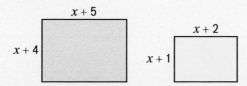

1   Factorise
    $x^2 - 2x - 8$
    (2 marks)

Adapted from 1MA1/3H, Specimen Papers, Set 1, Q6

3 Interpreting and representing data

3.1 Statistical diagrams 1

Key point

- A pie chart represents a set of data. Each sector represents a category within that set of data.

⚠ Purposeful practice

1 The pie charts show the favourite colours of students in two schools.

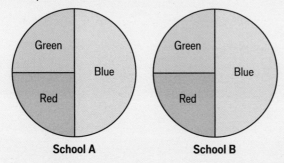

School A

School B

School A has 1400 students and school B has 960 students.

a Work out how many students in each school chose red.

b In which school did more students choose red?

2 The pie charts show the favourite flavour of crisps of students in two schools.
School A has 1400 students and school B has 960 students.

a Work out how many students in each school chose ready salted.

b In which school did more students choose ready salted?

3 The pie charts show the favourite fruit of students in two schools.
School A has 1400 students and school B has 960 students.
In which school did more students choose orange?

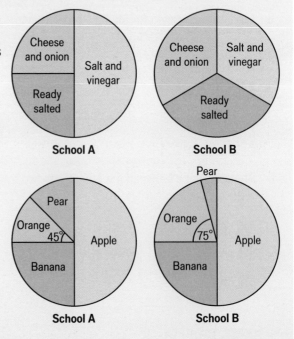

Reflect and reason

When comparing two pie charts, does a larger sector on one pie chart always represent a larger number? Use the questions on this page to explain your answer.

1   The pie charts show some information about the numbers of matches that a cricket team and a football team won, drew and lost last year.

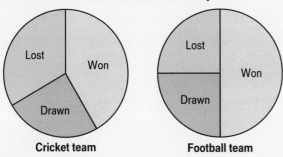

Jo says, 'These pie charts show the football team won more matches than the cricket team.'
Explain why Jo might not be correct.

2   The pie charts show the number of tennis matches Luke and Maisie each won and lost last year.

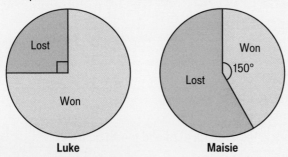

Luke played 56 matches.
Maisie played 120 matches.
Who won more matches?
How many more?

1   Pie chart A gives information about the location of the people who logged onto a website last week.
Pie chart B gives information about the location of the people who logged onto the same website this week.

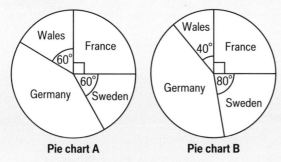

Diagrams not accurately drawn

Becky says, 'The pie charts show that more people in Sweden logged onto the website this week than last week.'
Is Becky correct?
Explain your answer.   **(1 mark)**

3.2 Time series

△ Purposeful practice

1   The time series graph shows the number of visitors to the UK for each quarter for the years 2015 to 2017.

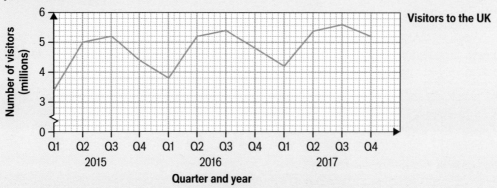

   a   Write the number of visitors for the first quarter of each year.
   Are these numbers increasing or decreasing?

   b   Repeat part **a** for the number of visitors in the second, third and fourth quarters.

   c   Describe the overall trend.

   d   Describe the variation in the number of visitors to the UK over the course of each year.

2   The time series graph shows the number of visitors to a theme park for each quarter for the years 2016 to 2018.

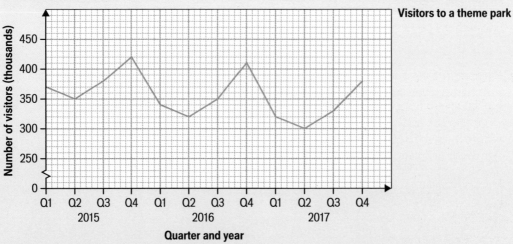

   a   Write down the number of visitors for the first quarter of each year.
   Are these numbers increasing or decreasing?

   b   Repeat part **a** for the number of visitors in the second, third and fourth quarters.

   c   Describe the overall trend.

   d   Describe the variation in the number of visitors to the theme park each year.

Reflect and reason

Explain the difference between describing the trend and the variation of the data.

1   The time series graph shows how much money UK residents spent when visiting abroad for each quarter for the years 2015 to 2017.

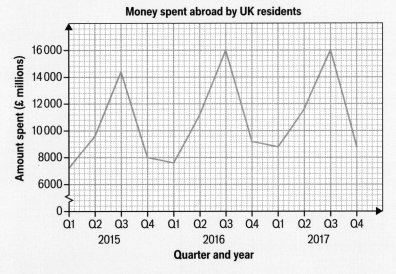

Mila is asked to describe the overall trend.
She says, 'Each year the amount spent is at its lowest in the first quarter then it increases for the second and third quarters and then decreases for the fourth quarter.'
Explain why Mila is incorrect.

2   The table shows the mean number of hours students spent watching TV each term from 2016 to 2018.

Year	2016			2017			2018		
Term	1	2	3	1	2	3	1	2	3
Hours	203	132	140	204	131	139	202	133	140

Describe the overall trend.

⊠ Exam practice

1   The time series graph gives some information about the number of visitors to an attraction in the first week of the school holidays.

The attraction predicted 750 visitors per day for the first week.
Did the attraction meet this predicted number?
You must show how you get your answer.
(3 marks)

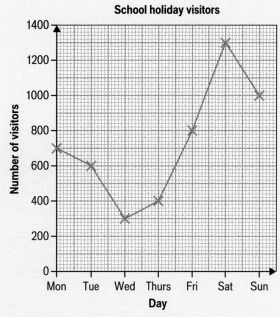

Adapted from 1MA1/2H, Specimen Papers, Set 1, Q3

Key points

- Bivariate data has two variables. Plotting these on a scatter graph can show whether there is a relationship between them.
- A scatter graph shows a relationship or correlation between variables.

△ Purposeful practice

1 The graph shows the heights (in cm) and weights (in kg) of 10 students.
One of the students has a height of 167 cm.

  a Write the weight of this student.

  b What type of correlation does the scatter graph show?

  c Describe the relationship between the height and the weight of these students.

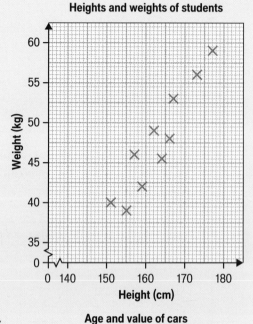

Heights and weights of students

2 The scatter graph shows the age and value of 8 cars.
One of the cars is two years old.

  a What is the value of the car?

  b What type of correlation does the scatter graph show?

  c Describe the relationship between the age and the value of the cars.

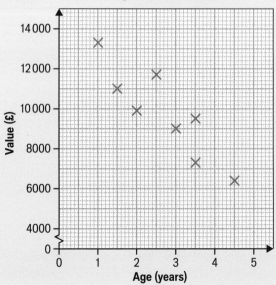

Age and value of cars

Reflect and reason

Explain the difference between stating the type of correlation and describing the relationship between the variables plotted on a scatter graph.

1 The scatter graph shows the height and test
  scores of 8 students.
  A teacher says, 'The shorter the student, the
  lower their test score.'
  Does the scatter graph support what the teacher
  says?
  Give a reason for your answer.

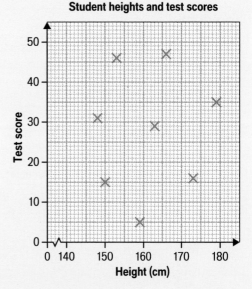

2 The table shows the length and width, in cm, of 10 leaves from the same tree.

Length (cm)	5.5	6.1	6.6	6.8	7.4	7.9	8.2	8.7	9.2	9.4
Width (cm)	2.8	3.2	3.1	3.5	3.7	3.3	4.2	3.7	4.2	4.7

  A biologist says, 'Longer leaves are wider.'
  Does the data support what the biologist says?
  Give a reason for your answer.

1 The scatter graph shows the hand length
  and foot length of 10 students.
  One of the students has a hand length of
  19.2 cm.
  a Write the foot length of this student.
    (1 mark)
  b Write the type of correlation for the
    scatter graph. **(1 mark)**
  A teacher says, 'Students with a greater
  hand length have longer feet.'
  c Does the scatter graph support what
    the teacher says?
    Give a reason for your answer.
    (1 mark)

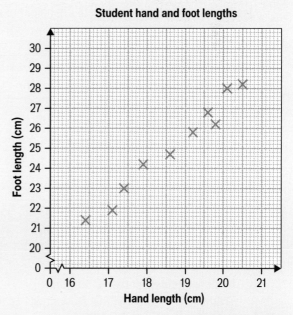

Adapted from 1MA1/1H, May 2017, Q1a, Q1b and Q1d

Exam feedback   ResultsPlus

Most students who achieved a **Grade 3** or above answered a similar question well.

3.4 Line of best fit

Key point

- A line of best fit is the line that passes as close as possible to the points on a scatter graph.

△ Purposeful practice

1   Tom recorded the height in cm and the weight in kg of 10 students.
    The scatter graph shows his results.

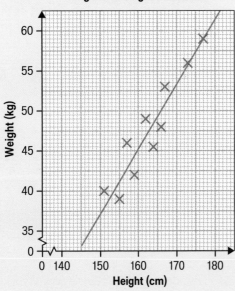

Height and weight of students

Use the line of best fit to estimate the height of a student weighing 44 kg.

2   The table shows the ages and values of 8 cars.

Age (years)	1	1.5	2	2.5	3	3.5	4.0	4.5
Value (£)	13300	11000	9900	11700	9000	7300	9500	6400

   a   Draw a scatter graph of this data.
   b   Draw a line of best fit on your scatter graph.
   c   Use your line of best fit to estimate the value of a four-year-old car.

3   The table shows the scores of two maths test papers for 10 students.

Paper 1	16	23	26	33	35	40	41	49	52	55
Paper 2	13	19	20	28	32	40	32	48	55	53

   a   Draw a scatter graph of this data.
   b   Another student scores 30 on Paper 1.
       Estimate the score that this student will achieve on Paper 2.

Reflect and reason

Try to estimate the answer to **Q3b** without using a line of best fit. Which is the most accurate estimate?
Explain your answer.

1   The scatter graph shows the length and width, in cm, of 10 leaves from the same tree.

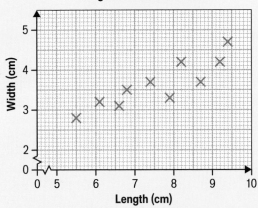

Nathan estimates the length of another leaf with a width of 4 cm.
Nathan says, 'This leaf will be 7.5 cm long.'
Use the scatter graph to explain why Nathan might not be correct.

✷ **Exam practice**

1   The scatter graph shows the hand length and foot length, in cm, of 10 students.

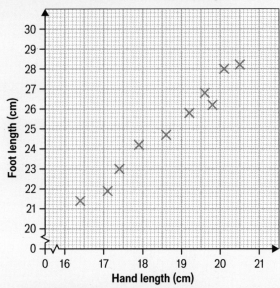

Another student measures their hand.
It is 18.8 cm long.
Estimate the length of this student's foot.   **(2 marks)**

Adapted from 1MA1/1H, May 2017, Q1c

Exam feedback   Results**Plus**

Most students who achieved a **Grade 3** or above answered a similar question well.

Key points

- The mean is the total of the set of values divided by the number of values.
- When data is grouped, you can calculate an estimate for the mean.

⚠ Purposeful practice

1   Sara asked some students how long they spent watching TV one weekend.
    The grouped frequency table shows her results.

Time, t (hours)	Frequency, f
$0 \leqslant t < 1$	15
$1 \leqslant t < 2$	13
$2 \leqslant t < 3$	18
$3 \leqslant t < 4$	20
$4 \leqslant t < 5$	14

   a   What single value best represents the group $0 \leqslant t < 1$?
   b   What single values best represent the groups $1 \leqslant t < 2$, $2 \leqslant t < 3$, $3 \leqslant t < 4$ and $4 \leqslant t < 5$?
   c   Work out an estimate for the total number of hours of TV watched.
   d   How many students took part in the survey?
   e   Estimate the mean number of hours the students spent watching TV.

2   The grouped frequency table shows the heights of some plants.

Height, h (cm)	Frequency, f
$0 < h \leqslant 5$	3
$5 < h \leqslant 10$	11
$10 < h \leqslant 15$	16
$15 < h \leqslant 20$	25
$20 < h \leqslant 25$	5

   a   Work out an estimate for the total heights of the plants.
   b   How many plants were measured?
   c   Estimate the mean height of the plants.

3   The grouped frequency table shows the ages of staff at a school.

Age, a (years)	Frequency, f
$20 < a \leqslant 30$	41
$30 < a \leqslant 40$	51
$40 < a \leqslant 50$	29
$50 < a \leqslant 60$	3
$60 < a \leqslant 70$	1

   a   How many staff are at the school?
   b   Estimate the mean age of the staff.
       Round your answer to 3 s.f.

Reflect and reason

When estimating the mean from a grouped frequency table, how do you work out the total number of values to divide by? Use one of the questions on this page to explain your answer.

For each of **Q1–3**, compare your estimate of the mean to the lowest and highest possible data values. Can the mean be outside the data values? Explain.

⊠ Problem-solving practice

1 Paul estimates the mean of the data in the grouped frequency table.

Length, l (cm)	Frequency, f
$80 < l \leqslant 100$	12
$100 < l \leqslant 120$	17
$120 < l \leqslant 140$	25
$140 < l \leqslant 160$	19
$160 < l \leqslant 180$	6

Paul writes

Total length = (80 × 12) + (100 × 17) + (120 × 25) + (140 × 19) + (160 × 6)
            = 9280
Estimate of mean = 9280 ÷ 5
            = 1856 cm

There are two errors in Paul's working.

a Explain how you know from Paul's answer of 1856 cm that he has made a mistake.

b Explain each error that Paul has made.

c Show the correct working and answer that Paul should have written.
   Give your answer to 1 d.p.

 ✦ Exam practice

1 The table shows information about the monthly salaries of 50 people who work at a company.

Monthly salaries, x (£)	Frequency, f
$1000 < x \leqslant 2000$	2
$2000 < x \leqslant 3000$	27
$3000 < x \leqslant 4000$	18
$4000 < x \leqslant 5000$	0
$5000 < x \leqslant 6000$	3

a Work out an estimate for the mean of the monthly salaries. **(3 marks)**

Arif says, 'The mean may **not** be the best average to use to represent this information.'

b Do you agree with Arif?
   You must justify your answer. **(1 mark)**

Adapted from 1MA1/1H, November 2017, Q5

Exam feedback ResultsPlus

Q1a: In a similar question, some students did not score full marks due to arithmetic errors, typically when finding fx.

Q1b: In a similar question, students did not give reasons to justify their answer.

Key point

• A two-way table divides data into groups in rows across the table and in columns down the table.

⚠ Purposeful practice

1 126 students went on an educational trip.
Each student went to a museum, to an art gallery or to the theatre.
71 of the students are female and the rest are male.
19 of the 47 students who went to the theatre are male.
32 of the students went to the art gallery. 29 males went to the museum.

a Copy and complete the two-way table to show this information.

	Museum	Art Gallery	Theatre	Total
Male				
Female				
Total				

b Work out the number of female students who went to the art gallery.

2 85 children each buy a piece of fruit.
They each buy an apple, a banana or an orange.
46 of these children are girls and the rest are boys.
18 boys buy an apple. 13 girls buy a banana.
11 of the 17 children who buy an orange are boys.

a Copy and complete the two-way table to show this information.

				Total
Girls				
Boys				
Total				

b Work out the number of children who buy an apple.

3 A teacher asked 30 children how they spent a school holiday.
The children either stayed at home, went on holiday in the UK or went on holiday abroad.
16 of the children were boys and the rest were girls.
5 of the boys went on holiday in the UK. 5 girls stayed at home.
5 of the 12 children who went abroad were boys.

a Work out the number of children who went on holiday in the UK, without drawing a two-way table.

b Draw and complete a two-way table to show this information and then write down the number of children who went on holiday in the UK.

Reflect and reason

Was it easier to work out the number of children who went on holiday in the UK in **Q3** with or without drawing a two-way table? Explain your answer.

1 The two-way table shows information about how some people travelled to work.

	Walk	Car	Cycle	Total
Full-time	124		7	179
Part-time		26		
Total			42	346

A person who works part-time is chosen at random.
Write the probability that they walked to work.
Give your answer as a fraction.

2 Cola is sold in $\frac{1}{2}$ litre bottles, in 1 litre bottles and in 2 litre bottles.
One weekend a shop sold 60 bottles of cola.
16 of the bottles were sold on Sunday.
7 of the bottles sold on Sunday were 2 litre bottles.
9 of the bottles sold on Saturday were $\frac{1}{2}$ litre bottles.
26 of the bottles sold were 2 litre bottles.
20 of the bottles sold were 1 litre bottles.
Which day did they sell the greatest number of 1 litre bottles?
Show your working to explain.

3 During a sport fundraising event at a college, students choose one sport.
They choose football or hockey or dance.
150 students are fundraising.
78 of the students are 16 years old and the rest are 17 years old.
12 of the 16-year-olds and 16 of the 17-year-olds play hockey.
55 of the students play football.
16 of the 55 students who play football are 17 years old.
How many more 17-year-olds than 16-year-olds dance?

✶ Exam practice

1 80 people were asked if they prefer to eat British, Italian or Indian food.
43 of the people were male and the rest were female.
23 of the 41 people who said British were female.
3 males said Italian.
25 people said Indian.
One of the females is chosen at random.
What is the probability that this female said Italian?   **(4 marks)**

Adapted from 1MA1/2H, June 2018, Q8

Exam feedback   Results**Plus**
Most students who achieved a **Grade 4** or above answered a similar question well.

4 Fractions, ratio and percentages

4.1 Fractions

Key points

- The reciprocal of the number n is $\frac{1}{n}$. You can also write this as n^{-1}.
- It is often easier to write mixed numbers as improper fractions before doing a calculation.

△ Purposeful practice 1

Find the reciprocal of these numbers.

1 a 2   b 3   c 4   d 5

2 a $\frac{1}{2}$ b $\frac{1}{3}$ c $\frac{1}{4}$ d $\frac{1}{5}$

3 a 0.2   b 0.3   c 1.3   d 1.7

   e 0.12   f 0.16   g 0.165   h 0.565

4 a $\frac{2}{7}$ b $\frac{3}{7}$ c $\frac{4}{7}$ d $\frac{5}{7}$

5 a $1\frac{1}{6}$ b $2\frac{2}{7}$ c $3\frac{4}{9}$ d $4\frac{5}{11}$

Reflect and reason

Look at the questions and answers for **Q1** and **Q2**.

What do you notice?

What do you need to do before you can find the reciprocal of a mixed number?

△ Purposeful practice 2

Work out

1 a $2\frac{3}{5} + 1\frac{2}{7}$ b $2\frac{2}{7} + 1\frac{4}{9}$ c $2\frac{3}{7} + 1\frac{4}{9}$ d $2\frac{3}{4} + 1\frac{4}{9}$

2 a $2\frac{4}{7} - 1\frac{2}{5}$ b $2\frac{3}{4} - 1\frac{4}{7}$ c $2\frac{4}{7} - 1\frac{2}{9}$ d $2\frac{2}{9} - 1\frac{3}{4}$

3 a $1\frac{1}{7} \times 1\frac{1}{5}$ b $1\frac{7}{8} \times 2\frac{2}{5}$ c $1\frac{1}{3} \times 3\frac{3}{5}$ d $1\frac{2}{7} \times 4\frac{3}{8}$

4 a $1\frac{1}{7} \div 1\frac{1}{14}$ b $2\frac{1}{7} \div 1\frac{2}{3}$ c $3\frac{2}{3} \div 1\frac{5}{7}$ d $4\frac{7}{8} \div 1\frac{1}{4}$

Reflect and reason

Mary writes this calculation

$$1\frac{1}{7} \times 2\frac{4}{5} = (1 \times 2) + \left(\frac{3}{7} \times \frac{4}{5}\right)$$
$$= 2\frac{12}{35}$$

What mistakes has she made?

1. The reciprocal of a number is 0.45
   What is the number?

2. A rectangle has side lengths $2\frac{3}{4}$ m and $3\frac{2}{7}$ m.
   Calculate its perimeter and area.

3. Sandra needs strips of ribbon $1\frac{2}{3}$ m long.
   She can buy a 12 m length of ribbon.
   How many strips can Sandra cut from the 12 m length?

4. John has a $5\frac{1}{4}$ m length of wood.
   He cuts $3\frac{2}{5}$ m from it.
   How long is the remaining piece?

5. A wall measuring $3\frac{1}{4}$ m by $2\frac{1}{5}$ m needs to be painted.
   A tin of paint covers $5\,\text{m}^2$.
   How many tins are required to cover the wall completely with two coats of paint?

6. $a^{-1} = 1.4$
   Find a.

7. $4\frac{3}{5} \div y = 1\frac{34}{35}$
   Find the value of y. Write y as a mixed number.

8. $x \times 2\frac{1}{3} = 4\frac{1}{9}$

   $y + 1\frac{2}{3} = 3\frac{1}{6}$

   Work out the value of xy. Give your answer as a mixed number.

✵ Exam practice

1. Find the reciprocal of 1.6.
   Give your answer as a decimal. **(1 mark)**

   Adapted from 1MA1/3H, November 2017, Q5a

2. a Work out

   $1\frac{1}{5} + 4\frac{1}{3}$ **(2 marks)**

   b Work out

   $2\frac{1}{6} \div \frac{2}{3}$

   Give your answer as a mixed number in its simplest form. **(2 marks)**

   Adapted from 1MA1/1H, May 2018, Q1

Exam feedback

Q2a: Most students who achieved a **Grade 5** or above answered a similar question well.

Q2b: Most students who achieved a **Grade 7** or above answered a similar question well.

Key points

- You can compare ratios by writing them as unit ratios. In a unit ratio, one of the numbers is 1.
- You can share amounts in a ratio.

△ Purposeful practice 1

1 Write each ratio in the form $1 : n$
   a 2 : 3   b 2 : 5   c 2 : 7
   d 4 : 3   e 4 : 5   f 4 : 7

2 Write each ratio in the form $n : 1$
   a 2 : 3   b 2 : 5   c 2 : 7
   d 4 : 3   e 4 : 5   f 4 : 7

3 Write each ratio in the form $1 : n$
   a 1 cm : 3 m   b 2 cm : 4 m   c 3 m : 0.3 km
   d 20 g : 0.8 kg   e 400 g : 5 kg   f 300 ml : 7 litres
   g 500 ml : 8 litres

Reflect and reason

The instructions on a car shampoo bottle read, 'Mix 100 ml of shampoo with 4 litres of water.'
Rob says, 'That is a ratio of 25 : 1.'
Rob is not correct.
What has he done wrong?

△ Purposeful practice 2

1 Share £240 in each ratio. Round your answers to the nearest penny.
   a 1 : 2   b 1 : 3   c 1 : 7
   d 2 : 3   e 5 : 7   f 4 : 11

2 Share £360 in each ratio. Round your answers to the nearest penny.
   a 1 : 2 : 3   b 1 : 3 : 4   c 1 : 4 : 5
   d 2 : 3 : 5   e 2 : 3 : 7   f 4 : 3 : 11

3 Share £100 in each ratio. Round your answers to the nearest penny.
   a 1 : 2 : 3   b 1 : 3 : 4   c 1 : 4 : 5
   d 2 : 3 : 7   e 1 : 3 : 14   f 3 : 2 : 4

Reflect and reason

When you have shared an amount in a ratio, what quick check can you do to see if your answer is correct?
Is it always possible to share a sum of money exactly in a given ratio?
What effect does rounding to the nearest penny have?

⊠ Problem-solving practice

1 Ann, Bert and Callum's ages are in the ratio 1 : 2 : 4.
The total of their ages is 42 years.
Find each of their ages.

2 Doris, Ed and Frank's ages are in the ratio 3 : 5 : 8.
The total of their ages is 80 years.
Find each of their ages.

3 Fran is twice the age of George, who is one third the age of Heather.
The sum of their ages is 72 years.
How old is Fran?

4 A cake recipe states that the ratio of flour, sugar and butter should be 5 : 3 : 4.
The total mass of the three ingredients should be 480 g.
Sandi has
250 g of flour
150 g of sugar
150 g of butter
Does she have enough to make the cake?

5 The perimeter of a rectangle is 63 cm.
The width and length of the rectangle are in the ratio 2 : 5.
Find the length of the rectangle.

6 Tom walks along an 8.4 km route.
The route measures 3 cm on a map.
Work out the scale of the map.
Write it as the ratio of distance on the map to real distance in the form $1 : n$.

7 Henna mixes white, green and blue paint in the ratio 1 : 2 : 5 to make a new shade.
She has
100 ml of white paint
240 ml of green paint
500 ml of blue paint
How much more of each colour does Henna need to make 1 litre of the new shade of paint?

⊲ Exam practice

1 The perimeter of a right-angled triangle is 81 cm.
The length of its sides are in the ratio 2 : 3 : 4.
Work out the area of the triangle.   **(4 marks)**

Adapted from 1MA1/1H, May 2018, Q8

Exam feedback   Results**Plus**

Most students who achieved a **Grade 5** or above answered a similar question well.

4.3 Ratio and proportion

Key point

- When two quantities are in direct proportion, as one is multiplied by a number, n, so is the other.

△ Purposeful practice 1

These ratios are in the form P : Q.

1 Write each ratio in the form 1 : n and then write a formula Q = ☐ P.
   The first one has been done for you.

   a $2 : 3 = 1 : 1.5$, so Q = 1.5P

   b $2 : 5$ **c** $4 : 3$ **d** $4 : 5$ **e** $8 : 3$ **f** $8 : 5$

2 Write each ratio in the form n : 1 and then write a formula P = ☐ Q.

   a $2 : 3$ **b** $2 : 5$ **c** $4 : 3$ **d** $4 : 5$ **e** $8 : 3$ **f** $8 : 5$

Reflect and reason

The ratio of A to B is 5 : 6.
Archie worked out that the formula would be

A = 1.2B

This is wrong. Explain why.

△ Purposeful practice 2

1 R is directly proportional to D.
   Write a formula R = ☐ D for each pair of values.

   a When R is 8, D is 4.

   b When R is 12, D is 4.

   c When R is 4, D is 8.

   d When R is 15, D is 10.

   e When R is 5, D is 20.

2 The tables show quantities in direct proportion.
   For each pair of quantities, copy and complete the formula.
   Use the formula to find the missing value.

   a Y = ☐ X

X	2	5	10
Y	6	15	

   b N = ☐ M

M	2	5	10
N	5	12.5	

   c T = ☐ S

S	3	7	
T	10.5	24.5	56

   d V = ☐ W

W	3	7	
V	0.75	1.75	15.2

Reflect and reason

Look at **Q2c** and **Q2d**. What did you have to do differently, compared to **Q2a** and **Q2b**, to work out the missing values?

☒ Problem-solving practice

1   $H = 1.2D$
    Write the ratio $D : H$ in its simplest form where D and H are integers.

2   Decide whether each of these tables shows quantities in direct proportion.
    For those that do, write a formula $Y = \square\, X$

a
X	6	8	15	25
Y	8.4	11.2	21	40

b
X	7.5	10	12.5	15
Y	45	60	75	90

c
X	120	140	230	450
Y	84	98	184	315

3   A conversion ratio for miles : kilometres is 5 : 8.
    The distance from Southampton to Edinburgh is 430 miles.
    What is the distance in kilometres?

4   £1 = 147 Japanese yen.
    $1 = 113 Japanese yen.
    Convert $250 to pounds (£).
    Round your answer to the nearest pence.

5   A pet shop sells dog food in bags of different sizes.
    A 5 kg bag of dog food costs £12.
    An 8 kg bag of dog food costs £20.
    Which is the better value?

6   The cost of rope, C, is directly proportional to its length, L.
    4 metres of rope costs £5.
    Mark buys some rope and pays £7.60.
    How long is Mark's piece of rope?

7   The price of a pizza, P, is directly proportional to its diameter, D.
    An 8 inch pizza has a price of £6.40.
    What is the diameter of a pizza with a price of £9.60?

⬡ Exam practice

1   In England, 1 pint of milk costs 49p.
    In Australia, 1 litre of milk costs 1.44 Australian dollars ($).
    1 pint = 0.568 litres
    £1 = $1.76
    In which country is milk better value for money, England or Australia?
    You must show your working.   **(3 marks)**

    Adapted from 1MA1/3H, November 2017, Q2

Exam feedback   Results**Plus**

In a similar question, students often used the wrong operation when converting units.

Key points

- You can calculate a percentage change using the formula

  $$\text{percentage change} = \frac{\text{actual change}}{\text{original amount}} \times 100$$

- You can use inverse operations to find the original amount after a percentage increase or decrease.

⚠ Purposeful practice 1

1 Find the percentage increase.

   a From 50 to 60   **b** From 50 to 75   **c** From 50 to 100

   d From 80 to 90   **e** From 80 to 100   **f** From 80 to 120

   g From 30 to 75   **h** From 30 to 90   **i** From 30 to 126

2 Find the percentage decrease.

   a From 40 to 30   **b** From 40 to 25   **c** From 40 to 5

   d From 200 to 190   **e** From 200 to 160   **f** From 200 to 20

   g From 750 to 150   **h** From 750 to 187.5   **i** From 750 to 15

3 Find the percentage change. State whether it is an increase or a decrease.

   a From £300 to £390   **b** From £500 to £470   **c** From £1250 to £1500

   d From £20 000 to £18 500   **e** From £250 to £1000   **f** From £5000 to £200

Reflect and reason

John bought a car for £5000. A year later he sold the car for £4000.

He calculated his percentage loss.

$5000 - 4000 = 1000$

$$\frac{1000}{4000} \times 100 = 25\%$$

What mistake has John made?

⚠ Purposeful practice 2

1 Find the original price before the decrease.

   a £72 after a 10% decrease   **b** £72 after a 20% decrease

   c £240 after a 25% decrease   **d** £240 after a 60% decrease

2 Find the original price before the increase.

   a £72 after a 20% increase   **b** £72 after a 50% increase

   c £240 after a 25% increase   **d** £240 after a 60% increase

3 Find the original price before the change.

   a £72.80 after a 12% increase   **b** £73.92 after a 12% decrease

   c £65.25 after a 45% increase   **d** £5060 after an 8% decrease

Reflect and reason

Hasif wants to know how to find the original amount after a percentage change.

Write in your own words how to find the number to divide by.

⊠ Problem-solving practice

1. Bob bought an antique clock for £75 and sold it for £92.
   Jim bought an antique jug for £32 and sold it for £39.
   Who made the largest percentage profit?

2. Freda sold a coat for £12 that she originally bought for £30.
   She also sold a handbag for £15 that she originally bought for £40.
   What was her overall percentage loss considering the two purchases together?

3. The price of a house increased by 5% followed by another increase of 10%.
   It is now worth £288 750.
   What was the original price?

4. Jenny sold a wardrobe for £120, making a 20% loss.
   She also sold a table for £630, making a 5% profit.
   What was her overall profit or loss?

5. An amount is increased by 25% and then decreased by 30%.
   What do you need to divide by to find the original amount?

6. An amount was decreased by 15% twice, then increased by 15% three times. It is now 263.72
   Find the original amount correct to the nearest integer.

⬡ Exam practice

1. Maria buys a washing machine.
   20% VAT is added to the price of the washing machine.
   Maria then has to pay a total of £480.
   What is the price of the washing machine with no VAT added?   **(2 marks)**

   Adapted from 1MA1/1H, May 2017, Q9

2. Seb buys a pack of 8 bottles of water.
   The pack costs £2.94.
   Seb sells all 8 bottles for 40p each.
   Work out Seb's percentage profit.
   Give your answer to 1 decimal place.   **(3 marks)**

   Adapted from 1MA1/2H, November 2017, Q2

3. In 2004, Peter bought a house.
   In 2008, Peter sold the house to Lana.
   He made a profit of 30%.
   In 2015, Lana sold the house for £172 800.
   She made a loss of 20%.
   Work out how much Peter paid for the house in 2004.
   Give your answer to the nearest pound.   **(4 marks)**

   Adapted from 1MA1/3H, June 2018, Q11

Exam feedback   Results**Plus**

Q1: Most students who achieved a **Grade 7** or above answered a similar question well.

Q2: In a similar question, students earned a mark for correctly finding how much Seb paid for 1 bottle or how much he got for selling 8.

Q3: Most students who achieved a **Grade 8** or above answered a similar question well.

4.5 Fractions, decimals and percentages

Key point

- All recurring decimals can be written as exact fractions.

△ Purposeful practice 1

Write each of these fractions as a recurring decimal.

1 $\frac{1}{3}$ 2 $\frac{2}{3}$ 3 $\frac{1}{6}$ 4 $\frac{5}{6}$ 5 $\frac{1}{9}$

6 $\frac{4}{9}$ 7 $\frac{2}{11}$ 8 $\frac{7}{11}$ 9 $\frac{1}{7}$ 10 $\frac{3}{7}$

Reflect and reason

Anne tried to work out the decimal for $\frac{7}{9}$

Look at her working out.

$$7\overline{)9.0000000} \quad \frac{1.2857142}{^{2}6^{6}4^{4}5^{5}1^{1}3^{3}2}$$

$= 1.\dot{2}8571\dot{4}$

What mistake has Anne made?

△ Purposeful practice 2

1 Convert each of these recurring decimals to a fraction in its simplest form.

   a $0.\dot{7}$ b $0.\dot{2}$ c $0.\dot{8}$ d $0.\dot{5}$

   e $0.\dot{1}\dot{3}$ f $0.3\dot{1}$ g $0.5\dot{4}$ h $0.\dot{4}\dot{5}$

   i $0.\dot{1}2\dot{3}$ j $0.\dot{3}2\dot{1}$ k $0.1\dot{3}\dot{2}$ l $0.\dot{3}1\dot{2}$

2 Convert each of these recurring decimals to a fraction in its simplest form.
   The first one has been started for you.

   a $0.6\dot{1}$

$$0.6\dot{1} = 0.611111\ldots$$
$$\text{So } 100n = 61.11111\ldots$$
$$10n = 6.11111\ldots$$
$$90n =$$

   b $0.6\dot{3}$

   c $0.5\dot{1}$

   d $0.5\dot{7}$

Reflect and reason

To convert a recurring decimal to a fraction, what do you multiply the recurring decimal by when it is in each of these forms?

1   $0.\dot{a}$

2   $0.\dot{a}\dot{b}$

3   $0.\dot{a}b\dot{c}$

4   $0.a\dot{b}$

Problem-solving practice

1 Write these numbers in order, from smallest to largest.

$\frac{7}{25}$ $\frac{3}{11}$ $0.2\dot{6}$ 27%

2 Work out

$0.3\dot{6} \times \frac{3}{8}$

Give your answer as a simplified fraction.

3 Work out

$\frac{1}{4} + \frac{7}{36}$

Give your answer as a recurring decimal.

4 Work out

$0.5\dot{1} \div 0.\dot{2}$

Give your answer as a mixed number in its simplest form.

5 Work out

$0.3\dot{4} + 0.\dot{7}$

Give your answer as a mixed number in its simplest form.

6 Work out

$6 \times 0.2\dot{7}$

Give your answer as a mixed number in its simplest form.

7 $x = 0.8\dot{7}$

Show

$x = \frac{29}{33}$

8 $x = 0.6\dot{5}$

Ryan writes

$x = \frac{65}{90}$

Sarah writes

$x = \frac{59}{90}$

Who is correct? Explain why.

Exam practice

1 $x = 0.2\dot{1}\dot{8}$

Prove algebraically x can be written as $\frac{12}{55}$ **(3 marks)**

Adapted from 1MA1/1H, November 2017, Q15

2 Using algebra, prove that $0.1\dot{3}\dot{6} \times 0.\dot{4}$ is equal in value to $\frac{2}{33}$ **(3 marks)**

Adapted from 1MA1/2H, June 2017, Q16

Exam feedback   ResultsPlus

Q1: In a similar question, most students understood the need to find multiples of x.

Q2: Most students who achieved a **Grade 7** or above answered a similar question well.

Mixed exercises A

1 Helen is going to choose a main course and a dessert from a menu.
She can choose from 7 main courses and 5 desserts.
Helen says, 'To work out the number of different ways of choosing a main course and a dessert you add 7 and 5.'
Is Helen correct? You must give a reason for your answer.

2 20 teams play in a competition.
Each team plays the other teams exactly once.
Work out the total number of games played.

3 Buses to Cardiff leave a bus station every 30 minutes.
Buses to Bristol leave the same bus station every 18 minutes.
A bus to Cardiff and a bus to Bristol both leave the bus station at 7 am.
When will buses to Cardiff and to Bristol next leave the bus station at the same time?

4 Can you use the pie charts to determine which team won the greatest number of matches? If so, which team was it?
Explain your answer.

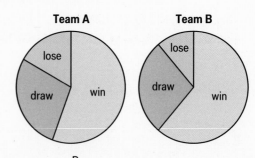
Team A   Team B

5 PQR is a triangle.
Angle PQR = angle PRQ.
The length of side PQ is $(2x - 9)$ cm.
The length of side PR is $(15 - x)$ cm.
The length of side QR is x cm.
Work out the perimeter of the triangle. Give your answer in centimetres.

6 Here are the first five terms of an arithmetic sequence.
2   9   16   23   30

a Find an expression, in terms of n, for the nth term of this sequence.

Emma says, '200 is in the sequence.'

b Is Emma right? You must explain your answer.

7 The table shows information about the length of time, t, in minutes, of the phone calls Lynne had in a week.

a Work out an estimate for the mean length of time of the phone calls.

Lynne says, 'The mean may not be the best average to use to represent this information.'

b Do you agree with Lynne? You must justify your answer.

Time, t (minutes)	Frequency
$0 < t \leqslant 10$	12
$10 < t \leqslant 20$	15
$20 < t \leqslant 30$	5
$30 < t \leqslant 40$	0
$40 < t \leqslant 60$	8

8 Mercury is approximately 5.8×10^7 km from the Sun.
Saturn is approximately 1.427×10^9 km from the Sun.
Jo says, 'Saturn is over a hundred times further away from the Sun than Mercury is.'
Is Jo right? You must show how you get your answer.

9 Harry went to a football match in Madrid.
His ticket cost €130.
The exchange rate was £1 = €1.15

a Work out the cost of his ticket in pounds.

Harry bought a football shirt in Madrid.
The shirt cost €73.40
In London, the same type of shirt cost £60.
The exchange rate was £1 = €1.15

b Compare the cost of the shirt in Madrid with the cost of the shirt in London.

10 Karen works out $4\frac{2}{3} + 3\frac{1}{5}$
Karen writes

$$4\frac{2}{3} + 3\frac{1}{5} = 7\frac{2}{15} + \frac{1}{15} = 7\frac{3}{15} = 7\frac{1}{5}$$

Karen is incorrect. What is Karen's mistake?

11 Monty makes 350 sandwiches.
He makes only four types: ham, cheese, tuna, egg.

$\frac{4}{7}$ of the sandwiches are ham.

24% of the sandwiches are cheese.
The ratio of the number of tuna sandwiches to the number of egg sandwiches is 4 : 7.
Work out the number of tuna sandwiches Monty makes.

12 In a sale, normal prices are reduced by 30%.
A television has a sale price of £546.
By how much money is the normal price of the television reduced?

13 Prove algebraically that the recurring decimal $0.3\dot{1}\dot{5}$ can be written as the fraction $\frac{52}{165}$

14 Here are the first five terms of a sequence.
1   8   19   34   53
Find an expression, in terms of n, for the nth term of this sequence.

✧ Exam practice

15 A force of 80 newtons acts on an area of 30 cm².
The force is increased by 10 newtons.
The area is increased by 10 cm².
Jay says, 'The pressure decreases by less than 20%.'
Is Jay correct? You must show how you get your answer.

$\text{pressure} = \dfrac{\text{force}}{\text{area}}$

(3 marks)

Adapted from 1MA1/2H, June 2018, Q6

Exam feedback

ResultsPlus

Most students who achieved a **Grade 4** or above answered a similar question well.

✦ Exam practice

16 On Saturday, some adults and some children were in a cinema.

The ratio of the number of adults to the number of children was 5 : 2.

Each person had a seat in screen 1 or a seat in screen 2.

$\frac{1}{4}$ of the children had seats in screen 1.

108 children had seats in screen 2.

There are only two screens in the cinema. There are exactly 800 seats in the cinema.

On this Saturday, were there people on more than 60% of the seats?

You must show how you get your answer. **(5 marks)**

Adapted from 1MA1/2H, June 2017, Q2

Exam feedback `ResultsPlus`

Most students who achieved a `Grade 6` or above answered a similar question well.

✦ Exam practice

17 The scatter graph shows the mean weight and life expectancy for eight different breeds of dog.

One of the breeds of dog has a weight of 16 kg.

a Write down the life expectancy of this dog. **(1 mark)**

b Write down the type of correlation for the scatter graph. **(1 mark)**

A vet says, 'Heavier dogs have a lower life expectancy.'

c Does the scatter graph support what the vet says? Give a reason for your answer. **(1 mark)**

d Another breed of dog has an average weight of 20 kg. Estimate the life expectancy of this breed of dog. **(2 marks)**

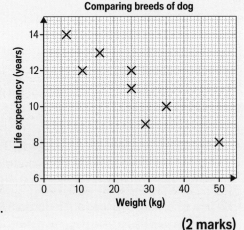

Adapted from 1MA1/1H, May 2017, Q1

Exam feedback `ResultsPlus`

Most students who achieved a `Grade 3` or above answered a similar question well.

✦ Exam practice

18 $T = \sqrt{\dfrac{x}{y}}$

$x = 7.2 \times 10^{-6}$

$y = 1.8 \times 10^{-4}$

a Work out the value of T. **(2 marks)**

x is increased by 5%.

y is increased by 10%.

Kieran says, 'The value of T will increase because both x and y are increased.'

b Kieran is wrong. Explain why. **(2 marks)**

Adapted from 1MA1/3H, June 2018, Q9

Exam feedback `ResultsPlus`

Q18a: Most students who achieved a `Grade 7` or above answered a similar question well.

✦ **Exam practice**

19 Solve

$$\frac{2x - 3}{2} - \frac{5x + 2}{9} = \frac{1 - x}{6}$$

(4 marks)

Adapted from 1MA1/2H, June 2017, Q11

Exam feedback

ResultsPlus

Most students who achieved a **Grade 8** or above answered a similar question well.

✦ **Exam practice**

20 a Factorise $p^2 - q^2$ **(1 mark)**
 b Hence, or otherwise, simplify fully $(x^2 + 9)^2 - (x^2 - 3)^2$ **(3 marks)**

Adapted from 1MA1/1H, June 2018, Q15

Exam feedback

ResultsPlus

Q20a: Most students who achieved a **Grade 8** or above answered a similar question well.
Q20b: Most students who achieved a **Grade 9** answered a similar question well.

 ✦ **Exam practice**

21 $8^{\frac{2}{5}} \times 2^x = 4^{\frac{1}{4}}$
Work out the exact value of x. **(3 marks)**

Adapted from 1MA1/2H, June 2017, Q18

Exam feedback

ResultsPlus

Most students who achieved a **Grade 9** answered a similar question well.

 ✦ **Exam practice**

22 Kate rationalised the denominator of $\frac{3}{\sqrt{20}}$

Here is Kate's answer.

$$\frac{3}{\sqrt{20}} = \frac{3\sqrt{20}}{\sqrt{20} \times \sqrt{20}}$$

$$= \frac{3 \times 5\sqrt{2}}{20}$$

$$= \frac{3\sqrt{2}}{4}$$

Kate's answer is wrong.
Find Kate's mistake. **(1 mark)**

Adapted from 1MA1/2H, June 2018, Q20b

Exam feedback

ResultsPlus

Most students who achieved a **Grade 8** or above answered a similar question well.

5 Angles and trigonometry

5.1 Angle properties of triangles and quadrilaterals

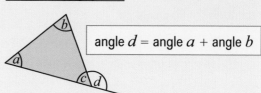
⚠ Purposeful practice 1

Work out the sizes of the angles marked with letters.

1
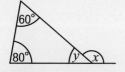

2
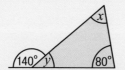

3
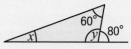

4

5
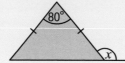

6
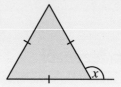

Reflect and reason

In **Q1–4**, was it always necessary to calculate the size of angle y to find the size of angle x?

⚠ Purposeful practice 2

Work out the sizes of the angles marked x in each of the diagrams. Give reasons for your working.

1
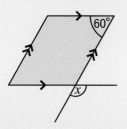

2
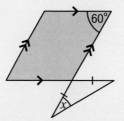

3
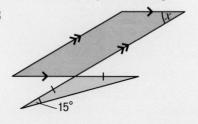

Reflect and reason

Compare your methods for **Q2** and **Q3**. What is the same and what is different?

1   Mia says x is $50 + 70 = 120°$.
    Mia is not correct.
    a   Explain what Mia's mistake is.
    b   Find the value of x.

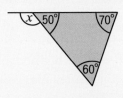

2   Work out the size of the angle marked x.
    Give reasons for your working.

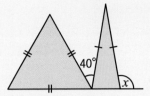

3   In this diagram, AB = BC and angle AED = 43°.
    Is the quadrilateral AFCB a rectangle?
    Show working to explain.

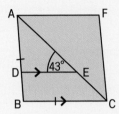

4   Work out the size of the angle marked x.
    Give reasons for your working.

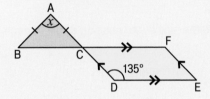

5   Calculate the size of angle y.
    Give reasons for your working.

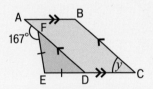

1   ABCD is a parallelogram.
    EDC is a straight line.
    F is the point on AD so that BFE is a straight line.
    Angle EFD = 40°
    Angle BCE = 65°
    Show that angle ABF = 75°.
    Give a reason for each stage of your working.

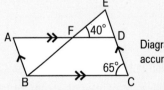

Diagram NOT
accurately drawn

(4 marks)

Adapted from 1MA1/1H, November 2017, Q3

Exam feedback   ResultsPlus

In a similar question, students lost marks due to stating incorrect reasons.

Unit 5 Angle properties of triangles and quadrilaterals   56

5.2 Interior angles of a polygon

Key point

- The sum of the interior angles of a polygon with n sides $= (n - 2) \times 180°$

△ Purposeful practice 1

Calculate the size of one interior angle of a regular polygon with

1   15 sides   **2**   16 sides   **3**   17 sides

4   18 sides   **5**   19 sides

Where necessary, give your answers to 1 d.p.

> **Reflect and reason**
>
> When you increase the number of sides by 1, does the interior angle always increase by the same amount?
>
> What is the largest an interior angle can be?

△ Purposeful practice 2

Calculate the size of the missing angle in each irregular polygon.

1
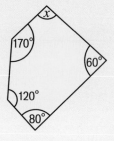

2
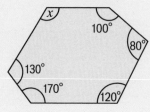

3
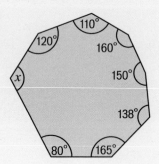

> **Reflect and reason**
>
> In what ways did the number of sides affect your method for **Q1–3**?

△ Purposeful practice 3

Find the number of sides for each polygon.

1   Polygon with sum of interior angles of 720°

2   Polygon with sum of interior angles of 1800°

3   Polygon with sum of interior angles of 3960°

> **Reflect and reason**
>
> When the number of sides doubles, does the sum of the interior angles double?
>
> Is there any limit to the possible size of the angle sum?

Problem-solving practice

1   Sammy says a regular polygon can never have a non-integer interior angle.
    Give an example to show that Sammy is wrong.

2   An interior angle of an octagon is measured as 105°.
    Is this a regular octagon?
    Show working to explain.

3   A pentagon has two right angles.
    What size could its other angles be?

4   The diagram shows a regular hexagon, with centre A.

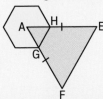

AEF is a triangle where AE = AF.
Work out the size of angle FEA.
Give reasons for your working.

5   The diagram shows a regular pentagon and a regular nonagon.
    Work out the size of the angle marked x.

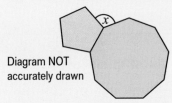

Diagram NOT
accurately drawn

6   Here is a tessellation of regular hexagons.
    A tessellation is a repeating pattern that covers the space
    with no gaps.
    Is it possible to make a tessellation of regular pentagons?
    Show working to explain.

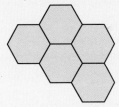

 Exam practice

1   ABCDE is a pentagon.
    Angle BCD = 3 × angle ABC
    Work out the size of angle BCD.
    You must show all your working.

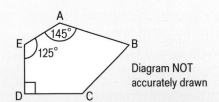

Diagram NOT
accurately drawn

(5 marks)

Adapted from 1MA1/3H, June 2018, Q8

Exam feedback   ResultsPlus

Most students who achieved a **Grade 6** or above answered a similar question well.

5.3 Exterior angles of a polygon

△ Purposeful practice 1

1 Which of these angles are exterior angles?

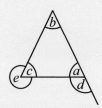 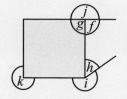

Reflect and reason

Why can an exterior angle never be reflex?

△ Purposeful practice 2

Work out the sizes of the angles marked with letters.
Check that the exterior angles of each shape add up to 360°.

1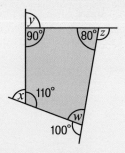

2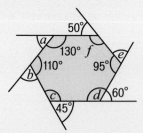

3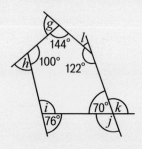

Reflect and reason

In **Q3**, do you need to add all the angles you found to calculate the exterior angle? Explain.

△ Purposeful practice 3

Calculate, giving your answers to 1 d.p. where necessary, the size of one exterior angle of a regular polygon with

1 10 sides   2 11 sides   3 12 sides   4 13 sides

Reflect and reason

When you increase the number of sides by 1, does the exterior angle always decrease by the same amount? What is the smallest an interior angle can be?

1   Sketch and name a regular polygon with obtuse exterior angles.
    Is there more than one regular polygon with obtuse exterior angles?
    Give reasons for your answer.

2   One exterior angle of a regular polygon is 5°.
    How many sides does the polygon have?
    Show your working to explain.

3   The diagram shows a regular pentagon.
    Two sides are extended to create an isosceles triangle.
    What is the size of the angle marked y?
    Show your working to explain.

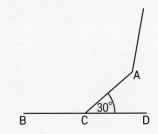

4   In this diagram, BCD is a straight line.
    A, B and C are the vertices of a regular polygon.
    The angle ACD is 30°.
    How many sides does the polygon have?
    Show your working to explain.

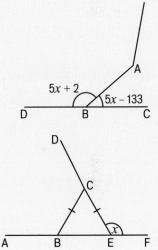

5   ABC is the exterior angle of a regular polygon.
    How many sides does the polygon have?
    Show your working to explain.

6   A, B, C and D are vertices of a regular decagon.
    Calculate the size of the angle marked x.
    Show your working to explain.

1   In the diagram, AB, BC and CD are three sides of a regular
    polygon P.
    The triangles are equilateral triangles.
    Show that polygon P is a 10-sided polygon.
    You must show all your working.

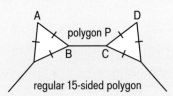

polygon P

regular 15-sided polygon

(4 marks)

Adapted from 1MA1/3H, June 2017, Q5

Exam feedback

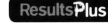

Most students who achieved a **Grade 7** or above answered a similar question well.

5.4 Pythagoras' theorem 1

Key points

- In a right-angled triangle, the longest side is called the hypotenuse.
- Pythagoras' theorem states that, in a right-angled triangle, the square of the hypotenuse is equal to the sum of the squares of the other two sides: $c^2 = a^2 + b^2$
- A triangle with sides a, b and c, where c is the longest side, is right-angled only if $c^2 = a^2 + b^2$.

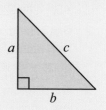

△ Purposeful practice 1

1 Which of these missing lengths are hypotenuses?

    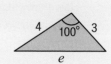

Reflect and reason

What is the same and what is different about the lengths d and e?

△ Purposeful practice 2

Calculate the length of the hypotenuse in each triangle. Where necessary, give your answers to 1 d.p.

1   **2** 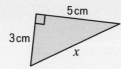 **3**   **4**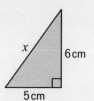

Reflect and reason

As the sides lengthen, what happens to the hypotenuse?

△ Purposeful practice 3

Giving reasons, state whether each triangle is right-angled.

1 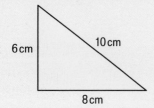 **2** 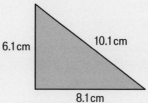 **3**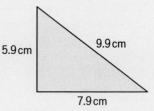

Reflect and reason

Does increasing or decreasing the length of the sides of a right-angled triangle by the same amount give another right-angled triangle? Use your answers to **Q1–3** to explain.

⊠ Problem-solving practice

Where necessary, give your answers to 1 d.p.

1   Two ladders are leaning against a wall.
    They both reach 6 m up the wall.
    The base of one is 2 m away from the wall.
    The base of the other is 1 m away from the wall.
    What is the difference in length between the two ladders?

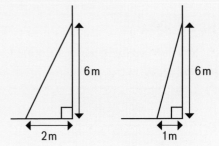

2   A ramp is being built to access the door of a school.
    The ramp starts 1.5 m from the building.
    It rises to a vertical height of 25 cm.
    The top of the ramp is a rectangle 75 cm wide and must
    be covered with non-slip material.
    The non-slip material costs £15 per m².
    What is the total cost of the non-slip material?

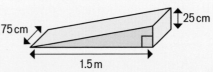

3   A right-angled triangle has a base of 8 cm.
    The area of the triangle is 48 cm².
    Calculate the perimeter of the triangle.

4   In this kite, AB is 85 cm and CD is 60 cm.
    CD is bisected by AB.

    CD crosses AB $\frac{1}{5}$ of the way along AB.
    What is the perimeter of the kite?

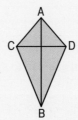

5   Two roads, AB and BC, meet at right angles.
    A new road is built from A to C.
    The length of road AB is double that of BC.
    The length of the new road is 2.5 km.
    How much shorter is the distance on the new road than
    travelling along the sections of the old roads?

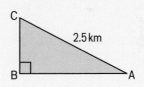

✦ Exam practice

1   This rectangular frame is made from 5 straight pieces of wood.
    The weight of the wood is 1.2 kg per metre.
    Work out the total weight of wood in the frame.

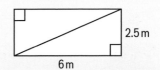

(5 marks)

Adapted from 1MA1/1H, June 2017, Q5

Exam feedback

ResultsPlus

Most students who achieved a **Grade 6** or above answered a similar question well.

5.5 Pythagoras' theorem 2

Key point

- You can use Pythagoras' theorem to work out the length of a shorter side in a right-angled triangle.

◁ Purposeful practice 1

Calculate the missing lengths. Where necessary, give your answers to 1 d.p.

1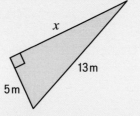

2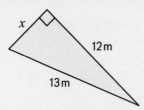

3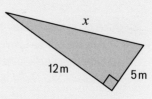

4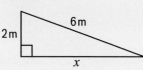

5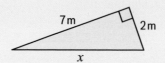

6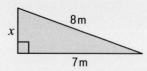

Reflect and reason

Why did your method change for some of the questions?
How did you recognise that you had to change your method?

◁ Purposeful practice 2

Calculate the missing lengths.
Give each answer   **a** as a surd   **b** to 1 d.p.

1

2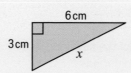

3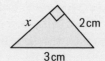

Reflect and reason

Which answers are more accurate, surds or to 1 decimal place?

◁ Purposeful practice 3

Calculate the height of each triangle. Give your answers to 1 d.p.

1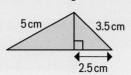

2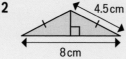

3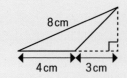

Reflect and reason

What is special about any triangle where the line indicating its perpendicular height bisects the base?

Problem-solving practice

Where necessary, give your answers to 1 d.p.

1 Calculate the height of this isosceles trapezium.

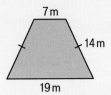

7 m
14 m
19 m

2 An equilateral triangle has a perimeter of 30 cm.
Calculate the area.

3 Two ladders are leaning against a wall.
Their bases are both 1.3 m from the wall.
One reaches 40 cm higher up the wall than the other.
The shorter ladder is 5 m long.
How long is the other ladder?

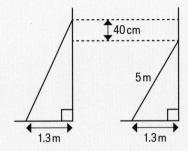

40 cm
5 m
1.3 m   1.3 m

4 Calculate the area of the shaded part of this regular hexagon.

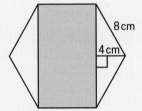

8 cm
4 cm

5 A ramp is built to reach the door to a school.
The ramp starts 3 m away from the doorstep.
The top of the ramp is a rectangle. The rectangle is 98 cm wide.
The ramp is covered in anti-slip material, costing £13 per m².
The anti-slip material cost £39.
What is the height of the doorstep above the ground?

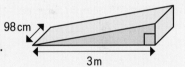

98 cm
3 m

Exam practice

1 This diagram shows a triangle DEF inside a rectangle ABCD.

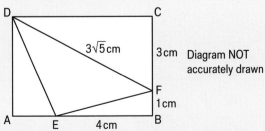

D   C
$3\sqrt{5}$ cm   3 cm   Diagram NOT
                          accurately drawn
F
1 cm
A   E   4 cm   B

Show that the area of triangle DEF is 9 cm². **(4 marks)**

Adapted from 1MA0/1H, June 2016, Q26

5.6 Trigonometry 1

Key points

- The side opposite the right angle is called the hypotenuse.
- The side opposite the angle θ is called the opposite.
- The side next to the angle θ is called the adjacent.
- In a right-angled triangle:

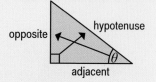

the sine of angle θ is the ratio of the opposite side to the hypotenuse, $\sin \theta = \dfrac{\text{opp}}{\text{hyp}}$

the cosine of angle θ is the ratio of the adjacent side to the hypotenuse, $\cos \theta = \dfrac{\text{adj}}{\text{hyp}}$

the tangent of angle θ is the ratio of the opposite side to the adjacent, $\tan \theta = \dfrac{\text{opp}}{\text{adj}}$

△ Purposeful practice 1

Find x in each triangle. Give your answers to 1 d.p.

1 4 cm, x, 30° **2** 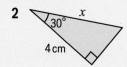 **3** 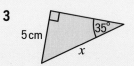 **4**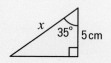

Reflect and reason

How did you decide when to use sine and when to use cosine for **Q1–4**? Could you use the tangent ratio? Explain your answer.

△ Purposeful practice 2

Find x in each triangle. Give your answers to 1 d.p.

1 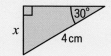 **2** x, 4 cm, 30° **3** 5 cm, x, 35° **4**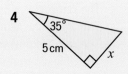

Reflect and reason

What is the same and what is different about your use of the sine ratio in **Q1** in Purposeful practice 1 and Purposeful practice 2? Could you use the cosine ratio to find the opposite side? Explain your answer.

△ Purposeful practice 3

Find x in each triangle. Give your answers to 1 d.p.

1 4 cm, 30°, x **2** 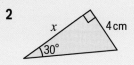 **3** 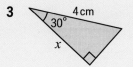 **4**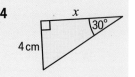

Reflect and reason

Which side were you finding in each triangle – opposite, adjacent or hypotenuse?
How did this help you choose which trigonometric ratio to use?

1 Calculate the area of this triangle.
Give your answer to 1 d.p.

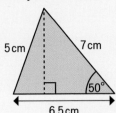

2 Two planks are leaning against a wall.
One meets the wall at a 30° angle and one meets the
ground at a 30° angle.
They are both 6 m long.

What is the difference between the heights they reach
up the wall?
Give your answer to 1 d.p.

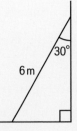

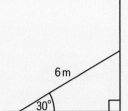

3 The diagram shows a right-angled trapezium.
Calculate its height, to 3 s.f.

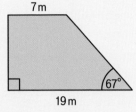

4 The area of this isosceles triangle is double the area of a square.
Give the side length of the square, to 2 d.p.

5 An aeroplane takes off from a runway at an angle of 10° to the ground.
In the first 20 minutes of its journey, the aeroplane travels 50 km.
How high above the ground is it after 20 minutes?
Give your answer to 1 d.p.

 ⬨ **Exam practice**

1 AB = 12 cm
Angle BAD = 74°
Angle BCD = 31°
Work out the length of side BC.
Give your answer correct to 1 decimal place.

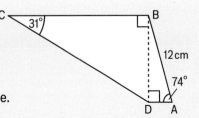

Diagram NOT
accurately drawn

(5 marks)

Adapted from 1MA0/2H, November 2016, Q15

5.7 Trigonometry 2

Key points

- If the lengths of two sides of a right-angled triangle are given, you can find a missing angle using the inverse trigonometric functions: $\sin^{-1}$ $\cos^{-1}$ $\tan^{-1}$
- The angle of elevation is the angle measured upwards from the horizontal.
- The angle of depression is the angle measured downwards from the horizontal.

△ Purposeful practice 1

Calculate the size of the angle labelled x in each triangle. Give your answers to 1 d.p.

1

2

3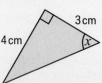

4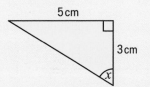

5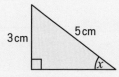

6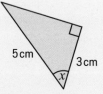

Reflect and reason

For **Q6**, Tom writes, $\cos\theta = \frac{3}{5}$ so $\theta = \frac{3}{\cos 5}$

Explain the mistake Tom has made.

△ Purposeful practice 2

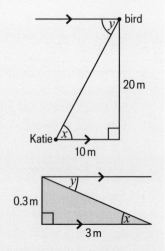

Give your answers to 1 d.p.

1 Katie is standing 10 m away from a 20 m tree.
There is a bird at the top of the tree.
Work out
  a the angle of elevation x from Katie to the bird.
  b the angle of depression y from the bird to Katie.

2 A ramp starts 3 m away from a doorstep.
It joins the step 0.3 m above the ground.
Work out
  a the angle of elevation x from the bottom of the ramp to the top of the step.
  b the angle of depression y from the top of the step to the bottom of the ramp.

Reflect and reason

Explain the relationship between the angles of elevation and depression in each diagram.

⊠ Problem-solving practice

1 Two ladders are leaning against a wall.
One ladder is 4.5 m long and leans against the wall at an angle of 80°.
The other ladder is 4.7 m long.
The ladders reach the same height on the wall.
What is the angle between the 4.7 m ladder and the ground?
Give your answer to 1 d.p.

2 Show that the triangle ABC is not an isosceles triangle.

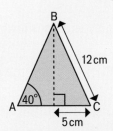

3 Millie is looking at a bird in a tree.
The tree is 10 m away from Millie.
The tree is 27 m tall.
The bird is two thirds of the way up the tree.
What is the angle of elevation of the bird from Millie's feet?
Give your answer to 1 d.p.

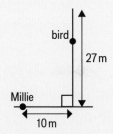

4 Calculate the size of angle ABC, to 1 d.p.

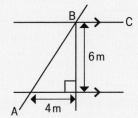

5 The area of this triangle is 11 cm²
Calculate the sizes of the angles in the triangle, to 1 d.p.

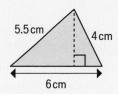

⬙ Exam practice

1 ABCD is a trapezium.
Work out the size of angle CDA.
Give your answer correct to 1 decimal place.

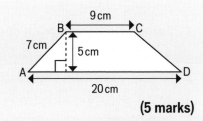

(5 marks)

Adapted from 1MA1/2H, November 2017, Q7

Exam feedback

ResultsPlus

In a similar question, a common error was for students to subtract 9 from 20 to find the missing base length of the right-angled triangle needed to find angle CDA.

6 Graphs

6.1 Linear graphs

Key points

- A linear equation generates a straight-line (linear) graph. The equation for a straight-line graph can be written as $y = mx + c$ where m is the gradient and c is the y-intercept.
- To find the y-intercept of a graph, find the y-coordinate where $x = 0$.
  To find the x-intercept of a graph, find the x-coordinate where $y = 0$.
- To compare the gradients and y-intercepts of two straight lines, make sure their equations are in the form $y = mx + c$.

△ Purposeful practice 1

1 Which of these lines

   a have a negative gradient?   **b** have a positive gradient?

   c have a y-intercept of 0?   **d** are parallel to each other?

   A $y = 3x$ **B** $y = -3x$ **C** $y = 3x + 4$ **D** $y = 3x - 4$

   E $y = -3x + 4$ **F** $y = 4x$ **G** $y = -4x$ **H** $y = -4x - 3$

2 Put these lines in order of steepness, starting with the steepest.

   A $y = 3x + 4$ **B** $y = 5x + 4$ **C** $y = \frac{1}{2}x + 4$ **D** $y = -2x + 4$ **E** $y = -3x$

3 Match each line to an equation.

   $\boxed{y = 2x - 1}$ $\boxed{y = 2x + 4}$ $\boxed{y = 2x + 3}$ $\boxed{y = 2x}$

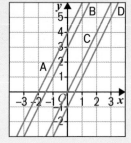

Reflect and reason

Larry says, 'To put lines in order of steepness, starting with the steepest, you have to order the coefficients of x from smallest to largest.' Explain why Larry is wrong.

△ Purposeful practice 2

1 Find the y-intercept for each of these graphs.
   a $2y = 3x + 24$ **b** $3y = 3x + 24$ **c** $4y = 3x + 24$ **d** $8y = 2x + 24$

2 Find the coordinates where each of these graphs crosses the x-axis.
   a $y = 2x + 12$ **b** $y = 3x - 12$ **c** $y = 4x + 12$ **d** $y = 6x - 12$

3 Here are the equations of some linear graphs. Find the gradients of these lines.
   a $2y = 8x + 6$ **b** $3y = 12x + 15$

Reflect and reason

How do you know that the line in part **a** and the line in part **b** in **Q3** are parallel?

Problem-solving practice

1 Peter says, 'All these equations contain $2x$, so all these lines have a gradient of 2.'
   Is Peter correct? If not, explain why.

   A $2x + y = 8$ **B** $2x - y = 8$ **C** $2x + 8 = y$ **D** $2x + 8 = 4y$

2 Three students are studying the equation $8x + 5y = 20$.
   Sarah says, 'The line crosses the y-axis at $(0, 5)$.'
   Theresa says, 'The line crosses the x-axis at $(5, 0)$.'
   Rebecca says, 'The line will go through $(1, 2.4)$.'
   Who is correct?

3 Write the equations of these lines.

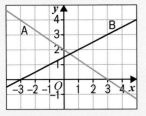

4 Put these equations in order of their y-intercepts, starting with the graph that crosses the y-axis
   nearest to the origin.

   A $2y = 4x + 8$ **B** $3y = 4x + 13$
   C $5x + 6y = 21$ **D** $3y + 2x + 15 = 0$

5 Here are two equations.

   $y = \square x + \square$ $2y = \square x + \square$

   a Complete these equations so the lines are parallel.

   b Complete these equations so their lines have the same y-intercept.

   c Complete these equations so their lines have the same x-intercept.

Exam practice

1 The equation of the line L1 is $y = 2x + 3$
   The equation of line L2 is $4y - 8x = 2$
   Show that these two lines are parallel.   **(2 marks)**

   Adapted from 1MA1/1H, June 2017, Q6

2 Here are the equations of four straight lines.
   Line A $y = 3x - 1$
   Line B $3y = x - 1$
   Line C $3x + 3y = -1$
   Line D $3x - y = -1$
   Two of the lines are parallel.
   Write down the two parallel lines.   **(1 mark)**

   Adapted from 1MA1/3H, Specimen Papers, Set 1, Q7

Exam feedback   Results**Plus**

Q1: Most students who achieved a **Grade 7** or above answered a similar question well.

6.2 More linear graphs

△ Purposeful practice 1

1 Draw these graphs from their equations.
Use a coordinate grid from −5 to +5 on both axes.

   a $y = 3x + 4$ **b** $y = 3x − 1$ **c** $y = 2x + 1$ **d** $y = 2x − 4$

2 Match each equation to one of these sketch graphs.

| $y = 5x + 2$ | $y = 5x − 3$ | $y = 2 − 3x$ | $y = 4 − 3x$ |

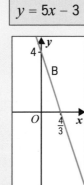
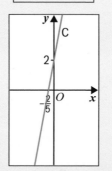
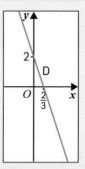

3 Sketch these graphs.
Show clearly where the graphs intercept the x-axis and y-axis.

   a $x + y = 6$ **b** $2x + y = 6$ **c** $2x + 3y = 6$

Reflect and reason

What is different and what is the same about drawing a graph and sketching a graph?

△ Purposeful practice 2

1 (3, 9)   (3, 15)   (3, 14)

   Which of these points lies on these lines?

   a $y = 3x + 5$ **b** $y = 3x + 6$ **c** $y = 3x$

2 (8, 8)   (8, 4)   (8, 0)   (0, 8)   (0, −4)
   (0, −8)   (−8, −4)   (−8, −8)   (8, −8)   (12, 2)

   Which of these points lies on these lines?

   a $y = \frac{1}{2}x + 4$ **b** $y = −\frac{1}{2}x + 4$ **c** $y = −\frac{1}{2}x − 4$

   d $y = −\frac{1}{2}x + 8$ **e** $y = \frac{1}{2}x − 4$ **f** $y = −\frac{1}{2}x − 8$

Reflect and reason

James answered **Q1** and **Q2** by drawing each graph.
Describe a quicker method.

⊠ Problem-solving practice

1   Each pair of coordinates represents the graph of a line joining those two points.
    Which of the graphs has a gradient of $\frac{1}{2}$?
    A (1, 2) to (5, 6)   **B** (1, 2) to (5, 4)   **C** (1, 2) to (5, −6)
    Show your working.

2   Work out the equations of these straight-line graphs.
    a   The line with gradient 2 that passes through (3, 5)
    b   The line with gradient $\frac{1}{2}$ that passes through (4, 5)
    c   The line with gradient −3 that passes through (4, 0)
    d   The line that joins the points (1, 2) to (2, 5)
    e   The line that joins the points (2, 5) to (3, 1)
    f   The line that joins the points (3, 1) to (1, 2)

3   **a**   Draw the graphs of $x + y = 5$ and $4y = 5x - 16$
    b   Write where the two graphs intersect.

4   A square is made using four straight lines.
    The equations of three of these lines are
    $$y = -2x + 1 \qquad y = -2x + 4 \qquad y = \frac{1}{2}x + 1$$

    Point D lies on the fourth side of the square and its
    coordinates are (0.6, 2.8)
    Find the equation of the fourth side of the square.

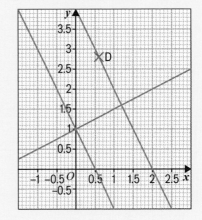

⊠ Exam practice

1   The line L is shown on the grid.
    Find an equation for L.

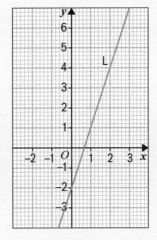

(3 marks)

Adapted from 1MA1/2H, June 2018, Q3

Exam feedback   ResultsPlus

Most students who achieved a **Grade 6** or above answered a similar question well.

6.3 Graphing rates of change

Key points

- The gradient of a straight-line graph is the rate of change.
- A velocity–time graph has time on the x-axis and velocity on the y-axis.
- The gradient is the rate of change of velocity, or acceleration.
- A positive gradient means an object is speeding up.
- Acceleration $= \dfrac{\text{change in velocity}}{\text{time}}$
- The area under a velocity–time graph is the distance travelled.

△ Purposeful practice 1

1 A scientist records the speed of a particle on a graph.

   a   What speed is the particle travelling at 0.5 seconds?

   b   How long does the particle travel at 20 m/s?

   c   When is the particle at its fastest?

   d   When are the two periods when the particle is accelerating?

   e   What is happening to the particle between D and E?

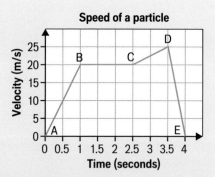

Reflect and reason

What is it about the graph that shows you the particle's speed is constant for a period?

△ Purposeful practice 2

1 The flight recorder on a transatlantic flight produced this velocity–time graph.

   a   What is the acceleration during the first $\frac{1}{2}$ hour?

   b   How far does the aeroplane travel during the first $\frac{1}{2}$ hour?

   c   How far does the aeroplane travel between B and C?

   d   How far does the aeroplane travel between C and D?

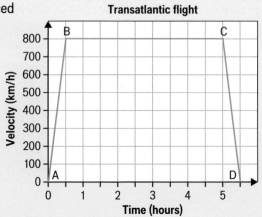

Reflect and reason

Why does the velocity–time graph of an entire flight always give a closed shape?

1 This is the velocity–time graph for part of a car journey.

   a How long is the car travelling at 20 m/s?

   b How far does it travel at this speed of 20 m/s?
     Note that time is measured in minutes on the graph.
     Give your answer in km.

   c What is the acceleration between 12 and
     16 minutes?
     Give your answer in m/s².

   d How far does the car travel between 12 and
     16 minutes?
     Give your answer in km.

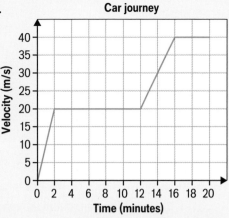

Car journey

2 Shankar records the velocity of a car travelling on an oval
  racetrack and produces this graph.

   a How fast is the car going after 10 seconds?

   b What is the acceleration between 40 and
     43 seconds?

   c How many times is the car driving at a velocity of
     40 m/s?

   d Work out the total distance the car travels round the
     track.

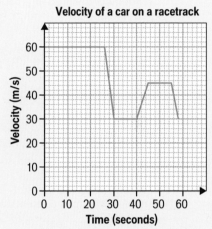

Velocity of a car on a racetrack

3 A train travelling between London and Birmingham leaves
  London at 3 pm and accelerates to 100 mph in 5 minutes.
  It maintains this speed until taking 10 minutes to slow down before arriving in Birmingham at 4.30 pm.
  Draw a velocity–time graph and work out the distance between London and Birmingham.

Exam practice

1 This is a velocity–time graph for 2 minutes of a train's journey.

Train journey

   a Work out the acceleration during the first 40 seconds.
     Give the units in your answer.   (2 marks)

   b Estimate how far the train has travelled in 2 minutes.
     Give your answer in km.   (3 marks)

Key point

- Graphs can be used to display information from a variety of real-life situations.

△ Purposeful practice

1 This graph shows the conversion from British pounds (£) to Australian dollars ($).

   a How many dollars do you get for £10?

   b How many pounds do you get for $30?

   c i Work out the gradient of the graph.

   ii What does the gradient mean, in the context of the two currencies?

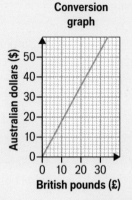

Conversion graph

2 This graph shows the charge to hire a hall for a number of hours.

   a How much does it cost to hire the hall for 4 hours?

   b Andre paid £210 to hire the hall.
   How long did he hire the hall for?

   c i What is the y-intercept?

   ii In this context, what does the y-intercept mean?

   d i What is the gradient?

   ii In this context, what does the gradient mean?

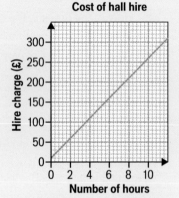

Cost of hall hire

3 Gary has a new freezer delivered and turned on.
Gary monitors the freezer's temperature and records his results on a graph.

   a i What is the y-intercept?

   ii What does the y-intercept mean in the context of the freezer?

   b What is the temperature 6 hours after delivery?

   c To work correctly the freezer has to be at $-12\,°C$.
   How long does this take?

   d i What is the gradient of the graph?

   ii What does this mean in the context of the freezer?

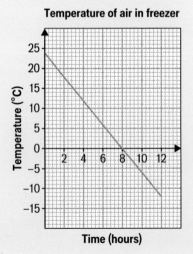

Temperature of air in freezer

Reflect and reason

Why does the graph in **Q3** have a negative gradient?

1 The table shows the largest quantity of sugar s in grams that will dissolve in a cup of tea at temperature $t\,°C$.

$t\,(°C)$	30	45	60	75	90
s (grams)	258	394	523	616	751

   a Plot these results on a scatter graph and draw a line of best fit.

   b Find the largest quantity of sugar that will dissolve in an 80 °C cup of tea.

   c Find the lowest temperature that 700 g of sugar will dissolve in.

   d What does the gradient of your line of best fit tell you?

2 The graph shows the cost of hiring a car from two different companies, Company A and Company B.

   a What is the set-up charge for each company?

   b Work out the gradient of each line and explain what this means in the context of the graph.

   c Which company is cheaper after 12 months?

   d Which company is cheaper after 2 years?

   e At what time is the cost of hiring a car the same from both companies?

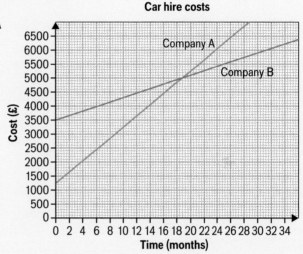

Car hire costs

 ✎ **Exam practice**

1 The graph shows the volume of liquid, L litres in a container at time, t seconds.

   a Find the gradient of the graph.   **(2 marks)**

   b Explain what the gradient represents.   **(1 mark)**

   c The line intercepts the volume axis at $L = 12$. Explain what this intercept represents.   **(1 mark)**

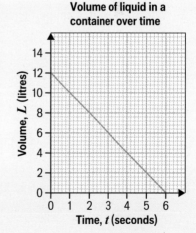

Volume of liquid in a container over time

Adapted from 1MA1/3H, June 2018, Q12

Exam feedback   Results**Plus**

Q1a: Most students who achieved a **Grade 6** or above answered a similar question well.

Q1b: Most students who achieved a **Grade 8** or above answered a similar question well.

Key points

- The coordinates of the midpoint of a line segment joining (x_1, y_1) to (x_2, y_2) are $\left(\dfrac{x_1 + x_2}{2}, \dfrac{y_1 + y_2}{2}\right)$
- When two lines are perpendicular, the product of their gradients is -1.
  When a graph has gradient m, a graph perpendicular to it has gradient $\dfrac{-1}{m}$

⚠ Purposeful practice 1

Find the midpoint of these pairs of coordinates.

1 $(1, 2)$ and $(3, 6)$ 2 $(1, 2)$ and $(5, 8)$ 3 $(1, 2)$ and $(4, 7)$

4 $(3, 4)$ and $(-3, 6)$ 5 $(3, 4)$ and $(5, -4)$ 6 $(3, 4)$ and $(-4, 5)$

7 $(-3, 4)$ and $(-3, -6)$ 8 $(-3, 4)$ and $(-5, -4)$ 9 $(-3, 4)$ and $(-4, 5)$

10 $(3\frac{1}{2}, 4\frac{1}{2})$ and $(3, -6)$ 11 $(3\frac{1}{2}, 4\frac{1}{2})$ and $(-5, 4)$ 12 $(3\frac{1}{2}, 4\frac{1}{2})$ and $(-4, -5)$

Reflect and reason

How could a simple sketch help you check your answers?

⚠ Purposeful practice 2

1 Which of these equations are perpendicular to $y = 2x + 5$?

   A $y = -\dfrac{1}{2}x + 5$

   B $y = \dfrac{1}{2}x + 5$

   C $y = -2x + 5$

   D $y = 2x - 5$

2 Which equations are perpendicular to each other?

   A $y = 3x + 5$

   B $y = \dfrac{1}{4}x + 6$

   C $y = -4x + 11$

   D $y = -\dfrac{1}{2}x + 4$

3 Find the equation of the line that passes through $(4, 3)$ and is perpendicular to $y = 2x + 1$

4 Find the equation of the line that passes through $(4, 3)$ and is perpendicular to $y = -\dfrac{1}{2}x + 5$

Reflect and reason

Stephanie says, 'The equation in **Q4** is the answer to **Q3**, so the equation in **Q3** must be the answer to **Q4**.' What has Stephanie got wrong?

1   Find the equation of the perpendicular bisector of the line segment that joins $(-3, 2)$ to $(4, 3)$.

2   Tim tries to find the equation of the perpendicular bisector of the line segment that joins $(-3, 4)$ to $(4, 5)$.

$(-3, 4)$ to $(4, 5)$
gradient is $\frac{5-4}{4--3} = \frac{1}{7}$
perpendicular gradient $= 7$
$-3 = 7 \times 4 + c$
$-3 = 28 + c$
$c = -31$
So $y = 7x - 31$

Tim has made some mistakes.
What has Tim done wrong?

3   Find the midpoints of each side of each shape.
   a   A triangle with vertices at $(2, 1)$, $(2, 5)$ and $(6, 1)$.
   b   A rectangle with vertices at $(2, 4)$, $(6, 6)$, $(7, 4)$ and $(3, 2)$.
   c   The quadrilateral formed from the four midpoints in part **b**.

4   Two vertices of a rectangle have coordinates $(-3, 2)$ and $(-1, 5)$.
    David says, '$(-2, -2)$ is a possible third vertex of the rectangle.'
    Eliza says, 'David's answer is wrong and $(-2, 1\frac{1}{3})$ is correct.'
    Work out who is correct.

5   Two consecutive vertices of a square have coordinates $(3, 1)$ and $(5, 2)$.
   a   Find the equations of the two sides of the square that pass through $(5, 2)$.
   b   Find the coordinates of the two possible locations for the other two vertices.
   c   Find the length of the diagonal of the square.
       Give your answer to 1 decimal place.

✵ Exam practice

1   ABCD is a square.
    The coordinates of A are $(2, 9)$.
    The equation of the diagonal DB is $y = x + 2$
    Find the equation of the diagonal AC.   **(4 marks)**

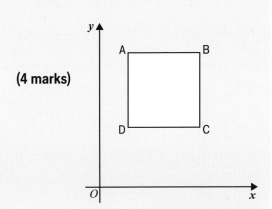

Adapted from 1MA1/1H, June 2017, Q18

Exam feedback   Results**Plus**

Most students who achieved a Grade 8 or above answered a similar question well.

Key points

- A quadratic equation contains a term in x^2 but no higher power or negative powers of x.
  The graph of a quadratic equation is a curved shape called a parabola.
- A quadratic graph has either a minimum point or a maximum point where the graph turns.

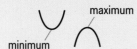

- A quadratic graph can have 0, 1 or 2 solutions.

Purposeful practice

1 Which of these are quadratic graphs?

A

B

C

D

2 Which of these are quadratic equations?

A $y = x^2 + x^3$ **B** $y = x^2 + 3x$ **C** $y = 5 + x + x^2$ **D** $y = x^2 + \dfrac{1}{x}$

3 Match each equation to a graph.

   i $y = x^2 + 3x + 4$ **ii** $y = x^2 + 3x - 4$ **iii** $y = 4 - x^2 + 3x$ **iv** $y = 3x - 4 - x^2$

A

B

C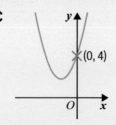

D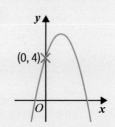

4 Write down the number of solutions for each of these graphs.

a

b

c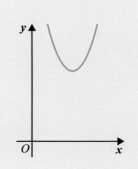

Reflect and reason

How does the graph tell you how many solutions the equation will have?

⊠ Problem-solving practice

1 Use the graphs to solve the equations.

a $x^2 - 3x - 2.5 = 0$

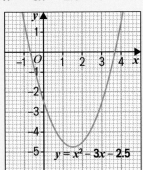

b $x = 2 - 2x^2 = 0$

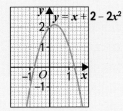

c $x^2 - 6x + 9 = 0$

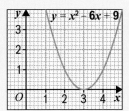

2 The graph shows four equations.

$y = x^2 + x - 6$ $y = x - 4$

$y = 3x - 8$ $x + y = 2$

a Use the graph to solve

   i $x^2 + x - 6 = 0$

   ii $x^2 + x - 6 = x - 4$

   iii Where $y = x^2 + x - 6$ meets $x + y = 2$

b Explain how you can tell from the graph that there are no solutions to $x^2 + x - 6 = 3x - 8$

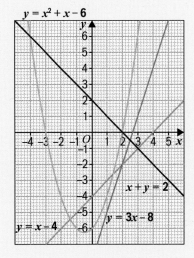

✦ Exam practice

1 Ali needs to draw the graph of $y = x^2 + 3$
The graph he draws is shown.
Write down one thing that is wrong with Ali's graph. **(1 mark)**

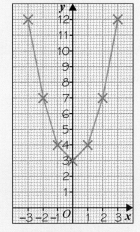

Adapted from 1MA1/1H, November 2017, Q7

Exam feedback   Results**Plus**

In a similar question, some students thought the wrong points had been plotted, which is incorrect.

Key points

- A cubic function contains a term in x^3 but no higher power of x.
  It can also have terms in x^2 and x, and number terms.
- A cubic equation can have 1, 2 or 3 solutions.
- A reciprocal function is in the form $\frac{k}{x}$ where k is a number.
- For reciprocal functions, the x and y axes are asymptotes to the curve.
  An asymptote is a line that the graph gets very close to, but never actually touches.

△ Purposeful practice

1 Which of these are cubic graphs?

A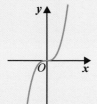

B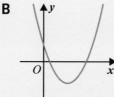

C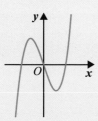

D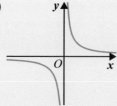

2 Identify whether each equation is quadratic, cubic or reciprocal.

   a $y = x^3 + 2x^2 + x + 6$ **b** $y = 3x^2 + 2x + 1$

   c $y = \frac{1}{x}$ **d** $y = (x - 1)(x + 1)(x - 2)$

3 Write down the number of solutions for each of these graphs.

a

b

c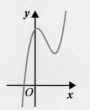

d

Reflect and reason

Geraldine says, 'A cubic function always has a term in x^3. Therefore, a cubic graph always has 3 solutions.'
Is Geraldine correct? Explain.

⊠ Problem-solving practice

1 a Draw the graph of $y = \frac{2}{x}$
where $x \neq 0$, for $-4 \leq x \leq 4$

b Draw the graph of $y = -\frac{2}{x}$
where $x \neq 0$, for $-4 \leq x \leq 4$

2 This is the graph of
$y = x^3 + 2x^2 - 3x - 1$
Use it to solve

a $x^3 + 2x^2 - 3x - 1 = 0$

b $x^3 + 2x^2 - 3x = 0$

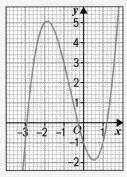

3 These are graphs of $y = (x - a)^2(x - b)$
For each graph, work out the values of a and b.

a
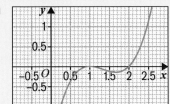

b
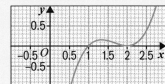

c
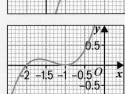

d
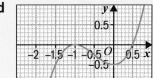

✦ Exam practice

1 Here are some equations. Match each equation with the letter of its graph.

i $y = x^2 - 3$ **ii** $y = x^3$ **iii** $y = \frac{3}{x}$ **iv** $y = -x^2$

A

B

C
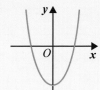

D

E

F

(3 marks)

Adapted from 1MA1/2H, June 2017, Q14

Key points

- No correlation or weak correlation shows that there is **no** linear relationship between two quantities, because their graph is not close to a straight line.

- The equation of a circle with centre (0, 0) and radius r is $x^2 + y^2 = r^2$

⚠ Purposeful practice 1

1 The table shows the sales of shoes and the average temperature over 10 days.
   Plot a scatter graph and comment on the relationship between the shoe sales and the average temperature each day.

Temperature (°C)	24	30	27	10	10	23	17	16	21	13
Shoe sales	113	126	85	146	82	64	74	69	72	104

2 The table shows the number of visitors at a theme park and the daily temperature forecast over 10 days.
   Plot a scatter graph and comment on the relationship between the number of visitors and the forecast temperature.

Temperature (°C)	18	24	22	27	28	20	27	25	22	15
Visitors	2089	2422	2335	2751	2942	2273	2890	2546	2360	2040

Reflect and reason

James says, 'The graph in **Q2** can be used to predict, with confidence, the number of visitors given the weather forecast.'
Comment on James's statement.

⚠ Purposeful practice 2

1 Which of these equations will give a circle?
   A $x + y = 5$ **B** $x^2 + y = 5$ **C** $x + y^2 = 5$
   D $x^2 + y^2 = 5$ **E** $x^3 + y^2 = 5$ **F** $x^3 + y^3 = 5$

2 What is the radius of the circles given by these equations?
   a $x^2 + y^2 = 4$ **b** $x^2 + y^2 = 16$ **c** $x^2 + y^2 = 64$
   d $x^2 + y^2 = 100$ **e** $x^2 + y^2 = 7$

3 Which of these points lies on the circle $x^2 + y^2 = 25$?
   A (4, 3)   **B** (3, 4)   **C** (6, 1)
   D (25, 0)   **E** (5, 5)

Reflect and reason

Mark says that the equation $x^2 + y^2 = 25$ will be a circle with a radius of 25.
Is Mark correct?
Explain.

⊠ Problem-solving practice

1 The graph shows the number of alpha particles given off by a radioactive material.

  a How many particles are given off at the start?

  b How many particles are given off after 10 minutes?

  c When are 500 particles given off?

  d How long does it take for the number of particles given off to halve?

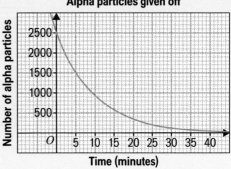

Alpha particles given off

2 Match these graphs to their equations.

  i $x^2 + y^2 < 36$ **ii** $x^2 + y^2 = 36$ **iii** $x^2 + y^2 > 36$

A
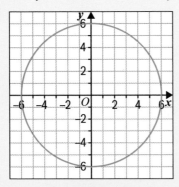

B
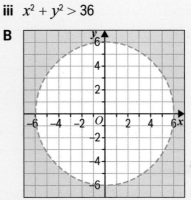

C
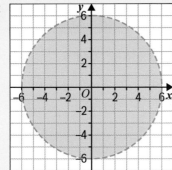

▨ Exam practice

1 On a copy of the grid, draw the graph of $x^2 + y^2 = 20.25$

      (2 marks)

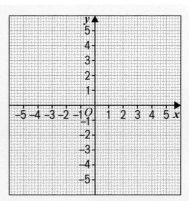

Adapted from 1MA1/2H, June 2018, Q16a

Exam feedback

    Results**Plus**

In a similar question, some students recognised this as being the equation of a circle and although they were unable to get the correct radius, they scored a single mark for drawing a circle with centre (0, 0).

7 Area and volume

7.1 Perimeter and area

Key points

- This trapezium has parallel sides, a and b, and perpendicular height, h.
- Area of a trapezium = $\frac{1}{2}(a + b)h$

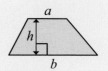

△ Purposeful practice 1

Calculate the areas of these trapezia.

1
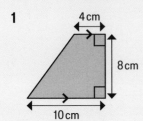

2
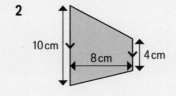

3
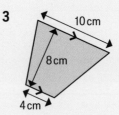

Reflect and reason

For these three trapezia, what is the same and what is different?

△ Purposeful practice 2

Calculate the areas of these trapezia. Round your answers to 1 d.p. where necessary.

1

2
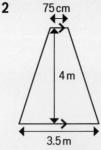

3
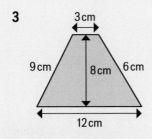

4
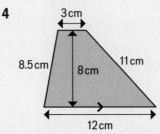

Reflect and reason

For **Q4**, Lily writes,

$\frac{1}{2}(3 + 12) \times 8.5$

What mistake has Lily made?

1 These trapezia each have an area of 30 cm².
   Work out the missing measurements.

   a
   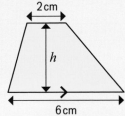

   b
   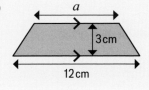

   c
   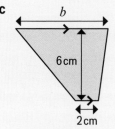

2 James works out the area of this trapezium incorrectly.
   James writes,

   Area = (6 + 10) × 8 = 6 + 80 = 86 cm²

   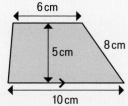

   a Identify James's three mistakes.
   b Find the correct area.

3 The areas of trapezia B, C, and D are the same as the area of trapezium A.
   Find the missing measurement for each trapezium.

   A
   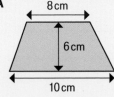

   B
   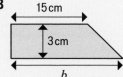

   C
   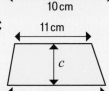

   D
   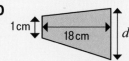

✪ **Exam practice**

1 Here is a trapezium.

   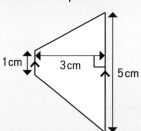

   On a centimetre grid, draw a triangle equal in area to this trapezium.   **(2 marks)**

   Adapted from 1MA1/3H, June 2018, Q3

Exam feedback   Results**Plus**

Most students who achieved a Grade 6 or above answered a similar question well.

Key points

- A 10% error interval means that a measurement could be up to 10% larger or smaller than the one given.

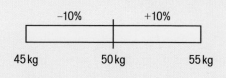

- Measurements rounded to the nearest unit could be up to half a unit smaller or larger than the rounded value.
- The upper bound is half a unit greater than the rounded measurement.
- The lower bound is half a unit smaller than the rounded measurement.

$$12.5 \leqslant x < 13.5$$

lower bound   upper bound

⚠ Purposeful practice 1

For each rectangle

   a use measurements in cm to calculate the area in cm²

   b use measurements in mm to calculate the area in mm²

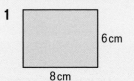

1

6 cm

8 cm

2

35 mm

50 mm

3

28 mm

4 cm

Reflect and reason

Look at your answers in cm² and mm².

How do you convert from mm² to cm²? How do you convert from cm² to mm²?

⚠ Purposeful practice 2

1 Wood is cut into these lengths with the error interval given.

   Write an inequality $\square \leqslant l \leqslant \square$ for each, to show the possible lengths l.

   a 10% error interval

     i 15 mm   **ii** 150 cm   **iii** 1.5 m   **iv** 15 m

   b 5% error interval

     i 15 mm   **ii** 150 cm   **iii** 1.5 m   **iv** 15 m

   c 2.5% error interval

     i 15 mm   **ii** 150 cm   **iii** 1.5 m   **iv** 15 m

2 Write the lower and upper bounds of each measurement as an inequality $\square \leqslant l < \square$

   a 18 cm (to the nearest cm)   **b** 180 mm (to the nearest mm)

   c 1.8 m (to the nearest cm)   **d** 1.8 m (to the nearest 10 cm)

   e 2.3 m (to 1 d.p.)   **f** 2.30 m (to 2 d.p.)

   g 2.0 km (to 1 d.p.)   **h** 2.00 km (to 2 d.p.)

Reflect and reason

What is different about the inequality signs you use for upper and lower bounds, and the inequality signs you use for error intervals?

Explain why they are different.

⊠ Problem-solving practice

1   Holly is asked to calculate the area, in cm², of a square with sides 8 mm.
    Here is her answer.

    8 mm is 0.8 cm, so the area is 0.8 × 0.8
             = 6.4 cm²

    Holly's answer is wrong.

    a Write what Holly has done wrong and find the correct answer.

    b Suggest an improvement to her method.

2   Work out the missing lengths in these triangles.

    a   Area = 1200 mm²   **b**   Area = 2.4 cm²

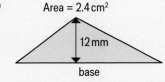

3   Several students work out and round the answer to a calculation to the nearest whole number.
    Adam: 56   Bella: 68   Charlie: 60   Daisy: 59
    The correct answer is 60.48 (to 2 d.p.)
    Which students are within 10% of the correct answer?

4   Jessica measures the school hockey field to be a rectangle 91 m by 55 m, with measurements
    correct to the nearest metre.

    a Using Jessica's measurements, what are the upper and lower bounds for the area of the
       hockey field?

    Ali measures the hockey field to be 91.4 m by 54.5 m to 1 d.p.

    b Using Ali's measurements, what are the upper and lower bounds for the area of the
       hockey field?

5   Liam has measured his classroom floor to be 4 m by 5 m, recording each measurement to the
    nearest metre.
    He buys 20 carpet tiles.
    Each carpet tile is a square with sides of 1 m.
    Will 20 carpet tiles definitely be enough to cover the whole floor?
    Show working to explain your answer.

✦ Exam practice

1   The length, L cm, of a line is measured as 5 cm correct to the nearest cm.
    Complete the following sentence to show the possible values of L.

    $\square \leqslant L < \square$ **(2 marks)**

    Adapted from 1MA1/3H, Specimen Papers, Set 1, Q2

Key points

- The surface area of a 3D solid is the total area of all its faces.
- A prism is a 3D solid that has the same cross-section all through its length.

- Volume of a prism = area of cross-section × length
- Volume is measured in mm³, cm³ or m³
- Capacity is measured in ml and litres. 1 cm³ = 1 ml, 1000 cm³ = 1 litre

△ Purposeful practice 1

Find the surface area of each prism.

1

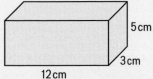

5 cm
3 cm
12 cm

2

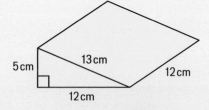

5 cm 13 cm 12 cm
12 cm

3

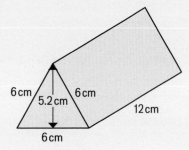

6 cm 6 cm
5.2 cm
12 cm
6 cm

4

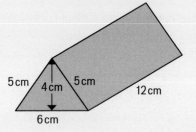

5 cm 5 cm
4 cm 12 cm
6 cm

Reflect and reason

Pat says, 'In **Q3**, I only had to calculate the areas of 2 different faces to work out the surface area.'
Explain how Pat did this.

△ Purposeful practice 2

1   Find the volumes of the four solids in **Q1–4** in Purposeful practice 1.

2   Four containers are shaped like the solids in **Q1–4** in Purposeful practice 1.
    Find the capacity of each container. (1 cm³ = 1 ml)

Reflect and reason

How could you use some of your area calculations from Purposeful practice 1 in your volume calculations in Purposeful practice 2?

The formula for the volume of a cuboid is $l \times w \times h$.

Is this different to the volume of a prism (cross-section area × length)? Explain.

1 The volume of a cube is numerically the same as its surface area.
What is the side length of the cube?

2 An octagon with an area of 80 cm² is used as the base of a prism-shaped container.
The prism needs to hold 500 ml.
How tall should it be?

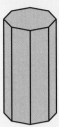

3 A small container of paint will cover 20 000 cm².
Luke wants to paint all the faces of fifty 8 cm cubes.
Is one container of paint enough?

4 A cuboid has a square base.
Its height is 4 times the width of the base.
Its surface area is 450 cm²
Work out the volume of the cuboid.

5 The width of a cuboid is 3 cm.
Its length is double this.
The height of the cuboid is the same as the height of a cube with a volume of 64 cm³.
Find the surface area of the cuboid.

✵ **Exam practice**

1 The diagram shows a flower bed.
The flower bed is in the shape of a cuboid.

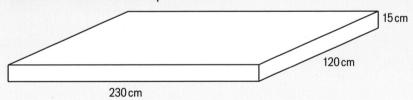

15 cm

120 cm

230 cm

A gardener wants to fill the flower bed with compost.
A bag of compost costs £7.
There are 50 litres of compost in each bag.
The gardener says, 'The compost will cost less than £60.'
Show that the gardener is wrong.   **(5 marks)**

Adapted from 1MA1/1H, Specimen Papers, Set 1, Q5

> ### Key points
>
> - The circumference of a circle is its perimeter.
> - For any circle, circumference $= \pi \times$ diameter: $C = \pi d$ or $C = 2\pi r$
> - The formula for the area, A, of a circle with radius r is $A = \pi r^2$

△ Purposeful practice 1

1 Work out the circumference of each circle.
   Give your answers to 1 d.p.

   a

   18 cm

   b
   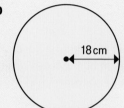
   18 cm

   c

   7 mm

   d
   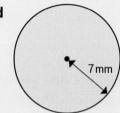
   7 mm

   e

   15 m

   f
   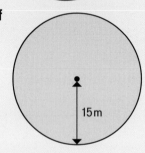
   15 m

2 Work out the circumference of each circle in **Q1**.
   Give your answers in terms of π.

> ### Reflect and reason
>
> When you double the diameter, what happens to the circumference?

△ Purposeful practice 2

1 Work out the area of each circle in **Q1** of Purposeful practice 1, giving your answers to 1 d.p.

2 Work out the area of each circle in **Q2** of Purposeful practice 1, giving your answers in terms of π.

> ### Reflect and reason
>
> Tim is struggling to remember whether $2\pi r$ is the circumference and πr^2 is the area, or whether $2\pi r$ is the area and πr^2 is the circumference.
> Laila suggests that thinking about units would help.
> What do you think Laila means?

⊠ **Problem-solving practice**

1 A circle has a radius of 8 cm.
   Find its circumference, to 1 d.p.

2 The area of a circle is numerically the same as its circumference.
   What is the diameter of the circle?

3 A child's bicycle wheel has a diameter of 30 cm.
   An adult's bicycle wheel has a diameter of 700 mm.
   A father and daughter ride their bikes for 5 km.
   How many more times does the daughter's wheel turn round than the father's?
   Give your answer to the nearest whole number.

4 A rectangular lawn measures 8 m by 5 m.
   In the lawn, there is a circular pond with a diameter of 3 m.

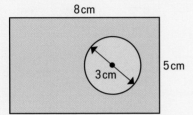

   What is the area of the grass?
   Give your answer to 2 d.p.

5 A circular hole with diameter 2 cm is cut from a larger circle with radius 2 cm.
   Calculate the area of the remaining shape. Give your answer to 2 d.p.

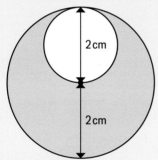

 ✳ **Exam practice**

1 A square, with sides of length x cm, is inside a circle.
   Each vertex of the square is on the circumference of the circle.
   The area of the circle is 64 cm².
   Work out the value of x.
   Give your answer correct to 3 s.f.   **(4 marks)**

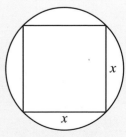

area of circle = 64 cm²

Adapted from 1MA1/3H, June 2017, Q8

Exam feedback   Results**Plus**

Most students who achieved a **Grade 9** answered a similar question well.

Key point

- For a sector with angle $x°$ of a circle with radius r

  Arc length $= \frac{x}{360} \times 2\pi r$

  Area of sector $= \frac{x}{360} \times \pi r^2$

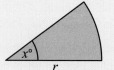

⚠ Purposeful practice 1

1 Work out the arc length for each sector.
   Give your answers to 1 d.p.

a
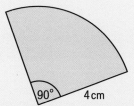

b
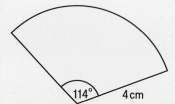

c
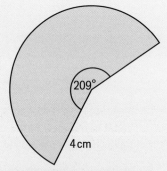

2 Find the perimeter of each sector.
   Give your answers to 1 d.p.

a

b
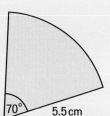

c
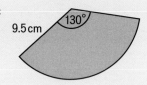

d
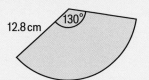

e
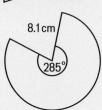

f
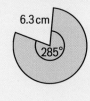

Reflect and reason

Harry gets these two answers for **Q2c** and **Q2d**. 40.6 cm and 54.6 cm

He cannot remember which perimeter is which. Explain how he can work it out.

⚠ Purposeful practice 2

1 Find the area of each sector in **Q1** in Purposeful practice 1, giving your answers to 1 d.p.

2 Find the area of each sector in **Q1** in Purposeful practice 1, giving your answers in terms of π.

Reflect and reason

Which are more accurate, your answers to **Q1** or your answers to **Q2**?

1   Graham is calculating the perimeter of this sector.
    He writes,
    Arc length = $\frac{110}{360} \times \pi \times 26.2 = 25.15$ cm
    a Identify Graham's three mistakes.
    b Work out the correct answer.

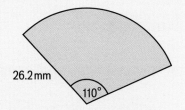

2   The diagram shows an unshaded sector with an angle of 250° and
    radius of 3 m inside a shaded sector with an angle of 40° and
    radius of 12 m.
    Work out the shaded area, to 1 d.p.

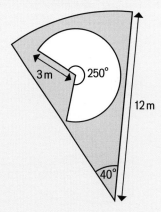

3   Circles are drawn on a regular hexagon.
    Each side of the hexagon is 10 m.
    Each circle is centred on a vertex of the hexagon and has
    radius half the side length of the hexagon.
    Calculate the shaded area inside the hexagon taken up by
    the sectors of the circles.
    Give your answer to 1 d.p.

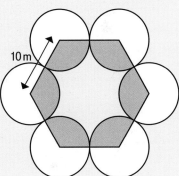

Exam practice

1   The diagram shows a sector of a circle of radius 7 cm, centre O.

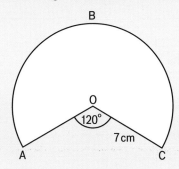

Work out the length of the arc ABC.
Give your answer correct to 3 significant figures.   **(2 marks)**

Adapted from 1MA1/3H, Specimen Papers, Set 2, Q16

7.6 Cylinders and spheres

Key points

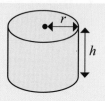

- The volume of a cylinder of radius r and height h is $V = \pi r^2 h$
- The total surface area of a cylinder of radius r and height h is $2\pi r^2 + 2\pi rh$

- For a sphere of radius r, surface area $= 4\pi r^2$ and volume $= \frac{4}{3}\pi r^3$

 △ Purposeful practice 1

Work out the volume of each cylinder. Give your answers to 1 d.p.

1 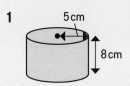   **2** 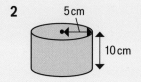   **3**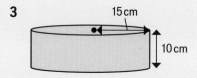

Reflect and reason

How is the formula for the volume of a cylinder similar to the formula for the volume of a prism?
Volume of a prism = cross-section area × length

 △ Purposeful practice 2

Work out the total surface area of each cylinder, giving your answers to the nearest whole mm².

1 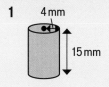   **2** 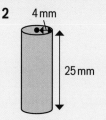   **3**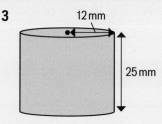

Reflect and reason

How could you work out the surface area of a cylinder if you forget the formula?

△ Purposeful practice 3

For each sphere, calculate   **a** the volume to 2 d.p.   **b** the surface area to 2 d.p.

1   **2**   **3**

Reflect and reason

How can you use units to remember whether the formula $4\pi r^2$ gives the volume of a sphere and $\frac{4}{3}\pi r^3$ gives the surface area, or whether the formula $4\pi r^2$ gives the surface area and $\frac{4}{3}\pi r^3$ gives the volume?

⊠ Problem-solving practice

1 Here are two cylinders.
Every length in cylinder B is twice as long as cylinder A.

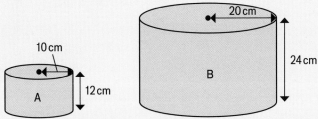

Maria says, 'The volume of cylinder B will be twice the volume of cylinder A.'
Calculate the volume of each cylinder and write the correct version of Maria's statement.

2 The moon is roughly spherical and has a radius of 1737 km.
What is its surface area?
Give your answer to 3 significant figures.

3 A chocolate hemisphere has an internal radius of
10 cm and is 0.25 cm thick.
Imagine this to be a hemisphere of radius 10.25 cm
with a hemisphere of radius 10 cm cut from it.
What volume of chocolate is the hemisphere made
from?
Give your answer to 3 s.f.

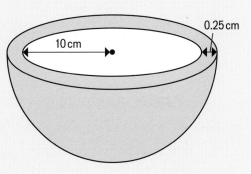

4 A gold cylinder has radius 3 cm and height 5 cm.
The cylinder is melted down and then reformed as a sphere.
What is the radius of the sphere to 3 s.f.?

✧ Exam practice

1 Shape P is one half of a solid sphere, centre O.

Volume of sphere $= \frac{4}{3}\pi r^3$

Surface area of sphere $= 4\pi r^2$

The volume of P is $\frac{250}{3}\pi$ cm^3.
Find the surface area of P.
Give your answer correct to 3 significant figures.
You must show your working.

(5 marks)

Adapted from 1MA1/2H, June 2018, Q19

Exam feedback

Results Plus

In a similar question, few students managed to arrive at a radius of 5 cm, even if a correct formula was
used, as they made mistakes in rearranging equations.

7.7 Pyramids and cones

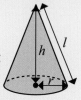

Key points

- Volume of pyramid $= \frac{1}{3} \times$ area of base $\times$ vertical height

- Volume of cone with base radius r and height $h = \frac{1}{3} \times$ area of base $\times$ vertical height
$$= \frac{1}{3}\pi r^2 h$$

- Curved surface area of a cone $= \pi r l$, where r is the base radius and l is the slant height.

- Total surface area of a cone $= \pi r l + \pi r^2$

△ Purposeful practice 1

1 Find the volume of each pyramid.

a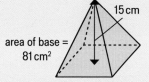
15 cm
area of base = 81 cm²

b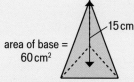
15 cm
area of base = 60 cm²

c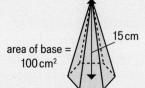
15 cm
area of base = 100 cm²

2 Find the volume of each cone. Give your answers in terms of π.

a
27 cm
5 cm

b
18 cm
5 cm

c
12 cm
5 cm

Reflect and reason

How is the formula for the volume of a cone similar to the formula for the volume of a pyramid?

△ Purposeful practice 2

1 Find the curved surface area of these cones, giving your answers in terms of π.

a
12 cm
8 cm

b
20 cm
8 cm

c
20 cm
15 cm

2 Find the total surface area of these solid cones. Give your answers in cm², correct to 1 d.p.

a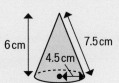
6 cm 7.5 cm
4.5 cm

b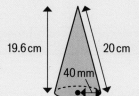
19.6 cm 20 cm
40 mm

c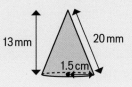
13 mm 20 mm
1.5 cm

Reflect and reason

Jim calculates the total surface area for **Q2a**.
What has he done wrong?

> Total surface area = $\pi \times 4.5 \times 6 + \pi \times 4.5^2$

Problem-solving practice

1 An Egyptian pyramid was built out of $1\,m^3$ stones.
It is a square-based pyramid.
Each side of the base is $230\,m$.
The height of the pyramid is $147\,m$.
How many stones were needed?

2 A gold square-based pyramid has a base with
sides of $5\,cm$ and has a height of $10\,cm$.
It is melted down and recast into a sphere.
What is the radius of the sphere to 1 d.p.?

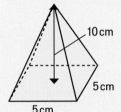

3 A filled ice cream cone has a height of $15\,cm$.
An ice cream seller completely fills each cone, and adds a hemisphere,
with radius $33\,mm$, on the top.
How many filled ice cream cones can she sell from a 5 litre container?

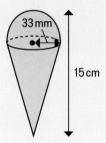

4 A solid metal sphere with radius $6\,cm$ is melted and recast as a cone with the same radius.

What is the total surface area of the cone? Give your answer to 2 d.p.

 Exam practice

1 A square-based pyramid has volume $2\,600\,000\,m^3$.
Its vertical height is $147\,m$.

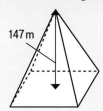

Find the length of a side of the base.   **(3 marks)**

8 Transformations and constructions

8.1 3D solids

Key points

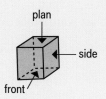

- The plan is the view from above the solid.
- The front elevation is the view of the front of the solid.
- The side elevation is the view of the side of the solid.

⚠ Purposeful practice 1

1 On squared paper, draw and label the plan, front elevation and side elevation of the cube.

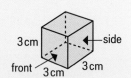

2 On squared paper, draw and label the plan, front elevation and side elevation of these solids.

a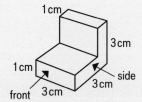

b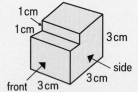

c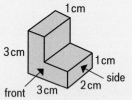

Reflect and reason

What is the same and what is different about the views of the 3D solids with one 'stair' in **Q2**?
Predict how the views would be different for a 3D solid with two 'stairs'.

⚠ Purposeful practice 2

1 On squared paper, draw and label the plan, front elevation and side elevation for each solid.

a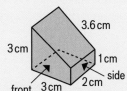

b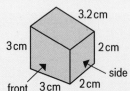

2 On squared paper, draw and label the plan, front elevation and side elevation for each solid.

a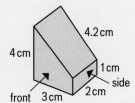

b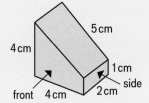

c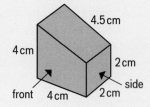

Reflect and reason

What is the same and what is different between your diagrams for **Q2**?

1 The plan, front elevation and side elevation of a solid prism
   are drawn on a centimetre square grid.

   a Draw a sketch of the solid prism.
       Write the dimensions of the prism on your sketch.

   b Name the solid prism.

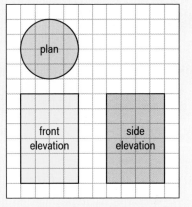

2 The front elevation and plan of a solid prism are shown on
   the grid.
   Draw the side elevation from the direction of the arrow.

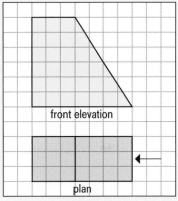

1 The diagram shows a prism with a cross-section in the shape of a trapezium.

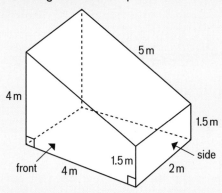

   On centimetre squared paper, draw the front elevation and the side elevation
   of the prism.
   Use a scale of 1 cm to 1 m.   **(4 marks)**

   Adapted from 1MA1/2H, June 2017, Q3

Exam feedback   ResultsⓅlus

Most students who achieved a **Grade 4** or above answered a similar question well.

8.2 Reflection and rotation

△ Purposeful practice 1

1 Describe fully the single transformation that maps

a shape A onto shape B

b shape C onto shape D

c shape E onto shape F

d shape G onto shape H

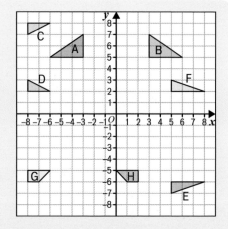

Reflect and reason

How do you decide the position of the mirror line? How do you know when the equation of the mirror line starts with '$x = ...$' or '$y = ...$' for vertical and horizontal mirror lines?

△ Purposeful practice 2

1 Describe fully each single transformation that maps shape A onto shape B.

a
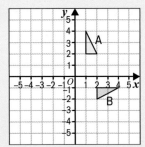

b
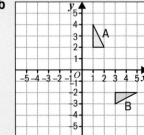

c
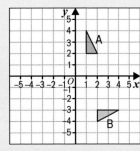

d
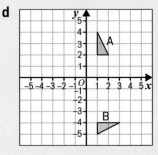

Reflect and reason

Write an alternative answer for each transformation in **Q1**.

1 In an exam, Sophie is asked to describe fully the single
   transformation that maps triangle A onto triangle B.
   Sophie says, 'This has centre (0, 1), 90° anticlockwise.'
   Explain why Sophie only scored 1 of the 3 marks for her
   answer.

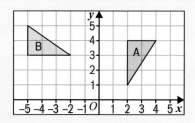

2 Draw a coordinate grid from −6 to +6 on both axes.
   a Draw triangle P with vertices at coordinates (1, 3), (1, 5) and (2, 5).
   b Reflect triangle P in the y-axis. Label the image Q.
   c Reflect triangle Q in the line $y = 1$. Label the image R.
   d Describe the transformation that takes triangle P to triangle R.

✩ Exam practice

1

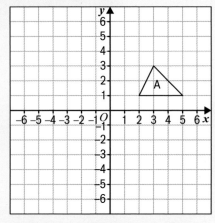

Triangle A is reflected in the line $x = -1$ to give triangle B.
Triangle B is reflected in the line $y = -1$ to give triangle C.
Describe the single transformation that maps triangle A onto triangle C. **(2 marks)**

Adapted from 1MA1/1H, June 2018, Q7

2

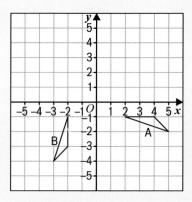

Describe the single transformation that maps triangle A onto triangle B. **(2 marks)**

Adapted from 1MA1/2H, Specimen Papers, Set 2, Q1

Exam feedback ResultsPlus

Q1: Most students who achieved a Grade 7 or above answered a similar question well.

Key points

- An enlargement is a transformation where all the side lengths of a shape are multiplied by the same scale factor.
- To describe an enlargement you need to give the centre of enlargement and the scale factor.
- To enlarge a shape by a fractional scale factor, multiply all the side lengths by the scale factor. When a centre of enlargement is given, multiply the distance from the centre to each point on the shape by the scale factor.
- A negative scale factor takes the image to the opposite side of the centre of enlargement.

△ Purposeful practice 1

1   Each triangle B, C, D, E and F is an enlargement of triangle A with centre (0, 0). Write the scale factor for each enlargement.

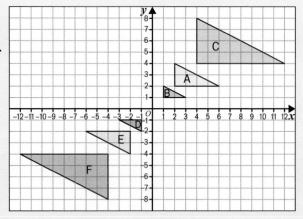

Reflect and reason

How do you know which are scale factors less than 1? How do you know which are negative scale factors?

△ Purposeful practice 2

Copy the diagram.

1   Enlarge shape P by scale factor −2 with centre of enlargement (0, 0). Label your image Q.

2   Enlarge shape P by scale factor $-\frac{1}{2}$ with centre of enlargement (0, 0). Label your image R.

3   Enlarge shape P by scale factor −2 with centre of enlargement (0, 2). Label your image S.

4   Enlarge shape P by scale factor $-\frac{1}{2}$ with centre of enlargement (1, 2). Label your image T.

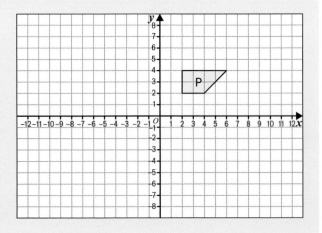

Reflect and reason

Describe fully the enlargements that map shape Q onto P, R onto P, S onto P and T onto P. What do you notice?

1   Olivia says, 'The transformation that maps triangle P onto triangle Q is an enlargement of scale factor −2, centre of enlargement (0, 0).'

   a What two mistakes has Olivia made?

   b Give the correct transformation.

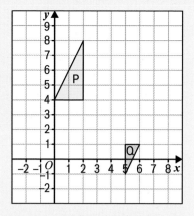

2   Enlarge the triangle by scale factor −1½, centre (0, 2).

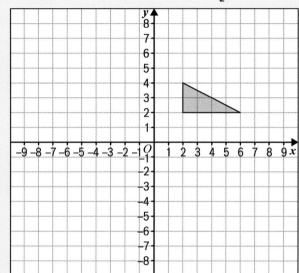

1   Enlarge shape A by scale factor −½ with centre of enlargement (0, 0).
   Label your image B.   **(2 marks)**

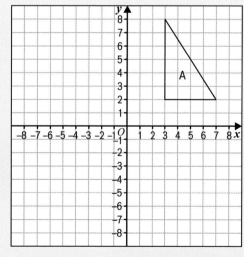

Adapted from 1MA1/2H, June 2018, Q7

Exam feedback

ResultsPlus

Most students who achieved a **Grade 6** or above answered a similar question well.

8.4 Translations and combinations of transformations

△ Purposeful practice 1

Triangle B is a translation of triangle A by the vector $\begin{pmatrix} -3 \\ -2 \end{pmatrix}$.
Copy the diagram.

1 Translate triangle A by the vector $\begin{pmatrix} 4 \\ 0 \end{pmatrix}$. Label the image C.

2 Translate triangle A by the vector $\begin{pmatrix} 0 \\ -5 \end{pmatrix}$. Label the image D.

3 Translate triangle A by the vector $\begin{pmatrix} 4 \\ -5 \end{pmatrix}$. Label the image E.

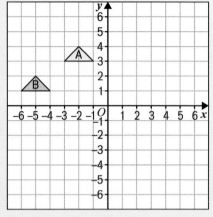

Reflect and reason

What do the top and bottom numbers of the column vector represent?

What is the difference between a positive and negative number in the column vector?

△ Purposeful practice 2

Copy the diagram.

1 Translate triangle P by the vector $\begin{pmatrix} -1 \\ 1 \end{pmatrix}$. Label the image Q.

2 Translate triangle Q by the vector $\begin{pmatrix} -6 \\ -3 \end{pmatrix}$. Label the image R.

3 What is the resultant vector that takes P directly to R?

4 Translate triangle P by the vector $\begin{pmatrix} -3 \\ -3 \end{pmatrix}$. Label the image S.

5 Translate triangle S by the vector $\begin{pmatrix} 1 \\ -6 \end{pmatrix}$. Label the image T.

6 What is the resultant vector that takes P directly to T?

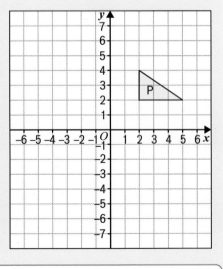

Reflect and reason

Crista says, 'The translation of triangle T to triangle P is $(-1, 6)$.'

What mistake has Crista made?

Problem-solving practice

1. Shape A is translated by the vector $\begin{pmatrix} 4 \\ -5 \end{pmatrix}$ to give shape B.

   Write the vector that translates shape B to shape A.

2. Triangle P is translated by one vector, followed by a second vector.
   Triangle Q shows its final position.
   Give two possible pairs of vectors that could translate triangle P to triangle Q.

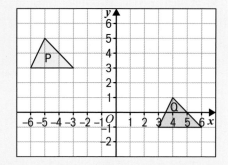

3. Shape P is translated by the vector $\begin{pmatrix} -5 \\ 3 \end{pmatrix}$ to give shape Q.

   Shape Q is then translated by the vector $\begin{pmatrix} -2 \\ -1 \end{pmatrix}$ to give shape R.
   Describe the resultant vector that maps shape P onto shape R.

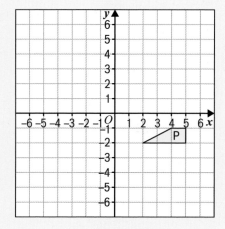

Exam practice

1. The diagram shows triangle A drawn on a grid.
   Helen reflects triangle A in the x-axis to get triangle B.

   She then translates triangle B by vector $\begin{pmatrix} -5 \\ 3 \end{pmatrix}$ to get triangle C.

   Zach translates triangle A by vector $\begin{pmatrix} -5 \\ 3 \end{pmatrix}$ to get triangle D.

   He is then going to reflect triangle D in the x-axis to get triangle E.
   Zach says, 'Triangle E should be in the same position as triangle C.'
   Is Zach correct?
   You must show how you get your answer.

   (3 marks)

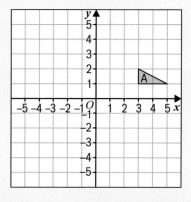

Adapted from 1MA1/2H, June 2017, Q9

Exam feedback

ResultsPlus

Most students who achieved a **Grade 8** or above answered a similar question well.

Key point
- A bearing is an angle in degrees, clockwise from north. A bearing is always written using three digits.

△ Purposeful practice 1

1 For each diagram, describe the bearing of
   i B from A   **ii** A from B

a
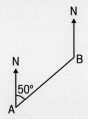

b
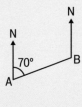

c

2 For each diagram, describe the bearing of
   i B from A   **ii** A from B

a
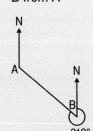

b
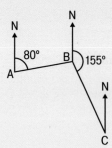

c
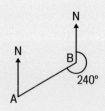

3 Write down the bearing of
   a B from A
   b B from C

Reflect and reason
In **Q1**, the angle at A was marked. In **Q2**, the angle at B was marked.
How did this change your answers to parts **i** and **ii**?

△ Purposeful practice 2

1 Work out the bearing of A from B when the bearing of B from A is
   a 030°   **b** 065°   **c** 135°

2 Work out the bearing of B from A when the bearing of A from B is
   a 190°   **b** 225°   **c** 305°

Reflect and reason
Did you draw a sketch to help you answer these questions? If so, why? If not, how did you work them out?

⊠ Problem-solving practice

1 The bearing of an aeroplane from an airport is 040°.
   Work out the bearing of the airport from the aeroplane.

2 The bearing of a boat from a rock is 234°.
   Work out the bearing of the rock from the boat.

3 Sam and Paul are asked to work out the bearing of A from B using the diagram.
   Sam says, 'The bearing of A from B is 110° as it is marked on the diagram.'

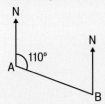

   a Sam is incorrect.
      Explain why Sam is incorrect.

   Paul says, 'The bearing of A from B is 070° as 70° is the complementary angle to 110°.'

   b Paul is incorrect.
      Explain why Paul is incorrect.

4 The diagram shows the position of school A.

   School B is 47 km from school A on a bearing of 080°.
   Copy the diagram and mark the position of school B with a cross.
   Use a scale of 1 cm to represent 10 km.

✦ Exam practice

1 The diagram shows the positions of three points, A, B and C, on a map.

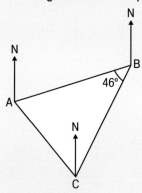

   The bearing of B from A is 065°.
   Angle ABC is 46°.
   AB = CB
   Work out the bearing of C from A.   **(3 marks)**

   Adapted from 1MA1/2H, Specimen Papers, Set 1, Q9

Unit 8 Bearings and scale drawings   108

Key points

- To 'construct' means to draw accurately using a ruler and compasses.
- A perpendicular bisector cuts a line in half at right angles.

△ Purposeful practice

1 Copy or trace each line.
Use a ruler and compasses to construct the perpendicular bisector of each line.

a ────────────────

b

c

d

2 Copy or trace each triangle.
Use a ruler and compasses to construct the perpendicular bisector of line AB in each triangle.

a

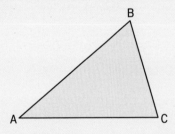

b

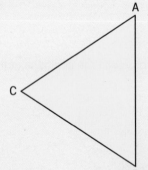

3 Copy or trace the rectangle ABCD.
Use a ruler and compasses to construct the perpendicular bisector of
CD in the rectangle.

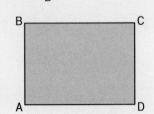

Reflect and reason

How was the method you used to construct the perpendicular bisectors the same or different in **Q1** to
Q2 and **Q3**?

1 AB is a straight line.
   Emily and Jake are asked to construct the
   perpendicular bisector of the line AB.

   a This diagram shows Jake's construction.
   Explain what Jake has done wrong.

   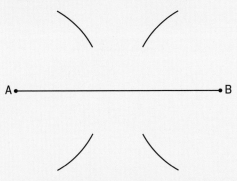

   b This diagram shows Emily's perpendicular bisector.
   Explain what Emily has done wrong.

   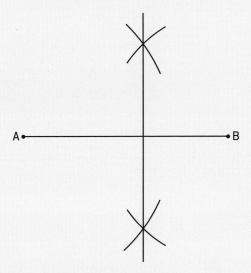

2 Draw an equilateral triangle with sides 7 cm.
   Label your triangle ABC.
   a Use a ruler and compasses to construct the perpendicular bisectors of AB, BC and AC.
   b What do you notice about your three perpendicular bisectors?
   c Does this work for isosceles and scalene triangles?
   Draw one of each to help you decide.

1 Use a ruler and compasses to construct
   the perpendicular bisector of line AB. **(2 marks)**

Adapted from 1MA1/2H, Spring 2017, Mock Set 2, Q3

Key point

- An angle bisector cuts an angle exactly in half.

△ Purposeful practice

1 Copy or trace each angle.
   Use a ruler and compasses to construct the angle bisector of each angle.

   a

   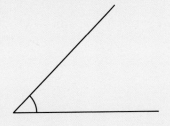

   b

   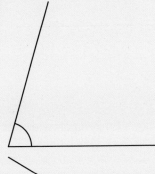

   c

   d

   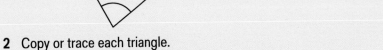

2 Copy or trace each triangle.
   Use a ruler and compasses to bisect angle ABC in each triangle.

   a

   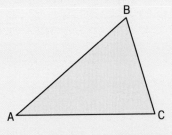

   b

   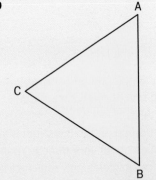

3 Copy or trace the parallelogram.
   Use a ruler and compasses to construct the angle bisector
   of angle ABC in the parallelogram.

   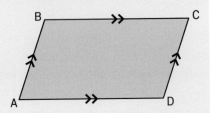

Reflect and reason

How was the method you used to construct the angle bisectors the same or different in **Q1**, **Q2** and **Q3**?

1 Angle ABC is an obtuse angle.
   George is asked to construct the angle bisector of the
   angle ABC.
   The diagram shows George's angle bisector.
   Explain what George has done wrong.

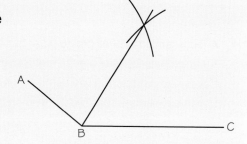

2 Draw a line 7 cm long.
   Construct the perpendicular bisector of your line in order to construct an angle of 90°.
   Now use your diagram to construct an angle of 135°.

3 ABCD is a rectangle.
   Copy or trace the rectangle.
   Construct the line that is equal distance from the lines AB and BC.

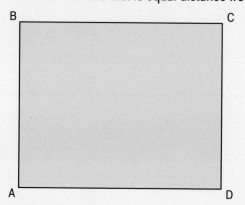

1 Use a ruler and compasses to bisect the angle at X.
   You must show all your construction lines.

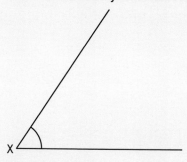

(2 marks)

Adapted from 1MA0/1H, May 2016, Q14a

Exam feedback

ResultsPlus

In a similar question, some students lost marks where it was clear the compass settings were changed or adjusted mid construction. Compasses should be well maintained. The most common error was to draw arcs from the ends of the given lines.

Key points

- A locus is the set of all points that obey a certain rule. Often a locus is a continuous path.
- A circle is the locus of a point that moves so that it is always a fixed distance from a fixed point.
- Points equidistant from two points lie on the perpendicular bisector of the line joining the two points.
- Points equidistant from two lines lie on the angle bisector.

⚠ Purposeful practice

1 Copy or trace the rectangle.

   a Construct the locus of points equidistant from the points A and B.

   b Construct the locus of points equidistant from the lines BC and CD.

2 Copy or trace the parallelogram.

   a Construct the locus of points equidistant from the points B and C.

   b Construct the locus of points equidistant from the lines AD and CD.

3 Copy or trace the triangle.

   a Construct the locus of points equidistant from the points A and B.

   b Construct the locus of points equidistant from the lines AB and BC.

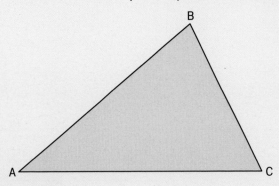

Reflect and reason

How did you decide when to use the perpendicular bisector and angle bisector in **Q1–3**?

1   The map shows the positions of two schools, A and B. They are 8 km apart.

×
B

×
A

Scale: 1 cm represents 1 km

A new swimming pool is going to be built.
It will be less than 5 km from school A.
It will be nearer to school B than to school A.
Copy or trace the map.
Shade the region where the new swimming pool can be built.

2   Copy or trace this scale drawing of a rectangular garden ABCD.
Alex wants to plant a tree in the garden that is
   at least 8 m from point B
   nearer to fence AD than to fence CD
   less than 3 m from AB
On the diagram, shade the region where Alex can plant the tree.

Scale: 1 cm represents 2 m

Exam practice

1   Here is an accurate scale drawing of a classroom.
1 cm represents 2 m.
Sameer is going to put a computer in the classroom.
The computer has to be
   less than 6 m from D
   closer to AD than to AB
   more than 2 m from AB
Show, by shading on the diagram, the region where Sameer can put the computer.   **(4 marks)**

Adapted from 1MA0/2H, June 2015, Q10

Exam feedback

In a similar question, a common error was to replace what should have been an arc with a vertical line.

Mixed exercises B

Mixed problem-solving practice B

1 Sean draws this graph of $y = x^2 - 3$
Write down one thing that is wrong with Sean's graph.

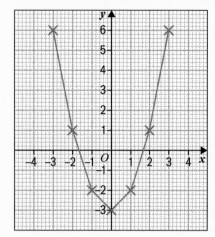

2 Here are some graphs.

A
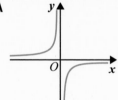

B
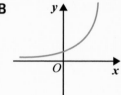

C
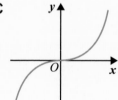

D
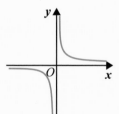

E
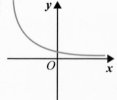

F
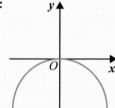

G
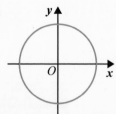

H
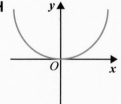

I
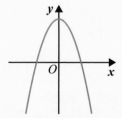

Match each equation with the letter of its graph.

a $y = 4 - x^2$ **b** $y = x^3$ **c** $y = \dfrac{2}{x}$ **d** $x^2 + y^2 = 25$

3 The graph shows the volume of water, L, (litres) in a barrel after time, t (seconds).

Water in a barrel

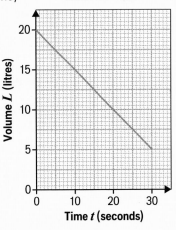

   a Find the gradient of the graph.

   b Explain what this gradient represents.

The graph intersects the volume axis at $L = 20$

   c Explain what this intercept represents.

4 The diagram shows the plan, front and side elevations of a 3D solid.
Draw a sketch of this solid.

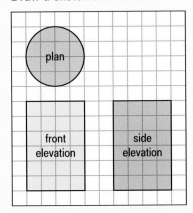

5 The diagram shows the plan of Charlotte's patio.
Charlotte is going to use tiles to make the patio.
The tiles cost £28 per square metre.
Charlotte gets a discount of 20% off the cost of the tiles.
Charlotte has £300.
Does Charlotte have enough money to buy all the tiles she needs?
You must show all your working.

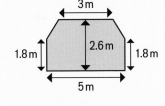

6 Describe fully the single transformation that maps triangle A onto triangle B.

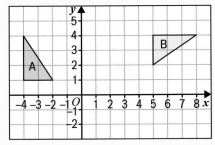

7 The equation of line L_1 is $y = 4x - 3$

The equation of line L_2 is $3y - 12x + 7 = 0$

Show that the lines L_1 and L_2 are parallel.

8 The diagram shows a solid made from a hemisphere and a cone.
   The radius of the hemisphere is 6 cm.
   Calculate the volume of the solid.
   Give your answer correct to 3 s.f.

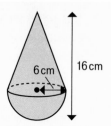

9 Here is a scale drawing of an office.
   The scale is 1 cm to 2 m
   A security camera is going to be put in the office.
   The security camera has to be closer to A than it is to B.
   The security camera also has to be less than 8 metres from D.
   Show, by shading, the region where the security camera can be put on a copy of the drawing.

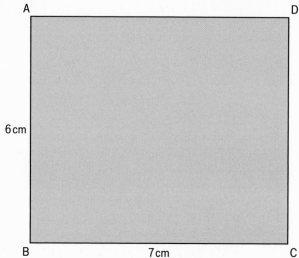

10 OAB is a sector of a circle, centre O.
    OCD is a sector of a circle, centre O.
    OCA and ODB are straight lines.
    Angle AOB = 65°, OD = 5 cm, DB = 3 cm
    Calculate the perimeter of the shaded region.
    Give your answer correct to 3 s.f.

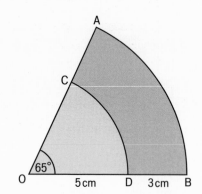

✦ Exam practice

11 The line L is shown on the grid.

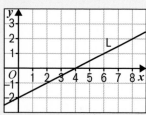

    Find an equation for L.   **(3 marks)**

Adapted from 1MA1/2H, June 2018, Q3

Exam feedback   ResultsPlus

Most students who achieved a **Grade 6** or above answered a similar question well.

12 Enlarge shape A by scale factor $\frac{1}{3}$ centre (2, 0).

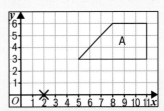

(2 marks)

Adapted from 1MA1/2H, June 2018, Q7

Exam feedback

ResultsPlus

Most students who achieved a **Grade 6** or above answered a similar question well.

 Exam practice

13 AB and BC are 2 sides of a regular 10-sided polygon.
AC is a diagonal of the polygon.
Work out the size of angle ABC.
You must show your working.

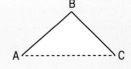

(3 marks)

Adapted from 1MA1/2H, November 2017, Q12

Exam feedback

ResultsPlus

In a similar question, many students were able to gain one mark by finding the interior or exterior angle of the polygon.

 Exam practice

14 A square, with sides of length x cm, is inside a circle.
Each vertex of the square is on the circumference of the circle.
The area of the circle is $64\,\text{cm}^2$.
Work out the value of x.
Give your answer correct to 3 significant figures.

(4 marks)

Adapted from 1MA1/3H, June 2017, Q8

Exam feedback

ResultsPlus

Most students who achieved a **Grade 9** answered a similar question well.

 Exam practice

15 Shape S is one quarter of a solid sphere, centre O.
The volume of S is $243\pi\,\text{cm}^3$.
Find the surface area of S.
Give your answer correct to
3 significant figures.
You must show your working.

Shape S

Volume of sphere = $\frac{4}{3}\pi r^3$
Surface area of sphere = $4\pi r^2$

(5 marks)

Adapted from 1MA1/2H, June 2018, Q19

Exam feedback

ResultsPlus

Most students who achieved a **Grade 9** answered a similar question well.

9 Equations and inequalities

9.1 Solving quadratic equations 1

⚠ Purposeful practice 1

1 Show that $x = 3$ is a solution for each of the quadratic equations.

   a $x^2 + 2x = 15$

   b $x^2 + x = 12$

   c $x^2 - 3x = 0$

2 Use the graphs to write the roots of the quadratic equations.

   a $x^2 + x - 6 = 0$

   b $x^2 + 5x + 6 = 0$

   c $x^2 - 4x + 4 = 0$

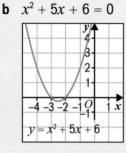

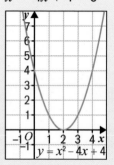

Reflect and reason

How can you find the roots of a quadratic equation from its graph?

Do all quadratic equations have two different roots?

⚠ Purposeful practice 2

1 Find the roots of the quadratic equations.

   a $(x + 3)(x - 2) = 0$

   b $(x - 3)(x + 2) = 0$

   c $(x + 3)(x + 2) = 0$

   d $(x - 3)(x - 2) = 0$

2 Find the roots of the quadratic equations.

   a $x^2 + 7x + 12 = 0$

   b $x^2 + x - 12 = 0$

   c $x^2 - x - 12 = 0$

   d $x^2 - 7x + 12 = 0$

Reflect and reason

Romesh says, 'The roots of $(x + 5)(x - 2) = 0$ are -2 and 5.'

What mistake has Romesh made?

⊠ Problem-solving practice

1 Salma is solving $x(x - 1) = 12$
She says, 'I know that 12 is equal to 4×3, so the answer is $x = 4$.'

   a What mistake has Salma made?

   b Find both solutions to the original equation.

2 Solve
$x^2 - 2x - 15 = 0$

3 Find the roots of $y = x^2 - 1$

4 Show that $y = x^2 - 8x + 16$ has one repeated root.

5 Match each graph to its equation.

$\boxed{y = x^2 - 9}$ $\boxed{y = x^2 - 6x + 9}$ $\boxed{y = x^2 + 6x + 9}$

a 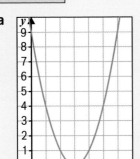   **b** 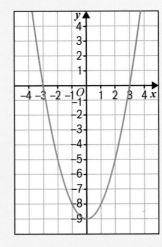   **c**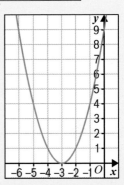

6 Find all the possible values of a such that $y = x^2 + ax + 9$ has one repeated root.

7 What root do these two equations have in common?
$y = x^2 + 8x + 12$ $y = x^2 + 11x + 30$

8 Work out the equation that will have roots that are double the roots of
$y = x^2 + 9x + 18$

9 Jason sketches the graph of $y = x^2 + 10x + 25$, as shown.

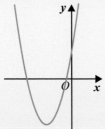

Find the roots of the equation $y = x^2 + 10x + 25$ and use your answer to show why Jason cannot be correct.

✦ Exam practice

1 Find the roots of the quadratic equation.
$x^2 + x - 20 = 0$ **(2 marks)**

Key point

- You can use the quadratic formula

$$x = \frac{-b \pm \sqrt{b^2 - 4ac}}{2a}$$

to find solutions to a quadratic equation $ax^2 + bx + c = 0$

△ Purposeful practice 1

1 Find the roots of the quadratic equations.

a $(2x + 3)(x - 2) = 0$ **b** $(x - 3)(3x + 2) = 0$

c $(2x + 3)(x + 2) = 0$ **d** $(x - 3)(3x - 2) = 0$

2 Find the roots of the quadratic equations.

a $2x^2 - 5x - 3 = 0$ **b** $2x^2 - 7x + 3 = 0$

c $2x^2 - 3x - 2 = 0$ **d** $2x^2 + 5x + 2 = 0$

Reflect and reason

When the x^2 term is $2x^2$, what are the x terms in the brackets in the factorisation?

△ Purposeful practice 2

1 Use the quadratic formula to solve the equations, giving your answers to 2 d.p. where necessary.

a **i** $2x^2 + 8x + 3 = 0$ **ii** $3x^2 + 8x + 3 = 0$ **iii** $4x^2 + 7x + 1 = 0$

b **i** $x^2 + 3x + 1 = 0$ **ii** $x^2 + 5x + 1 = 0$ **iii** $x^2 + 7x + 1 = 0$

c **i** $x^2 + 5x + 3 = 0$ **ii** $x^2 + 5x + 4 = 0$ **iii** $x^2 + 5x + 5 = 0$

d **i** $5x^2 - 11x - 3 = 0$ **ii** $11x^2 - 3x - 5 = 0$ **iii** $3x^2 - 5x - 11 = 0$

e **i** $16x^2 + 8x + 1 = 0$ **ii** $25x^2 - 30x + 9 = 0$ **iii** $64x^2 + 80x + 25 = 0$

Reflect and reason

Look at the values of $b^2 - 4ac$ in your solutions to **Q1e**.

Why does this mean there is only one (repeated) solution?

△ Purposeful practice 3

Use the quadratic formula to solve the equations, giving your answers in surd form.

1 **a** $x^2 + 6x + 7 = 0$ **b** $x^2 - 6x + 7 = 0$ **c** $x^2 - 6x - 1 = 0$

2 **a** $2x^2 - 8x + 5 = 0$ **b** $3x^2 + 3x - 1 = 0$ **c** $2x^2 - 9x - 4 = 0$

Reflect and reason

Which solutions are more accurate: your answers to Purposeful practice 2 or Purposeful practice 3?

1 Mark is solving $2x^2 + 3x - 4 = 0$
Here is his working.

$$x = \frac{3 \pm \sqrt{3^2 - 4 \times 2 \times 4}}{2 \times 2}$$

$$x = \frac{3 \pm \sqrt{-23}}{2 \times 2}$$

It is impossible to square root a negative number.
So this equation must have no solutions.

a Find the two errors in Mark's working.

b Work out the correct answers, to 2 d.p.

2 a Work out the value of $b^2 - 4ac$ in the equations.

i $4x^2 + 3x - 4 = 0$

ii $4x^2 + 3x + 4 = 0$

iii $4x^2 + 8x + 4 = 0$

b Match each equation in part **a** to the correct graph.

A 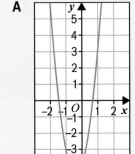   **B** 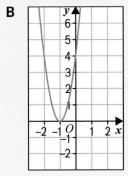   **C**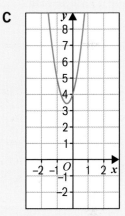

3 Find the roots of the quadratic equations.

a $x^2 + 12x = -35$

b $x^2 + 12x + 5 = -30$

c $x^2 + 50 = 15 - 12x$

d $3x^2 + 120 = 15 - 36x$

4 a Show that $1 + \frac{1}{x} = x$ can be rearranged to $x^2 - x - 1 = 0$

b Find two solutions for x.
Give your answers to 3 d.p.

 ✦ **Exam practice**

1 Solve $x^2 - 4x + 1 = 0$
Write your answer in the form $a \pm \sqrt{b}$ where a and b are integers. **(3 marks)**

Adapted from 1MA1/1H, Specimen Papers, Set 2, Q17

Key points

- Expressions such as $(x + 3)^2$, $(x - 1)^2$ and $\left(x + \frac{1}{2}\right)^2$ are called perfect squares.

- $x^2 + bx + c$ can be written in the form $\left(x + \frac{b}{2}\right)^2 - \left(\frac{b}{2}\right)^2 + c$
  This is called completing the square.

- $ax^2 + bx + c$ can be written in the form $a\left(x^2 + \frac{b}{a}x\right) + c$ before completing the square for the expression inside the brackets.

△ Purposeful practice

1 Expand

  a $(x + 3)^2$ **b** $(x - 3)^2$

  c $2(x + 3)^2$ **d** $2(x - 3)^2$

  e $5(x + 3)^2$ **f** $5(x - 3)^2$

2 Expand and simplify

  a $(x + 3)^2 + 3$ **b** $(x + 3)^2 - 4$

  c $(x + 3)^2 - 15$ **d** $(x - 3)^2 + 3$

  e $(x - 3)^2 - 4$ **f** $(x - 3)^2 - 15$

3 Write these in the form $(x + p)^2 + q$

  a $x^2 + 6x + 12$ **b** $x^2 + 6x + 10$

  c $x^2 + 6x + 15$ **d** $x^2 + 6x - 1$

  e $x^2 + 6x - 11$ **f** $x^2 + 6x - 91$

4 Write these in the form $(x + p)^2 + q$

  a $x^2 - 6x + 12$ **b** $x^2 - 6x - 12$

  c $x^2 - 6x$ **d** $x^2 + 6x + 12$

  e $x^2 + 6x - 12$ **f** $x^2 + 6x$

5 Write these in the form $a(x + p)^2 + q$

  a $2x^2 + 12x + 20$ **b** $2x^2 + 12x + 8$

  c $2x^2 + 12x - 18$ **d** $3x^2 + 12x + 21$

  e $3x^2 + 12x + 18$ **f** $3x^2 + 12x - 18$

6 Write these in the form $a(x + p)^2 + q$

  a $9x^2 + 18x - 3$ **b** $9x^2 + 18x$

  c $9x^2 + 18x + 19$ **d** $16x^2 + 32x + 4$

  e $16x^2 + 32x$ **f** $16x^2 + 32x + 64$

7 Write these in the form $(x + p)^2 + q$ or $a(x + p)^2 + q$

  a $x^2 + 8x + 17$ **b** $4x^2 - 20x + 15$

  c $2x^2 + 6x - 1$ **d** $x^2 + 5x + 1$

  e $x^2 + x + 1$ **f** $10x^2 + 2x + 1$

Reflect and reason

How does the number inside the bracket in the completed square form compare to the coefficient of x in the expression?

1 Jenny has made two errors when completing the square for $x^2 + 8x + 50$.

$$x^2 + 8x + 50 = (x + 8)^2 - 8x - 14$$

   a Identify her mistakes.

   b Work out the correct solution.

2 The area of rectangle C is given by $x^2 + 4x + 10$.
   The rectangle is split into a square (A) and a rectangle (B).
   The area of rectangle B is independent of x (the expression for its area is just a number).
   Work out the dimensions of square A in terms of x, and the area of rectangle B.

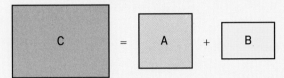

3 Look at the two methods (**a** and **b**) showing a starting strategy for completing the square with $3x^2 + 12x + 7$.
   Finish each method.

   a $3x^2 + 12x + 7 = 3\left(x^2 + 4x + \frac{7}{3}\right)$

   b $3x^2 + 12x + 7 = 3(x^2 + 4x) + 7$

4 **a** Complete the square for the expression $3x^2 + 18x + 21$.

   b Show that one solution of $3x^2 + 18x + 21 = 0$ is $x = -3 + \sqrt{2}$ and find the other solution.

5 **a** Write $x^2 + 6x + 1$ in completed square form.

   b Use a substitution for y in terms of x to write $4y^2 + 12y + 1$ in completed square form, and use this form to solve the equation $4y^2 + 12y + 1 = 0$
   Give your answers to 2 s.f.

6 **a** Write $x^2 + 4x + 10$ in completed square form.

   b Use your answer to **a** to explain why $x^2 + 4x + 10 = 0$ has no solutions.

7 **a** Show that $n^2 + n + 0.25$ can be written as a perfect square.

   b Write $n^2 + n + 0.25$ in the form $n(n + 1) + a$, where a is a decimal number.

   c Anna says, 'You can find 2.5^2 by working out 2×3 and adding 0.25.'
   Substitute $n = 2$ into your answers to parts **a** and **b**, and calculate the solutions, to show Anna is correct.

   d Use your answers from parts **a** to **c** to work out 5.5^2.

1 Write $x^2 + 8x - 5$ in the form $(x + a)^2 + b$ where a and b are integers.   **(2 marks)**

   Adapted from 1MA1/3H, November 2017, Q13

Exam feedback   Results**P**lus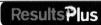

In a similar question, students were often able to score one mark for $(x + 4)^2$ but errors were frequently made when finding b.

9.4 Solving simple simultaneous equations

Key points

- When there are two unknowns, you need two equations to find their values. These are called simultaneous equations.
- You can solve simultaneous equations by
  substitution: substituting an expression for x or y from one equation into the other equation
  elimination: making the coefficients of one variable the same in both equations, and then either adding or subtracting the equations to eliminate this variable

⚠ Purposeful practice 1

1 Solve the simultaneous equations by substitution.

a $y = 4x$
$x + y = 10$

b $y = 2x$
$x + y = 12$

c $y = 3x$
$x + y = 16$

2 Solve the simultaneous equations.

a $y = 2x + 4$
$2x + y = 10$

b $y = 3x + 5$
$2x + y = 10$

c $y = 4x - 8$
$2x + y = 10$

Reflect and reason

How can you check your solutions to a pair of simultaneous equations?

⚠ Purposeful practice 2

1 Solve the simultaneous equations by elimination.

a $4x + 2y = 20$
$3x - 2y = 8$

b $4x + 2y = 20$
$3x + 2y = 8$

c $y = 5x$
$x + y = 18$

d $y = 9x$
$x + y = 20$

2 Solve the simultaneous equations by elimination.

a $4x + 2y = 20$
$3x - y = 5$

b $4x + 2y = 20$
$3x - 4y = -7$

c $4x + y = 16$
$3x - 4y = -7$

d $4x + 2y = 14$
$3x + y = 9$

e $4x + 2y = 14$
$3x + 4y = 18$

f $4x + y = 11$
$3x + 4y = 18$

3 Solve the simultaneous equations by elimination.

a $x + 2y = 8$
$3x + 5y = 22$

b $2x + 2y = 16$
$4x + 3y = 26$

c $6x + 8y = 1$
$18x + 4y = 8$

4 Solve the simultaneous equations by elimination.

a $3x + 2y = 11$
$6x - 5y = 13$

b $4x + 3y = 1$
$6x + 9y = 15$

c $-2x + 3y = -13$
$6x + 4y = -13$

Reflect and reason

How do you decide whether to add or subtract equations to eliminate a variable?

1   Two numbers, x and y, add up to 6 and have a difference of 1.
    Find the two numbers.

2   The diagram shows a rectangle.
    All sides are measured in centimetres.
    Find the area of the rectangle.

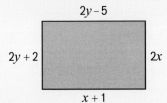

3   Two cups of coffee and one cake cost £7.29.
    One cup of coffee costs 81p more than one cake.
    Find the cost of a cup of coffee and the cost of a cake.

4   Jason and Louise both have pay-as-you-go phones, where they pay a fixed cost for each text or
    phone call they make. (There is no monthly fee.)
    In one month, Jason pays £52.80 for 300 texts and 240 calls.
    Louise pays £54.40 for 500 texts and 120 calls.
    Work out the cost of

    a   one text

    b   one call

5   An electricity company charges a fixed cost per day, as well as a cost for each unit of
    electricity used.
    A customer uses 1000 units of electricity in their first 40 days and receives a bill for £22.
    The customer uses 600 units of electricity over the next 30 days and is charged £13.50.
    Work out the cost per day and the cost for each unit of electricity used.

6   In a fair game, you roll three dice to play.
    You win the jackpot if the following criteria are met.
    Two of the dice show the same result.
    The numbers on the dice add up to 12.
    The difference between the larger and the smaller number is 3.
    Use this information to form two sets of simultaneous equations, and use them to determine the
    two possible combinations of dice that win the jackpot.

1   Solve the simultaneous equations.
    $5x - y = 11$
    $5x + 2y = 23$ **(3 marks)**

    Adapted from 1MA1/3H, June 2017, Q2

Exam feedback   Results**Plus**

Most students who achieved a **Grade 6** or above answered a similar question well.

9.5 More simultaneous equations

Key point

- To solve simultaneous equations, you may need to multiply the equations by different numbers so that you can add or subtract to eliminate a variable.

⚠ Purposeful practice 1

1 Solve the simultaneous equations, by multiplying first as shown.

 a $3x + 4y = 2$ Multiply by 3   **b** $3x + 4y = 2$ Multiply by 5
      $5x + 3y = 7$ Multiply by 4 $5x + 3y = 7$ Multiply by 3

2 $4x + 3y = -9$ ①
   $3x - 7y = -16$ ②

 a What could you multiply equations ① and ② by

    i so you could add to eliminate y **ii** so you could subtract to eliminate x?

 b Solve the simultaneous equations.

Reflect and reason

Does it matter whether you multiply both equations to get the same number in the x terms, or to get the same number in the y terms?

⚠ Purposeful practice 2

1 Solve the simultaneous equations.

 a $2x + 3y = 20$ **b** $2x - 3y = 11$ **c** $2x + 3y = -8$
      $3x - 4y = -4$ $3x + 4y = -9$ $3x + 5y = -11$

2 Solve the simultaneous equations by eliminating the x variable first.

 a $6x + 5y = 23$ **b** $4x + 2y = 16$ **c** $6x - 5y = -7$
      $4x - 3y = 9$ $6x + 5y = 20$ $4x + 3y = 8$

Reflect and reason

In **Q2a**, Sara multiplied ① by 4 and ② by 6. Hassan multiplied ① by 2 and ② by 3.

Do both methods give the same solutions?

How did Hassan use the LCM of 4 and 6 to decide what to multiply by?

⚠ Purposeful practice 3

Solve the simultaneous equations. Give your answers as fractions.

1 $6x + 8y = 23$ 2 $8x + 9y = 6$ 3 $14x + 10y = 19$
   $9x - 10y = -17.75$ $10x + 6y = 5\frac{3}{4}$ $-21x - 15y = 34.5$

Reflect and reason

In **Q1** and **Q2**, fraction solutions are more accurate than decimal solutions to 2 decimal places. Explain why.

1 The maximum load a small van can carry is 400 kg.
The maximum load is reached with 12 bags of cement and 5 bags of sand.
When the van carries 8 bags of cement and 9 bags of sand, it is 20 kg less than the maximum load.
When there is no cement, how many bags of sand can the van carry?

2 At a cinema
two adult and three child tickets cost £33.50
three adult and two child tickets cost £36.50
Next week the cinema has a special offer where two adult and four child tickets cost £35.00.
How much less than the full price is this for two adult and four child tickets?

3 A straight line has the form $y = mx + c$
A straight line joins (4, 19) to (8, 31).
a Show that this would produce the simultaneous equations
$4m + c = 19$
$8m + c = 31$

b Find the equation of the line.

c Is the point (6, 25) on the line?

4 A farmer has some sheep and some chickens and wants to know how many of each he has.
Some unhelpful friends count 115 heads in total, and 310 feet.
How many of each animal does the farmer have?

5 A curve has the form $y = ax^2 + b$ and goes through the points (2, 31) and (3, 56).
Find the equation of the curve.

6 Solve
$17x + 18y = 15$
$15x + 16y = 13$

7 James and his friend buy some shorts and t-shirts from a discount store.
Each type of item has a fixed price.
James buys 3 pairs of shorts and 5 t-shirts for £44.92.
His friend buys 5 pairs of shorts and 3 t-shirts for £42.92.
How much does each item of clothing cost?

8 A square grid is placed over a map, so that two roads on the map follow straight lines
with equations $3y = 4x - 5$ and $2y + 5x = 12$.
Without drawing the graph, determine the coordinates on the map where the two roads meet.

⬡ Exam practice

1 Solve the simultaneous equations.
$3x + 4y = 6$
$4x - 5y = -23$

(4 marks)

Adapted from 1MA1/3H, Specimen Papers, Set 2, Q11

9.6 Solving linear and quadratic simultaneous equations

- A pair of quadratic and linear simultaneous equations can have two possible solutions.

- To find the coordinates where two graphs intersect, solve their equations simultaneously.

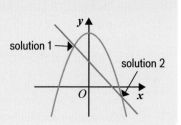

⚠ Purposeful practice 1

1 Solve the simultaneous equations.

  a $y = x$
    b $y = -x$
    c $y = 2x$
    d $y = -2x$

    $y = x^2 - 6$
    $y = x^2 - 6$
    $y = 2x^2 - 12$
    $y = 2x^2 - 12$

2 Solve the simultaneous equations.

  a $y = x + 2$
    b $y = x - 2$
    c $y = 3x + 2$
    d $y = 3x - 2$

    $y = x^2 + 6x + 8$
    $y = x^2 + 8x + 10$
    $y = x^2 - 5x + 9$
    $y = x^2 + 4x + -32$

3 Solve the simultaneous equations, giving your answers to 2 d.p.

  a $y = 2x^2 + x - 2$
    b $y = 2x^2 + 3x - 2$
    c $y = 2x^2 + 3x - 2$

    $y = x + 3$
    $y = x + 3$
    $y = x + 5$

Reflect and reason

When do you need to use the quadratic formula to solve the simultaneous equations?

⚠ Purposeful practice 2

1 Solve the simultaneous equations.
Give your answers to an appropriate degree of accuracy.

  a $y = x^2 + 6x - 1$
    b $y = x^2 + 6x - 1$

    $y = 3x - 1$
    $y = 3x + 1$

  c $y = x^2 + 10x + 3$
    d $y = x^2 + 14x + 16$

    $y = 2x + 3$
    $y = 2x - 3$

2 Solve the simultaneous equations.

  a $x^2 + y^2 = 5$
    b $x^2 + y^2 = 5$

    $y = x + 1$
    $y = x - 1$

  c $x^2 + y^2 = 5$
    d $x^2 + y^2 = 5$

    $y = 2x + 4$
    $y = 2x - 4$

3 Solve the simultaneous equations.
Give your answers to an appropriate degree of accuracy.

  a $y = x^2 - 2x + 15$
    b $y = 2x^2 - 6x + 19$
    c $y = 2x^2 + x - 5$

    $y = 4x + 6$
    $y = 2x + 11$
    $y = -15x - 37$

Reflect and reason

What does each solution in **Q3** reveal about the two graphs of the equations?

Problem-solving practice

1 Consider the pair of simultaneous equations
   $y = x^2 + x + 7$
   $y = 5x + a$
   What value of a is required so that the equations have only one solution?

2 Solve
   $y = x^2 + x + 4$
   $y = x + 10$
   Give your answers to 2 d.p.

3 The height of a hill, in metres, is modelled by the equation
   $$y = 1500 - 2x - \frac{x^2}{500}$$
   A tunnel cuts through the hill following a path represented by the equation
   $$y = \frac{-2}{5x} + 1100$$
   Solve the equations simultaneously to work out how much the height of the tunnel changes between the entrance and exit.

4 a Find the two points of intersection where the curve $y = x^2 + 3x - 1$ meets the line $y = 4 - x$.
   b Find the distance between these two points.
      Give your answer to 2 d.p.
   c A second line, $y = 3x - 1$, only meets the curve $y = x^2 + 3x - 1$ once.
      Find the coordinates of this point.

5 Solve algebraically the simultaneous equations.
   $x^2 + y^2 = 25$
   $y = x + 1$

6 Find the value of a so that $4x + 3y = a$ is a tangent to $x^2 + y^2 = 25$.

7 Find the positive value of c such that the line $y = 10 - cx$ is a tangent to the curve
   $x^2 + y^2 = 64$.

Exam practice

1 Solve algebraically the simultaneous equations.
   $x^2 + y^2 = 34$
   $3y - x = 12$

   (5 marks)

   Adapted from 1MA1/1H, June 2017, Q20

Exam feedback
Most students who achieved a Grade 9 answered a similar question well.

ResultsPlus

Key points

- You can show inequalities on a number line.
- An empty circle ○ shows that the value is not included.
- A filled circle ● shows that the value is included.
- An arrow ○——→ shows that the solution continues towards infinity.
- You can rearrange an inequality in the same way as you rearrange an equation.
- You can write the solution to an inequality using set notation.

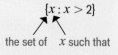

$\{x : x > 2\}$

the set of x such that

⚠ Purposeful practice 1

1. Represent the inequalities on a number line.

   a $n < 2$ **b** $n > 2$ **c** $n \leq 2$ **d** $n \geq 2$

2. Represent the inequalities on a number line.

   a $\{x : x < 5\}$ **b** $\{x : x \geq 5\}$ **c** $\{x : x \leq 5\}$

3. Complete the inequalities for the set of x values $\{x : x < 5\}$.

   a $3x <$ **b** $4x <$ **c** $4x + 3 <$ **d** $4x - 1 <$

4. Complete the inequalities for the set of x values $\{x : x \geq 5\}$.

   a $3x \geq$ **b** $4x \geq$ **c** $4x + 3 \geq$ **d** $4x - 1 \geq$

5. Solve the inequalities. Write the solution set using set notation.

   a $3x + 1 < 13$ **b** $3x + 1 \leq -5$ **c** $4x - 3 \geq 13$ **d** $4x - 3 < 29$

Reflect and reason

Look back at **Q5**. How can you tell which inequality sign is needed in the solution?

⚠ Purposeful practice 2

1. For each inequality, multiply both sides by -1 and change the sign to make the inequality correct.

   a $2 < 5$ **b** $4 > 1$ **c** $-3 < 7$ **d** $-2 > -6$

2. Write each inequality for x, instead of $-x$.

   a $-x < 5$ **b** $-x > 1$ **c** $-x < 7$ **d** $-x > -6$

3. Solve the inequalities.

   a $7 - x > 4$ **b** $5 - x \leq 12$ **c** $-2x > 8$ **d** $-3x \leq 12$

   e $-4x \geq 20$ **f** $-5x \leq -20$ **g** $-\frac{x}{3} \leq 2$ **h** $-\frac{x}{2} > 3$

   i $5 - 3x > 14$ **j** $-7 - 3x < 14$ **k** $11 - 2x \geq -3$ **l** $6 - 4x \geq -10$

Reflect and reason

When you multiply or divide all the terms in an inequality by a negative number, what do you need to do to the inequality sign?

⊠ Problem-solving practice

1 Match the inequalities with their solutions.

A $3x + 2 \geqslant 20$	1 $\{x : x < 6\}$
B $5x - 5 < 25$	2 $\{x : x > 6\}$
C $4x + 6 \leqslant 30$	3 $\{x : x \leqslant 6\}$
D $3x - 3 > 15$	4 $\{x : x \geqslant 6\}$

2 a Solve

    i $3x + 1 < 9$

    ii $2x + 3 \geqslant 5$

  b Using a number line, show the region where both inequalities are satisfied.

3 Find the integer solutions to
$4 \leqslant 2x + 3 \leqslant 12$.

4 The sides of a right-angled triangle are $3x$, $4x$ and $5x$.
The perimeter is greater than or equal to 60 cm.
Find the minimum possible area.

5 The perimeter of this rectangle is less than or equal to 52 cm.
Find the maximum possible area.
All measurements are in cm.

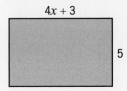

6 Write an inequality with solution set
$\{x : x > -2\}$.

7 Esther is solving $5x + 2 \geqslant 8x - 22$ as follows

$5x + 2 \geqslant 8x - 22$
$-3x \geqslant -20$
$x \geqslant 6.666$

Work out the answer yourself and identify the two errors in her method.

8 Work out the value of x^2 using values of x from -4 to $+4$ and write down the two inequalities needed if $x^2 > 9$.

✦ Exam practice

1 Solve $7(2x - 3) > 7$ **(2 marks)**

Adapted from 1MA0/2H, June 2014, Q13

Exam feedback   Results**Plus**

In a similar question, some students replaced the inequality sign with an equals sign and lost marks because they did not replace with the inequality sign in the answer.

10 Probability

10.1 Combined events

Key points

- A sample space diagram, or possibility space diagram, shows all the possible outcomes of two events.

- Probability $= \dfrac{\text{number of successful outcomes}}{\text{total number of possible outcomes}}$

△ Purposeful practice 1

Write all the possible outcomes when

1 a the coin is flipped
   b the spinner is spun
   c the coin is flipped **and** the spinner is spun

2 a the coin is flipped
   b the dice is rolled
   c the coin is flipped **and** the dice is rolled

3 a the spinner is spun
   b the dice is rolled
   c the spinner is spun **and** the dice is rolled

Reflect and reason

How can you use the number of possible outcomes from two separate events to work out the number of possible outcomes when both events happen together?

△ Purposeful practice 2

Fay spins each spinner once. Both spinners are fair.
She adds the two numbers together to get her score.

1 Make a possibility space diagram for each possible score.

2 Find the probability that Fay's score is

   a 8
   b less than 8
   c more than 8
   d 8 or more
   e 8 or less

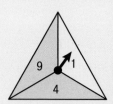

Reflect and reason

Which of your answers to **Q2** can you add together to make 1? Explain why.

⊠ Problem-solving practice

1   Mel rolls two ordinary dice.
    He adds the two scores.
    What is the probability that Mel's total score is a prime number?

2   When you roll two ordinary dice at the same time, what is the probability that both dice show
    the same score?

3   Box 1 contains a £5 note, a £10 note and a £20 note.
    Box 2 contains a £10 note and a £20 note.
    Dan picks a note from each box at random.
    What is the probability he gets a total of less than £30?

4   Amy has a set of cards labelled 1 to 10.
    She picks one card at random.
    She also throws an ordinary dice once.

    a   How many possible outcomes include 5 on the dice?

    b   Work out the probability of picking an even number and rolling a 5.

5   Kim and Zoe play a game.
    They roll two dice and multiply the numbers to get a score.
    Kim wins if the score is less than 12.
    Zoe wins if the score is 12 or more.
    Is this game fair?
    Explain.

6   Arrange these cards into two sets, so that there are 15 different possible outcomes for 'pick one
    card from set A and one card from set B'.

✿ Exam practice

1   Paul has a bag of stationary.
    There are 40 pens in the bag.
    The table shows the types of pens in the bag.

	Red	Green	Blue
Ballpoint pen	4	7	9
Felt tip pen	2	5	4
Fountain pen	1	0	8

Paul takes at random a pen from the bag.

    a   Write down the probability that the pen is a red ballpoint pen.   **(1 mark)**

    b   Work out the probability the pen is a felt tip.   **(2 marks)**

Adapted from 1MA0/2H, June 2015, Q1a and b

Key points

- When events are mutually exclusive, you can add their probabilities.
  For mutually exclusive events, P(A or B) = P(A) + P(B)
- The probabilities of an exhaustive set of mutually exclusive events sum to 1.
- For mutually exclusive events A and not A, P(not A) = 1 − P(A)

△ Purposeful practice 1

For this set of counters, write down these probabilities

1 P(R)	**2** P(B)	**3** P(Y)	**4** P(W)
5 P(R or Y)	**6** P(R or W)	**7** P(R or B or Y)	**8** P(R or B or W)
9 P(B or Y or W)	**10** P(not B)	**11** P(not Y)	**12** P(not W)
13 P(not B or R)	**14** P(not B or W)	**15** P(not W or Y)	

Reflect and reason

Use your answers to **Q1–15** to show that

    P(R or W) = P(R) + P(W)
    P(B or Y or W) = P(B) + P(Y) + P(W)
    P(not W) = 1 − P(W)

△ Purposeful practice 2

In each question, there are only blue (B), yellow (Y), red (R) and green (G) counters in a bag.

1 The table shows the probabilities of getting a blue or yellow or green counter.
Work out the probability of getting a red counter.

Colour	B	Y	R	G
Probability	0.1	0.2		0.3

2 The table shows the probabilities of getting a blue or yellow or red counter.
Work out the probability of getting a green counter.

Colour	B	Y	R	G
Probability	0.1	0.25	0.6	

3 The table shows the probabilities of getting a blue or red or green counter.
Work out the probability of getting a yellow counter.

Colour	B	Y	R	G
Probability	$\frac{3}{8}$		$\frac{1}{4}$	$\frac{1}{4}$

4 The table shows the probabilities of getting a blue or yellow or red counter.
Work out the probability of getting a green counter.

Colour	B	Y	R	G
Probability	15%	15%	25%	

Reflect and reason

For **Q2** Karl writes,
0.1 + 0.25 + 0.6 = 0.95, so P(green) = 0.5
Explain what Karl has done wrong.

1 The probability that a train is late is 0.03.
   What is the probability that the train is not late?

2 The weather forecast says the probability of rain is <10%.
   What is the probability that it does not rain?

3 A counter is picked at random from a bag.
   The table shows the probabilities of getting a blue or yellow counter.
   The probability of getting a red counter is the same as the probability of getting a green counter.
   Work out the probability of getting a green counter.

Colour	blue	yellow	red	green
Probability	0.15	0.25		

4 The table shows the probabilities of getting a blue or yellow counter.
   The probability of getting a red counter is twice the probability of getting a green counter.
   Work out the probability of getting a red counter.

Colour	blue	yellow	red	green
Probability	0.3	0.4		

5 The probability of picking a black counter from a bag of counters is $\frac{1}{12}$.
   Alex says there are 6 counters in the bag.
   Explain why there cannot be only 6 counters in the bag.

6 The table shows the probabilities of getting different colours of counters.

Colour	pink	black	white	green
Probability	0.3	0.15	0.45	0.1

   There are 12 pink counters in the bag.
   a Which colour counter is half as likely as pink?
   b Work out the numbers of black, white and green counters in the bag.

1 There are some cubes in a bag.
   The cubes are red or blue or green or white.
   Sam is going to take a cube at random from the bag.
   The table shows each of the probabilities that the cube will be red or will be white.

Colour	red	blue	green	white
Probability	0.4			0.45

   There are 8 red cubes in the bag.
   The probability that the cube Sam takes will be blue is twice the probability that the cube will be green.
   Work out the number of green cubes in the bag.   **(4 marks)**

   Adapted from 1MA1/3H, June 2018, Q6a

Exam feedback   ResultsPlus

Most students who achieved a **Grade 5** or above answered a similar question well.

Key points

- Experimental probability of an outcome = $\dfrac{\text{frequency of outcome}}{\text{total number of trials}}$

- Expected number of outcomes = number of trials × probability

△ Purposeful practice 1

1 The table shows the experimental probabilities of each score on dice A. Freya rolls dice A 100 times. Work out an estimate for the total number of times the dice will land on

Score	1	2	3	4	5	6
Experimental probability	0.12	0.15	0.21	0.17	0.15	0.2

a 3 b 5

c 1 or 6 d an even number

2 The table shows the scores for a number of rolls of dice B.

Score	1	2	3	4	5	6
Frequency	30	35	46	40	32	17

a Work out the experimental probability of each score.

Dice B is now rolled 300 times.

b Work out an estimate for the number of times the dice will land on

i 3 ii 5

iii 1 or 6 iv an even number

Reflect and reason

Which dice, A or B, is most likely to be fair? How did you decide?

△ Purposeful practice 2

1 Ben, Carla and Deb each flip the same coin a number of times. The table shows their results.

	Ben	Carla	Deb
Head	15	49	12
Tail	18	61	8

Work out the experimental probability of flipping a head with this coin based on

a Ben's results b Carla's results

c Deb's results d all the results combined

Give your answers to 2 d.p.

Reflect and reason

Jake says, 'Carla flipped the coin more times than Ben or Deb. So, I am going to use Carla's results to give an estimate for the experimental probability.'

Explain how Jake could get an even better estimate for the experimental probability.

⌧ Problem-solving practice

1 A train company advertises, 'The probability that one of our trains is late is only 2%.'
   The company runs 1400 trains each week.
   Work out an estimate for the number of these trains that are likely to be late each week.

2 In a probability experiment, Shan picks a ball from a bag, records its colour, and then replaces it in the bag.
   She does this 50 times. Here are her results.
   There are 20 balls in the bag.
   Calculate an estimate for the number of each colour.

Colour	Red	Blue	Green	White
Frequency	15	20	5	10

3 **a** Which of these probabilities need to be estimated from a probability experiment?
       The probability that
       i a drawing pin lands point up when you drop it
       ii a spinner with 6 equal sections, A–F, lands on a vowel
       iii a light bulb lasts more than 1 year in normal use
       iv a card picked at random from a normal pack is a picture card
       v more than one egg breaks when you drop a box of 6 eggs
       vi a cuboid-shaped matchbox lands on one of its smallest faces when dropped

   b Which of the probabilities in **a** can be calculated as a theoretical probability?

4 The table shows the probabilities that a biased dice lands on 1, 2, 3, 4 and 5.

Score	1	2	3	4	5	6
Probability	0.21	0.13	0.15	0.24	0.11	

   This dice is rolled 120 times. Work out an estimate for the number of times it will land on 6.

5 The table shows the results of spinning this five-sided spinner 80 times.

Score	1	2	3	4	5
Frequency	18	14	19	13	16

   a Is the spinner likely to be fair? Show your working to explain.
   b Explain how you could improve the experiment to test whether the spinner is fair.

⊠ Exam practice

1 When a piece of buttered toast is dropped, it can land butter side up or butter side down.
   Kay, Jay and Min each dropped a piece of buttered toast a number of times.
   Their results are shown in the table.
   Dane is going to drop a piece of buttered toast once.
   Whose results will give the best estimate for the probability that the toast will land butter side down? Give a reason for your answer.   **(1 mark)**

	Kay	Jay	Min
Butter side up	7	15	36
Butter side down	12	13	54

Adapted from 1MA1/3H, November 2017, Q8

Exam feedback

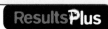

In a similar question, students identified the best estimate for the probability, but did not give the correct reasons.

Key points

- Two events are independent if one event does not affect the probability of the other.
- To find the probability of two independent events, multiply their probabilities.
- A tree diagram shows two or more events and their probabilities.

△ Purposeful practice

1   Alex spins both these spinners.

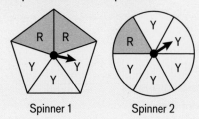

Spinner 1   Spinner 2

   a   Copy and complete the probability tree diagram.

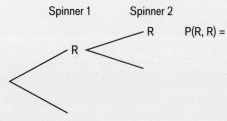

Spinner 1   Spinner 2

   R   P(R, R) =

   R

   b   Which outcome is most likely from spinning these two spinners?

Alex spins spinner 1 and then spinner 2. He does this 75 times.

   c   Work out an estimate for the number of times both spinners land on red.

2   Bella spins both these spinners.

   a   For each spinner, write P(Red) as a decimal.

   b   Draw a tree diagram to show the probabilities
when Bella spins spinner 1 and then spinner 2.
Write the probabilities as decimals.

   c   Calculate the probability that the two spinners land on
different colours.

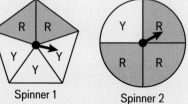

Spinner 1   Spinner 2

   d   Bella spins spinner 1 and then spinner 2. She does this 100 times.
Work out an estimate for the number of times both spinners land on the same colour.

Reflect and reason

Use the terms 'add' and 'multiply' to complete these sentences.

- The two spinners are independent, so you _____ along the branches to calculate the probability
of P(Red and Red).

- Outcomes are mutually exclusive, so you _____ the probabilities down the side to calculate
P(Red and Red) or P(Yellow and Yellow).

1 The tree diagram shows the probabilities when two spinners, each with a number of blue and green sections, are spun.

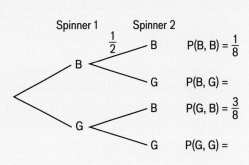

a Work out
 i the probability of G on spinner 1
 ii the probability of G on spinner 1 and G on spinner 2.

b Draw two spinners that give these probabilities.

2 Jack has two spinners, A and B.
Each spinner can only land on an even number or an odd number.
The probability that spinner A lands on an odd number is 0.3.
The probability that spinner B lands on an odd number is 0.8.
The probability tree diagram shows this information.
Jack spins spinner A once and then spinner B once. He does this a number of times.
The number of times **both** spinners land on odd numbers is 24.
Work out an estimate for the number of times **both** spinners land on even numbers.

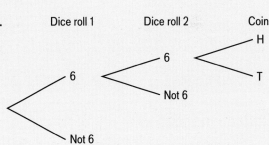

3 Anna rolls a fair dice twice and then flips a coin.
She starts to draw this tree diagram.
Work out the probability that she rolls 2 sixes and the coin shows Heads.

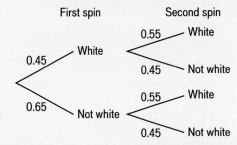

1 When a biased spinner is spun, the probability that it will land on white is 0.45.
Jake spins the biased spinner twice.
He draws this tree diagram.
The tree diagram is not correct.
Write down two things that are wrong with the probability tree diagram. **(2 marks)**

First spin Second spin
0.45 White
  0.55 White
  0.45 Not white
0.65 Not white
  0.55 White
  0.45 Not white

Adapted from 1MA1/3H, June 2018, Q4

Exam feedback **Results Plus**
Most students who achieved a Grade 4 or above answered a similar question well.

Key points

- If one event depends on the outcome of another event, the two events are dependent events.
- A conditional probability is the probability of a dependent event. The probability of the second outcome depends on what has already happened in the first outcome.

△ Purposeful practice 1

There are 6 red and 2 yellow balls in a bag.
Lucy takes a ball. She does not replace it in the bag.
Then she takes another ball.

1 Copy and complete this tree diagram to show the probabilities.

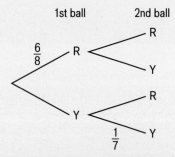

2 Work out the probability that she takes 2 yellow balls.

Reflect and reason

What do you notice about the probabilities on each pair of branches like this?

△ Purposeful practice 2

1 There are 10 chocolates in a box.
6 are milk and 4 are plain.
Max takes a chocolate and eats it.
Then he takes another chocolate and eats it.

   a Draw a tree diagram to show the probabilities.

   b Work out the probability that he eats one milk and one plain chocolate.

2 There are 12 pens in a box.
7 are red and the rest are black.
Sofia takes 2 pens from the box.

   a Draw a tree diagram to show the probabilities.

   b Work out the probability that she takes at least one red pen.

Reflect and reason

Problems where items are picked 'without replacement' lead to conditional probabilities.
Which parts of the questions on this page tell you they are 'without replacement' problems?

1st sweet   2nd sweet

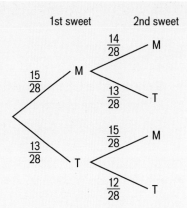

1   There are 28 sweets in a bag.
    15 of them are toffees and the rest are mints.
    Mary is going to pick two sweets at random.
    She draws this tree diagram to show the probabilities.
    Write down **one** thing that is wrong with the probabilities in her
    tree diagram.

2   There are 5 red and 7 green marbles in a bag.
    Lin takes 3 marbles.
    Work out the probability that she takes 3 green marbles.

3   The probability diagram shows the probabilities when Amir
    takes two socks from his drawer.
    If Amir takes one black and one white sock from the drawer,
    he has to take a third sock to make a pair.
    a   Work out the probability he has to take a third sock.
    b   Explain why, when he takes a third sock, he will have a pair
        of socks the same colour.

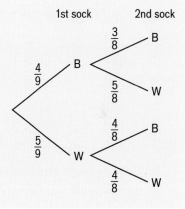

 ⊛ **Exam practice**

1   A hockey team is going to play a match on Wednesday and on Saturday.
    The probability that the team will win on Wednesday is 0.4
    If they win on Wednesday, the probability that they will win on Saturday is 0.72
    If they do **not** win on Wednesday, the probability that they will win on Saturday is 0.25
    a   Copy and complete the tree diagram.   **(2 marks)**

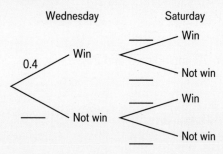

    b   Find the probability that the team will win exactly one of the two matches.   **(3 marks)**

Adapted from 1MA1/2H, June 2018, Q15

Exam feedback   Results**Plus**

Q1a: Most students who achieved a `Grade 3` or above answered a similar question well.
Q1b: Most students who achieved a `Grade 6` or above answered a similar question well.

10.6 Venn diagrams and set notation

Key points

- Curly brackets { } show a set of values.
  $\in$ means 'is an element of'.

- A $\cap$ B means 'A intersection B'. This is all the elements that are in A **and** B.

- A $\cup$ B means 'A union B'. This is all the elements that are in A **or** B **or** both.

- A′ means the elements **not** in A.

- ξ means the universal set — all the elements being considered.

⚠ Purposeful practice

1 ξ is the set of numbers from 10 to 30 (including 10 and 30).
   A = {11, 13, 18, 20, 25}
   B = {11, 12, 15, 18, 20, 22, 24, 29}
   a Which numbers are in A $\cap$ B?
   b Copy and complete this Venn diagram for ξ, A and B.
   c Write down the numbers that are in set

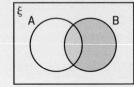

   i A $\cup$ B ii A′
   iii A′ $\cap$ B iv (A $\cup$ B)′

Repeat **Q1** for these sets

2 ξ is the numbers from 10 to 30 (including 10 and 30).
   A = multiples of 3
   B = even numbers

3 ξ is the numbers from 1 to 20 (including 1 and 20)
   A = odd numbers
   B = square numbers

4 ξ is the numbers from 5 to 20 (including 5 and 20).
   A = NOT multiples of 4
   B = NOT factors of 60

5 ξ is the numbers from 1 to 15 inclusive.
   A = prime numbers
   B = factors of 210

Reflect and reason

How does starting with the numbers in A $\cap$ B help you to fill in the Venn diagram?
How many times should each number in ξ appear in the Venn diagram?

1 The numbers 9, 15, 17, 20, 26 are put into a Venn diagram with two sets, P and Q.

$9 \in P' \cap Q$
$15 \in P \cap Q$
$17 \in P \cap Q$
$20 \in (P \cup Q)'$
$26 \in P \cap Q'$

a Draw the Venn diagram.

A number is chosen at random from the Venn diagram.

b Write down the probability that this number is **not** in set P.

2 40 people were asked whether they owned a fridge, a washing machine and a TV.
26 people owned all three.
1 person did not own any of the items.
34 people owned a washing machine. Of these:

1 also owned a fridge but not a TV
3 also owned a TV but not a fridge

31 people in total owned a fridge.
2 people owned a TV and a fridge but not a washing machine.

a Draw a Venn diagram to represent this information.

A person is chosen from this group at random.

b What is the probability that this person owns a TV?

3 The Venn diagram shows the numbers of students who own a tablet (T) and a laptop (L).
Work out

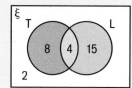

a $P(T \cup L)$ **b** $P(T \cup L')$ **c** $P(T' \cup L')$ **d** $P(T \cup L)'$

---

1 $\xi = \{\text{even numbers less than } 30\}$

$A = \{10, 20, 28\}$

$B = \{2, 14, 16, 20, 22, 26\}$

a Complete the Venn diagram to represent this information.   **(4 marks)**

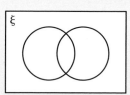

A number is chosen at random from the universal set ξ.

b What is the probability that the number is in the set $A \cup B'$?   **(2 marks)**

Adapted from 1MA1/3H, June 2017, Q1

Exam feedback   ResultsPlus

Q1a: Most students who achieved a Grade 4 or above answered a similar question well.

11 Multiplicative reasoning

11.1 Growth and decay

> **Key point**
>
> - You can calculate an amount after n years' compound interest using the formula
>
> $$\text{amount} = \text{initial amount} \times \left(\frac{100 + \text{interest rate}}{100}\right)^{n}$$

△ Purposeful practice 1

1 Carla invests £50 in an account at 5% per annum compound interest.
  Calculate the total amount in Carla's account after

  a 1 year   **b** 2 years   **c** 3 years

  d 10 years   **e** 11 years   **f** 20 years

2 Deepak invests £50 in an account at 10% per annum compound interest.
  Calculate the total amount in Deepak's account after

  a 1 year   **b** 2 years   **c** 3 years

  d 10 years   **e** 11 years   **f** 20 years

> **Reflect and reason**
>
> Why is it not possible to get the answers to **Q2** by doubling your answers to **Q1**?

△ Purposeful practice 2

1 A painting is valued at £50. Its value depreciates by 5% per annum.
  Work out the value of the painting after

  a 1 year   **b** 2 years   **c** 3 years

  d 10 years   **e** 11 years   **f** 20 years

2 A painting is valued at £100. Its value depreciates by 5% per annum.
  Work out the value of the painting after

  a 10 years   **b** 11 years   **c** 20 years

> **Reflect and reason**
>
> Will the value of the painting ever reach £0, if the depreciation continues at the same rate?
> Explain your answer.

△ Purposeful practice 3

Give the total percentage change after

1 a 10% increase followed by a 5% increase

2 a 10% increase followed by a 5% decrease

3 a 10% increase followed by a 10% decrease

> **Reflect and reason**
>
> Explain why the total percentage change in **Q3** is not 0%.

⊠ Problem-solving practice

1 The value of a company's share price shows an overall rise of 3% at the end of a 3 hour period.
The share price increased in value by 50% in the first hour and by 5% in the second hour.
By what percentage did it decrease in value in the third hour?

2 A car has an initial value of £31 000.
The value of the car depreciates by the same percentage each year.
After 4 years, the car is worth 60% of the initial value.
How much was the car worth after 3 years?

3 Tasfia has inherited some money.
She can choose to invest in shares or to put it into a savings account.
The shares are expected to increase in value by 10% in 2 years.
The savings account pays 5% per annum compound interest.
Which option would be the best for Tania financially over the next 2 years?

4 A radioactive isotope has a half-life of 3 days.
What percentage of the isotope will be left after 15 days?

5 A winner of a raffle is given two options.

Option 1: If the raffle pays out on the first day you get £200, but if the raffle pays out on subsequent days you get 25% less each day.

Option 2: If the raffle pays out on the first day you get 1p, but if the raffle pays out on subsequent days you get double the previous amount every day.

a If the raffle pays on the fourth day, which is the better option?

b If the raffle pays out after 4 weeks, which is the better option?

c How many days does it take before the better option changes?

Show working to explain your answers to parts **a** and **b**.

6 A colony of bacteria increases in size by 10% every 2 minutes.
When a timer is started, there are 1378 bacteria.

a How many bacteria will there be after 18 minutes?

b What will be the total percentage increase in the number of bacteria after 12 minutes?

c Rounding up to the nearest 2 minutes, how long will it take for the colony to double in size?

7 Marigold bought a new computer for £3500.
She read that its price decreases by 30% as soon as it is bought, and then by a further 20% for each year she owns it.
How much should Marigold expect to sell it for, 5 years after purchasing it?

✦ Exam practice

1 Dean invests £20 000 in an account paying compound interest for 3 years.
In the first year the rate of interest is x%.
At the end of the first year the value of Dean's investment is £20 800.
The rate of increase each year is $\frac{x}{2}$%.
What is the value of Dean's investment at the end of 3 years? **(4 marks)**

Adapted from 1MA1/2H, June 2018, Q9

Exam feedback   Results**Plus**

Most students who achieved a **Grade 6** or above answered a similar question well.

11.2 Compound measures

Key point

- These are kinematics formulae.

$$v = u + at \qquad s = ut + \frac{1}{2}at^2 \qquad v^2 = u^2 + 2as$$

where a is constant acceleration, u is initial velocity, v is final velocity, s is displacement from the position where $t = 0$ and t is time taken.

Velocity is speed in a given direction, and possible units are m/s.

Initial velocity is speed in a given direction at the start of the motion.

Acceleration is the rate of change of velocity, i.e. a measure of how the velocity changes with time, and possible units are m/s^2.

 ⚠ **Purposeful practice 1**

1   Calculate the average rate of writing in words per minute.

   a 300 words in 20 minutes   **b** 1000 words in 2 hours   **c** 20 words in 10 seconds

Reflect and reason

Which part shows the fastest writing speed? What do you need to do to be able to compare them?

 ⚠ **Purposeful practice 2**

1   Convert these speeds to m/h.

   a 60 m/s   **b** 30 m/s   **c** 6 m/s   **d** 0.6 m/s

2   Convert these speeds to km/h.

   a 60 m/s   **b** 30 m/s   **c** 6 m/s   **d** 0.6 m/s

Reflect and reason

What is the same and what is different about the process of converting units of time and units of distance in measures of speed?

 ⚠ **Purposeful practice 3**

1   Calculate the acceleration when

   a $v = 5$ m/s $u = 10$ m/s $t = 15$ s
   b $v = 8$ m/s $u = 13$ m/s $t = 15$ s

2   Calculate the acceleration when

   a $s = 5$ m $u = 10$ m/s $t = 15$ s
   b $s = 8$ m $u = 13$ m/s $t = 15$ s

3   Calculate the acceleration when

   a $v = 5$ m/s $u = 10$ m/s $s = 15$ m
   b $v = 8$ m/s $u = 13$ m/s $s = 15$ m

Reflect and reason

How did you decide which formula to use for **Q1–3**?

Problem-solving practice

1 Jahidul writes 140 words every 5 minutes.
  Angela writes 1570 words in one hour.
  They both have to complete a 5000-word essay.
  Who will finish it sooner?
  Show working to explain.

2 A car starts from rest and accelerates at $6\,\text{m/s}^2$.
  How many seconds does it take for its velocity to reach $90\,\text{km/h}$?

3 A cheetah has an acceleration of $8.93\,\text{m/s}^2$.
  A gazelle has an acceleration of $4.2\,\text{m/s}^2$.
  The cheetah is $300\,\text{m}$ behind the gazelle when they both start to run.
  Will the cheetah catch the gazelle in 11 seconds?
  Show working to explain.

4 Rowan starts from rest and accelerates to a speed of $3.5\,\text{m/s}$ after $2.5\,\text{s}$.
  Nurhad starts from rest and accelerates to a speed of $3.8\,\text{m/s}$ after $3\,\text{s}$.
  Assuming the acceleration is constant in each case, which of them has the greater acceleration?
  Show working to explain.

5 A cyclist is racing a car driver down a mountain.
  They both start from rest at the same point.
  The car travels along a road that is $21.48\,\text{m}$ long.
  The cyclist travels along a track that is $12.3\,\text{m}$ long.
  The car has a constant acceleration of $2\,\text{m/s}^2$.
  The cyclist has a constant acceleration of $1.4\,\text{m/s}^2$.
  Who will win the race?

6 Amra has a 16-week-old kitten.
  Kittens up to 24 weeks old should be fed 3 times a day.
  Kittens over 24 weeks old should be fed 2 times a day.
  Each feed uses one pouch of cat food, which costs £2.25 for 12 pouches.
  How much will it cost to feed the kitten for the next 20 weeks?

7 Two gardeners are planting their gardens.
  Archie plants $5y$ flowers in 2 minutes.
  Grant plants $178y$ flowers in an hour.

  a If they both needed to plant the same number of flowers, who would finish first?
    Explain your answer.

  b On one morning, Archie and Grant plant 224 flowers each.
    Grant spends a total of 30 minutes planting flowers.
    How much longer does Archie spend planting flowers than Grant?

Exam practice

1 A car has an initial speed of p m/s.
  The car accelerates to a speed of $3p$ m/s in 10 seconds.
  The car then travels at a constant speed of $3p$ m/s for 20 seconds.
  Assuming that the total acceleration in the first 10 seconds is constant, show that the total
  distance travelled by the car is $80p$. **(3 marks)**

11.3 More compound measures

△ Purposeful practice 1

1 Calculate the pressure in N/cm^2 when
    a force = 6 N, area = 2 cm^2 **b** force = 12 N, area = 2 cm^2 **c** force = 12 N, area = 4 cm^2

2 Calculate the density in g/cm^3 when
    a mass = 6 g, volume = 2 cm^3 **b** mass = 3 g, volume = 2 cm^3 **c** mass = 3 g, volume = 1 cm^3

Reflect and reason

What happened to the answer when the numerator doubled?

What about when the denominator doubled?

△ Purposeful practice 2

1 Calculate the mass in g when
    a density = 6 g/cm^3, volume = 2 cm^3 **b** density = 3 g/cm^3, volume = 2 cm^3
    c density = 3 g/cm^3, volume = 1 cm^3

2 Calculate the force in newtons when
    a pressure = 6 N/cm^2, area = 2 cm^2 **b** pressure = 12 N/cm^2, area = 2 cm^2
    c pressure = 12 N/cm^2, area = 4 cm^2

3 Calculate the volume in cm^3 when
    a mass = 6 g, density = 2 g/cm^3 **b** mass = 3 g, density = 2 g/cm^3
    c mass = 3 g, density = 1 g/cm^3

4 Calculate the area in cm^2 when
    a force = 6 N, pressure = 2 N/cm^2 **b** force = 12 N, pressure = 2 N/cm^2
    c force = 12 N, pressure = 4 N/cm^2

Reflect and reason

For **Q1**, Marie rearranged the formula to make mass the subject, $M = D \times V$. She used this in all the **Q1** calculations.

Dan substituted the numbers into $D = \frac{M}{V}$ for each **Q1** calculation and solved the equation.

Which method do you prefer, and why?

Problem-solving practice

1 Feathers have a density of $0.0025\,g/cm^3$.
   Steel has a density of $8050\,kg/m^3$.
   What volume of feathers is equal in mass to $5\,cm^3$ of steel?
   Give your answer in cm^3.

2 A litre of a mixed drink has a density of $1.06\,g/ml$.
   It is made from $300\,ml$ of orange juice, $200\,ml$ of cranberry juice and $500\,ml$ of lemonade.
   The density of orange juice is $1.25\,g/ml$.
   The density of cranberry juice is $1.07\,g/ml$.
   A new mixed drink is made from $500\,ml$ of cranberry juice and $500\,ml$ of lemonade.
   Work out the density of the new drink.

3 Weight is a measure of downwards force exerted by a body and is calculated by multiplying mass by 9.8.
   A person with a mass of $67\,kg$ is wearing heeled shoes.
   The area of each heel is $0.25\,cm^2$.
   A person with a mass of $75\,kg$ is also wearing heeled shoes.
   The area of each heel is $0.7\,cm^2$.
   The area of the rest of the sole of each shoe is $40\,cm^2$.
   Who exerts the greater pressure through their shoes?
   Show working to explain.

4 Gold has a density of $19.3\,g/cm^3$.
   A gold-coloured cube measures $6\,cm$ on each side and weighs $70\,g$.
   Is it gold?

5 A swimming pool is built on the first floor of a leisure centre.
   The swimming pool measures $25\,m$ by $10\,m$ and is $1.2\,m$ deep.
   Water has a density of $1060\,kg/m^3$.
   The force exerted by the water on the base of the swimming pool = mass of water $\times$ 9.8
   The ceiling beneath the swimming pool can withstand a maximum pressure of $300\,N/cm^2$.
   Can the ceiling withstand the pressure of the swimming pool?

6 Objects will float if their density is less than the density of water.
   The density of water is $997\,kg/m^3$.
   Will a cube of wood with side lengths $5\,cm$ and a mass of $81.25\,g$ float?
   Explain your answer.

Exam practice

1 A cake mix contains 4 ingredients, butter, flour, sugar and yogurt.
   The density of butter is 0.87 grams per cm^3.
   The density of flour is 0.59 grams per cm^3.
   The density of sugar is 0.85 grams per cm^3.
   The density of yogurt 1.03 grams per cm^3.
   70 grams of butter are combined with 175 grams of flour, 60 grams of sugar and 45 grams of yogurt to make 350 grams of cake mix.
   Work out the density of the cake mix. Give your answer to 2 d.p.   **(3 marks)**

Adapted from 1MA1/3H, June 2017, Q6

Exam feedback

ResultsPlus

Most students who achieved a **Grade 7** or above answered a similar question well.

Key points

- When x and y are in direct proportion
  $y = kx$ where k is the gradient of the graph of y against x
  $\frac{y}{x} = k$, a constant.

- When x and y are in inverse proportion, y is proportional to $\frac{1}{x}$

  $x \times y = k$, a constant, $\qquad y = \frac{k}{x}$, where k is a constant.

 △ **Purposeful practice 1**

1 3 nurses can treat 8 patients in 6 hours.

  a How many patients can 6 nurses treat in 6 hours?

  b How many nurses are needed to treat 24 patients in 6 hours?

  c How many patients can 4 nurses treat in 6 hours?
    Give your answer to a sensible degree of accuracy.

  d How many nurses are needed to treat 23 patients in 6 hours?

  e How long will it take 6 nurses to treat 8 patients?

  f How many nurses are needed to treat 8 patients in 1.5 hours?

Reflect and reason

When the time stays the same, what happens to the number of patients treated when you double the number of nurses?
When the number of patients stays the same, what happens to the number of nurses needed when you halve the time?

 △ **Purposeful practice 2**

1 x and y are in direct proportion. When $x = 5$, $y = 20$.

  a Write an equation linking x and y. b What is the value of y when $x = 3$?

  c What is the value of x when $y = 3$?

2 x and y are inversely proportional. When $x = 5$, $y = 20$.

  a Write an equation linking x and y. b What is the value of y when $x = 3$?

  c What is the value of x when $y = 3$?

3 x and y are in direct proportion. When $x = 10$, $y = 42$.

  a Write an equation linking x and y. b What is the value of y when $x = 3$?

  c What is the value of x when $y = 3$?

4 x and y are inversely proportional. When $x = 10$, $y = 42$.

  a Write an equation linking x and y. b What is the value of y when $x = 3$?

  c What is the value of x when $y = 3$?

Reflect and reason

For direct proportion (**Q1**, **Q3**), how does doubling the given values affect the equation linking x and y?

For inverse proportion (**Q2**, **Q4**), how does doubling the given values affect the equation linking x and y?

⊠ Problem-solving practice

1   Dora can groom 18 cats in 7 hours.
    Dora's 7 cats have an average of 3 kittens each.
    How long will it take Dora to groom all of her cats and kittens?

2   The number of a vegetable that can grow in a field is inversely proportional to the number of worms in the soil.
    The number of worms in the soil is directly proportional to the depth of the soil in the field.
    A field that has a soil depth of 3 m has 165 worms and can grow 24 vegetables.

    a   Find the number of worms when there are 36 vegetables growing.

    b   Find the depth of soil when there are 36 vegetables growing.

3   At a nursery, 2 carers are needed for every 8 children. The number of carers to children is in direct proportion.
    The carers are paid £15.60 an hour.
    The nursery cares for the children from 9.00 am to 6.00 pm, 5 days a week.
    There are 24 children in the nursery.
    How much does it cost to pay the carers for one week?

4   It takes 3 gamers 2.5 hours to clear one boss on a video game.
    How long would it take 4 gamers to clear 3 bosses (assuming they are the same difficulty and time taken is proportional to the number of players)?

5   It takes 19 workers 6 hours to build an 18 m long wall.
    Each worker is paid £9.70 per hour of work.
    Is it cheaper to hire 10 workers or 12 workers to build a 9 m long wall (assuming that all workers build at the same rate)?

6   Mrs Roberts teaches 5 different classes over the course of a week, and the mean average of students in each class is 29.2. She can mark 30 books in 2.5 hours.

    a   How long does Mrs Roberts spend marking books each week, assuming she always marks every book once during the week?

    b   One week, Mrs Roberts shares her marking with Mr Lewis, who takes half of the books.
        Mr Lewis can mark 8 books in 45 minutes.
        How long will it take Mr Lewis to mark his share of the books?

7   A group of 6 friends are working on a project.
    They have to write a total of 8000 words.
    On a different project, it took 2 of the group 3 hours to complete 2000 words in total.
    Assuming all of the friends work at the same rate as the previous project, how long will it take them to complete this project?

✦ Exam practice

1   On Monday it took 4 painters $3\frac{1}{2}$ hours to paint a classroom in a school.
    There are 5 painters to paint another room the same size on Tuesday.
    Each painter is paid £12.40 for each hour or part of an hour they work.
    How much will each painter be paid on Tuesday?   **(3 marks)**

    Adapted from 1MA1/2H, November 2017, Q9

Exam feedback   Results**Plus**

In a similar question, students made mistakes by using direct proportion rather than inverse proportion.

12 Similarity and congruence

12.1 Congruence

Key points

- Congruent triangles have exactly the same size and shape. Their angles are the same and corresponding sides are the same length.
- Two triangles are congruent when one of these conditions of congruence is true.
    - SSS (all three sides equal)
    - SAS (two sides and the included angle are equal)
    - AAS (two angles and a corresponding side are equal)
    - RHS (right angle, hypotenuse and one other side are equal)

△ Purposeful practice 1

Each pair of triangles is congruent. Explain why.

1

2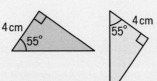

3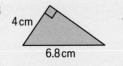

4

5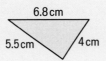

6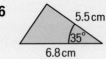

Reflect and reason

How did you know which condition of congruence to choose for each pair of triangles?

△ Purposeful practice 2

1 Which of these triangles are congruent to triangle A? Give reasons for your answers.

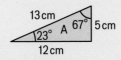 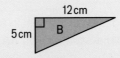 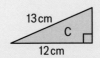

Reflect and reason

Ross says, 'Triangle A and triangle E have exactly the same angle sizes. Therefore they are congruent.'

Explain why Ross may not be correct.

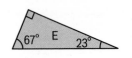

1 Write true or false for each statement.
Give reasons for your answers.

   a Two triangles, both with sides 6 cm, 7 cm and 8 cm, are always congruent.

   b Two right-angled triangles, both with one side 6 cm and another 8 cm, are always congruent.

   c Two triangles, both with sides 7 cm and 10 cm and an angle of 55°, are always congruent.

   d Two triangles, both with angles of 25°, 45° and 110°, are always congruent.

2 Tiff is asked if triangle X is congruent to triangle Y.

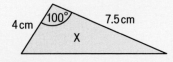 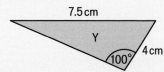

Tiff says, 'Yes, they are congruent because both triangles have an angle of 100°, a side of 4 cm and a side of 7.5 cm.'
Is Tiff correct?
Explain your answer.

3 Are triangles ABC and DEF congruent?
Give reasons for your answer.

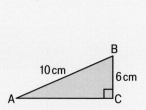 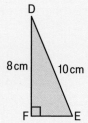

4 PQ and RS are parallel lines.
Show that triangle PQM and triangle RSM are congruent.

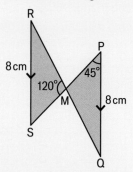

1 ABCD is a parallelogram
AB = DC
Prove that triangles ABE and DEC are congruent.

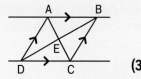

(3 marks)

Adapted from 1MA1/3H, June 2018, Q21

Exam feedback   Results**Plus**

In a similar question, few students used the congruency of the triangles to start their explanation.

12.2 Geometric proof and congruence

Key points

- Conditions of congruence (SSS, SAS, AAS, RHS) can be used for geometric proof.
- Write each statement of a proof on a new line. Give a reason for every statement you make.

△ Purposeful practice

1 AB and CD are parallel lines.

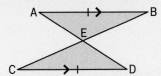

   a Copy and complete the sentences.
   Angle AEB = angle _____ because _____ angles are equal.
   Angle BAE = angle _____ because _____ angles are equal.
   AB = _____

   b The three statements in **Q1a** prove that triangle ABE is congruent to triangle CDE.
   Which condition has been used to prove congruence?

2 ABCD is a rhombus.

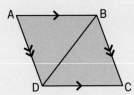

   a Identify two equal corresponding sides in triangle ABD and triangle BCD.

   b Identify another pair of equal corresponding sides in triangle ABD and triangle BCD.

   c Is the included angle between the two sides you chose in triangle ABD equal to the included
   angle between the two corresponding sides in triangle BCD?
   Give a reason for your answer.

   d Your answers to **Q2a–c** prove that triangle ABD is congruent to triangle BCD.
   Which condition has been used to prove congruence?

3 ABCD is a rectangle.

   a Identify three pairs of equal corresponding sides in
   triangle ABE and triangle CDE.
   Give reasons why they are equal.

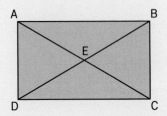

   b The three pairs of equal corresponding lines in **Q3a** prove that
   triangle ABE is congruent to triangle CDE.
   Which condition has been used to prove congruence?

Reflect and reason

For **Q1–3**

Prove congruence again, but using a different condition.

Prove congruence a third time, using a third condition.

Which condition of congruence is it not possible to use? Explain.

1   ABC is an equilateral triangle.
    BD is perpendicular to AC.
    Prove that triangle ABD is congruent to triangle BCD.

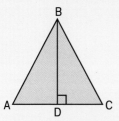

2   PQRS is a parallelogram.
    The diagonals PR and QS meet at the point M.
    Prove that triangle PSM is congruent to triangle QRM.

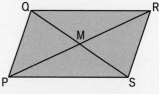

3   ABC is an isosceles triangle.
    AB = BC.
    M is the midpoint of AB.
    N is the midpoint of BC.
    Prove triangle AMC is congruent to triangle CNA.

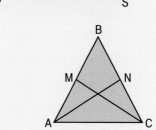

4   ADG is an isosceles triangle.
    AD = DG.
    ABCD and DEFG are squares.
    Prove that triangle ADE is congruent to triangle GDC.

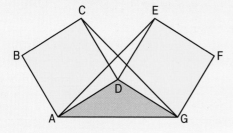

Exam practice

1   ABCD is a kite.
    X and Y are points on AC such that AX = YC.
    Prove that triangle ADX is congruent to triangle CDY.   **(3 marks)**

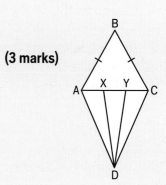

Adapted from 1MA1/3H, Specimen Papers, Set 2, Q12

Key point

- Shapes are similar when one shape is an enlargement of the other. Corresponding angles are equal and corresponding sides are all in the same ratio.

⚠ Purposeful practice 1

1 Here are two rectangles A and B.

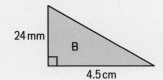

a Work out

 i $\dfrac{\text{length of B}}{\text{length of A}}$ ii $\dfrac{\text{width of B}}{\text{width of A}}$

b Are the rectangles similar? Explain how you know.

2 a Work out

 i $\dfrac{\text{base of B}}{\text{base of A}}$ ii $\dfrac{\text{height of B}}{\text{height of A}}$

b Are the triangles similar? Explain how you know.

3 Are the shapes in each pair similar? Explain how you know.

a

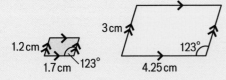

b

Reflect and reason

In **Q1**, are the angles in rectangle B bigger than the angles in rectangle A?

In **Q2**, are the angles in triangle B bigger than the angles in triangle A?

Explain how you know.

⚠ Purposeful practice 2

1 Rectangles A, B, C and D are similar. Work out each value of x.

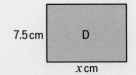

2 Triangles A, B, C and D are similar. Work out each value of x.

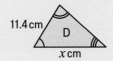

Reflect and reason

Which of the four operations $+, -, \times$ and $\div$ did you use to work out the value of each x?

Why don't the other operations work for finding lengths of similar shapes?

⊠ Problem-solving practice

1   The smallest angle of a triangle is 30°.
The triangle is enlarged by scale factor 2.
Ben says, 'The smallest angle of the enlarged triangle is 60° because 30 × 2 = 60.'
Is Ben right? Explain your answer.

2   A photograph has a length of 6 cm and a width of 4 cm.
Rhiannon enlarges the photograph to make a larger photograph.
The larger photograph has a width of 15 cm.

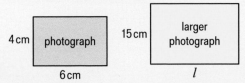

The two photographs are similar rectangles.
Work out the length l of the larger photograph.

3   Josh has a postcard and a rectangular piece of card.

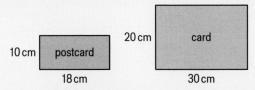

Josh cuts the card along the dotted line shown in the diagram.

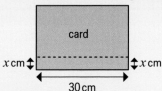

Josh throws away the piece of card that is 30 cm by x cm.
The piece of card he has left is mathematically similar to the postcard.
Work out the value of x.

✩ Exam practice

1   Show that these two triangles are mathematically similar.   **(2 marks)**

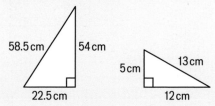

Adapted from 1MA1/3F, June 2017, Q21

Exam feedback   ResultsPlus

In a similar question, some students found the correct scale factor but did not apply it to all 3 sides, so they lost a mark.

12.4 More similarity

Key points

- Angles in parallel lines can be used to show that shapes are similar.

- Similar shapes that are inside each other sometimes share angles and/or sides.

- Sometimes you are not told that two shapes are similar, but you want to use similarity to find a missing side. Then, first of all you must prove that the shapes are similar by showing that all corresponding angles are equal.

△ Purposeful practice 1

1 a Work out the sizes of angle ECD, angle CDE and angle CED.
Give reasons for your answers.

b Are triangles ABE and CDE similar?
Explain how you know.

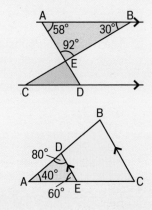

2 a Work out the sizes of angle ABC and angle ACB.
Give reasons for your answers.

b Are triangles ADE and ABC similar?
Explain how you know.

Reflect and reason

If angles A and D are equal and angles B and E are equal, then explain why triangles ABC and DEF must be similar.

△ Purposeful practice 2

1 a Show that triangles ABE and DCE are similar.

b Work out the value of x.

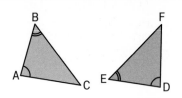

2 a Show that triangles ABC and ADE are similar.

b Work out the length of BD.

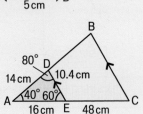

Reflect and reason

Draw and label the two triangles in **Q1** separately. Does this help show they are similar? Explain.

Draw and label the two triangles in **Q2** separately. Does this help show they are similar? Explain.

⊠ Problem-solving practice

1 ABCD and WXYZ are two rectangles.
Rectangle ABCD is 30 cm by 20 cm.
There is a space 5 cm wide between the perimeter of
rectangle ABCD and the perimeter of rectangle WXYZ.
Are rectangle ABCD and rectangle WXYZ mathematically
similar?
You must show how you got your answer.

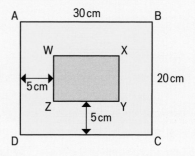

2 PQRS and STUV are mathematically similar parallelograms.

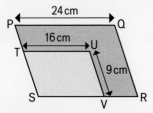

UV = 9 cm
TU = 16 cm
PQ = 24 cm
Work out the length of PT.

3 ABC and CDE are straight lines.
BD is parallel to AE.
AC = 13.5 cm
BC = 5.4 cm
BD = 7.6 cm

a Work out the length of AE.

CE = 17.5 cm

b Work out the length of CD.

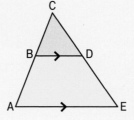

⊠ Exam practice

1 The two triangles in the diagram are similar.

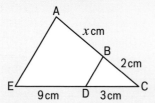

There are two possible values of x.
Work out each of these values.
State any assumptions you make in your working. **(5 marks)**

Adapted from 1MA1/1H, November 2017, Q22

Exam feedback

ResultsPlus

In a similar question, students showed a good understanding of similar shapes but were unable to find
two values of x and find the second assumption.

12.5 Similarity in 3D solids

Key point

*   When the linear scale factor is k:

    Lengths are multiplied by k Area is multiplied by k^2 Volume is multiplied by k^3

△ Purposeful practice 1

Copy and complete the table. The first question has been completed for you.

Question	Linear scale factor	Surface area of A	Surface area of B	Area scale factor	Volume of A	Volume of B	Volume scale factor
1	2	$6\,cm^2$	$24\,cm^2$	4	$1\,cm^3$	$8\,cm^3$	8
2							
3							
4							

1

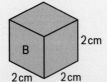

2

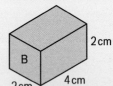

3

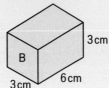

4

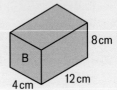

Reflect and reason

Write the area and volume factors as a power of the linear scale factors.

What do you notice about the area scale factors? What do you notice about the volume scale factors?

△ Purposeful practice 2

1 A and B are similar cuboids, where B is larger than A. Copy and complete the table.

Linear scale factor	Area scale factor	Surface area of A	Surface area of B	Volume scale factor	Volume of A	Volume of B
2		$52\,cm^2$			$24\,cm^3$	
3		$52\,cm^2$			$24\,cm^3$	
5		$52\,cm^2$			$24\,cm^3$	
7		$52\,cm^2$			$24\,cm^3$	

Reflect and reason

Draw diagrams to explain why

   the area scale factor (two dimensions) is the linear scale factor (one dimension) squared

   the volume scale factor (three dimensions) is the linear scale factor (one dimension) cubed.

⊠ Problem-solving practice

1   A company makes teddy bears.
    The company makes small bears with a height of 8 cm.
    Making a small bear requires a 180 cm² area of cloth.
    The company also makes large bears with a height of 60 cm.
    A small bear and a large bear are mathematically similar.
    Work out the area of cloth required to make a large bear.

2   The diagram shows two boxes, A and B.
    The boxes are mathematically similar.
    The height of box A is 4 cm.
    The total surface area of box A is 100 cm².
    The total surface area of box B is 625 cm².
    Work out the height of box B.

3   The diagram shows two similar solids, A and B.
    Solid A has a volume of 40 cm³.

    a Work out the volume of solid B.

    Solid B has a total surface area of 290 cm².

    b Work out the total surface area of solid A.

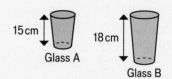

4   Here are two glasses.
    Glass A and glass B are mathematically similar.
    The area of the base of glass B is 80 cm².
    Work out the area of the base of glass A.
    Give your answer to 3 s.f.

5   Two solid cones are mathematically similar.
    Cone A has a volume of 140 cm³.
    Cone B has a volume of 3780 cm³.
    Work out the ratio of the total surface area of cone A to the total surface area of cone B.

6   Tins A and B are mathematically similar.
    Tin A has a total surface area of 180 cm².
    Tin B has a total surface area of 405 cm² and a volume of 540 cm³.
    Work out the volume of tin A.

⊗ Exam practice

1   A factory makes bowls in two sizes, small and large.
    The bowls are similar in shape.
    The height of the small bowl is 6 cm.
    The volume of the small bowl is 450 cm³.
    The volume of the large bowl is 1600 cm³.
    Work out the height of the large bowl.
    Give your answer correct to 3 significant figures.

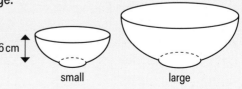

    (2 marks)

Adapted from 1MA1/2H, Autumn 2017, Mock Set 3, Q17

Mixed exercises C

Mixed problem-solving practice C

1 There are only red, blue, green and yellow counters in a bag.
Samir takes a counter from the bag at random.
The table shows each of the probabilities.

Colour	red	blue	green	yellow
Probability	0.3	0.25	$2x$	x

a Work out the value of x.

Samir takes a counter from the bag.
He writes down the colour of the counter.
He puts the counter back in the bag.
Samir does this 200 times.

b Work out an estimate for the number of times that Samir takes a red counter from the bag.

2 Write a function with roots $x = 3$ and $x = -5$.

3 A swimming pool is in the shape of a prism.
To begin with, the swimming pool is completely full of water.
Water is pumped out of the swimming pool.
The volume of water in the swimming pool decreases at a
constant rate.
The level of the water goes down by 20 cm in the first 30 minutes.
Work out the total time it will take for the pump to completely empty the swimming pool.

4 Sasha wants to invest £8000 in a savings account for 3 years.
She finds information about savings accounts at two different banks.

Bank A
Compound interest of
2.8% per annum

Bank B
Compound interest of
4% per annum in year 1
2.2% per annum for each extra year

Sasha wants to choose the bank that pays the greatest total amount of interest for the 3 years.
Which bank should she choose?
You must show all your working.

5 ABC is a triangle.
D is a point on AB and E is a point on AC.
DE is parallel to BC.
AD = 6 cm, DB = 10.5 cm, DE = 8 cm, AE = 5 cm.
Calculate the perimeter of the trapezium DBCE.

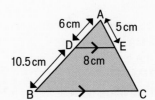

6 Lauren says, 'Triangles A and B are congruent because all of the
angles are the same in both triangles.'
Is Lauren correct?
Explain your answer.

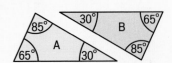

7 Sasha rolls a 4-sided dice and Tom spins the spinner.
The player with the highest number wins a point. If the numbers
are the same, neither player wins.

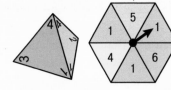

   a List the possible outcomes.

   b Is the game fair? Explain why.

   c Sasha and Tom win 120 points between them. How many points would you expect each player
to win?

8 Paper clips are sold in tubs and in boxes.
There is a total of 520 clips in 4 tubs and 5 boxes.
There is a total of 264 clips in 3 tubs and 2 boxes.
Work out the number of clips in each tub and in each box.

9 100 people were asked if they speak French or German or Spanish.
Of these people,
62 speak French
4 speak French, German and Spanish
8 speak French and Spanish but not German
14 speak German and Spanish
16 do not speak any of the languages at all
The 20 people who speak German all speak at least one other language

   a Draw a Venn diagram to represent this information.

   Two of the people who speak Spanish are chosen at random.

   b Work out the probability that they both only speak Spanish.

10 Daisy says, 'I think of an integer, double it and then subtract 7.
The answer is greater than 5 but smaller than 12.'

   a Write an inequality to represent this information.

   b Solve the inequality.

   c Write down all of the numbers Daisy could have chosen.

11 Tristan uses the quadratic formula to solve a quadratic equation.
He correctly substitutes the values into the formula to give

$$x = \frac{9 \pm \sqrt{33}}{6}$$

Work out the quadratic equation that Tristan is solving.
Give your answer in the form $ax^2 + bx + c = 0$, where a, b and c are integers.

12 Kit tries to solve the simultaneous equations

   $y = x^2 + 3x - 9$ $y = 4x + 3$

The first line of Kit's working is

$y = (4x + 3)^2 + 3(4x + 3) - 9$

Kit has made a mistake.

   a What mistake has Kit made?

   b Solve the simultaneous equations.

13 There are only red, blue and green marbles in a bag.
The ratio of the number of red marbles to the number of blue marbles is 7 : 3.
The probability that a counter is green is 0.4.
Suri takes a counter from the bag at random and then replaces it.
Suri then takes another counter from the bag at random.
Work out the probability that Suri takes two counters of the same colour.

14 ABCD and AEFG are mathematically similar kites.
AE = 5 cm
EF = 8 cm
BC = 20 cm

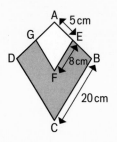

a Work out the length of AB.

Kite AEFG has an area of 32 cm².

b Work out the area of the shaded region.

15 q is directly proportional to p.
$q = 14$ when $p = 5$
Calculate the value of q when $p = 1.3$

 🌐 **Exam practice**

16 Jason invests £14 000 in an account paying compound interest for 2 years.
In the first year the rate of interest is x%.
At the end of the first year the value of Jason's investment is £14 364.

In the second year the rate of interest is $\frac{x}{2}$%

What is the value of Jason's investment at the end of 2 years? **(4 marks)**

Adapted from 1MA1/2H, June 2018, Q9

Exam feedback Results**Plus**

Most students who achieved a **Grade 6** or above answered a similar question well.

🌐 **Exam practice**

17 3 teas and 2 coffees have a total cost of £10.40.
5 teas and 4 coffees have a total cost of £19.20.
Work out the cost of one tea and the cost of one coffee. **(4 marks)**

Adapted from 1MA1/1H, November 2017, Q11

Exam feedback Results**Plus**

In a similar question, many students found forming and solving simultaneous equations difficult. Many students attempted to solve this problem through a trial and improvement method, normally with little or no success.

 🌐 **Exam practice**

18 Cone A and cone B are mathematically similar.
The ratio of the volume of cone A to the volume of cone B is 64 : 27.
The surface area of cone A is 592 cm².
Show that the surface area of cone B is 333 cm². **(3 marks)**

Adapted from 1MA1/3H, November 2017, Q14

Exam feedback Results**Plus**

In a similar question, many students assumed the result they were given instead of proving it.

19 There are 9 counters in a bag.
5 of the counters are green.
4 of the counters are blue.
Helen takes at random two counters from the bag.
Work out the probability that Helen takes one counter of each colour.
You must show your working. **(4 marks)**

Adapted from 1MA1/1H, June 2017, Q17

Exam feedback **ResultsPlus**

Most students who achieved a **Grade 6** or above answered a similar question well.

 ⬡ **Exam practice**

20 Jordan is trying to find the density, in g/cm³, of a block of wood.
The block of wood is in the shape of a cuboid.
He measures
   the length as 14.2 cm, correct to the nearest mm
   the width as 17.0 cm, correct to the nearest mm
   the height as 22.7 cm, correct to the nearest mm
He measures the mass as 1980 g, correct to the nearest 5 g.
By considering bounds, work out the density of the wood.
Give your answer to a suitable degree of accuracy.
You must show all your working and give a reason for your final answer. **(5 marks)**

Adapted from 1MA1/2H, June 2018, Q21

Exam feedback **ResultsPlus**

Most students who achieved a **Grade 9** answered a similar question well.

⬡ **Exam practice**

21 PQRS is a parallelogram.
TPQ and SRU are straight lines.
Angle TRQ = angle SPU

   a Prove that triangle TRQ is congruent to triangle SPU. **(3 marks)**
   b Explain why TS is parallel to QU. **(2 marks)**

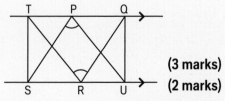

Adapted from 1MA1/1H, June 2018, Q21

Exam feedback **ResultsPlus**

Q21a: In a similar question, students more often than not lost a mark because their reasons for congruency were incomplete or poorly expressed.
Q21b: In a similar question, students often stated that TQUS was a parallelogram without any or without sufficient justification.

13 More trigonometry

13.1 Accuracy

Key points

- The upper bound of a fraction = $\dfrac{\text{upper bound of the numerator}}{\text{lower bound of the denominator}}$

- The lower bound of a fraction = $\dfrac{\text{lower bound of the numerator}}{\text{upper bound of the denominator}}$

 △ **Purposeful practice 1**

Here are three triangles.
Measurements are given to 1 d.p.

a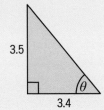

b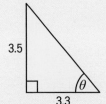

c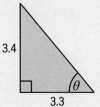

1 For each triangle, find the upper and lower bounds of the side lengths.

2 For each triangle, use the upper and lower bounds to find four possible sizes of angle θ.

Reflect and reason

Explain how it is possible for two of the triangles to have the same angle size despite different written measurements.

△ **Purposeful practice 2**

Here are three triangles.
Each side is rounded to the nearest integer.

a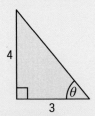

b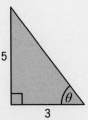

c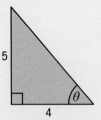

1 Use Pythagoras' theorem to find the upper and lower bounds for the hypotenuse.

2 Use the tangent ratio to find the upper and lower bounds for the size of the angle θ.

Reflect and reason

What do you think are the true upper and lower bounds for the angle in triangle **a**?
Explain your answer.

⊠ Problem-solving practice

1 The upper bound of an angle in a right-angled triangle is 32°.
   The side opposite this angle is 8.7 cm, correct to 1 d.p.
   What is a possible length for the hypotenuse?
   Write your answer correct to 1 d.p.

2 The angle a ramp makes with the floor must be less than 67° to be compliant with safety
   regulations.

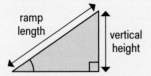

   An inspector measures the vertical height of the ramp as 2 m.
   She knows her measurement could be up to 5 cm wrong.
   She measures the length of the ramp as 3 m.
   This could be up to 7 cm wrong.
   Could the ramp be too steep?

3 The hypotenuse of a right-angled triangle is 0.80 m to the nearest cm.
   One of the other sides is 0.73 m to the nearest cm.
   What are the upper and lower bounds of the length of the remaining side?

4 Simon says, 'The difference between the upper and lower bounds of an angle in a right-angled
   triangle will be the same, no matter what accuracy is used to round the side lengths.'
   Simon tests this by measuring the hypotenuse of a triangle and the side adjacent to an angle.
   The hypotenuse measures 3.2 cm (correct to 1 d.p.) and 3 cm (correct to 1 s.f.).
   The adjacent side measures 0.9 cm (correct to 1 d.p.) and 0.9 cm (correct to 1 s.f.).
   Is Simon right? Give reasons.

5 All of the sides of this triangle have been measured correct to the nearest cm.
   What is the maximum possible area of this triangle?

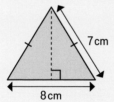

✹ Exam practice

1

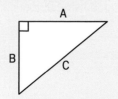

A is 4.2 cm correct to the nearest mm.
C is 7.6 cm correct to the nearest mm.
Calculate the upper bound for B.
You must show your working.

(4 marks)

Adapted from 1MA1/2H, Specimen Papers, Set 2, Q17

Key point

- The diagram shows the circle of radius 1 unit with centre at (0, 0).

  $\sin 30° = \dfrac{PQ}{1} = PQ = 0.5$

  The length of PQ gives the sine of the angle.

  This is shown on the vertical axis by the position of the arrow.

  You can find the sine of any angle using this method.

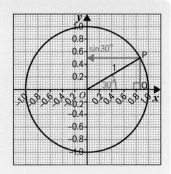

△ Purposeful practice 1

Find the value of $\sin\theta$ in each diagram.

1

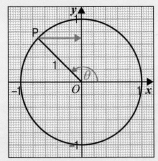

2

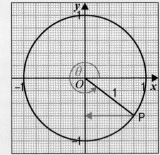

Reflect and reason

Use the inverse sine on your calculator to find the size of θ in **Q1** and **Q2**.

For each question, how does the angle you found on your calculator relate to the angle in the diagram?

△ Purposeful practice 2

Use a calculator to find the sine of

1 30° **2** 210° **3** 390° **4** 5° **5** 95° **6** 185° **7** 275° **8** 365°

Reflect and reason

Which questions in Purposeful practice 2 give the same numerical answer, ignoring positive or negative signs?

What do you notice about the differences between the angle sizes that give you the same numerical answer? How does this relate to the graph of $\sin\theta$?

△ Purposeful practice 3

1 Solve each equation for x in the interval 0° to 540°.

   a $2\sin x = 1.2$ **b** $2\sin x + 3 = 4.2$ **c** $3\sin x = 1.2$

2 How many solutions are there for each equation in **Q1** in the interval 540° to 720°?

Reflect and reason

Explain why it is not possible to solve $2\sin x = 4$.

⊠ Problem-solving practice

1   State two pairs of angles where the sine ratio has the same numerical value but opposite signs.

2   Give a possible length for the hypotenuse, and the corresponding possible opposite length, given that $3 \sin x = 1.8$.

Here is a sketch of the graph of $y = \sin x$ for $0° \leqslant x \leqslant 360°$.
Use it to help you answer **Q3–6**.

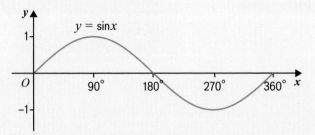

3   State three values of x such that $\sin x$ is between 0.9 and 1, where $180° < x < 540°$.

4   State one range of values of x such that $\sin x < 0$.

5   State two ranges of values of x such that $-0.5 < \sin x < 0.5$.

6   State one range of values of x such that $0 < 5 \sin x < 4$.

7   Here is a sketch of $y = \sin x$.
Write the coordinates for each point shown.

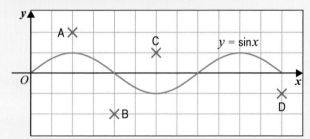

8   The line $y = 0.75$ is drawn on the same set of axes as a sine curve.
What is the greatest possible vertical distance between the sine curve and the line?

9   The graphs of $y = x$ and $y = \sin x$ are plotted on the same set of axes.
Write down the coordinates of all the points of intersection between the two graphs.

✦ Exam practice

1   Sketch the graph of $y = \sin x$ for $0° \leqslant x \leqslant 360°$.

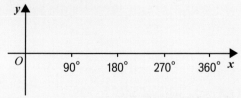

(2 marks)

Adapted from 1MA1/2H, Specimen Papers, Set 2, Q19a

Key point

- The diagram shows the circle of radius 1 unit with centre at $(0, 0)$.

$\cos 60° = \frac{OQ}{1} = OQ = 0.5$

The length of OQ gives the cosine of the angle.
This is shown on the horizontal axis by the position of the arrow.
You can find the cosine of any angle using this method.

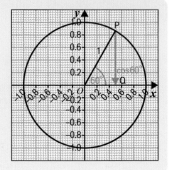

△ Purposeful practice 1

Find the value of $\cos \theta$ in each diagram.

1

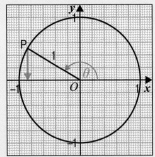

2

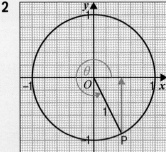

Reflect and reason

Use the inverse cosine on your calculator to find the size of θ in **Q1** and **Q2**.
For each question, how does the angle you found on your calculator relate to the angle in the diagram?

△ Purposeful practice 2

Use your calculator to find the cosine of

1 $30°$ **2** $210°$ **3** $390°$ **4** $5°$ **5** $95°$ **6** $185°$ **7** $275°$ **8** $365°$

Reflect and reason

Which questions in Purposeful practice 2 give the same numerical answer, ignoring positive and negative signs?
What do you notice about the differences between the angle sizes that give you the same numerical answer? How does this relate to the graph of $\cos \theta$?

△ Purposeful practice 3

1 Solve each equation for x in the interval $0°$ to $540°$.

    a $2 \cos x = 1.2$ **b** $2 \cos x - 3 = -1.2$ **c** $3 \cos x = -1.2$

2 How many solutions are there for each equation in **Q1** in the interval $540°$ to $720°$?

Reflect and reason

In the interval $0°$ to $\infty°$, how many solutions would there be for each equation in **Q1**? Explain your answer.

1   State two pairs of angles where the cosine ratio has the same numerical value but opposite signs.

2   Give a possible length for the hypotenuse, and the corresponding possible adjacent side, given that $3\cos x = 1.8$

Here is a sketch of the graph of $y = \cos x$ for $0° \leqslant x \leqslant 360°$.
Use it to help you answer **Q3–6**.

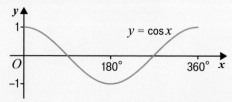

3   State three values of x such that $\cos x$ is between 0.8 and 0.9, where $180° < x < 540°$.

4   State one range of values of x such that $\cos x < 0$.

5   State one range of values of x such that $-0.5 < \cos x < 0.5$.

6   State one range of values of x such that $0 < 5\cos x < 4$.

7   Here is a sketch of $y = \cos x$.
Write down the coordinates for each point shown.

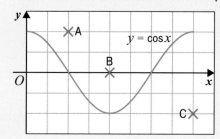

8   The graphs of $y = x$ and $y = \cos x$ are plotted on the same set of axes.
How many points of intersection there are between the two graphs?

9   The line $y = 0.75$ is drawn on the same set of axes as the line $y = \cos x$.
How many intersections are there in the interval $-360° \leqslant x \leqslant 360°$?

10 Give the equation of a line that would have no intersections with the curve $y = \cos x$.

11 Explain why there are no possible solutions to $\cos x = 3$.

1   Sketch the graph of $y = \cos x$ for $-360° \leqslant x \leqslant 360°$.

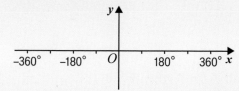

(2 marks)

Adapted from 1MA1/2H, Specimen Papers, Set 2, Q19a

Key point

- The diagram shows a circle of radius 1 unit with centre at $(0, 0)$.

$\tan \theta = \dfrac{0.8}{1} = 0.8$

Extending OP to hit the vertical tangent line gives the value of $\tan \theta$.

You can find the tangent of any angle using this method, except for angles of the form $90° \pm 180n°$.

Unlike sine and cosine, the tangent can take on **any** value, positive or negative, not just values between -1 and 1.

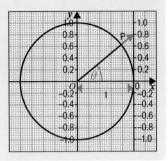

△ Purposeful practice 1

Find the value of $\tan \theta$ in each diagram.

1

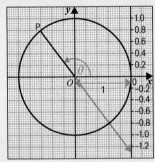

2

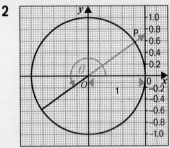

Reflect and reason

Using the unit circle, explain why it is not possible to find the value of $\tan 90°$.
What about $90° \pm 180°$? Or $90° \pm$ a multiple of $180°$?

△ Purposeful practice 2

Use your calculator to find the tangent of

1 $30°$ **2** $210°$ **3** $390°$ **4** $5°$ **5** $95°$ **6** $185°$ **7** $275°$ **8** $365°$

Reflect and reason

Which of the questions in Purposeful practice 2 give the same numerical answer, ignoring positive or negative signs? What do you notice about the differences between the angle sizes that give you the same numerical answer? How does this relate to the graph of $\tan \theta$?

△ Purposeful practice 3

1 Solve each equation for x in the interval $0°$ to $540°$.

  a $2 \tan x = 1.2$ **b** $2 \tan (x) - 3 = 12$ **c** $3 \tan x = -120$

2 How many solutions are there for each equation in **Q1** in the interval $540°$ to $720°$?

Reflect and reason

What is the same and what is different about solving these two equations?
  $2y - 3 = 12$ $2 \tan (x) - 3 = 12$

1 State a pair of values that have the same numerical value of $\tan x$ but opposite signs.

2 Give possible lengths for the adjacent and opposite sides of the right-angled triangle where $13 \tan x = 18$

Here is a sketch of the graph of $y = \tan x$ for $0° \leqslant x \leqslant 360°$.
Use it to help you answer **Q3–6**.

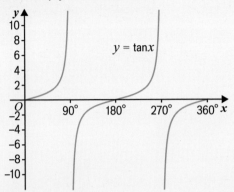

3 State three values of x such that $\tan x$ is between 8 and 9, where $180° < x < 540°$.

4 State one range of values of x such that $\tan x < 0$.

5 State one range of values of x such that $-0.5 < \tan x < 0.5$.

6 State one range of values of x such that $0 < 5 \tan x < 4$.

7 For the tangent function
   a State four values for which x is undefined.
   b Find the sine of those values.
   c Find the cosine of those values.

8 State how many times each line would intersect the curve $y = \tan x$ in the interval $-360° < x < 360°$ and $-10 < y < 10$
   a $y = 1$
   b $y = 2$

9 State the equation of a line that would not intersect with the curve $y = \tan x$.

Exam practice

1 Sketch the graph of $y = \tan x$ for $-180° \leqslant x \leqslant 180°$.

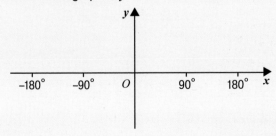

(2 marks)

Adapted from 1MA1/2H, Specimen Papers, Set 2, Q19a

13.5 Calculating areas and the sine rule

Key points

- The area of this triangle $= \frac{1}{2}ab\sin C$

  a is the side opposite angle A.

  b is the side opposite angle B.

- The sine rule can be used in any triangle.

  Use this to calculate an unknown side: $\dfrac{a}{\sin A} = \dfrac{b}{\sin B} = \dfrac{c}{\sin C}$

  Use this to calculate an unknown angle: $\dfrac{\sin A}{a} = \dfrac{\sin B}{b} = \dfrac{\sin C}{c}$

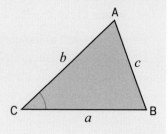

Purposeful practice 1

Find the area of each triangle.

1
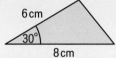

2
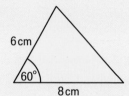

3
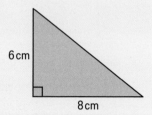

Reflect and reason

How did your calculation for **Q3** compare to using the formula Area $= \frac{1}{2} \times$ base $\times$ height?

Purposeful practice 2

1 Use the sine rule to find the length of the side labelled x in each triangle.

a
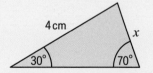

b
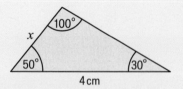

c
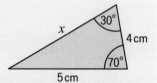

2 Find the size of angle θ in each diagram.

a

b
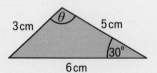

c
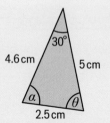

Reflect and reason

Did you need to use all the given lengths and angles in **Q1** and **Q2**?

Explain how you identified any lengths/angles you did not need to use in your calculation.

1 Calculate the perimeter of the triangle.

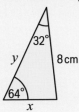

2 A is the centre of the circle.
The angle BAC is 120°.
The radius of the circle is 6.2 cm.
Calculate the area of triangle ABC.

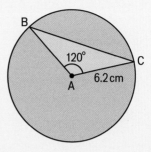

3 Calculate the perimeter of this scalene triangle.

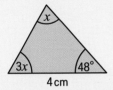

4 An isosceles triangle has an interior angle of 43°.
One of the side lengths is 25 cm.

   a What are the three possible lengths of the base of the triangle?

   b What area does the triangle have if it has the smallest possible base?

5 The area of this triangle is 2 cm². What is its perimeter?

 ✦ **Exam practice**

1

$(x+2)$ cm, $60°$, $(x-5)$ cm

The area of the triangle is $2\sqrt{3}$ cm².
Calculate the value of x.

(5 marks)

Adapted from 1MA1/3H, June 2017, Q15

Exam feedback

Results**Plus**

Most students who achieved a **Grade 8** or above answered a similar question well.

13.6 The cosine rule and 2D trigonometric problems

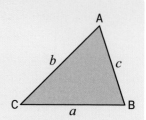

△ Purposeful practice 1

Find the length of the side labelled x in each diagram.

1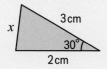

2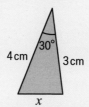

3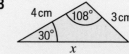

> **Reflect and reason**
>
> How do you decide which angle to label A? Does it matter which side you label b and which you label c?

△ Purposeful practice 2

Calculate the size of the angles labelled with letters in each diagram.

1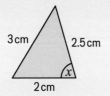

2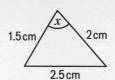

3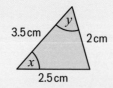

> **Reflect and reason**
>
> How could you prove that the triangle in **Q2** is a right-angled triangle?
> How does this relate to the cosine rule?

△ Purposeful practice 3

Find the length of the side labelled x in each diagram.

1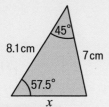

2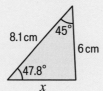

3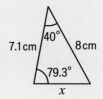

> **Reflect and reason**
>
> How did you decide which sides and angles you needed to use with the cosine rule?

1   The area of this triangle is 86.7 cm² to 1 d.p.
    Is the numerical value of the perimeter greater than the numerical
    value of the area? Give reasons.

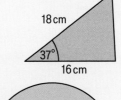

2   What percentage of the circle is shown by the shaded area?
    Show your working.

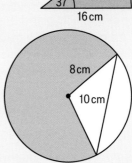

3   The length of the diagonal of this parallelogram is 27 cm.
    Calculate the perimeter.

4   Townley to Barnehurst is 18 miles on a bearing of 037°.
    Barnehurst to Syden is 16 miles on a bearing of 143°.
    All North lines are parallel.
    What is the distance between Townley and Syden?

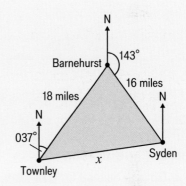

1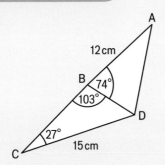

    Work out the length of AD.
    Give your answer correct to 3 significant figures.   **(5 marks)**

    Adapted from 1MA1/3H, June 2018, Q17

Exam feedback   Results**Plus**

Most students who achieved a **Grade 7** or above answered a similar question well.

Key point

- A plane is a flat surface. For example, the surface of your desk lies in a horizontal plane; the surface of a wall in your classroom lies in a vertical plane.
  In the diagram, BC is perpendicular to the plane WXYZ.
  Triangle ABC is in a plane perpendicular to the plane WXYZ.
  θ is the angle between the line AB and the plane WXYZ.

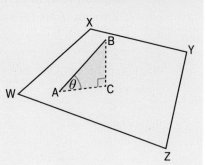

△ Purposeful practice 1

Here are two cuboids.

a
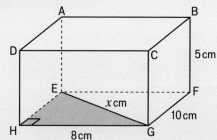

b
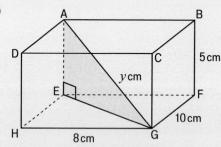

1   For each cuboid, draw the right-angled triangle containing the unknown length.

2   Work out the lengths marked x and y.

Reflect and reason

How did your method for **Q2a** relate to your method for **Q2b**?

△ Purposeful practice 2

Work out the size of the angles labelled θ and α.

1
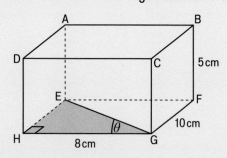

2
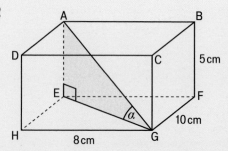

Reflect and reason

What was the same and what was different about your method for **Q2** compared to your method for **Q1**?

⊠ **Problem-solving practice**

1 ABCDEFGH is a cuboid.
The length AG is 18 cm.
The length AE is 5 cm.
The angle EGH is 60°.
What is the volume of this cuboid?

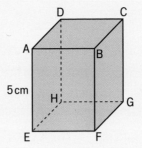

5 cm

2 The volume of this cube is 125 cm³.
What is the length of the diagonal AF?

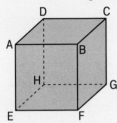

3 A cylindrical pencil pot with a diameter of 4.5 cm has a height of 10 cm.
Will a 15 cm long pencil fit diagonally into the pot without showing over the top?

4 ABCDE is a square-based pyramid.
Point A is vertically above point M,
which is the centre of the square base.
The length AD is 32 cm.
The length CD is 22 cm.
Calculate the angle ADM.

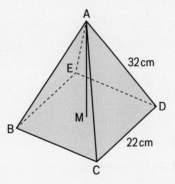

32 cm

22 cm

5 Marisa's tent is shaped like a cone.
The top of the tent is 1.9 m above the floor.
The diagonal height of the tent is 2.1 m.
Marisa's sleeping bag is 195 cm long.
Will Marisa be able to fit her sleeping bag on the floor? Explain your answer.

✦ **Exam practice**

1 ABCDEFGH is a cuboid.
AB = 6.2 cm
CH = 7.5 cm
Angle BCA = 34°
Find the size of the angle between AH and the plane ABCD.
Give your answer correct to 1 decimal place. **(4 marks)**

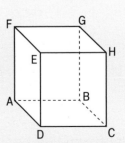

Adapted from 1MA1/2H, June 2018, Q18

Exam feedback

ResultsPlus

Most students who achieved a **Grade 9** answered a similar question well.

Key points

- The graph of $y = -f(x)$ is the reflection of the graph of $y = f(x)$ in the x-axis.
- The graph of $y = f(-x)$ is the reflection of the graph of $y = f(x)$ in the y-axis.
- The graph of $y = -f(-x)$ is a reflection of the graph of $y = f(x)$ in the x-axis and then the y-axis, or vice versa. These two reflections are equivalent to a rotation of $180°$ about the origin.

△ Purposeful practice 1

1 Copy and complete the table.

x	$\sin x$	$-\sin x$	$\sin(-x)$
0°			
45°			
90°			
135°			
180°			
270°			
360°			

2 On the same set of axes, sketch the graphs of
   a $y = \sin x$
   b $y = -\sin x$
   c $y = \sin(-x)$

Reflect and reason

Which two of your graphs are the same?
How are they related to the graph of $\sin x$?
Explain why they are the same.

△ Purposeful practice 2

1 On the same set of axes, sketch the graphs of
   a $y = \cos x$
   b $y = -\cos x$
   c $y = \cos(-x)$

2 On the same set of axes, sketch the graphs of
   a $y = \tan x$
   b $y = -\tan x$
   c $y = \tan(-x)$

Reflect and reason

Were the important angles to check for cos and tan the same angles as they were for sin? Explain.
Which two of the cosine graphs are the same? How are they related to the graph of $\cos x$? Explain why they are the same.

⊠ **Problem-solving practice**

1 For which values of x are $y = \sin x$ and $y = -\sin x$ the same, given $0° < x < 540°$?

2 Draw the graphs of $y = \cos x$ and $y = \tan x$ on the same axes.
Multiply the values of $\cos x$ and $\tan x$ at 5 different points and show, by drawing another trigonometric graph, that all these points lie on that graph.
What is the equation of the third graph?

3 $y = \tan x$ is reflected in the y-axis.
What is the equation of the new function?

4 What combination of transformations of $y = \sin x$ will reproduce the $y = \sin x$ graph?

5 What is the equation of this line?

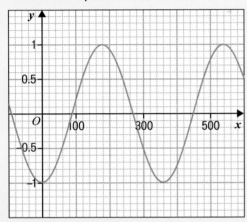

6 The graph shows $f(x) = \cos x$.
The graph is transformed to $f(-x)$.
Give the new coordinates of the point marked on the diagram.

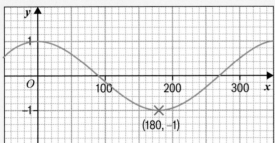

⊠ **Exam practice**

1 Here is the graph of $y = \sin x$ for $0° \leqslant x \leqslant 360°$

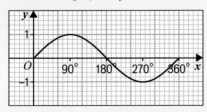

Copy the grid and draw the graph of $y = -\sin x$ for $0° \leqslant x \leqslant 360°$ **(1 mark)**

Adapted from 1MA1/2H, Specimen Papers, Set 2, Q19b

Key points

- The graph of $y = f(x) + a$ is the translation of the graph of $y = f(x)$ by $\begin{pmatrix} 0 \\ a \end{pmatrix}$.

- The graph of $y = f(x + a)$ is the translation of the graph of $y = f(x)$ by $\begin{pmatrix} -a \\ 0 \end{pmatrix}$.

△ Purposeful practice 1

1 Copy and complete the table.

x	$y = \sin x$	$y = \sin(x + 90°)$	$y = \sin(x) + 90°$
0°			
90°			
180°			
270°			
360°			

2 Draw the graphs of $y = \sin x$ and $y = \sin(x + 90°)$, between 0° and 360°.
For each graph, state
  a the maximum and minimum values on the y-axis
  b the intercepts with the x-axis.

Reflect and reason

Use the order of operations to explain why $f(x + a)$ produces a shift of negative a but $f(x) + a$ produces a positive shift.

△ Purposeful practice 2

1 Sketch, between $x = 0°$ and $x = 360°$, the graphs of
  a $y = \cos x$
  b $y = \cos(x + 90°)$
  c $y = \cos(x) + 1$
  For each graph, state
  i The maximum and minimum values on the y-axis.
  ii The intercepts with the x-axis.

2 Sketch, between $x = 0°$ and $x = 360°$, the graphs of
  a $y = \tan x$
  b $y = \tan(x + 90°)$
  c $y = \tan(x) + 1$
  For each graph, state the intercepts with the x-axis.

Reflect and reason

What was the same and what was different about the effect of the transformations on the tangent graph compared to their effects on the sine and cosine graphs?

1   Describe fully the single transformation that maps $y = \sin x$ onto $y = \cos x$.

2   Sketch the curve $y = -\cos(x) + 6$ and label any intersections with the axes.

3   The diagram shows $f(x) = \sin x$.

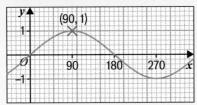

Give the new coordinates for the point marked under the transformation which maps $f(x)$ onto:

a $f(x + 3)$

b $f(x - 3)$

c $f(x) + 3$

d $f(x) - 3$

4   Estimate from graphs a point of intersection of $y = \tan x$ and $y = \sin(x) + 2$.

5   The graph of $y = \sin x$ has been transformed such that it no longer intersects with the graph of $y = \cos x$.
    Give a possible transformation that would do this.

6   The tangent function has been translated by $\begin{pmatrix} 5 \\ 6 \end{pmatrix}$.
    What is the new equation?

7   Write one possible equation for this curve.

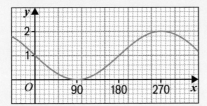

1   Here is the graph of $y = \cos x$ for $0° \leqslant x \leqslant 360°$.

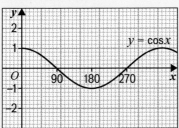

Copy the grid and draw the graph of $y = \cos x + 1$ for $0° \leqslant x \leqslant 360°$.   **(2 marks)**

Adapted from 1MA1/1H, June 2018, Q18

Exam feedback   ResultsPlus

Most students who achieved a **Grade 7** or above answered a similar question well.

14 Further statistics

14.1 Sampling

- To estimate the size of the population N of an animal species:
  Capture and mark a sample size n. Recapture another sample of size M. Count the number marked (m).
  $$\frac{n}{N} = \frac{m}{M} \quad \text{So, } N = \frac{n \times M}{m}$$
  This is the Peterson capture-recapture method.

Purposeful practice 1

For each question

  a Write an expression for the proportion of the population N that are marked.

  b Write down the proportion of the recaptured sample that are marked.

  c Assume the two proportions are equal and write an equation.

  d Solve to find an estimate for the total population N.

1 50 are caught and marked. The recapture sample size M is 50 and the number of these marked m is 5.

2 50 are caught and marked. The recapture sample size M is 50 and the number of these marked m is 10.

3 50 are caught and marked. The recapture sample size M is 40 and the number of these marked m is 10.

4 30 are caught and marked. The recapture sample size M is 40 and the number of these marked m is 5.

Reflect and reason

Tom says, 'The Peterson capture-recapture method works by comparing proportions.'
Explain why Tom is correct. Why do you need to assume that marks or tags are not lost, to use this method?

Purposeful practice 2

Estimate the size of the population when

1 the sample size caught and marked is 80, the recapture sample size is 50 and the number of these marked is 10

2 the sample size caught and marked is 50, the recapture sample size is 60 and the number of these marked is 12

3 the sample size caught and marked is 70, the recapture sample size is 60 and the number of these marked is 15

Reflect and reason

For the Peterson capture-recapture method, why do you need to assume that the population does not change between capture and recapture, and that the probability of being captured is the same for each individual?

1 The image shows the results from four
population studies using the Peterson
capture-recapture method. Match each
set of results to the correct estimate of the
population size, N.

A $n = 120$
$M = 30$
$m = 4$

B $n = 120$
$M = 50$
$m = 6$

C $n = 120$
$M = 45$
$m = 10$

D $n = 120$
$M = 70$
$m = 5$

$N = 1000$ $N = 1680$ $N = 900$ $N = 540$

2 Andy wants to estimate the number of mice in a field.
On Saturday Andy catches 180 mice.
He puts a mark on each mouse.
He then puts all 180 mice back in the field.
On Sunday Andy catches 100 mice.
2 of these mice have a mark on them.
Work out an estimate for the total number of mice in the field.
You must write down any assumptions you have made.

3 A biologist wants to estimate the number of rabbits in a National Park.
On Monday she catches 150 rabbits.
She puts a tag on each rabbit and then releases them.
On Tuesday the biologist catches 80 rabbits.
6 of these rabbits have a tag on them.
Work out an estimate for the total number of rabbits in the National Park.
You must write down any assumptions you have made.

4 Charley wants to estimate the number of frogs in a pond.
Charley catches 20 frogs from the pond.
She marks each frog and then lets them go.
The next day, Charley catches 12 frogs from the pond.
3 of these frogs have been marked.

   a Work out an estimate for the number of frogs in the pond.

   b Write down any assumptions you have made.

5 Jonathan is asked to estimate the number of counters in a bag.
He takes 10 counters from the bag at random.
He puts a mark on each counter and then puts them back in the bag.
Jonathan shakes the bag and then takes 20 of the counters at random.
There are marks on 5 of the counters.
Jonathan says, 'The total sample is 30 because $10 + 20 = 30$ and $30 \times 5 = 150$, so there are
150 counters in the bag.'
Jonathan is incorrect. Explain what Jonathan has done wrong.

⊞ ✳ **Exam practice**

1 Emily wants to find out how many chickens there are on a farm.
One day she puts a tag on 50 of the chickens.
The next day she catches 80 chickens.
10 of these chickens have tags on them.

   a Work out an estimate for the number of chickens on the farm. **(3 marks)**

   Emily assumed that none of the tags fell off during the night.

   b If Emily's assumption is wrong, explain how this could affect your answer to part a. **(1 mark)**

   Adapted from 1MA1/2H, Autumn 2016, Mock Set 1, Q13

Key points

- A cumulative frequency table shows how many data values are less than or equal to the upper class boundary of each data class. The upper class boundary is the highest possible value in each class.
- A cumulative frequency diagram has data values on the x-axis and cumulative frequency on the y-axis.
- For a set of n data values on a cumulative frequency diagram, the estimate for the median is the $\frac{n}{2}$th value.

△ Purposeful practice

a Draw a cumulative frequency graph for the information in each table. The first one is done for you.

b Use each graph to find an estimate for the median.

1

Value	Frequency
$0 < x \leqslant 10$	3
$10 < x \leqslant 20$	8
$20 < x \leqslant 30$	15
$30 < x \leqslant 40$	10
$40 < x \leqslant 50$	4

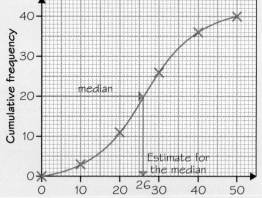

Cumulative frequency graph

2

Value	Frequency
$40 < x \leqslant 50$	3
$50 < x \leqslant 60$	8
$60 < x \leqslant 70$	15
$70 < x \leqslant 80$	10
$80 < x \leqslant 90$	4

3

Value	Frequency
$40 < x \leqslant 50$	2
$50 < x \leqslant 60$	11
$60 < x \leqslant 70$	17
$70 < x \leqslant 80$	12
$80 < x \leqslant 90$	8

4

Value	Frequency
$110 < x \leqslant 120$	2
$120 < x \leqslant 130$	11
$130 < x \leqslant 140$	17
$140 < x \leqslant 150$	12
$150 < x \leqslant 160$	8

5

Value	Frequency
$50 < x \leqslant 55$	2
$55 < x \leqslant 60$	11
$60 < x \leqslant 65$	17
$65 < x \leqslant 70$	12
$70 < x \leqslant 75$	8

Reflect and reason

Explain where you plot the points for a cumulative frequency graph.

How do you work out an estimate for the median?

1 Ewan is asked to draw a cumulative frequency graph for the results given in the table.

Time, m (minutes)	Frequency
$0 < m \leqslant 10$	3
$10 < m \leqslant 20$	8
$20 < m \leqslant 30$	22
$30 < m \leqslant 40$	7

He has made mistakes when drawing his cumulative frequency graph.
What two mistakes has Ewan made?

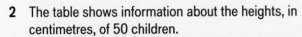

Cumulative frequency graph

2 The table shows information about the heights, in centimetres, of 50 children.

a Draw a cumulative frequency graph for the heights.

b Louise says, 'The estimate for the median is 25 because the median is half.'
Louise is wrong.
Explain what Louise has done wrong and give the correct estimate for the median.

c What does the estimate of the median value show you?

Height, h (cm)	Frequency
$100 < h \leqslant 110$	5
$110 < h \leqslant 120$	11
$120 < h \leqslant 130$	16
$130 < h \leqslant 140$	12
$140 < h \leqslant 150$	6

3 The table shows information about the weights of some apples.

a Draw a cumulative frequency graph for the weights.

b Find an estimate for the number of apples with a weight greater than 148 g.

Weight, w (grams)	Frequency
$110 < w \leqslant 120$	10
$120 < w \leqslant 130$	29
$130 < w \leqslant 140$	36
$140 < w \leqslant 150$	18
$150 < w \leqslant 160$	7

 ✩ Exam practice

1 Lisa carried out a survey about the ages of the people at her company.
The table shows information about her results.

Age, a (years)	Cumulative frequency
$20 < a \leqslant 30$	12
$20 < a \leqslant 40$	31
$20 < a \leqslant 50$	59
$20 < a \leqslant 60$	76
$20 < a \leqslant 70$	80

a Draw a cumulative frequency graph for this information. **(2 marks)**

b Use your graph to find an estimate for the median age. **(1 mark)**

Lisa says, 'More than 60% of the people at the company are between 35 and 55 years old.'

c Use your graph to determine if Lisa is correct. **(3 marks)**

Adapted from 1MA1/3H, Autumn 2017, Mock Set 3, Q9

Key points

- A box plot, sometimes called a box-and-whisker diagram, displays a data set to show the median and quartiles.

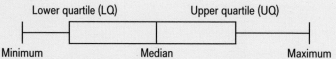

- Summary statistics for a set of data are the averages, ranges and quartiles.

⚠ Purposeful practice 1

1 The summary statistics for exam scores of students in different schools are given in the table.
   On graph paper, draw a box plot for each school.

	Minimum score	Lower quartile	Median	Upper quartile	Maximum score
School A	13	18	20	30	45
School B	23	32	37	47	57
School C	20	25	28	38	46
School D	17	21	25	28	35

Reflect and reason

Which values do you use to draw the 'box'? Where do you put the other values?

⚠ Purposeful practice 2

80 students sat the exam in school A.   200 students sat the exam in school B.
120 students sat the exam in school C.   40 students sat the exam in school D.

Using your box plots from Purposeful practice 1, estimate the following.
The first one has been started for you.

1 The number of students in school A who scored more than 30 marks.

   30 = upper quartile, so 25% of students scored more than 30 marks,
   25% of ___ = ___

2 The number of students in school B who scored more than 47 marks.

3 The number of students in school C who scored more than 38 marks.

4 The number of students in school D who scored more than 28 marks.

5 The number of students in school A who scored between 18 and 30 marks.

6 The number of students in school A who scored less than 30 marks.

7 The number of students in school B who scored between 32 and 47 marks.

8 The number of students in school C who scored less than 25 marks.

Reflect and reason

What percentage of the results in Purposeful practice 2 are less than the LQ? Greater than the LQ?
Between the LQ and UQ? Between the LQ and median?

⊠ Problem-solving practice

1 The table shows some information about the weights, in kg, of some dogs.

Lightest weight	Lower quartile	Median	Upper quartile	Range
5 kg	20 kg	32 kg	40 kg	52 kg

A vet uses this information to draw the box plot below.

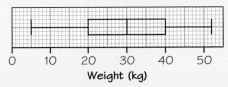

Weights of dogs

Weight (kg)

Write down two mistakes the vet has made.

2 Pasha recorded the heights of 80 students.
The incomplete table and box plot give information about his results.

Shortest height	Lower quartile	Median	Upper quartile	Range
152 cm		168 cm	173 cm	

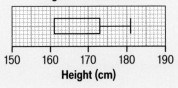

Heights of 80 students

Height (cm)

a i Use the information in the table to complete the box plot.

   ii Use the information in the box plot to complete the table.

b Find an estimate for the number of students between 152 cm and 173 cm tall.

3 The table gives some information about the weights of 100 children.

   a Draw a box plot to show this information.

   b Work out an estimate for the number of children with a weight between 20.1 kg and 29.5 kg.

Lowest	19.0 kg
Highest	29.5 kg
Lower quartile	20.1 kg
Upper quartile	25.8 kg
Median	23.4 kg

✳ Exam practice

1 The table gives some information about the heights of 120 boys.

   a Draw a box plot to represent this information. **(3 marks)**

   b Work out an estimate for the number of these boys with a height between 165 cm and 183 cm. **(2 marks)**

Least height	148 cm
Greatest height	183 cm
Lower quartile	165 cm
Upper quartile	172 cm
Median	168 cm

Adapted from 1MA1/1H, June 2018, Q10

Exam feedback   Results**Plus**

Q1a: Most students who achieved a **Grade 3** or above answered a similar question well.

Q1b: Most students who achieved a **Grade 8** or above answered a similar question well.

Key point

- A histogram is a type of frequency diagram used for grouped continuous data. In a histogram the area of the bar represents the frequency. The height of each bar is the frequency density.

$$\text{Frequency density} = \frac{\text{frequency}}{\text{class width}}$$

△ Purposeful practice

1 a Copy and complete the table.

Height, x (cm)	Frequency	Class width	Frequency density
$0 < x \leqslant 10$	5	10	$5 \div 10 = 0.5$
$10 < x \leqslant 15$	12		
$15 < x \leqslant 30$	15		
$30 < x \leqslant 50$	6		

b Copy and complete the histogram.

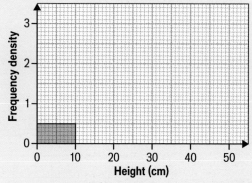

Histogram showing heights

c Calculate the area of each bar in your histogram to check it is equal to the frequency for that class.

2 a Work out the frequency densities for the data given in the table.

b Draw a histogram to display the data.

c Calculate the area of each bar in your histogram to check it is equal to the frequency for that class.

Height, x (cm)	Frequency
$0 < x \leqslant 10$	8
$10 < x \leqslant 15$	14
$15 < x \leqslant 30$	9
$30 < x \leqslant 50$	7

3 a Draw a histogram to display the data given in the table.

b Calculate the area of each bar in your histogram to check it is equal to the frequency for that class.

Height, x (cm)	Frequency
$0 < x \leqslant 10$	8
$10 < x \leqslant 25$	18
$25 < x \leqslant 35$	9
$35 < x \leqslant 60$	7

Reflect and reason

Why do you need to use frequency density to draw a histogram rather than drawing the bars to the height of the frequency?

⊠ Problem-solving practice

1 Megan recorded the lengths of time, in hours, that 30 students took to complete a puzzle.
The table shows information about her results.

Length of time, t (hours)	Frequency
$0 < t \leqslant 10$	5
$10 < t \leqslant 15$	9
$15 < t \leqslant 20$	13
$20 < t \leqslant 40$	3

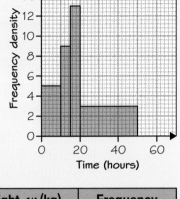
Time to complete a puzzle

Megan draws a histogram for this information.
Write down two mistakes Megan has made.

2 The weights, in kilograms, of babies born at a hospital are recorded during a week.
The table shows information about the results.
Draw a histogram for this information.

Weight, w (kg)	Frequency
$1.0 < w \leqslant 2.5$	6
$2.5 < w \leqslant 3.0$	13
$3.0 < w \leqslant 3.5$	17
$3.5 < w \leqslant 3.75$	14
$3.75 < w \leqslant 4.5$	9

3 a Ashiok records the heights of 100 students, in centimetres.
His results are shown in the table.
Draw a histogram for this information.

b Ashiok realises that he made a mistake and the height of the tallest student is actually 190 cm, not 180 cm.
What effect would this have on the final bar, assuming nothing else on the histogram changes?

Height, h (cm)	Frequency
$140 < h \leqslant 150$	10
$150 < h \leqslant 155$	20
$155 < h \leqslant 160$	34
$160 < h \leqslant 165$	24
$165 < h \leqslant 180$	12

⬡ Exam practice

1 The table gives information about the heights of 100 students.
Draw a histogram for this information. **(3 marks)**

Height, h (cm)	Frequency
$140 < h \leqslant 150$	5
$150 < h \leqslant 155$	20
$155 < h \leqslant 160$	41
$160 < h \leqslant 165$	26
$165 < h \leqslant 180$	8

Adapted from 1MA1/2H, November 2017, Q17a

Exam feedback

ResultsPlus

In a similar question, some students did not label the vertical axis correctly. Class intervals were sometimes used on the horizontal axis instead of a linear scale.

14.5 Interpreting histograms

 △ **Purposeful practice**

1 The histogram shows information about the height of some plants.

   a Copy and complete the table.   **b** How many plants were measured?

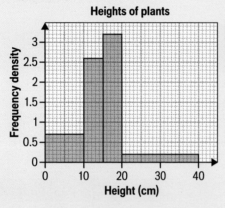

Heights of plants

Height, x (cm)	Frequency density	Class width	Frequency
$0 < x \leqslant 10$	0.7	10	$0.7 \times 10 = 7$

2 The histogram shows information about the height of some plants.

   a Copy and complete the table.   **b** How many plants were less than or equal to 25 cm tall?

Heights of plants

Height, x (cm)	Frequency density	Class width	Frequency
$0 < x \leqslant 10$			
$10 < x \leqslant 15$			
$15 < x \leqslant 25$			
$25 < x \leqslant 40$			

3 The histogram shows information about the height of some plants.
   Work out how many plants are

   a less than or equal to 20 cm

   b between 20 cm and 30 cm (inclusive of 30 cm)

   c less than or equal to 30 cm

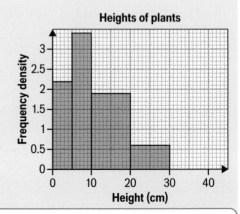

Heights of plants

Reflect and reason

How do you work out the frequency from a histogram? Explain why you do this calculation.

1 The histogram gives information about house
   prices in a village in 2018.
   30 houses in the village have a price between
   £300 000 and £400 000.
   Work out the number of houses in the village with
   a price under £300 000.

2 The histogram shows information about the time taken
   by sprinters to finish a race.
   11 sprinters took between 50 and 60 seconds to finish
   the race.

   a Work out an estimate for the number of sprinters who
       took more than 80 seconds to finish the race.

   b Explain why your answer to part **a** is only an estimate.

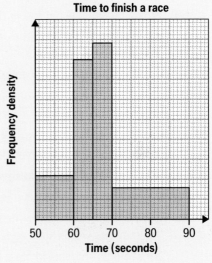

1 The histogram shows some information about the ages
   of the 84 members of a golf club.

   20% of the members of the golf club who are over
   50 years of age are female.
   Work out an estimate for the number of female
   members who are over 50 years of age.   **(3 marks)**

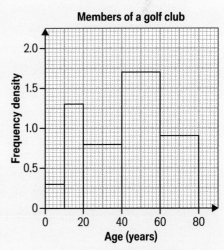

Adapted from 1MA1/2H, June 2017, Q13

Exam feedback   ResultsPlus

Most students who achieved a **Grade 8** or above answered a similar question well.

14.6 Comparing and describing populations

Key points

- The interquartile range measures the spread of the middle 50% of the data.
  To describe a data set (or population) give a measure of average and a measure of spread.
  To compare data sets, compare a measure of average and a measure of spread.
- The median and interquartile range are not affected by extreme values or outliers.

△ Purposeful practice

1 Year 11 students in school A have a median height of 164 cm and an interquartile range of 10 cm.
  Year 11 students in school B have a median height of 167 cm and an interquartile range of 14 cm.

   a Which school has the higher median height for Year 11 students?

   b Which school has the higher interquartile range, therefore a larger spread of heights for Year 11 students?

   c Copy and complete the sentence comparing the two sets of data.

   On average, Year 11 students in school ___ are taller and Year 11 students in school ___ have a larger spread of heights.

2 Students in class A have a median test score of 47 and an interquartile range of 25.
  Students in class B have a median test score of 41 and an interquartile range of 20.

   a Which class has the higher average test score?

   b Which class has the greater spread of scores?

   c Copy and complete the sentence.
   You may use words such as higher, lower, greater and smaller.

   On average, students in class A have _____ test scores and a _____ spread of test scores than students in class B.

3 Students in class A have a median weight of 55 kg and an interquartile range of 12 kg.
  Students in class B have a median weight of 52 kg and an interquartile range of 16 kg.

   a Which class has the higher average weight?

   b Which class has the greater spread of weights?

   c Compare the two sets of data.

4 Students in class A have a median height of 159 cm and an interquartile range of 15 cm.
  Students in class B have a median height of 161 cm and an interquartile range of 11 cm.
  Compare the two sets of data.

5 Students in class C have a median height of 163 cm and an interquartile range of 10 cm.
  Students in class D have a median height of 160 cm and an interquartile range of 17 cm.
  Compare the two sets of data.

6 Students in class E have a median height of 174 cm and an interquartile range of 22 cm.
  Students in class F have a median height of 169 cm and an interquartile range of 18 cm.
  Compare the two sets of data.

Reflect and reason

In **Q1–6**, which average and measure of spread did you use to compare the sets of data?

Why are these good measures to use when comparing two sets of data?

⊠ Problem-solving practice

1 Jordan digs up the potatoes from all 46 potato plants on his allotment.
For each plant, he records the total weight of its potatoes.
The table shows some information about these total weights in kg.

Least weight	0.9 kg
Greatest weight	2.25 kg
Median	1.35 kg
Lower quartile	1.15 kg
Upper quartile	1.5 kg

Ben has 58 potato plants.
The box plot shows the distribution of the total weights of the potatoes Ben digs up from each of his potato plants.

Weights of Ben's potatoes

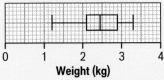

Weight (kg)

Compare the distribution of the weights of potatoes Jordan picks with the distribution of the weights of potatoes Ben picks.

✦ Exam practice

1 The table shows information about the heights, in cm, of a group of Year 11 girls.

Least height	152 cm
Median	164 cm
Lower quartile	160 cm
Interquartile range	8 cm
Range	22 cm

a Draw a box plot for this information. **(3 marks)**

The box plot below shows information about the heights, in cm, of a group of Year 7 girls.

Heights of Year 7 girls

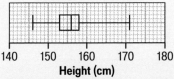

Height (cm)

b Compare the distribution of heights of the Year 7 girls with the distribution of heights of the Year 11 girls. **(2 marks)**

Adapted from 1MA1/1H, November 2017, Q12

Exam feedback ResultsPlus

Q1a: In a similar question, many students gained at least one mark for 3 correct values on the box plot.
Q1b: In a similar question, many students did not make any comparisons, and those students that did lost marks as they did not put their comparisons in context.

15 Equations and graphs

15.1 Solving simultaneous equations graphically

Key point

- You can solve a pair of simultaneous equations by plotting the graph of both equations and finding the point(s) of intersection.

⚠ Purposeful practice 1

1   Draw a coordinate grid from -10 to 10 on both axes.
On the same axes, draw the graph of $x + y = 6$ and the graphs of
   a $y = x$ **b** $y = 2x$ **c** $y = 5x$ **d** $y = -3x$
For each graph, write down the coordinates of the points of intersection with $x + y = 6$

2   Draw a coordinate grid from -5 to 15 on both axes. Draw these three graphs on the same axes.
   $x + y = 4$ $y = 3x$ $y = \frac{1}{3}x$
Hence write down the solutions to these simultaneous equations.
   a $x + y = 4$ **b** $x + y = 4$
      $y = 3x$ $y = \frac{1}{3}x$

3   On the same coordinate grid you used for **Q2**, draw the graph of $x + y = 8$
Hence write down the solutions to these simultaneous equations.
   a $x + y = 8$ **b** $x + y = 8$
      $y = 3x$ $y = \frac{1}{3}x$

4   On the same coordinate grid you used for **Q2**, draw the graph of $x + y = 12$
Hence write down the solutions to these simultaneous equations.
   a $x + y = 12$ **b** $x + y = 12$
      $y = 3x$ $y = \frac{1}{3}x$

Reflect and reason

Predict the solutions to these simultaneous equations.
   1 $x + y = 16$ **2** $x + y = 16$ **3** $x + y = -4$ **4** $x + y = -4$
      $y = 3x$ $y = \frac{1}{3}x$ $y = 3x$ $y = \frac{1}{3}x$
Explain how you made your predictions.

⚠ Purposeful practice 2

Draw graphs to solve these simultaneous equations.
   1 $x + y = 5$ **2** $x + y = 5$ **3** $x = 7y + 13$
      $y = 3x + 1$ $x = 7y + 13$ $y = 3x + 1$

Reflect and reason

Ruth says, 'I can use **Q1** to find the solution to the simultaneous equations $x = -y + 5$ and $x = \frac{1}{3}y - \frac{1}{3}$.'
What is the solution? How did Ruth use **Q1**?
Use **Q2** to write a pair of simultaneous equations you can find the answer to.

1. Solve the simultaneous equations graphically.
   Use a coordinate grid with −10 to 10 on both axes.

   a $x + y = 3$

   $y = x^2 + 2x - 1$

   b $x + y = 3$

   $y = 3 - x^2$

   c $x^2 + y^2 = 25$

   $y = \frac{3}{4}x$

   d $x^2 + y^2 = 5$

   $x = y + 1$

2. A mobile phone company offers two ways to buy a phone.
   Purchase: Buy the phone for £100 and then pay £5 per month for calls and data.
   Rent: Pay £15 per month.
   At what point do both ways of buying the phone have the same cost?

3. Use a graphical method to find approximate solutions to this pair of simultaneous equations.
   $y = x^2 - 4x + 3$
   $y = x + 1$

4. Aaron buys 4 pears and 2 pineapples for £5.86.
   In the same shop Ceris buys 3 pears and 5 pineapples for £11.22.
   What is the cost of

   a 1 pear?

   b 2 pears and 1 pineapple?

5. Andrew buys 3 coffees and 2 teas for £10.
   In the same shop, Matt buys 1 coffee and 5 teas for £7.
   James drew this graph to find the cost of 1 tea.
   How can you tell he has made a mistake?

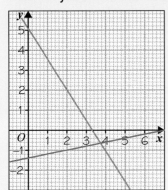

1. **a** Copy the grid and draw the graph of $x^2 + y^2 = 15$.

   (2 marks)

   b Hence find estimates for the solution of the simultaneous equations

   $x^2 + y^2 = 15$
   $2x - y = 2$

   (3 marks)

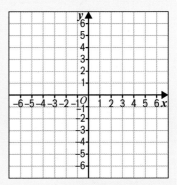

Adapted from 1MA1/2H, June 18, Q16b

Exam feedback   Results**Plus**

Q1a: Most students who achieved a `Grade 7` or above answered a similar question well.

Q1b: Most students who achieved a `Grade 9` answered a similar question well.

Key points

- The points that satisfy an inequality can be represented by shading a region on a graph. A solid line means that the shaded region includes the points on the line; a dotted line means that the shaded region does **not** include the points on the line.

- You can write solution sets using set notation.
  The inequality $x^2 - 9 \leqslant 0$ is satisfied when $-3 \leqslant x \leqslant 3$
  This is written: $\{x : -3 \leqslant x \leqslant 3\}$
  The inequality $0 < x^2 - 4$ is satisfied when $x < -2$ or $x > 2$
  This is written: $\{x : x < -2\} \cup \{x : x > 2\}$
  The symbol $\cup$ means that the solution includes all the values satisfied by either inequality.

⚠ Purposeful practice 1

1 Draw a coordinate grid with -5 to 5 on both axes.

   a Draw the graph of $y = x + 2$ **b** Shade the region of points whose coordinates satisfy $y < x + 2$

2 Draw a coordinate grid with -5 to 5 on both axes.

   a Shade the region of points whose coordinates satisfy $x + y > 3$

   b Shade the region of points whose coordinates satisfy $x + y < 1$

3 Draw a coordinate grid with -5 to 5 on both axes.

   a Shade the region of points whose coordinates satisfy $y < 2x + 1$

   b Shade the region of points whose coordinates satisfy $y > 4x + 1$

4 Look at **Q3b** again.

   a Does $(0, 0)$ satisfy $y > 4x + 1$?   **b** Does $(-1, -1)$ satisfy $y > 4x + 1$?

Reflect and reason

How does **Q4** help you check your answer to **Q3b**?

⚠ Purposeful practice 2

1 Write the solutions to the following inequalities using set notation.

   a $4x < 20$ **b** $4x + 1 < 25$ **c** $4x - 1 < 15$

   d $4x > 32$ **e** $4x + 1 > 41$ **f** $4x - 1 > 47$

2 Write the solutions to the following inequalities using set notation.

   a $x^2 - 16 \leqslant 0$ **b** $x^2 - 81 < 0$ **c** $x^2 - 256 > 0$ **d** $x^2 - 64 \geqslant 0$

3 Sketch graphs to find the values of x that satisfy these inequalities.
   Give your answers using set notation.

   a $x^2 - 11x + 24 \leqslant 0$ **b** $x^2 - 10x + 24 \leqslant 0$

   c $x^2 - 14x + 24 \geqslant 0$ **d** $x^2 - 25x + 24 \geqslant 0$

Reflect and reason

After Henry had completed **Q3a** and **Q3b**, he decided it was unnecessary to sketch the graphs. He did not sketch a graph for **Q3c**, and wrote the answer, $\{x : 2 \leqslant x \leqslant 12\}$.
What mistake has Henry made? Why would a sketch of the graph be helpful?

1   Draw a coordinate grid with 0 to 5 on both axes.
    Draw the graphs of $y = 2$, $x + y = 5$ and $x = 1$
    Mark the points with integer coordinates that satisfy the inequalities $y \geqslant 2$, $x + y < 5$ and $x \geqslant 1$

2   Draw a coordinate grid with 0 to 6 on both axes.
    Draw the region that satisfies the inequalities $x < 4$, $y > 2$ and $x + 2y < 12$
    Considering only integer coordinates, find the largest possible value of $x + y$ inside the region.

3   Each diagram shows a shaded region bounded by three lines.
    For each diagram, write down the three inequalities satisfied by the coordinates of the points in the shaded region.

a
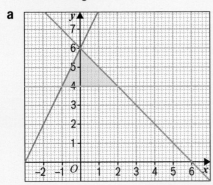

b
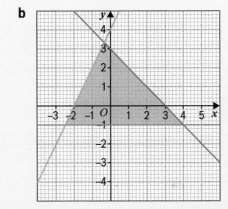

c
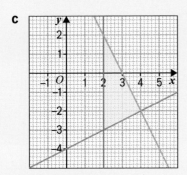

4   Draw the graph of $y = x^2 - 7x + 12$
    Use the graph to help you write the values of x that satisfy $x^2 - 7x + 12 < 0$
    Write your answer using set notation.

⋇ Exam practice

1   Write down three inequalities that define the shaded region.
    (4 marks)

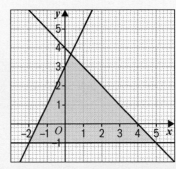

Adapted from 1MA1/3H, June 2017, Q13

Exam feedback

Most students who achieved a **Grade 8** or above answered a similar question well.

ResultsPlus

Key points

- The lowest or highest point of the parabola, where the graph turns, is called the turning point. The turning point is either a minimum or maximum point.
  The x-values where the graph intersects the x-axis are the solutions, or roots, of the equation $y = 0$.
- To find the coordinate of the turning point, write the equation in completed square form:
  $y = a(x + b)^2 + c$
- When a quadratic is written in completed square form $y = a(x + b)^2 + c$, the coordinate of the turning point is $(-b, c)$
- To sketch a quadratic function
  calculate the solutions to the equation '$y = 0$'
  calculate the point at which the graph crosses the y-axis
  find the coordinates of the turning point and whether it is a maximum or a minimum.

Purposeful practice 1

1 Factorise the expression on the right-hand side of each equation.
   Then write down the roots of the equation $y = 0$.

   a $y = x^2 - 4x + 3$ **b** $y = x^2 - 1$ **c** $y = x^2 + 2x - 3$

2 Factorise the expression on the right-hand side of each equation.
   Then write down the roots of the equation $y = 0$.

   a $y = 4x^2 - 5x + 1$ **b** $y = 9x^2 + 9x - 4$ **c** $y = \frac{1}{4}x^2 + x - 3$

3 For each equation in **Q1** and **Q2**, complete the square.
   Then write down the coordinates of the turning point.

4 Sketch the graphs of the equations in **Q1** and **Q2**.

Reflect and reason

How did you use your answers to **Q1–3** to sketch your graphs?
What additional information did you need?

Purposeful practice 2

1 For each equation, complete the square.
   Then write down the coordinates of the turning point.

   a $y = 2x^2 + 4x + 6$ **b** $y = 3x^2 + 6x + 7$ **c** $y = 5x^2 + 10x + 9$

2 For each equation in **Q1**, state if the turning point is a maximum or a minimum.
   Explain how you know.

3 Sketch each graph.
   Write down its line of symmetry.

   a $y = x^2 - 6x + 8$ **b** $y = x^2 - 6x + 5$ **c** $y = 4x^2 - 8x + 3$

Reflect and reason

What is the relationship between
   the turning point of a quadratic graph and its line of symmetry?
   the x-coordinate of the turning point and the roots of the equation?

1   Match these graphs to their equations. Give reasons.

   a $y = x^2 - 7x + 6$ **b** $y = 6 - x - x^2$ **c** $y = x^2 + x - 6$ **d** $y = 6 + x - x^2$

   i 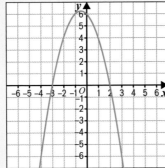   **ii**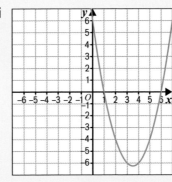

   iii 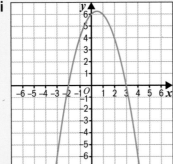   **iv**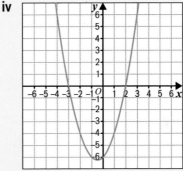

2   Give three reasons why this graph cannot be
   $y = 4 - 2x^2 + 3x$

   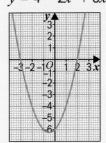

3   Find the equation of this quadratic graph.

   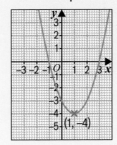

   (1, −4)

1   **a**   Complete the table of values for $y = x^2 - 4x + 3$ **(2 marks)**

x	−1	0	1	2	3	4	5
y		3					8

   b   On a coordinate grid with x-axis from −1 to 5 and y-axis from −1 to 9 draw the graph of
   $y = x^2 - 4x + 3$ for values of x from −1 to 5.   **(2 marks)**

   Adapted from 1MA1/2H, June 18, Q5a and b

Exam feedback   Results**Plus**

Q1a: Most students who achieved a   Grade 4   or above answered a similar question well.

Q1b: Most students who achieved a   Grade 5   or above answered a similar question well.

15.4 Solving quadratic equations graphically

Key points

- The quadratic equation $ax^2 + bx + c = 0$ is said to have no real roots if its graph does not cross the x-axis. If its graph just touches the x-axis, the equation has one repeated root.
- To find an accurate root of a quadratic equation, you can use an iterative process.

⚠ Purposeful practice 1

1 For each graph, state if it represents an equation with two roots, one repeated root, or no real roots.

a 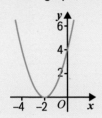   **b** 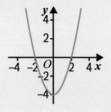   **c** 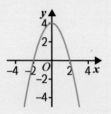   **d**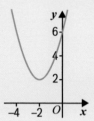

2 By completing the square, decide whether these quadratic equations have no roots, two roots or one repeated root.

  a $x^2 + 6x + 9$ **b** $x^2 + 6x + 12$ **c** $x^2 + 6x + 6$

  d $x^2 + 8x + 12$ **e** $x^2 + 8x + 16$ **f** $x^2 + 8x + 20$

3 Use the graph to find approximate solutions to $x^2 - 4x + 1 = 0$

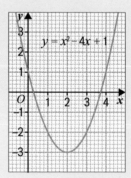

Reflect and reason

What algebraic method could you use to check your answers to **Q3**?

⚠ Purposeful practice 2

1 Calculate, to 2 d.p., the first three iterations of

  a $x = \sqrt{\dfrac{5x + 3}{3}}$ starting with $x = 1$ **b** $x = \sqrt{3x + 8}$ starting with $x = 4$

2 Use the iterative equation and the starting point given to find one root for each quadratic equation. Give each answer correct to 2 d.p.

  a $y = x^2 + 3x - 25$ $x = \sqrt{25 - 3x}$ $x_0 = 3.7$

  b $y = x^2 + 3x - 15$ $x = \sqrt{15 - 3x}$ $x_0 = 0.2$

  c $y = 9x^2 + 3x - 15$ $x = \dfrac{1}{3}\sqrt{15 - 3x}$ $x_0 = -2$

Reflect and reason

Sam says, 'The iterative equation in **Q1b** finds the roots of the quadratic equation $y = 9x^2 + 48x + 64$'. Sam is wrong. Explain the error he has made. What is the correct quadratic equation?

1 Match each graph to its equation.
Hence estimate the solutions to each equation.

a $5x^2 + x - 2 = 0$ **b** $x^2 + x - 2 = 0$

c $x^2 - x - 2 = 0$ **d** $(x - 2)^2 = 0$

i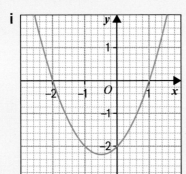

ii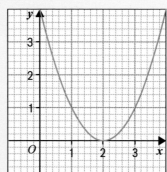

iii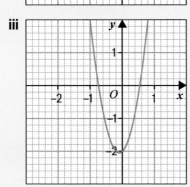

iv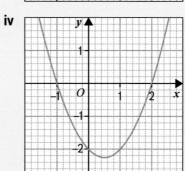

2 a By completing the square, find the roots of the equation
$x^2 - 8x + 2 = 0$
Give your answers in surd form.

b Show algebraically that $x^2 - 3x + 4 = 0$ has no real roots.

3 John is solving a quadratic equation using an iterative process.
Here is some of his working out.

$x_2 = 0.712793$

$x_3 = \frac{1}{4}\sqrt{10 - 2 \times 0.712793}$

a Continue John's method to find an iterative solution correct to 2 d.p.

b Find the quadratic equation that John is solving.

✦ Exam practice

1 a Show that the equation $2x^2 + x - 5 = 0$ can be rearranged to give the equation

$x = \sqrt{\dfrac{5 - x}{2}}$

(2 marks)

b Using $x_{n+1} = \sqrt{\dfrac{5 - x_n}{2}}$ with $x_0 = 1$, find the values of x_1, x_2 and x_3

(3 marks)

Key points

- A cubic function is one whose highest power of x is x^3. It is written in the form $y = ax^3 + bx^2 + cx + d$

  When $a > 0$ the function looks like this   When $a < 0$ the function looks like this

  The graph intersects the y-axis at the point $y = d$.

  The graph's roots can be found by finding the values of x for which $y = 0$.
- When the graph of a cubic function y crosses the x-axis three times, the equation $y = 0$ has three separate solutions.
- When the graph of a cubic function y crosses the x-axis once and touches the x-axis once, the equation $y = 0$ has three solutions but one of them is repeated.
- When the graph of a cubic function y crosses the x-axis only once, the equation $y = 0$ has only one real solution, or one solution repeated twice.

⚠ Purposeful practice 1

1 Which of these are cubic equations?

   a $y = (x - 1)(x - 2)(x - 3)$ **b** $y = (x - 1)^2(x - 2)(x - 3)$

   c $y = (x - 1)^3$ **d** $y = (x - 1)(x^2 - 5x + 6)$

2 For each equation, draw a table of values and plot a graph.

   a $y = x^3 - 4x^2 + x + 2$ (Use values of x from -2 to 4)

   b $y = x^3 + 4x^2 + x + 2$ (Use values of x from -4 to 2)

3 Write down the number of real solutions for each of these equations.

   a $(x - 1)(x - 2)(x - 3) = 0$ **b** $(x - 1)^2(x - 2) = 0$ **c** $(x - 1)(x - 2)^2 = 0$

   d $x^3 + 4x^2 + x + 2 = 0$ (Use **Q2b** to help you.)   **e** $(x + 1)^3$

> ### Reflect and reason
> What is the same and what is different about the graphs of these equations?
> $y = x + 1$ $y = (x + 1)^2$ $y = (x + 1)^3$

⚠ Purposeful practice 2

1 Find the x-values where these equations meet or cross the x-axis.

   a $y = (x - 1)(x - 2)(x - 3)$ **b** $y = (x - 1)(x + 2)(x - 3)$

   c $y = (x - 1)^2(x - 2)$ **d** $y = (x - 1)(x - 2)^2$

2 Match each equation to the correct graph.

   a $y = (x - 1)^2(x - 2)$ **b** $y = (x - 1)(x - 2)^2$ **c** $y = (x + 1)^2(x - 2)$ **d** $y = (x + 1)(x - 2)^2$

   i   **ii**   **iii**   **iv**

> ### Reflect and reason
> What is the same and what is different about graphs **ii** and **iii** in **Q2**?

1 Sketch these graphs.
$$y = (x - 2)^2(x + 2)$$
$$y = (x + 1)(x - 2)(x - 4)$$
Mark clearly the points of intersection with the x- and y-axes.
Write two similarities between the graphs.
Write two differences between the graphs.

2 A general cubic graph has the equation $y = ax^3 + bx^2 + cx + d$
Find the values of a, b, c and d for the graphs that satisfy these conditions.

   a The graph crosses the x-axis at $x = 2$, $x = 3$ and $x = -1$
      When $x = 4$, $y = 10$

   b The graph crosses the x-axis at $x = 2$ and $x = 3$
      $x = 2$ represents a repeated root.
      The graph passes through the point $(1, -2)$.

   c The graph crosses the x-axis at $x = -\frac{1}{2}$, $x = -4$ and $x = 8$
      It passes through the point $(0, -32)$.

3 Tim attempts to sketch the graph of $y = (x - 1)(x + 2)(x - 3)$
His working begins like this,
the graph crosses the y-axis when x = 0, so this means y = −1 × 2 × −3 = −6
the graph crosses the x-axis when y = 0 so this means (x − 1)(x + 2)(x − 3) = 0
which gives x = 1, 2, 3.

   a Tim has made two errors.
      Find and correct them.

   b Sketch the graph correctly.

1 **a** Copy and complete the table of values for $y = x^3 - 3x$

x	−3	−2	−1	0	1	2	3
y			2	0			18

                                                 (2 marks)

   b Copy the grid and draw the graph of $y = x^3 - 3x$ for $x = -2$ to $x = 3$

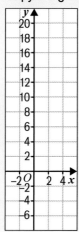

                                                 (2 marks)

Adapted from 1MAO/2H, November 2013, Q17

16 Circle theorems

16.1 Radii and chords

Key points

- A chord is a straight line connecting two points on a circle.
- The perpendicular from the centre of a circle to a chord bisects the chord and the line drawn from the centre of a circle to the midpoint of a chord is at right angles to the chord.

△ Purposeful practice 1

1   Look at the circles, each with centre, O. Which triangles are isosceles?

2   Each diagram shows a circle with centre O.
Work out the size of each angle marked with a letter.

Reflect and reason

How can you identify isosceles triangles in a circle?

△ Purposeful practice 2

Each diagram shows a circle with centre O.

1   Find the length AB.

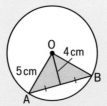

2   Find the length CD.

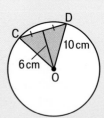

3   Find the distance from O to the midpoint of EF.

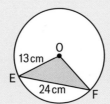

4   Find the perpendicular distance from O to GH.

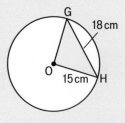

Reflect and reason

Explain why we can apply Pythagoras' theorem to **Q1–4**.

1   A circle has centre O and a radius of 12 cm.
    XY is a chord of length 18 cm.
    Find the shortest distance from the centre of the circle to the chord XY
    as a simplified surd.

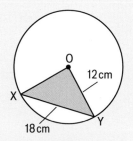

2   O is the centre of a circle.
    Work out the size of angle m.
    Give reasons for each step in your answers.

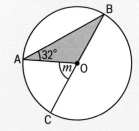

3   O is the centre of a circle.
    The radius of the circle is 13 cm.
    The point N is on the chord RQ.
    RQ is 16 cm.
    ON is 11 cm.
    Is N the midpoint of the chord? Show your working.

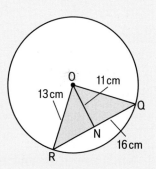

4   The diagram shows a circle with centre O and a radius of 7 cm.
    Find the length of the chord PQ to 1 d.p.
    Give reasons for each step in your working.

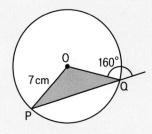

1   A and B are points on a circle, centre O with radius 5 cm.
    A, B and C lie on a straight line.
    Angle OBC is 140°.

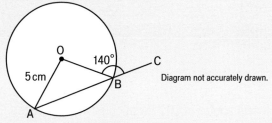

Diagram not accurately drawn.

    Find the length of AB.   (4 marks)

Key points

- A tangent is a straight line that touches a circle at one point only.
  The angle between a tangent and the radius is 90°.
- Tangents drawn to a circle from a point outside the circle are equal in length.

◭ Purposeful practice 1

Look at the circles, each with a centre O.
For each circle, state whether the line AB is a tangent.

1 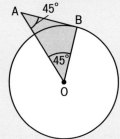 **2** 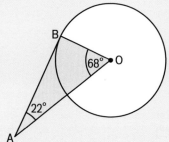 **3**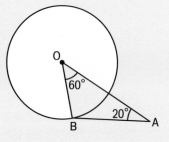

Reflect and reason

How can you identify the tangent to a circle?

◭ Purposeful practice 2

Each diagram shows a circle with centre O.
Work out the size of each angle marked with a letter.

1 **a** 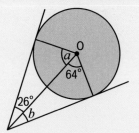 **b** 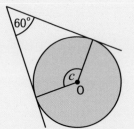 **c**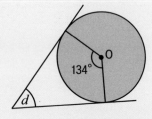

2 **a** 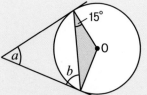 **b** 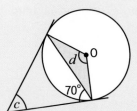 **c**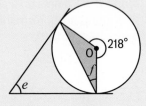

Reflect and reason

What knowledge of tangents helps you find the missing angles in **Q1**? What could you add to the diagrams to help you?

What other knowledge about tangents and chords helps you find the angles in **Q2**?

⊠ Problem-solving practice

1 The circle has centre O and a radius of 10 cm.
M is the point at which the tangent MN touches the circle.
MN is 24 cm.
Find the length of ON.
Give reasons for each step in your working.

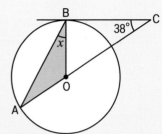

2 O is the centre of the circle.
Work out the size of angle x.
Give reasons for each step in your working.

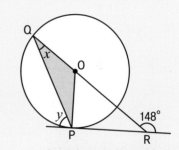

3 O is the centre of the circle.
Work out the size of angles x and y.
Give reasons for each step in your working.

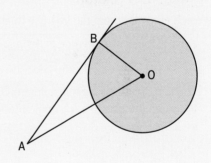

4 The circle has centre O and a radius of 4 cm.
OA is 8 cm.
Without using a calculator, find the size of angle OAB.
Give reasons for each step in your working.

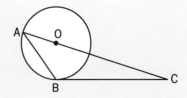

✳ Exam practice

1 A and B are points on a circle, centre O.
BC is a tangent to the circle.
AOC is a straight line.
Angle ACB = $x°$.
Find the size of angle OAB, in terms of x.
Give your answer in its simplest form.
Give reasons for each stage of your working.

(5 marks)

Adapted from 1MA1/1H, May 2018, Q11

Exam feedback

Most students who achieved a **Grade 9** answered a similar question well.

ResultsPlus

Key points

- The angle at the centre of a circle is twice the angle at the circumference when both are subtended by the same arc.
- The angle in a semicircle is a right angle.

△ **Purposeful practice 1**

The diagrams show circles, centre O.
Work out the size of each angle marked with a letter.

1
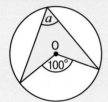

2
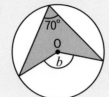

3
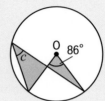

4
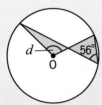

5

6
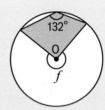

Reflect and reason

Which circle theorem did you use to find the missing angles in **Q1–6**?

△ **Purposeful practice 2**

The diagrams show circles, centre O.
Work out the size of each angle marked with a letter.

1
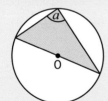

2
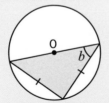

3
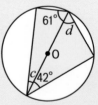

4
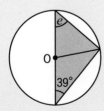

5
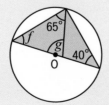

Reflect and reason

John says, 'The angle at the centre of a circle theorem applies to the angle in a semicircle theorem.'
What does John mean?

1 The diagram shows a circle, centre O.
Work out the size of angles a and b.
Give reasons for each step in your working.

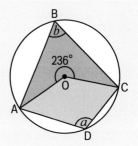

2 The diagram shows a circle, centre O.
Work out the size of angle x.
Give reasons for each step in your working.

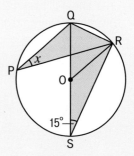

3 The diagram shows a circle, centre O.
Work out the size of angle x.
Give reasons for each step in your working.

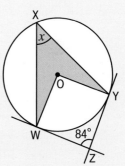

4 The diagram shows a circle, centre O.
Write an expression for n in terms of m.
Give reasons for each step in your working.

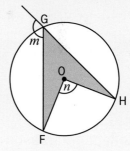

⭐ Exam practice

1 X, Y and Z are points on the circumference of a circle, centre O.
XOY is a diameter of the circle.
Prove that angle XZY is 90°.
You must not use any circle theorems in your proof. **(4 marks)**

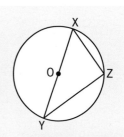

Adapted from 1MA1/3H, November 2017, Q20

Exam feedback ResultsPlus

Students should remember that this type of geometric proof requires full and correctly worded reasons
to be given.

16.4 Angles in circles 2

Key points

- Angles subtended at the circumference by the same arc are equal. Another form of the same theorem is that angles in the same segment are equal.
- A cyclic quadrilateral is a quadrilateral with all four vertices on the circumference of a circle.
- Opposite angles in a cyclic quadrilateral add up to 180°.
- An exterior angle of a cyclic quadrilateral is equal to the opposite interior angle.
- The angle between the tangent and the chord is equal to the angle in the alternate segment. This is called the alternate segment theorem.

△ Purposeful practice 1

Each diagram shows a circle. Work out the size of each angle marked with a letter.

1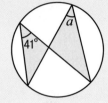

2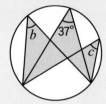

3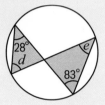

Reflect and reason

Which circle theorem did you use to find the missing angles in **Q1–3**?

△ Purposeful practice 2

Each diagram shows a circle. Work out the size of each angle marked with a letter.

1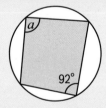

2

3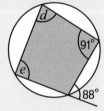

Reflect and reason

What property of the quadrilaterals makes them cyclic and therefore satisfy the cyclic quadrilateral theorem?

△ Purposeful practice 3

Each diagram shows a circle. Work out the size of each angle marked with a letter.

1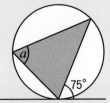

2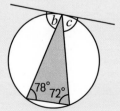

3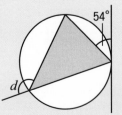

Reflect and reason

Which circle theorem did you use to find the missing angles in **Q1–3**?

1 The diagram shows a circle with points A, B, C and D on the
circumference.
Work out the size of angles x and y.
Give reasons for each step in your working.

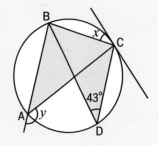

2 The diagram shows a circle, centre O. Points P, Q, R, S and T are
on the circumference.
Work out the size of angles a, b and c.
Give reasons for each step in your working.

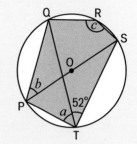

3 The diagram shows a circle. Points A, B, C and D are on the
circumference.
Is AB parallel to CD?
Give a reason for your answer.

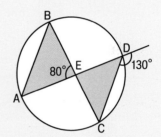

4 A, B, C and D are points on the circle. Write an expression for z in
terms of x and y.
Give reasons for each step in your working.

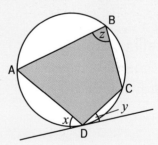

⊠ **Exam practice**

1 A, B, C and D are points on the circumference of a circle, centre O.
EDF is a tangent to the circle.
Show that angle BCD is $90 - x$.
You must give a reason for each stage of your working.   **(3 marks)**

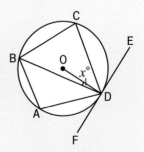

Adapted from 1MA1/2H, June 2018, Q13a

Exam feedback

ResultsPlus

Most students who achieved a **Grade 9** answered a similar question well.

Key points

- You can use the properties of tangents to find the equation of a tangent to a circle at a given point.
- The gradient of the radius is the negative reciprocal of the gradient of the tangent.

△ Purposeful practice 1

1 A circle has equation $x^2 + y^2 = 5$
Find the gradient of the radius at the points.

  a $(1, 2)$

  b $(2, -1)$

2 The diagrams show the circle with equation $x^2 + y^2 = 40$
Find the gradient of the tangents at the points shown.

a

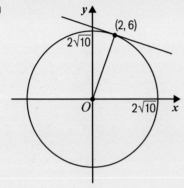

b

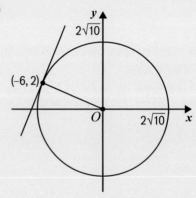

Reflect and reason

What shortcut can you use to find the gradient of the radius when a circle has a centre at the origin?

What circle theorem did you use to help you calculate the gradient of the tangent?

△ Purposeful practice 2

The diagrams show the circle with equation $x^2 + y^2 = 13$
Find the equation of the tangents at the points shown.

1

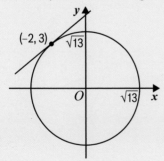

2

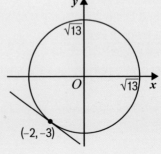

Reflect and reason

What knowledge of graphs of linear equations is required to find the equation of the tangent to a circle at a given point?

Problem-solving practice

1   Find the equation of the tangent to the circle $x^2 + y^2 = 25$ at the points

   a $(3, 4)$

   b $(4, 3)$

2   A circle has equation $x^2 + y^2 = 10$

   Find the coordinates where the tangent to the circle at the point $(1, -3)$ meets the y-axis.

3   A circle has equation $x^2 + y^2 = 34$

   Find the coordinates where the tangent to the circle at the point $(3, 5)$ meets the x-axis.

4   A circle has equation $x^2 + y^2 = 41$

   The tangent to the circle at the point $(4, 5)$ meets the x-axis at point R and the y-axis at point T.

   Find the area of the triangle ORT where O is the origin.

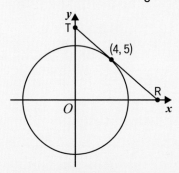

5   A circle has equation $x^2 + y^2 = 20$

   The tangent to the circle at the point $(-2, 4)$ meets the x-axis at point P and the y-axis at point Q.

   Find the distance PQ as a simplified surd.

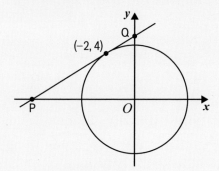

Exam practice

1   L is the circle with equation $x^2 + y^2 = 3$

   $P\left(\dfrac{3}{2}, \dfrac{\sqrt{3}}{2}\right)$ is a point on L.

   Find the equation of the tangent to L at the point P.   **(3 marks)**

Adapted from 1MA1/2H, June 2017, Q23

Exam feedback

In a similar question, students who understood the question gained at least two marks for the gradient of each of the normal and the tangent.

Mixed exercises D

Mixed problem-solving practice D

1   Here are some graphs.

A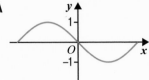

B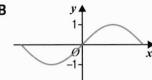

C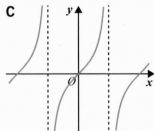

D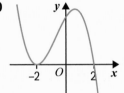

E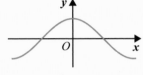

F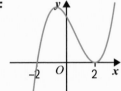

G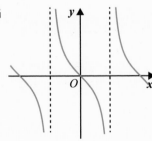

H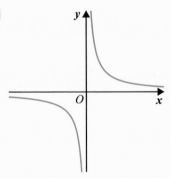

I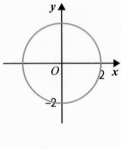

a   Match each equation with the letter of its graph.

   i $y = \sin x$ **ii** $y = \cos x$ **iii** $y = \tan x$

   iv $y = \dfrac{1}{x}$ **v** $x^2 + y^2 = 4$ **vi** $y = (x + 2)(x - 2)^2$

b   Write an equation for any graph you have not matched.

2   The cumulative frequency graph shows information about the heights of 60 students.

a   Use the graph to find an estimate for the median height.

Jane says, '190 − 160 = 30, so the range of the heights is 30 cm.'

b   Is Jane correct? You must give a reason for your answer.

c   Show that fewer than 25% of the students have a height greater than 175 cm.

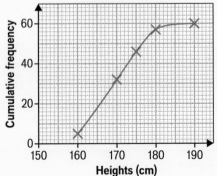

Heights of students

217

3 The expression $x^2 - 10x + 28$ can be written in the form $(x - a)^2 + b$ for all values of x.

a What is the value of a and the value of b?

The equation of a curve is $y = f(x)$ where $f(x) = x^2 - 10x + 28$
The diagram shows part of a sketch of the graph of $y = f(x)$.
The minimum point of the curve is M.

b Write down the coordinates of M.

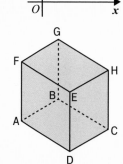

4 ABCDEFGH is a cuboid.
CD = 7.5 cm
BG = 8.3 cm
Angle BDC = 50°
Find the size of the angle between DG and the plane ABCD.
Give your answer correct to 1 d.p.

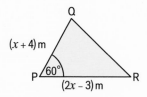

5 The area of triangle PQR is $8\sqrt{3}$ m².
Calculate the value of x.
Give your answer correct to 3 s.f.

6 The histogram shows information about the time, in minutes, taken by a group of students to travel to school in one day.

a Draw a frequency table for this information.

b Find an estimate for the lower quartile of the times taken to travel to school.

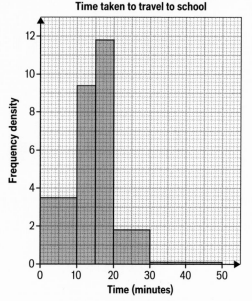

Time taken to travel to school

7 Write down the three inequalities that define the shaded region.

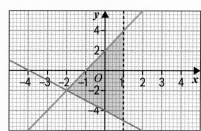

8 **a** Draw the graph of $y = \sin x$ for $0° \leqslant x \leqslant 360°$

b On the same axes, draw the graph of $y = 1 - \sin x$

9 The equation of a curve is $y = f(x)$ where $f(x) = 2x^2 - 12x + 7$
The diagram shows part of a sketch of the graph of $y = f(x)$
The minimum point of the curve is M.
Write down the coordinates of M.

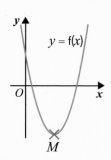

✦ Exam practice

10 The box plot shows information about the distribution of the weights of some cougars.

a Work out the interquartile range for the weights of these cougars. **(2 marks)**

Weights of cougars

The table below shows information about the distribution of the weights of some leopards.

	Smallest	Lower quartile	Median	Upper quartile	Range
Weight	43 kg	48 kg	55 kg	57 kg	26 kg

b Draw a box plot for the information in the table. **(2 marks)**

Tom says, 'The box plots show that the cougars weigh more than the leopards.'

c Is Tom correct? Give a reason for your answer. **(1 mark)**

Adapted from 1MA1/3H, June 2017, Q9

Exam feedback ResultsPlus

Q10a: Most students who achieved a **Grade 5** or above answered a similar question well.
Q10b: Most students who achieved a **Grade 3** or above answered a similar question well.

✦ Exam practice

11 a Copy the grid. Draw the graph of $x^2 + y^2 = 20.25$ **(2 marks)**

b Hence find estimates for the solutions of the simultaneous equations.
$x^2 + y^2 = 20.25$
$3x + y = 1$ **(3 marks)**

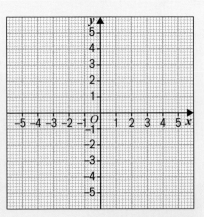

Adapted from 1MA1/2H, June 2018, Q16

Exam feedback ResultsPlus

Q11a: Most students who achieved a **Grade 7** or above answered a similar question well.
Q11b: Most students who achieved a **Grade 9** answered a similar question well.

12 Solve

$2x^2 + 5x - 3 > 0$ **(3 marks)**

Adapted from 1MA1/3H, June 2017, Q19

Exam feedback

Most students who achieved a **Grade 9** answered a similar question well.

ResultsPlus

 ⭐ **Exam practice**

13 a Show that the equation $x^3 + x = 17$ has a solution between 2 and 3. **(2 marks)**

b Show that the equation $x^3 + x = 17$ can be rearranged to give

$x = \sqrt[3]{17 - x}$ **(1 mark)**

c Starting with $x_0 = 3$, use the iteration formula $x_{n+1} = \sqrt[3]{17 - x_n}$ three times to find an estimate for a solution of $x^3 + x = 17$

Give your answer to 2 decimal places. **(3 marks)**

Adapted from 1MA1/3H, June 2018, Q18

Exam feedback

ResultsPlus

Q13a: Most students who achieved a **Grade 8** or above answered a similar question well.

Q13b and Q13c: Most students who achieved a **Grade 6** or above answered similar questions well.

⭐ **Exam practice**

14 The diagram shows a hexagon ABCDEF.

ABEF and CBED are congruent trapeziums where AB = BC = x cm

M is the point on AF and N is the point on CD such that BM = BN = 5 cm

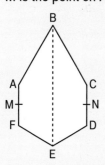

Given that angle ABC = 45°, prove that

$\cos MBN = 1 - \dfrac{x^2(2 - \sqrt{2})}{50}$ **(5 marks)**

Adapted from 1MA1/1H, June 2017, Q22

Exam feedback

ResultsPlus

Many students found a similar question difficult. They made errors in applying the cosine rule and wrote the wrong angle for $\cos 45°$.

17 More algebra

Key points

- When the letter to be made the subject is part of a term involving a power or root, rearrange so that this whole term is on its own on one side of the equation. You can then use inverse operations to eliminate the power or root.
- When the letter to be made the subject appears twice in the formula you will need to factorise.

⚠ Purposeful practice 1

Make k the subject of each formula.

1 $t = \dfrac{2ak}{5bc}$ **2** $t = \dfrac{2a + k}{5b}$ **3** $t = \dfrac{2a + 2k}{5b}$ **4** $t = \dfrac{2ak^2}{5b}$

5 $t = \dfrac{2a + k^2}{5b}$ **6** $t = \dfrac{2a + 3k^2}{5b}$ **7** $t = \dfrac{2a}{5b} + k$ **8** $t = \dfrac{2a}{5b} + \dfrac{k}{4}$

9 $t = \dfrac{2a}{5b} + k^2$ **10** $t = \dfrac{2a}{5b} + k^3$ **11** $t = 2a\sqrt{k}$ **12** $t = \dfrac{2}{5}a\sqrt{k}$

13 $t = \dfrac{2a\sqrt{k}}{5bc}$ **14** $t = \dfrac{2a}{5b} + \sqrt{k}$ **15** $t = \dfrac{2a}{5b} + \sqrt[3]{k}$ **16** $t = \sqrt{\dfrac{2a}{5b} + k}$

17 $t = \dfrac{\sqrt{2a + k}}{5b}$ **18** $t = \dfrac{\sqrt{2a + 7k}}{5b}$

Reflect and reason

Look at **Q9**. Tommy's working is shown opposite.

Tommy has made an error taking the square root of both sides.

Explain what he has done wrong.

$$t = \frac{2a}{5b} + k^2$$
$$t - \frac{2a}{5b} = k^2$$
$$\sqrt{t} - \sqrt{\frac{2a}{5b}} = \sqrt{k^2}$$
$$k = \sqrt{t} - \sqrt{\frac{2a}{5b}}$$

⚠ Purposeful practice 2

Make a the subject of each formula.

1 $a - ab = 3$ **2** $4a - ab = 3$ **3** $4a - 6ab = 3$

4 $4a - 6ab = 3 + c$ **5** $4a - 6ab = 3b + c$ **6** $4a = 3b + 6ab + c$

7 $2 = \dfrac{3b + c}{2a - 3ab}$ **8** $b(a + c) = ac$ **9** $b(a + c) = c(a - b)$

Reflect and reason

Arvin makes g the subject of each of these formulae

$$7g = 4g + 2f - 2g - 3a \qquad\qquad 7g = 4fg + 2f - 2g - 3a$$

His first step is to collect all the terms that contain g on the left-hand side.

Explain why he needs to factorise to help make g the subject in the second formula, but not in the first.

1 Jodie and Francis make h the subject of the formula $p = ah^2 + a$

Francis writes   The answer is $h = \sqrt{\dfrac{p - a}{a}}$

Jodie writes   The answer is $h = \sqrt{\dfrac{p}{a} - 1}$

Show that these two answers are equivalent to each other.

2 The formula for the volume of a cone is $V = \frac{1}{3}\pi r^2 h$

  a Find an expression for h in terms of π using $r = 10$ and $V = 200$.

  b Find an expression for r in terms of π using $h = 5$ and $V = 350$.

3 The cosine rule is $a^2 = b^2 + c^2 - 2bc \cos\theta$

Show that $\cos\theta = \dfrac{b^2 + c^2 - a^2}{2bc}$

4

The formula for the surface area of a cylinder is $2\pi r^2 + 2\pi rh$.
A cylinder has a total surface area A, radius r and height h.
Write h in terms of A and r.

5 Make g the subject of the formula.

$$h = \dfrac{\sqrt{g + 3}}{\sqrt{g}}$$

6 John's answer to a question is $b = \dfrac{3 - t}{7 - rt}$

The textbook answer is $b = \dfrac{t - 3}{rt - 7}$

What single step should John apply to his answer to transform it to the textbook answer?

7 Hannah is rearranging the formula $V + 1 = \dfrac{V}{x}$ to make V the subject.
Identify the two errors she has made.

$$V + 1 = \frac{V}{x}$$
$$x(V + 1) = V$$
$$xV + 1 = V$$
$$1 = V + xV$$
$$1 = V(1 + x)$$
$$\frac{1}{1 + x} = V$$

1 Make t the subject of the formula

$$k = \sqrt{\dfrac{(t^2 - 1)}{3}}$$

(3 marks)

Adapted from 1MA1/1H, Specimen Papers, Set 1, Q13

Key points

- The lowest common denominator of two fractions is the lowest common multiple of the denominators.
- When multiplying algebraic fractions, you can cancel common factors in numerators and denominators before multiplying the fractions together.

◿ Purposeful practice 1

Write as a single fraction in its simplest form.

1 $\dfrac{x}{2} + \dfrac{x}{3}$

2 $\dfrac{5x}{2} + \dfrac{x}{4}$

3 $\dfrac{5x}{2} - \dfrac{1}{3}$

4 $\dfrac{5x}{2} - 2$

5 $\dfrac{5x}{2} - 2x$

6 $\dfrac{5x}{2} - \dfrac{2x}{6}$

7 $\dfrac{x+2}{3} + \dfrac{x}{2}$

8 $\dfrac{x+2}{3} + \dfrac{x-4}{2}$

9 $\dfrac{x+2}{3} - \dfrac{3x-4}{2}$

10 $\dfrac{x+2}{4} - \dfrac{2x-4}{2}$

11 $\dfrac{1}{2x} + \dfrac{1}{3x}$

12 $\dfrac{1}{9x} + \dfrac{5}{3x}$

13 $\dfrac{5}{9x} - \dfrac{1}{3x}$

14 $\dfrac{1}{9x} - \dfrac{5}{3x}$

15 $\dfrac{1}{5x} + \dfrac{5}{3x}$

Reflect and reason

Joe says, 'The lowest common denominator of **Q11** is $6x^2$.'

Joe is wrong.

Explain his error.

◿ Purposeful practice 2

Write as a single fraction in its simplest form.

1 $\dfrac{x}{2} \times \dfrac{y}{3}$

2 $\dfrac{x}{2} \times \dfrac{x}{3}$

3 $\dfrac{9x}{2} \times \dfrac{x}{3}$

4 $\dfrac{9x}{2} \times \dfrac{x}{5}$

5 $\dfrac{9x}{2} \times \dfrac{y^2}{5}$

6 $\dfrac{9x^4}{2x^3} \times \dfrac{y^2}{3}$

7 $\dfrac{9x^4}{2y^5} \times \dfrac{y^2}{3x^3}$

8 $\dfrac{9x^4}{2x^5y^5} \times \dfrac{y^2}{3x^3}$

9 $\dfrac{9x^4}{2x^5y^5} \times \dfrac{y+6}{3x^3}$

10 $\dfrac{9x^4}{2x^5y^5} \times \dfrac{y+6}{x^4}$

11 $\dfrac{9x^4}{2x^5y^5} \times 6x^3y^2$

12 $\dfrac{1}{x} \div \dfrac{1}{y}$

13 $\dfrac{1}{y} \div \dfrac{1}{x}$

14 $\dfrac{x}{2} \div \dfrac{x}{3}$

15 $\dfrac{3x^2}{2} \div \dfrac{x}{3}$

16 $\dfrac{3x^2}{4} \div 5x$

17 $5x \div \dfrac{3x^2}{4}$

18 $\dfrac{5x}{15} \div \dfrac{x+5}{10}$

Reflect and reason

Look at **Q9**. Explain what you will need to do if you do not cancel all the factors before multiplying the two numerators and the two denominators.

⊠ Problem-solving practice

1 A train driver's journey is 300 miles in each direction.
   For the first half of the journey, he travels at x mph.
   On his return journey he travels 10 mph slower.

   Time $= \dfrac{\text{distance}}{\text{speed}}$

   Form an expression for the total time, T, the train spends travelling during this journey.
   Give your answer as a single fraction.

2 Fill in the missing values $\dfrac{\Box x + 3}{\Box} + \dfrac{x + 2}{4} = \dfrac{9x + 8}{4}$

3 Find an expression for the height, h, of each shape.
   Give your answer as a single fraction.

   a
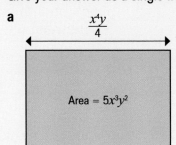

   $\dfrac{x^4 y}{4}$

   Area $= 5x^3 y^2$

   b

   Area $= 6\dfrac{x^2}{y^3}$

   $\dfrac{18x}{y}$

4 Fill in the missing terms.

   a $\dfrac{7}{2x} + \dfrac{5}{\Box} = \dfrac{\Box}{6x}$

   b $\dfrac{\Box x + 2}{3} - \dfrac{x - 5}{4} = \dfrac{5x + \Box}{12}$

   c $\dfrac{25x^2}{7\Box} \div \dfrac{\Box\Box}{21y^4} = \dfrac{15y}{2}$

✦ Exam practice

1 Write as a single fraction in its simplest form.

   $\dfrac{2x + 3}{5} - \dfrac{x - 4}{10}$ **(3 marks)**

2 Write as a single fraction in its simplest form.

   $\dfrac{2y^5}{3x} \times \dfrac{x^3}{6}$ **(3 marks)**

Key point

- You may need to factorise before simplifying an algebraic fraction:
  1 Factorise the numerator and denominator.
  2 Divide the numerator and denominator by any common factors.

△ Purposeful practice 1

Simplify

1 $\dfrac{3(x-6)}{x-6}$

2 $\dfrac{3(x-6)^2}{x-6}$

3 $\dfrac{3(x-6)}{(x-6)^2}$

4 $\dfrac{3x(x-6)}{(x-6)}$

5 $\dfrac{3x^2(x-6)}{x(x-6)}$

6 $\dfrac{(x+3)(x-2)}{(x+3)}$

7 $\dfrac{(x+3)^2}{(x+3)(x-2)}$

8 $\dfrac{(x+3)(x+4)}{(x+3)(x-2)}$

9 $\dfrac{(x+5)(x-4)}{(x+4)(x+5)}$

Reflect and reason

Carlos simplifies a fraction in his final answer to **Q7**.

$\dfrac{\cancel{x}+3}{\cancel{x}+2}$

Carlos has made a mistake.

Explain why the fraction cannot be cancelled in this way.

△ Purposeful practice 2

Simplify

1 $\dfrac{x^2+3x+2}{x^2+6x+8}$

2 $\dfrac{x^2+4x+3}{x^2+3x+2}$

3 $\dfrac{x^2+6x+9}{x^2+2x-3}$

4 $\dfrac{x^2-3x-4}{x^2+x-20}$

5 $\dfrac{x^2+x-6}{x^2+2x-8}$

6 $\dfrac{x^2-1}{x^2+2x+1}$

7 $\dfrac{x^2-1}{x^2+4x+3}$

8 $\dfrac{x^2+5x+6}{x^2-4}$

9 $\dfrac{x^2+x-2}{x^2-4}$

10 $\dfrac{4x^2-16}{2x^2+6x+4}$

11 $\dfrac{2x^2-2}{2x^2+4x-6}$

12 $\dfrac{4x^2+16x+16}{2x^2-6x-20}$

13 $\dfrac{6x^2-7x+2}{6x^2-x-2}$

14 $\dfrac{9x^2-4}{3x^2-17x+10}$

15 $\dfrac{5x^2+17x+6}{x^2-x-12}$

Reflect and reason

Fiona correctly factorises and cancels an algebraic fraction.

$$\dfrac{2x^2+10x+8}{x^2+5x+4}=\dfrac{(2x+8)\cancel{(x+1)}}{(x+4)\cancel{(x+1)}}=\dfrac{2\cancel{(x+4)}}{\cancel{(x+4)}}$$

Look at the original fraction.

What could Fiona have realised about the numerator, in relation to the denominator, that would have made the simplification easier?

1 Simplify the fraction $\dfrac{x^2 - y^2}{x + y}$

Use your result to work out the value of $\dfrac{625 - 169}{38}$

2 Show that $\dfrac{6x^2 + 10x + 4}{4x^2 - 2x - 6}$ can be written in the form $\dfrac{ax + b}{bx - a}$

3 Write an algebraic fraction, with quadratic expression in the numerator and denominator, that simplifies to $\dfrac{(x + 3)}{(x - 2)}$

4 Fill in the missing numbers.

$\dfrac{x^2 - 5x - \square}{x^2 - \square} = \dfrac{(x + 2)}{(x + 7)}$

5 Simplify

$\dfrac{2x^2 - 8}{4 - x^2}$

6 Work out expressions for the area of

a

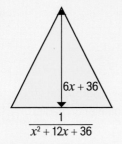

$\dfrac{1}{x^2 + 6x + 5}$

$x^2 - 25$

b

$6x + 36$

$\dfrac{1}{x^2 + 12x + 36}$

7 Simplify

$\dfrac{-x^2 + x + 6}{x + 2}$

8 Show that

$\dfrac{(9 - x^2)(x^2 - 3x - 10)(2x^2 + 14x + 24)}{(14x + 42)(x^2 - 2x - 15)(x + 4)} = \dfrac{(3 - x)(x + 2)}{7}$

1 Show that

$\dfrac{5x^2 - 9x - 2}{3x^2 - 8x + 4}$

can be written in the form $\dfrac{ax + b}{cx + d}$ where a, b, c and d are integers. **(3 marks)**

Adapted from MA1/1H, Specimen Papers, Set 1, Q15

Key points

- The lowest common denominator of two algebraic fractions is the lowest common multiple of the two denominators.
- You may need to factorise the numerator and/or denominator before you multiply or divide algebraic fractions.

△ Purposeful practice 1

Simplify

1 $\dfrac{4x + 1}{2} - \dfrac{x - 2}{3}$

2 $\dfrac{1}{x} + \dfrac{1}{2x}$

3 $\dfrac{1}{x} + \dfrac{1}{2x^2}$

4 $\dfrac{1}{x + 2} + \dfrac{1}{x - 4}$

5 $\dfrac{5}{x + 2} - \dfrac{2}{x - 4}$

6 $\dfrac{5}{3x - 12} - \dfrac{2}{x - 4}$

7 $\dfrac{5x + 2}{4x} + \dfrac{2x - 3}{2x}$

8 $\dfrac{2}{x + 4} + \dfrac{7}{(x + 4)(x + 1)}$

9 $\dfrac{2}{(x + 4)(x - 3)} + \dfrac{7}{(x + 4)(x + 1)}$

10 $\dfrac{4}{x^2 + 5x + 6} + \dfrac{3}{x + 2}$

11 $\dfrac{3}{2x^2 + 3x - 2} - \dfrac{2}{2x^2 - 7x + 3}$

12 $\dfrac{1}{x^2 - 1} + \dfrac{4}{x^2 + 2x - 3}$

Reflect and reason

Ian adds two fractions together.

$$\dfrac{8}{5x} + \dfrac{4}{7x} = \dfrac{8 \times 7x}{35x^2} + \dfrac{4 \times 5x}{35x^2} = \dfrac{56x + 20x}{35x^2} = \dfrac{76x}{35x^2} = \dfrac{76x}{35x^2} = \dfrac{76}{35x}$$

Look at Ian's common denominator.

Suggest another common denominator he could have used, to make the calculation easier.

Is his answer correct?

△ Purposeful practice 2

Write as a single fraction in its simplest form.

1 $\dfrac{x + 2}{x + 1} \times \dfrac{x + 1}{x - 3}$

2 $\dfrac{3(x + 2)}{6(x + 1)} \times \dfrac{(x + 1)^2}{x - 3}$

3 $\dfrac{x + 2}{5x + 5} \times \dfrac{4x + 4}{x - 3}$

4 $(x + 4) \times \dfrac{6}{x^2 + 5x + 4}$

5 $\dfrac{x^2 + 8x + 16}{x - 3} \times \dfrac{x^2 - 6x + 9}{x + 4}$

6 $\dfrac{4x^2 + 2x - 12}{x^2 - 9x + 20} \times \dfrac{x^2 - 8x + 16}{6x^2 + 14x + 4}$

Reflect and reason

Ethan is multiplying two fractions.

He says, 'I cannot factorise a cubic, so I cannot simplify this any further.'

Explain how you could simplify this expression without having to factorise a cubic.

$$\dfrac{x^2 + 5x + 4}{x + 1} \times \dfrac{x - 2}{x^2 + 8x + 16}$$

$$= \dfrac{(x^2 + 5x + 4)(x - 2)}{(x + 1)(x^2 + 8x + 16)}$$

$$= \dfrac{x^3 - 2x^2 + 5x^2 - 10x + 4x - 8}{x^3 + 8x^2 + 8x + x^2 + 8x + 16}$$

$$= \dfrac{x^3 + 3x^2 - 6x - 8}{x^3 + 9x^2 + 16x + 16}$$

⊠ Problem-solving practice

1 Work out the perimeter of each shape.
Give your answer as a fraction in its simplest form.

a
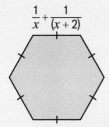
$\frac{1}{x} + \frac{1}{(x+2)}$

b
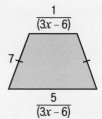
$\frac{1}{(3x-6)}$
7
$\frac{5}{(3x-6)}$

2 Work out the volume of each shape.
Give your answer as a fraction in its simplest form.

a
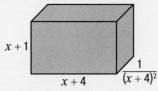
$x+1$
$x+4$
$\frac{1}{(x+4)^2}$

b
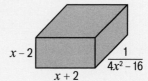
$x-2$
$x+2$
$\frac{1}{4x^2-16}$

3 a Work out the expression for the base of the rectangle.

$$\text{Area} = \frac{4x^2 - 2x - 12}{x - 8} \quad 4x^2 - 16$$

b Work out the total volume of the two cuboids.
Give your answers as fractions in their simplest form.

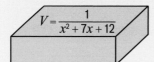
$V = \frac{1}{x^2 + 7x + 12}$

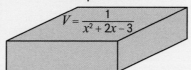
$V = \frac{1}{x^2 + 2x - 3}$

4 Fill in the missing terms.

$$\frac{1}{x^2 - \square} + \frac{2}{x + 5} = \frac{2x - 9}{\square - \square}$$

5 The lowest common multiple of two expressions is $x^2 - 1$.
Write down the two expressions.

6 Show that $\dfrac{1}{3x - 9} + \dfrac{1}{x^2 + 3x - 18} = \dfrac{x + A}{B(x - 3)(x + 6)}$
Find the values of A and B.

✦ Exam practice

1 Write as a single fraction in its simplest form.

$$\frac{3}{(x - 5)} - \frac{2}{x}$$

(3 marks)

Adapted from 1MA0/1H, November 2015, Q21a

Exam feedback   ResultsPlus

In a similar question, students made errors when finding the common denominator.

Key points

- To rationalise the fraction $\dfrac{1}{a\sqrt{b}}$, multiply by $\dfrac{\sqrt{b}}{\sqrt{b}}$

- To rationalise the fraction $\dfrac{1}{a \mp \sqrt{b}}$, multiply by $\dfrac{a \pm \sqrt{b}}{a \pm \sqrt{b}}$

△ Purposeful practice 1

Factorise these expressions.

1 $\sqrt{18} + 6$ 2 $\sqrt{12} + 6$ 3 $2\sqrt{18} + 6$

4 $\sqrt{72} + 6$ 5 $\sqrt{48} + \sqrt{72}$ 6 $\sqrt{96} + \sqrt{72}$

Reflect and reason

Look at **Q5**. Bobby's answer is $2\left(\sqrt{12} + \sqrt{18}\right)$

Explain why this should not be his final answer.

△ Purposeful practice 2

Expand and simplify

1 $4(\sqrt{3} + 2)$ 2 $\sqrt{2}(\sqrt{3} + 2)$ 3 $\sqrt{2}(\sqrt{3} - 8)$

4 $\sqrt{2}(6 - \sqrt{8})$ 5 $5\sqrt{2}(6 - \sqrt{8})$ 6 $5\sqrt{2}(6 - 4\sqrt{8})$

7 $(2 + \sqrt{3})^2$ 8 $(2 + 5\sqrt{3})^2$ 9 $(5 + \sqrt{6})(5 + \sqrt{6})$

10 $(8 + 2\sqrt{6})(8 - 2\sqrt{6})$ 11 $(10 - 4\sqrt{12})(10 - 4\sqrt{12})$ 12 $(10 - 4\sqrt{12})(10 + 4\sqrt{12})$

Reflect and reason

What pattern do you notice about the brackets that give a rational number when expanded and simplified?

△ Purposeful practice 3

Rationalise the denominators.

1 $\dfrac{1}{\sqrt{3} - 1}$ 2 $\dfrac{1}{1 + \sqrt{3}}$ 3 $\dfrac{1}{1 + \sqrt{2}}$

4 $\dfrac{1}{4 - \sqrt{2}}$ 5 $\dfrac{1}{4 - 2\sqrt{2}}$ 6 $\dfrac{6}{4 - 2\sqrt{2}}$

7 $\dfrac{1 + \sqrt{2}}{4 - \sqrt{2}}$ 8 $\dfrac{1 + \sqrt{2}}{4 - 2\sqrt{2}}$ 9 $\dfrac{1}{(1 + \sqrt{2})^2}$

Reflect and reason

Look at **Q6**.

Freya's answer is $\dfrac{24 - 12\sqrt{2}}{8}$

Freya is incorrect.

Explain what Freya forgot to do with her answer.

1 Simplify

a $\sqrt{2} + \dfrac{4}{\sqrt{8}} + \sqrt{72}$

b $3\sqrt{8} - 4\sqrt{50} + \dfrac{3}{\sqrt{2}} + 2\sqrt{5}$

2 Find the area of the rectangle.
Leave your answer in the form $a + b\sqrt{2}$

$5 + \sqrt{2}$

$2 + \sqrt{18}$

3 What is the missing length of this rectangle?
Leave your answer in the form $a + b\sqrt{2}$

Area $= 6 + \sqrt{8}$ $2 - \sqrt{2}$

4 Solve

a $x^2 + 2x - 5 = 0$ by completing the square.

b $3x^2 - 4x - 3 = 0$ using the quadratic formula.

Leave your answers in surd form.

5 Simplify

$$\dfrac{\sqrt{2}}{\left(2 - \sqrt{2}\right)^2}$$

6 Express $1 + \dfrac{1}{\sqrt{3}}$ as a single fraction, rationalising the denominator.

7 Andrew is rationalising the denominator of a fraction.

$$\dfrac{1 - \sqrt{3}}{2 + \sqrt{2}} = \dfrac{1 - \sqrt{3}}{2 + \sqrt{2}} \times \dfrac{2 - \sqrt{2}}{2 - \sqrt{2}}$$

$$= \dfrac{2 - \sqrt{2} - 2\sqrt{3} + \sqrt{5}}{4 - 2\sqrt{2} + 2\sqrt{2} - 2}$$

$$= \dfrac{\cancel{2} - \sqrt{2} - \cancel{2}\sqrt{3} + \sqrt{5}}{\cancel{2}}$$

$$= 1 - \sqrt{2} - \sqrt{3} + \sqrt{5}$$

a He has made two errors. Identify them.

b What should the answer be?

1 $\dfrac{1 + \sqrt{2}}{\left(\sqrt{2} - 3\right)^2}$ can be written in the form $\dfrac{a + b\sqrt{2}}{c}$

Find the value of a and the value of b. **(5 marks)**

Key points

- To solve equations involving algebraic fractions, first write one side as a fraction in its simplest form.
- To solve a quadratic equation, rearrange it into the form $ax^2 + bx + c = 0$.

△ Purposeful practice 1

Solve

1 $\dfrac{39}{x} + \dfrac{5}{x} = 11$

2 $\dfrac{1}{x} + \dfrac{1}{2x} = 2$

3 $\dfrac{4}{x} + \dfrac{1}{2x} = 6$

4 $\dfrac{3}{x} + \dfrac{5}{2x} = \dfrac{1}{2}$

5 $\dfrac{3}{5x} + \dfrac{6}{2x} = 12$

6 $\dfrac{1}{x + 2} + \dfrac{3}{x + 2} = 1$

7 $\dfrac{1}{x + 2} - \dfrac{4}{x + 2} = 3$

8 $\dfrac{1}{2x + 4} - \dfrac{4}{x + 2} = -\dfrac{7}{10}$

9 $\dfrac{1}{2x + 4} - \dfrac{4}{3x + 6} = \dfrac{1}{2}$

Reflect and reason

Benji starts to solve an equation

$$\frac{1}{2x - 4} - \frac{x - 4}{x - 2} = -\frac{7}{10}$$

$$\frac{1}{2x - 4} - \frac{2(x - 4)}{2(x - 2)} = -\frac{7}{10}$$

$$\frac{1 - 2x - 8}{2x - 4} = -\frac{7}{10}$$

Benji has made a mistake.

Explain Benji's error.

△ Purposeful practice 2

1 Solve

a $\dfrac{12}{x} + \dfrac{13}{x} = x$

b $\dfrac{2}{x} + \dfrac{12}{2x} = x$

c $\dfrac{x + 1}{x} + \dfrac{48}{x} = x + 1$

d $\dfrac{3x + 16}{x} = x + 3$

2 Solve these equations. Give your answers to 2 d.p.

a $\dfrac{1}{x - 3} - \dfrac{1}{x + 2} = 1$

b $\dfrac{1}{x - 3} - \dfrac{1}{x + 2} = 2$

c $\dfrac{3}{x - 3} - \dfrac{1}{x + 2} = 2$

d $\dfrac{3}{x - 3} - \dfrac{4}{x + 2} = 2$

e $\dfrac{3}{x - 3} - \dfrac{4}{x + 2} = \dfrac{2}{3}$

f $\dfrac{x}{x - 3} - \dfrac{4}{x + 2} = 2$

g $\dfrac{3}{x - 3} = \dfrac{x}{x + 2}$

h $\dfrac{x}{x - 19} + \dfrac{x}{x + 1} = 0$

i $\dfrac{x + 4}{x} + \dfrac{x + 3}{4x} = 1$

Reflect and reason

Alfie answers **Q2h**. The end of Alfie's working is

$2x^2 - 18x = 0$

$x^2 - 9x = 0$

He says, 'I can now divide all the terms by x to give $x - 9 = 0$, so $x = 9$.'

Explain why Alfie is wrong.

⊠ Problem-solving practice

1 The sum of a number and 6 times its reciprocal add to make 5.
Give the possible values of the number.

2 A third of my age plus three quarters of my age is 26.

  a Form an equation to represent this problem.

  b What is my age?

3 There are two resistors in an electrical circuit.
The resistance of resistor $R_1 = x$
The resistance of resistor $R_2 = 2x$
The formula for finding the total resistance, R_T, is $\dfrac{1}{R_1} + \dfrac{1}{R_2} = \dfrac{1}{R_T}$
The total resistance $R_T = 2000$ Ohms.
Work out R_1 and R_2

4 Two rectangles have areas $5\,\text{cm}^2$ and $10\,\text{cm}^2$.

a Area = $5\,\text{cm}^2$

$x - 3$

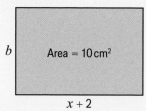

b Area = $10\,\text{cm}^2$

$x + 2$

The total of the length of a and b is $2\,\text{cm}$.

  a Work out the possible values of x.

  b Explain why one of these values of x is not relevant.

5 Edmund solves $\dfrac{3}{x + 1} - \dfrac{2}{2x + 1} = 1$.
Here is his working.

$$\frac{3(2x + 1)}{(x + 1)(2x + 1)} - \frac{2(x + 1)}{(2x + 1)(x + 1)} = 1$$

$$\frac{6x + 3 - 2x + 2}{2x^2 + 3x + 1} = 1$$

$$\frac{4x + 5}{2x^2 + 3x + 1} = 1$$

$$4x + 5 = 2x^2 + 3x + 1$$

$$0 = 2x^2 - x + 6$$

  a Find two errors in his working.

  b Correct the working and solve the equation.

6 Find the exact solutions of
$$2x + \frac{2}{x + 2} = 4$$

✦ Exam practice

1 Solve
$$\frac{x + 3}{4x} + \frac{x - 2}{3x} = 4$$

(3 marks)

Adapted from 1MA1/1H, Specimen Papers, Set 1, Q14

Key points

- A function is a rule for working out values of y for given values of x.
  For example, $y = 3x$ and $y = x^2$ are functions. The notation f(x) is read as 'f of x'. f is the function.
  f(x) = $3x$ means the function of x is $3x$.
- fg is a composite function. To work out fg(x), first work out g(x) and then substitute your answer into f(x).
- The inverse function reverses the effect of the original function.
- $f^{-1}(x)$ is the inverse of f(x).

△ Purposeful practice 1

1 h(x) = $x^2 + x$
   Work out

   a h(0)   **b** h(3)   **c** h(−4)   **d** h(0.5)   **e** h$\left(\dfrac{1}{3}\right)$ **f** h(−3.4)

2 k(x) = $\dfrac{x^2 + 8}{x + 2}$
   Work out

   a k(0)   **b** k(3)   **c** k(−4)   **d** k(0.5)   **e** k$\left(\dfrac{1}{3}\right)$ **f** k(−3.4)

Reflect and reason

f(x) = $x^2 + 4$
Tim works out f(−3). His calculator display is shown opposite.
Tim has made a mistake. Explain what he has done wrong.

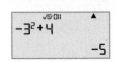

△ Purposeful practice 2

f(x) = $3x − 4$ g(x) = $x^2 + x$ h(x) = $7 − x$
Work out

1 fg(3)   **2** fg(5)   **3** fg(−4)   **4** gf(3)   **5** gf(5)   **6** gf(−4)

7 gh(3)   **8** gh(5)   **9** gh(−4)   **10** hg(3)   **11** hg(5)   **12** hg(−4)

Reflect and reason

Jamie has two functions, n(x) and y(x).
Explain how he would work out yn(3).

△ Purposeful practice 3

Find the inverse of each function.

1 f(x) = $3x$ **2** f(x) = $3x + 2$ **3** f(x) = $\dfrac{x}{3} + 2$

4 f(x) = $\dfrac{5x}{3} + 2$ **5** f(x) = $\dfrac{x + 2}{3}$ **6** f(x) = $\dfrac{4x + 2}{3}$

7 f(x) = $4(x + 3)$ **8** f(x) = $4(5x + 3)$ **9** f(x) = $\dfrac{4(5x + 3)}{7}$

Reflect and reason

Explain how the order of operations of f(x) helps you to find $f^{-1}(x)$.

1   $k(x) = \dfrac{2}{x + 3}$

    a Write as a single fraction.

      i $k(2x)$ **ii** $k(-x)$ **iii** $k(x) + 3$

    b Explain why we cannot work out $k(-3)$.

2   $d(x) = 5x - 4$

    a Work out $d^{-1}(x)$.

    b Work out the value of x such that $d(x) = d^{-1}(x)$

3   For which of these functions does $f(x) = f^{-1}(x)$?

    A $f(x) = 3 + x$ **B** $f(x) = 10 - x$ **C** $f(x) = \dfrac{10 - x}{2}$

    D $f(x) = \dfrac{6}{x}$ **E** $f(x) = 3x - 6$

4   $f(x) = x^2 - 16$

    $h(x) = x + 4$

    Find the values of x such that

    a $f(x) + h(x) = 8$ **b** $f(x) = 6h(x)$

5   $q(x) = 2x - 5$

    $t(x) = 6(x + 8)$

    Find the value of x such that $q^{-1}(x) = t^{-1}(x)$

6   $k(x) = x^2 - 2x$ and $c(x) = 10 - 2x^2$

    $k(a) + c(a) = 5$

    Find the two values of a.

    Leave your answers as simplified surds.

7   $d(x) = 2x + 4$

    $f(x) = x^2 - 1$

    Find the values of x such that $fd(x) + 1 = df(x)$

8   $f(x) = 3x - 4$

    Find the value of x such that $f^{-1}(x) = 33$.

9   $g(x) = ax + b$

    $g(2) = 11$ and $g(9) = 39$

    Form a pair of simultaneous equations. Find the values of a and b.

▦ ✧ **Exam practice**

1   The functions f and g are such that

    $f(x) = 5x + 1$

    $g(x) = ax + b$

    where a and b are constants.

    $g(3) = 20$ and $f^{-1}(81) = g(1)$

    Find the value of a and the value of b.   **(5 marks)**

Adapted from 1MA1/2H, November 2017, Q22

Exam feedback   Results**Plus**

In a similar question, only a small number of students were able to set up the correct simultaneous equations. Some students did not realise that they had to find the inverse function to $f(x)$.

Key point

- A proof is a logical argument for a mathematical statement. To prove a statement is true, you must show that it will be true in **all** cases.
  To prove a statement is not true you can find a counter-example – an example that does not fit the statement.

△ Purposeful practice 1

Give a counter-example to prove that these statements are not true.

1 A fraction multiplied by another fraction will always give an answer that is also a fraction.

2 When subtracting two numbers, changing their order will always give a different answer.

3 A number squared is always bigger than the original number.

4 The sum of two consecutive square numbers is always a prime number.

Reflect and reason

Explain why you only ever need to give one counter-example.

△ Purposeful practice 2

1 Explain how you know that $x^2 + 4$ will always give positive answers.

2 **a** Copy and complete.
   Even numbers are multiples of ☐.

   b Explain why $2a$ is an even number, for any non-zero integer value of a.

3 $2m$ is an even number.
   $2n$ is a second even number.
   Copy and complete the statement to prove a result about the sum of two even numbers.
   $2m + 2n = 2(m + n)$
   $m + n$ is either odd or even.
   $2(m + n)$ is odd/even/either odd or even because ☐.

4 $2m + 1$ and $2n + 1$ are two different odd numbers.
   Copy and complete the statements to prove a result about the product of two odd numbers.
   $(2m + 1)(2n + 1) = 4mn + 2m + 2n + 1 = 2(2mn + n + m) + 1$
   $2(2mn + n + m)$ is odd/even/either odd or even because ☐.
   Adding 1 to the previous expression will therefore be odd/even/either odd or even
   because ☐.

5 Explain why the nth term rule $2n + 3$ will never generate even numbers.

6 **a** Write expressions to represent three consecutive numbers.

   b Prove that the sum of three consecutive odd numbers is always odd.

7 Prove that the product of two consecutive numbers is even.

Reflect and reason

Emelia is writing an algebraic proof. She writes the expression $(a + b + c)^2$
a, b and c are integers.
Explain what type of number squaring the bracket will give.

1 **a** Choose any integer.
Add the next integer to it.
Add 9 to your total.
Now divide that answer by 2.
Subtract your original number.
What is your answer?

b Choose a different integer.
What is your answer now?

c Prove using algebra that the answer will always be the same.

2 Find a counter-example to these statements.

a A Fibonacci sequence starts with the numbers $\frac{1}{2}$ and $\frac{1}{3}$. The sequence will never have an integer term.

b If Lauren squares a number and adds 1, the answer will be a prime number.

c The sum of any two cube numbers is always even.

d The cube of an integer will always be greater than the integer.

3 Show that the sum of the squares of two consecutive even numbers will always be a number in the 4 times table.

4 Show by factorising that the sequence $4n^2 + 4n + 1$ will never have values that are a multiple of 2.

5 Prove that the sum of two consecutive square numbers will always be odd.

6 Show that $\dfrac{1}{2x^2 - 8} - \dfrac{1}{2x^2 + 4x} = \dfrac{A}{x(x^2 - 4)}$ and find the value of A.

7 The solution to $3x - a = 15$ is an integer value of x.
Explain why a is a number in the 3 times table.

8 The diagram shows a large triangle. A smaller triangle is cut out and removed.

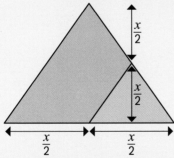

Show that the area of the shape that is left is represented by the expression $\dfrac{3x^2}{8}$

9 n is a positive integer.
Show that $(2n - 2)^2 - (4n - 4)(n - 2)$ will only give numbers that are a multiple of 4.

1 Prove, algebraically, that the difference between any two square numbers will be equal to the sum of the numbers multiplied by the difference of the two numbers. **(4 marks)**

Adapted from 1MA1/1H, Specimen Papers, Set 1, Q20

18 Vectors and geometric proof

18.1 Vectors and vector notation

Key points

- A vector is a quantity that has magnitude and direction.
  The magnitude of a vector is its size.
  Displacement is change in position. A displacement can be written as $\begin{pmatrix} 3 \\ 4 \end{pmatrix}$ where 3 is the x component and 4 is the y component.
- The displacement vector from A to B is written $\overrightarrow{AB}$.
  Vectors are written as bold lower case letters **a**, **b**, **c**.
  When handwriting, underline the letter <u>a</u>, <u>b</u>, <u>c</u>.
- Equal vectors have the same magnitude and the same direction.
- The magnitude of the vector $\begin{pmatrix} x \\ y \end{pmatrix}$ is its length, i.e. $\sqrt{x^2 + y^2}$
  |a| means the magnitude of the vector **a**. |OA| means the magnitude of vector $\overrightarrow{OA}$.

△ Purposeful practice 1

1 The point A is (5, 4).
   Find the coordinates of B where $\overrightarrow{AB}$ is

   a $\begin{pmatrix} 3 \\ 4 \end{pmatrix}$ **b** $\begin{pmatrix} -3 \\ 4 \end{pmatrix}$ **c** $\begin{pmatrix} 3 \\ -4 \end{pmatrix}$ **d** $\begin{pmatrix} -3 \\ -4 \end{pmatrix}$

   e $\begin{pmatrix} 4 \\ 3 \end{pmatrix}$ **f** $\begin{pmatrix} 4 \\ 4 \end{pmatrix}$ **g** $\begin{pmatrix} 0 \\ 4 \end{pmatrix}$ **h** $\begin{pmatrix} 4 \\ 0 \end{pmatrix}$

2 Write each displacement as a column vector.
   a (0, 0) to (3, 4)   **b** (1, 2) to (4, 6)   **c** (4, 7) to (1, 3)
   d (4, 7) to (2, 1)   **e** (7, 4) to (2, 1)   **f** (7, 4) to (1, 2)

Reflect and reason

Which column vectors in **Q2** are

   Equal? Explain how you know.
   Parallel, and in the same direction? Explain how you know.
   Equal and parallel, but in opposite directions? Explain how you know.

△ Purposeful practice 2

Work out the magnitude of each vector.
Where necessary, leave your answer as a surd.

1 $\begin{pmatrix} -3 \\ 4 \end{pmatrix}$ 2 $\begin{pmatrix} 3 \\ -4 \end{pmatrix}$ 3 $\begin{pmatrix} -3 \\ -4 \end{pmatrix}$ 4 $\begin{pmatrix} 6 \\ 8 \end{pmatrix}$ 5 $\begin{pmatrix} 8 \\ 6 \end{pmatrix}$ 6 $\begin{pmatrix} 8 \\ 3 \end{pmatrix}$

7 $\begin{pmatrix} 8 \\ 2 \end{pmatrix}$ 8 $\begin{pmatrix} 8 \\ 1 \end{pmatrix}$ 9 $\begin{pmatrix} 8 \\ 0 \end{pmatrix}$ 10 $\begin{pmatrix} 8 \\ -1 \end{pmatrix}$ 11 $\begin{pmatrix} 8 \\ -2 \end{pmatrix}$ 12 $\begin{pmatrix} -2 \\ 8 \end{pmatrix}$

Reflect and reason

Does the direction of the vector affect the magnitude? Explain your answer.

⊠ Problem-solving practice

1   A triangle has vertices A, B, C.

$$\overrightarrow{AB} = \begin{pmatrix} 0 \\ 3 \end{pmatrix} \qquad \overrightarrow{AC} = \begin{pmatrix} 4 \\ 0 \end{pmatrix}$$

   a   Find the column vector $\overrightarrow{BC}$.

   b   Work out the perimeter of the triangle.

   c   What type of triangle is triangle ABC?

2   Shape ABCD is a parallelogram.

$$\overrightarrow{AB} = \begin{pmatrix} 2 \\ 7 \end{pmatrix} \qquad \overrightarrow{BC} = \begin{pmatrix} 5 \\ 3 \end{pmatrix}$$

   A is the point (10, 10).

   a   Find the column vector $\overrightarrow{CD}$.

   b   Find the coordinates of D.

3   R is the point $(-3, -8)$.

   $\overrightarrow{RQ}$ is a vector such that Q has a negative x-coordinate and a positive y-coordinate.

   Write a possible column vector $\overrightarrow{RQ}$.

4   The magnitude of $\overrightarrow{ST}$ is 13.

$$\overrightarrow{ST} = \begin{pmatrix} 5 \\ h \end{pmatrix}$$

   S is the point $(-2, 3)$.

   Find the coordinates of T.

5   Vectors $\overrightarrow{LM}$ and $\overrightarrow{MN}$ each have a magnitude of 25.

   They are not parallel.

$$\overrightarrow{LM} = \begin{pmatrix} w \\ -7 \end{pmatrix}$$

   Give a possible vector for $\overrightarrow{MN}$.

✧ Exam practice

1   The vector **a** is shown on the grid.

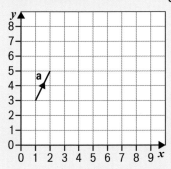

   Copy the grid. Draw and label the vector -2**a**.   **(1 mark)**

   Adapted from 1MA1/2H, June 2018, Q10a

Key points

- 2**a** is twice as long as **a** and in the same direction.
  −**a** is the same length as **a** but in the opposite direction.

- When a vector **a** is multiplied by a scalar k then the vector k**a** is parallel to **a** and is equal to k times **a**.

- A scalar is a number, e.g. $3, 2, \frac{1}{2}, -1 \ldots$

- The two-stage journey from A to B and then from B to C has the same starting point and the same finishing point as the single journey from A to C.
  So A to B followed by B to C is equivalent to A to C.
  $\overrightarrow{AB} + \overrightarrow{BC} = \overrightarrow{AC}$

  Triangle law for vector addition
  Let $\overrightarrow{AB} = $ **a**, $\overrightarrow{BC} = $ **b** and $\overrightarrow{AC} = $ **c**.
  Then **a** + **b** = **c** forms a triangle.

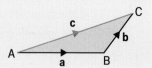

⚠ Purposeful practice 1

The vector **a** is $\begin{pmatrix} 2 \\ 3 \end{pmatrix}$. The vector **b** is $\begin{pmatrix} 0 \\ -3 \end{pmatrix}$.

1 Work out the column vector for

   a 2**a**   **b** 3**a**   **c** $\frac{1}{2}$**a**   **d** −**a**   **e** −2**a**

   f 2**b**   **g** 3**b**   **h** −3**b**   **i** −**b**   **j** **b** + $\begin{pmatrix} 1 \\ 1 \end{pmatrix}$

2 On squared paper, draw vectors to represent each vector from **Q1**.

Reflect and reason

Is it possible for a scalar multiple of vector **a** to be parallel to vector **b**?
Explain.

⚠ Purposeful practice 2

1 The vector **a** is $\begin{pmatrix} 2 \\ 1 \end{pmatrix}$. The vector **b** is $\begin{pmatrix} 3 \\ -1 \end{pmatrix}$. The vector **c** is $\begin{pmatrix} -2 \\ 3 \end{pmatrix}$.

   On squared paper, draw vectors to represent

   a **a** + **b**   **b** **a** + 2**b**   **c** **a** − **b**   **d** **b** − **a**

   e **a** + **c**   **f** **a** − **c**   **g** **a** − **c** + **b**   **h** **c** + **b** − **c**

2 Write a single column vector for each part of **Q1**.

3 Write a column vector that can be added to vector **a** to make it parallel to vector **b**.

4 Write the column vector that can be added to vector **b** to make it equal to **Q2c**.

Reflect and reason

Ali says, '2**a** = **a** − **c**.'
Is she correct?
Show your working.
If she is not correct, what mistake has she made?

⊠ Problem-solving practice

1 Vector $\overrightarrow{AC}$ is the result of adding two vectors $\overrightarrow{AB}$ and $\overrightarrow{BC}$.

$\overrightarrow{AC} = \begin{pmatrix} 9 \\ 18 \end{pmatrix}$ and $\overrightarrow{AB} = \begin{pmatrix} 3 \\ 8 \end{pmatrix}$

   a Find the column vector $\overrightarrow{BC}$.

   b Which of these vectors are parallel to $\overrightarrow{BC}$?

$\begin{pmatrix} 3 \\ 5 \end{pmatrix}$ $\begin{pmatrix} 3 \\ 7 \end{pmatrix}$ $\begin{pmatrix} 1 \\ 5 \end{pmatrix}$ $\begin{pmatrix} 9 \\ 15 \end{pmatrix}$

2 The vector $2\mathbf{a}$ is parallel and equal to the vector $\mathbf{a} + \mathbf{b}$.
What information can you state about the relationship between $\mathbf{a}$ and $\mathbf{b}$?

3 Sara draws the parallelogram TSRQ.

$\overrightarrow{TS} = \mathbf{a}$ $\overrightarrow{SR} = \mathbf{b}$

P is a point such that PQR is a straight line with Q at the midpoint of PR.

Is $\overrightarrow{SQ}$ parallel to $\overrightarrow{TP}$? Show your working.

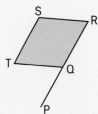

4 An isosceles trapezium is drawn such that the vector $\overrightarrow{AB} = \begin{pmatrix} 0 \\ -8 \end{pmatrix}$.

$\overrightarrow{DC} = \frac{1}{2}\overrightarrow{AB}$.

$\overrightarrow{BD} = -2\overrightarrow{AB} + \begin{pmatrix} 2 \\ -10 \end{pmatrix}$

What is the perimeter of the trapezium? Give your answer to 2 d.p.

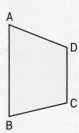

5 Shape ABCD is an isosceles trapezium.

The vector $\overrightarrow{AB}$ is $\begin{pmatrix} -1 \\ 6 \end{pmatrix}$.

The sides BC and AD are equal in length.
Give a possible column vector for $\overrightarrow{CD}$.

⊠ Exam practice

1 The vector $\mathbf{a}$ and the vector $\mathbf{b}$ are shown on the grid.

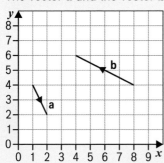

   a Copy the grid. Draw and label the vector $-3\mathbf{a}$ **(1 mark)**

   b Work out $\mathbf{a} + 3\mathbf{b}$ as a column vector.   **(2 marks)**

Adapted from 1MA1/2H, June 18, Q10

Exam feedback   Results**Plus**

Most students who achieved a **Grade 8** or above answered a similar question well.

Key points

- When **c** = **a** + **b**, the vector **c** is called the resultant vector of the two vectors **a** and **b**.
- In parallelogram PQRS where $\overrightarrow{PQ}$ is **a** and $\overrightarrow{PS}$ is **b**, the diagonal $\overrightarrow{PR}$ of the parallelogram is **a** + **b**. This is called the parallelogram law for vector addition.

△ Purposeful practice 1

In triangle ABC, M is the midpoint of BC.

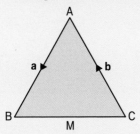

$\overrightarrow{AB}$ = **a** and $\overrightarrow{CA}$ = **b**

Write the resultant vector in terms of **a** and **b**.

1 $\overrightarrow{CB}$	2 $\overrightarrow{AC}$	3 $\overrightarrow{BA}$
4 $\overrightarrow{BA} + \overrightarrow{AC}$	5 $\overrightarrow{BC}$	6 $\overrightarrow{BM}$
7 $\overrightarrow{AB} + \overrightarrow{BM}$	8 $\overrightarrow{AM}$	9 $\overrightarrow{MA}$

Reflect and reason

Is it possible to find $\overrightarrow{AM}$ (**Q8**) without finding $\overrightarrow{BM}$ (**Q6**)?
Explain.

△ Purposeful practice 2

HIJK is a parallelogram.
$\overrightarrow{HI}$ = **h** and $\overrightarrow{HK}$ = **k**

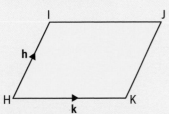

Write in terms of **h** and **k**

1 $\overrightarrow{KJ}$	2 $\overrightarrow{IJ}$	3 $\overrightarrow{HJ}$
4 $\overrightarrow{JH}$	5 $\overrightarrow{IK}$	

Reflect and reason

How did you use the information that HIJK is a parallelogram?

1 In trapezium ABCD, AD is triple the length of BC.
AD and BC are parallel.
$\overrightarrow{AB} = \mathbf{a}$ $\overrightarrow{BC} = \mathbf{b}$ $\overrightarrow{CD} = \mathbf{c}$

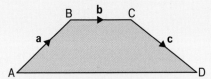

Show that $\mathbf{b} = \frac{1}{2}(\mathbf{a} + \mathbf{c})$

2 EFGH is a square.
M is the midpoint of EG.

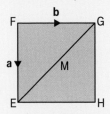

   a Write $\overrightarrow{MH}$ in terms of **a** and **b**.

   b $\mathbf{a} = \begin{pmatrix} -5 \\ 12 \end{pmatrix}$ and $\mathbf{b} = \begin{pmatrix} 12 \\ 5 \end{pmatrix}$

     Is triangle EMH an isosceles triangle?

3 IJKLMN is a regular hexagon.
O is the centre of the hexagon.
JO is parallel to KL.
KO is parallel to JI.
$\overrightarrow{IJ} = \mathbf{a}$ $\qquad$ $\overrightarrow{KL} = \mathbf{b}$

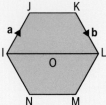

Show that IL is parallel to JK.

1 OPQR is a parallelogram.
$\overrightarrow{OP} = 2\mathbf{a}$
$\overrightarrow{OR} = 5\mathbf{b}$

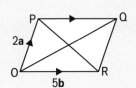

   a Find $\overrightarrow{OQ}$ in terms of **a** and **b**. **(1 mark)**

   b Find $\overrightarrow{PR}$ in terms of **a** and **b**.
     Give your answer in its simplest form. **(1 mark)**

Adapted from 1MA0/1H, June 2016, Q23a

18.4 Parallel vectors and collinear points

Key points

- With the origin O, the vectors $\overrightarrow{OA}$ and $\overrightarrow{OB}$ are called the position vectors of the points A and B. In general, a point with coordinates (p, q) has position vector $\begin{pmatrix} p \\ q \end{pmatrix}$.
- When $\overrightarrow{OA} = \mathbf{a}$ and $\overrightarrow{OB} = \mathbf{b}$, $\overrightarrow{AB} = \overrightarrow{AO} + \overrightarrow{OB} = \mathbf{b} - \mathbf{a}$
- $\overrightarrow{PQ} = k\overrightarrow{QR}$ shows that the lines PQ and QR are parallel. Also they both pass through point Q so PQ and QR are part of the same straight line. P, Q and R are said to be collinear (they all lie on the same straight line).

△ Purposeful practice 1

The points WXYZ have the coordinates (3, 4), (4, 5), (3, 5), (4, 4) respectively.
O is the origin.

1   Write the position vectors

    a $\overrightarrow{OW}$ **b** $\overrightarrow{OX}$ **c** $\overrightarrow{OY}$ **d** $\overrightarrow{OZ}$ **e** $\overrightarrow{WZ}$

2   Point V has coordinates (6, 10).

    a   Write the position vector $\overrightarrow{OV}$.

    b   OV is collinear with one of the position vectors in **Q1**.
        Which one?

Reflect and reason

Why will the position vectors for the vertices of a trapezium never be collinear equal vectors?

△ Purposeful practice 2

1   Work out the column vector $\overrightarrow{AC}$ for each set of coordinates.

    a   A(0, 0), B(2, 4), C(4, 8)

    b   A(1, 1), B(3, 5), C(5, 9)

    c   A(1, 1), B(3, 5), C(4, 8)

    d   A(0, 0), B(1, 1), C(2, 4)

    e   A(2, 4), B(3, 5), C(5, 9)

    f   A(2, 2), B(3, 5), C(4, 8)

2   Work out the column vector $\overrightarrow{AB}$ for each set of coordinates in **Q1**.

3   Using your answers from **Q1** and **Q2**, state whether each set of coordinates is collinear.

4   For each set of coordinates in **Q1**, state whether the position vector of point C is collinear with the vector $\overrightarrow{AC}$.

5   In which parts of **Q1** is the vector $\overrightarrow{AC}$ parallel to $\begin{pmatrix} 2 \\ 4 \end{pmatrix}$?

Reflect and reason

In **Q1a**, **Q1b** and **Q1f**, coordinate B is the midpoint of the two coordinates A and C.

Will three points, where one of the coordinates is the midpoint of the other two, always be collinear?
Explain.

1   KL is a line such that the vector $\overrightarrow{KL} = \begin{pmatrix} -6 \\ 5 \end{pmatrix}$.
    K is the point (3, 2).
    $\overrightarrow{LM} = \begin{pmatrix} -9 \\ 7.5 \end{pmatrix}$

    a Do the points KLM form a straight line?
       Give reasons.

    b Give the coordinates of the point M.

2   $\overrightarrow{RT}$ and $\overrightarrow{PW}$ are parallel.
    $\overrightarrow{PW} = 5\overrightarrow{RT}$.
    $\overrightarrow{PW} = \begin{pmatrix} g \\ 10 \end{pmatrix}$ $\overrightarrow{RT} = \begin{pmatrix} 12 \\ h \end{pmatrix}$
    Find the values of g and h.

3   Two vectors, **a** and **b** are not parallel.
    $\mathbf{a} = \begin{pmatrix} -5 \\ 6 \end{pmatrix}$
    Give a vector for **b** such that 2**a** + 3**b** is parallel to **a** − **b**.

4   Given that **a** and **b** are parallel

    a is **a** + **b** parallel to **a**?
       Give reasons.

    b is **a** − **b** parallel to **b**?
       Give reasons.

    c is 2**a** + **b** parallel to **a**?
       Give reasons.

5   GH is a line such that $\overrightarrow{GH} = \begin{pmatrix} 3 \\ x \end{pmatrix}$.

    HL is a line such that $\overrightarrow{HL} = 2\overrightarrow{GL}$ and the points GHL are collinear.
    G has coordinates (0, 0) and L has coordinates (9, 12).
    Work out the value of x.

6   The point P is (3, 0) and the point Q is (5, 8).
    Point R is such that its distance from Q is half the distance between P and Q.
    Give a point R such that it is collinear with P and Q, and show that it is collinear.

7   X is the point (3, 4), Y is the point (10, 12), W is the point (8, a).

    a Give the value of a such that $\overrightarrow{XY}$ and $\overrightarrow{YW}$ are collinear.

    b Z is the point (b, 18).
       Give values for b and a such that $\overrightarrow{WY}$ is collinear with $\overrightarrow{YZ}$ but not $\overrightarrow{XW}$.

1   **a** $= \begin{pmatrix} -2 \\ 3 \end{pmatrix}$ **b** $= \begin{pmatrix} 4 \\ 2 \end{pmatrix}$
    Vector **c** is parallel to the vector **a** + **b** and three times its size.
    Write the vector **c**.   **(3 marks)**

Key points

- Some vector problems involve ratios.
  The point M lies on AB such that AM : MB = 1 : 3.
  $AM = \frac{1}{4} AB$

  A—✕—————B
       M

- To find the vector asked for in the question, sometimes you need to find other vectors first.

△ Purposeful practice 1

The vector $\overrightarrow{AB}$ is $\begin{pmatrix} 20 \\ 20 \end{pmatrix}$.

1 The point Q divides the line AB in the ratio 1 : 3.
   Write the column vector
   a $\overrightarrow{AQ}$ **b** $\overrightarrow{QB}$ **c** $\overrightarrow{BQ}$

2 The point R divides the line AB in the ratio 3 : 2.
   Write the column vector
   a $\overrightarrow{AR}$ **b** $\overrightarrow{RB}$ **c** $\overrightarrow{BR}$

Reflect and reason

Is $\overrightarrow{RB}$ collinear with $\overrightarrow{QB}$? Explain.

△ Purposeful practice 2

ABCDEF is a regular hexagon.
G is the centre of the hexagon.

$\overrightarrow{AB} = \mathbf{a}$ $\overrightarrow{BC} = \mathbf{b}$ $\overrightarrow{AF} = \mathbf{c}$

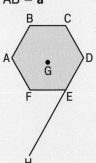

H is a point such that HED is a straight line.
E divides DH such that DE : EH = 1 : 3
Find in terms of **a**, **b** and **c**

1 $\overrightarrow{CD}$	2 $\overrightarrow{AD}$	3 $\overrightarrow{AG}$	4 $\overrightarrow{FG}$	5 $\overrightarrow{GF}$
6 $\overrightarrow{EH}$	7 $\overrightarrow{DH}$	8 $\overrightarrow{CH}$	9 $\overrightarrow{BH}$	10 $\overrightarrow{AH}$

Reflect and reason

Is it possible to find the vector $\overrightarrow{AH}$ without knowing the vector $\overrightarrow{EH}$? Explain.

1 The triangle ABC and the triangle ADE have side lengths in the ratio 5 : 2.
   E is a point such that AC is split into the ratio 2 : 3.
   The line DE is parallel to BC.
   $\overrightarrow{AD} = 2\mathbf{a}$ and $\overrightarrow{BC} = \mathbf{b}$

   Find the vector $\overrightarrow{BE}$ in terms of $\mathbf{a}$ and $\mathbf{b}$.

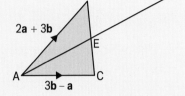

2 E is the midpoint of BC.
   E is the point such that AD is split in the ratio 1 : 4.
   Point A is $(-6, -2)$.
   $\overrightarrow{AB} = 2\mathbf{a} + 3\mathbf{b}$
   $\overrightarrow{AC} = 3\mathbf{b} - \mathbf{a}$

   a Find the vector $\overrightarrow{AD}$ in terms of $\mathbf{a}$ and $\mathbf{b}$.

   b $\mathbf{a} = \begin{pmatrix} 3 \\ 1 \end{pmatrix}$ and $\mathbf{b} = \begin{pmatrix} -2 \\ 5 \end{pmatrix}$

   Find the coordinates of the point D.

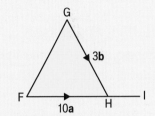

3 FI is a straight line.
   The point H is such that FI is split in the ratio 4 : 1.
   $\overrightarrow{GH} = 3\mathbf{b}$
   $\overrightarrow{FI} = 10\mathbf{a}$
   $\mathbf{a} = \begin{pmatrix} -3 \\ 4 \end{pmatrix}$ and $\mathbf{b} = \begin{pmatrix} 4 \\ -3 \end{pmatrix}$.

   a Find $\overrightarrow{FG}$ in terms of $\mathbf{a}$ and $\mathbf{b}$.

   b Find the perimeter of triangle FGH.

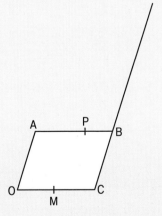

✦ Exam practice

1 OABC is a parallelogram.
   OMC, APB and CBN are straight lines.
   M is the midpoint of OC.
   BN = 2CB
   $\overrightarrow{OA} = \mathbf{a}$
   $\overrightarrow{OC} = \mathbf{b}$
   $\overrightarrow{AP} = k\overrightarrow{AB}$ where k is a scalar quantity.
   Given that MPN is a straight line, find the value of k. **(5 marks)**

Adapted from 1MA1/3H, November 2017, Q21

Exam feedback   ResultsPlus

In a similar question, mistakes were sometimes made with the direction sign of vectors. Also, many
students were unable to write the vector with the scalar quantity k.

19 Proportion and graphs

19.1 Direct proportion

△ Purposeful practice 1

1 Match the statements of proportionality.

$y \propto x$	x is directly proportional to y	$x = ky$
$x \propto y$	b is directly proportional to a	$b = ka$
$a \propto b$	y is directly proportional to x	$a = kb$
$b \propto a$	a is directly proportional to b	$y = kx$

Reflect and reason

Rupesh says, '$m \propto t$ means $m = t$.'

Explain what he has done wrong.

△ Purposeful practice 2

For each question, write the formula connecting the two variables.
The first one has been started for you.

1 y is directly proportional to x.
$y = 8$ when $x = 4$
$y \propto x$
$y = kx$
$8 = k \times 4$
$k = 2$
$y = \square$

2 y is directly proportional to x.
$y = 4$ when $x = 8$

3 y is directly proportional to x.
$y = 4$ when $x = -8$

4 y is directly proportional to x.
$x = 4$ when $y = -8$

5 a is directly proportional to b.
$a = 6$ when $b = 10$

6 a is directly proportional to b.
$a = -6$ when $b = 10$

7 a is directly proportional to b.
$a = -6$ when $b = -10$

8 a is directly proportional to b.
$a = 10$ when $b = 6$

9 p is directly proportional to q.
$p = 0.25$ when $q = 0.8$

10 p is directly proportional to q.
$p = 0.25$ when $q = 3.7$

11 h is directly proportional to d.
$h = \frac{1}{2}$ when $d = 3$

12 h is directly proportional to d.
$h = \frac{1}{2}$ when $d = \frac{3}{5}$

Reflect and reason

What types of number can the numerical constant k be?

In **Q8**, **Q10**, **Q11** and **Q12**, why is it better to write the value of k as a fraction rather than as a decimal?

⊠ Problem-solving practice

1 v is directly proportional to m.
$v = 15$ when $m = 3$
Find m when $v = 48$

2 y is directly proportional to x.
The table gives some values of x and y.

x	−5	−2	0	
y		3		−10.5

Work out the missing values of x and y.

3 r is directly proportional to z.
$r = -3.9$ when $z = 5$
Find a formula for r in terms of z.

4 The price of flour is directly proportional to its weight, so $p \propto w$.

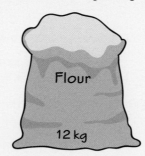

Work out the price of the 12 kg sack of flour.

5 y is directly proportional to x.
$y = 1\frac{1}{3}$ when $x = 2$
Find y when $x = 42$

6 The table gives some values for m and t.

m	0.7	0.9	1.6
t	2.66	3.42	6.08

Show that t is directly proportional to m.

✧ Exam practice

1 s is directly proportional to t.
When $t = 30$, $s = 7.5$
Find the value of s when $t = 24$

(3 marks)

Adapted from 1MA0/2H, June 2014, Q24

Exam feedback

ResultsPlus

In a similar question, some students incorrectly rearranged the equation to find the constant of proportionality, k.

Key point

- A quantity can be directly proportional to the square, the cube, or the square root of another quantity. For example

  if y is proportional to the square of x then $y \propto x^2$ and $y = kx^2$

  if y is proportional to the cube of x then $y \propto x^3$ and $y = kx^3$

  if y is proportional to the square root of x then $y \propto \sqrt{x}$ and $y = k\sqrt{x}$

 ## △ Purposeful practice 1

For each question, write a formula connecting the two variables.
The first has been started for you.

1 y is directly proportional to x^2.
$y = 8$ when $x = 4$
$y \propto x^2$
$y = kx^2$
$8 = k \times 4^2$
$k = \dfrac{1}{2}$
$y = \square$

2 y is directly proportional to x^3.
$y = 8$ when $x = 4$

3 y is directly proportional to $\sqrt{x}$.
$y = 8$ when $x = 4$

4 z is directly proportional to a^2.
$z = -5$ when $a = 1$

5 z is directly proportional to a^3.
$z = -5$ when $a = 1$

6 z is directly proportional to $\sqrt{a}$.
$z = -5$ when $a = 1$

7 f is directly proportional to g^2.
$f = 1.5$ when $g = 4$

8 f is directly proportional to g^3.
$f = 1.5$ when $g = 4$

9 f is directly proportional to $\sqrt{g}$.
$f = 1.5$ when $g = 4$

10 w is directly proportional to t^2.
$w = 1$ when $t = 3$

11 w is directly proportional to t^3.
$w = 1$ when $t = 3$

12 w is directly proportional to $\sqrt{t}$.
$w = 1$ when $t = 3$

Reflect and reason

What types of number can the numerical constant k be?

In **Q7** and **Q8**, how did you write the value of k? How else could you write it?

In **Q12**, what is the most accurate way to write the value of k?

△ Purposeful practice 2

1 y is directly proportional to x^2.
$y = 5$ when $x = 10$
Find y when $x = 0$

2 y is directly proportional to x^3.
$y = 5$ when $x = 10$
Find y when $x = 0$

3 y is directly proportional to $\sqrt{x}$.
$y = 5$ when $x = 10$
Find y when $x = 0$

Reflect and reason

Do you need to find the constant of proportionality to find the value of y when $x = 0$? Explain.

1   A stone is dropped from a tower.
    The distance the stone falls, d, is directly proportional to the square of the time, t, since it
    was dropped.
    After 4 seconds the stone has fallen 160 m.
    Write a formula for d in terms of t.

2   The volume, V, of a balloon is directly proportional to the cube of its radius, r.
    When the radius is 5 cm, the volume is 520 cm³.
    Write a formula for V in terms of r.

3   The cost, C, of a piece of carpet is directly proportional to the square root of its area, A.
    25 m² of carpet costs £180.00.
    Write a formula for C in terms of A.

4   The distance, d, travelled by a car at a constant speed is proportional to time, t.
    At time $t = 10$ seconds, the car has travelled a distance of 62 metres.

    a How far will the car have travelled after 1 minute?

    b How many seconds will it take for the car to travel 1 km?
       Give your answer to the nearest second.

5   The cost, C, of sending a parcel is directly proportional to the cube of its length, l.
    It costs £8.00 to send a parcel with a length of 0.2 m.
    Work out the cost of sending a parcel with a length of 0.3 m.

6   y is directly proportional to $\sqrt{x}$.
    $y = 1\frac{1}{5}$ when $x = 4$
    Find the value of y when $x = 9$

7   The width, w, of a tree is directly proportional to the square of its height, h.
    A tree with a height of 6 m has a width of 7.2 m.
    Find the height of a tree with a width of 4 m.
    Give your answer to the nearest centimetre.

8   The velocity, v, of an object is directly proportional to the square root of its kinetic energy, E.
    When $v = 6$ m/s, $E = 144$ J
    Find the kinetic energy of the object when its velocity is 10 m/s.

9   y is directly proportional to $\sqrt[3]{x}$.
    When $x = 1000$, $y = 140$
    Find the value of y when $x = 64$

1   y is directly proportional to $\sqrt[3]{x}$.
    y is $1\frac{1}{3}$ when $x = 27$
    Find the value of y when $x = 8$ **(3 marks)**

Adapted from 1MA1/1H, November 2017, Q16

Exam feedback   Results**Plus**

In a similar question, most students were not able to find the equation and many struggled with using
fractions.

Key point

- When y is inversely proportional to x, $y \propto \dfrac{1}{x}$ and $y = \dfrac{k}{x}$

  When y is inversely proportional to x^2, $y \propto \dfrac{1}{x^2}$ and $y = \dfrac{k}{x^2}$

  When y is inversely proportional to x^3, $y \propto \dfrac{1}{x^3}$ and $y = \dfrac{k}{x^3}$

  When y is inversely proportional to $\sqrt{x}$, $y \propto \dfrac{1}{\sqrt{x}}$ and $y = \dfrac{k}{\sqrt{x}}$

△ Purposeful practice 1

For **Q1–3**

    a find y when $x = 0.1$ **b** find y when $x = -0.1$

    c find y when $x = 0.01$ **d** find y when $x = -0.01$

1 y is inversely proportional to x. $y = 10$ when $x = 4$

2 y is inversely proportional to x^2. $y = 10$ when $x = 4$

3 y is inversely proportional to x^3. $y = 10$ when $x = 4$

4 y is inversely proportional to $\sqrt{x}$. $y = 10$ when $x = 4$

    a Find the positive value of y when $x = 0.1$ **b** Find the negative value of y when $x = 0.1$

    c Find the positive value of y when $x = 0.01$ **d** Find the negative value of y when $x = 0.01$

Reflect and reason

When y is inversely proportional to a power of x

    what happens to the value of y as positive values of x get closer and closer to zero?

    what happens to the value of y as negative values of x get closer and closer to zero?

Use your answers to **Q1–3** to explain.

△ Purposeful practice 2

For **Q1–3**

    a find y when $x = 100$ **b** find y when $x = -100$

    c find y when $x = 1000$ **d** find y when $x = -1000$

1 y is inversely proportional to x. $y = 10$ when $x = 4$

2 y is inversely proportional to x^2. $y = 10$ when $x = 4$

3 y is inversely proportional to x^3. $y = 10$ when $x = 4$

4 y is inversely proportional to $\sqrt{x}$. $y = 10$ when $x = 4$

    a Find the positive value of y when $x = 100$ **b** Find the positive value of y when $x = 100$

    c Find the positive value of y when $x = 1000$ **d** Find the negative value of y when $x = 1000$

Reflect and reason

When y is inversely proportional to a power of x

    how does the value of y approach zero as positive values of x get larger and larger?

    how does the value of y approach zero as negative values of x get smaller and smaller?

Use your answers to **Q1–3** explain. Can y ever be equal to zero?

⊠ **Problem-solving practice**

1   y is inversely proportional to the square of x.
    When $x = 5$, $y = 4$
    Find the positive value of x when $y = 25$

2   y is inversely proportional to the square root of x.
    When $x = 4$, $y = 3$
    Find the value of x when $y = 9$

3   The table shows a set of values for x and y.

x	1	4	9	16
y	5	$2\frac{1}{2}$	$1\frac{2}{3}$	$1\frac{1}{4}$

    y is inversely proportional to the square root of x.
    a   Find an equation for y in terms of x.
    b   Find the value of y when $x = 64$
    c   Find the value of x when $y = -7$

⊠ **Exam practice**

1   The graphs of y against x represent four different types of proportionality.
    Match each graph to a proportionality statement.

Graph A   **Graph B**   **Graph C**   **Graph D**

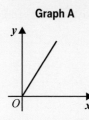   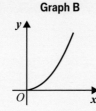   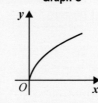   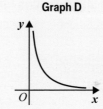

    i $y \propto \frac{1}{x}$
    ii $y \propto \sqrt{x}$
    iii $y \propto x^2$
    iv $y \propto x$
                                                                (2 marks)

Adapted from 1MA1/2H, May 2018, Q12

2   y is inversely proportional to d.
    When $d = 6$, $y = 3$
    d is directly proportional to x^2.
    When $x = 5$, $d = 50$
    Find a formula for y in terms of x.
    Give your answer in its simplest form.
                                                                (5 marks)

Adapted from 1MA1/1H, May 2018, Q14

Exam feedback   Results**Plus**

Q1: Most students who achieved a **Grade 6** or above answered a similar question well.
Q2: Most students who achieved a **Grade 8** or above answered a similar question well.

Key point

- Expressions of the form a^x, where a is a positive number, are called exponential functions.

⚠ Purposeful practice 1

1 Copy and complete the table of values for each exponential function.

   a $y = 2^x$ **b** $y = 3^x$ **c** $y = 4^x$

x	−5	−2	−1	0	1	2
y						

2 Copy and complete the table of values for each exponential function.

   a $y = \left(\frac{1}{2}\right)^x$ **b** $y = \left(\frac{1}{3}\right)^x$ **c** $y = \left(\frac{1}{4}\right)^x$

x	−2	−1	0	1	2	5
y						

Reflect and reason

For all the exponential functions in **Q1** and **Q2**, what is the value of y when $x = 0$?

Explain why all exponential graphs have the same y-intercept.

When y is an exponential function, can y ever be zero?

⚠ Purposeful practice 2

1 Draw the graphs of

   a $y = 2^x$

   b $y = \left(\frac{1}{2}\right)^x$

   Use your tables of values from Purposeful practice 1, **Q1** and **Q2**.

2 Which of your graphs shows

   a y values increasing as x increases?

   b y values decreasing as x increases?

3 a Draw the graph of $y = \left(\frac{1}{3}\right)^x$.

   Use your table of values from Purposeful practice 1, **Q2**.

   b Compare your graphs of $y = \left(\frac{1}{2}\right)^x$ and $y = \left(\frac{1}{3}\right)^x$.

   In which graph do the y values decrease the fastest?

   c Sketch the shape of the graph you expect for $y = \left(\frac{1}{4}\right)^x$.

   Draw the graph to check.

Reflect and reason

In the graphs you drew in **Q1**, y is the number of insects in a population and x is time.

Why is the graph of $y = a^x$ where $a > 1$ called an exponential growth curve?

Why is the graph of $y = a^x$ where $0 < a < 1$ called an exponential decay curve?

⊠ Problem-solving practice

1 The graph shows the decay curve for Strontium 90.
The half-life of Strontium 90 is the time it takes for
the mass of a sample to halve.

   a What is the half-life of Strontium 90?

   b What fraction of the original mass of Strontium
90 remains after 75 years?

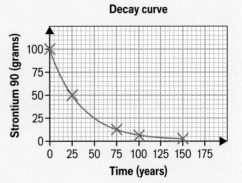

Decay curve

2 A bacterium cell divides to produce 2 cells every minute.

   a Copy and complete this table of values for the number of cells.

Time, t (minutes)	0	1	2	3	4	5
Number of cells, n	1	2				

   b Explain why this is an example of exponential growth.

3 There are 32 players in a tennis tournament.
Every player plays a match in the first round.
Each player who loses a match leaves the tournament.
The rest play a match in the second round.
Each player who loses a match leaves the tournament.

   a Explain why the number of players halves each round.

   b Show that the number of players, y, in the tournament after x rounds, is an exponential
function of the form $y = 32a^{x-1}$

   c Find the number of rounds needed to leave just one player – the winner of the tournament.

4 The graph shows the price of a brand of chocolate bar over 18 years.
A newspaper report says, 'Chocolate price grows exponentially'.
Give one reason why this statement is not accurate.

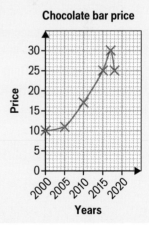

Chocolate bar price

⊛ Exam practice

1 The equation of a curve is $y = a^x$
Write down the coordinates of the y intercept of the curve.   **(1 mark)**

Adapted from 1MA1/3H, May 2017, Q20a

Exam feedback   ResultsPlus

Most students who achieved a **Grade 9** answered a similar question well.

Key points

- The tangent to a curved graph is a straight line that touches the graph at a point.
- The straight line that connects two points on a curve is called a chord.
- On a distance–time graph
  the gradient of the tangent at any point gives the speed at that time
  the gradient of a chord gives the average speed between two times
- On a velocity–time graph, the area under the curve shows the displacement or distance from the starting point.

 △ Purposeful practice 1

The distance–time graph shows information about part of a car journey.

1   Describe how the speed of the car changes as the time increases.

2   Copy or trace the graph. Draw tangents to the curve at
    a 1 second   **b** 4 seconds
    c 8 seconds

3   Use your tangents from **Q2** to estimate the speed of the car at
    a 1 second   **b** 4 seconds
    c 8 seconds

4   Draw chords to estimate the average speed
    a in the first 4 seconds   **b** in the first 8 seconds

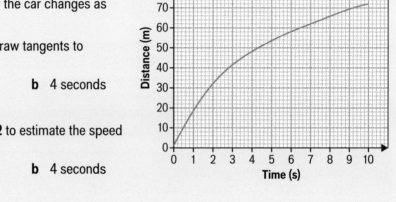

Car journey

Reflect and reason

Do the speeds you estimated in **Q3** and **Q4** fit with your answers to **Q1**?

How can you use the shape of the graph to check whether your answers are sensible?

 △ Purposeful practice 2

1   The two graphs show the speeds of two cars during the first 8 seconds of a journey.

    Each graph has 4 strips of equal width drawn on it.

    Calculate an estimate of the distance travelled by each car in the first 8 seconds.

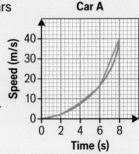

Car A

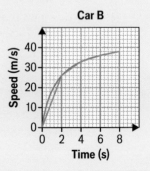

Car B

Reflect and reason

How can you tell from the shape of the graph whether your estimate for distance travelled is an overestimate or underestimate?

⬡ Problem-solving practice

1   The distance–time graph shows information about part of a
    train journey.
    Estimate the speed of the train at time 3 seconds.

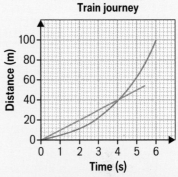

Train journey

2   For the distance–time graph in **Q1**, Fred drew a line like this
    to estimate the speed at 4 seconds.
    Explain what Fred has done wrong.

Train journey

3   The diagram shows part of the graph of
    $x^2 + 3x - 2$
    P is the point on the graph where $x = -3$
    Calculate an estimate for the gradient of the graph
    at the point P.

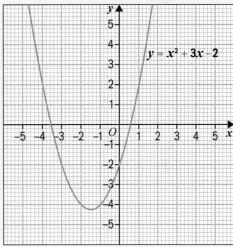

$y = x^2 + 3x - 2$

✸ Exam practice

1   The graph shows the speed of a motorbike, in metres per second,
    during the first 20 seconds of a journey.

    a Work out an estimate for the distance the motorbike travelled in
    the first 20 seconds.
    Use 4 strips of equal width.   **(3 marks)**

    b Is your answer to part **a** an underestimate or an overestimate of
    the actual distance the motorbike travelled in the first 20 seconds?
    Give a reason for your answer.   **(1 mark)**

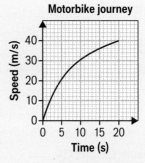

Motorbike journey

Adapted from 1MA1/3H, May 2018, Q15

Exam feedback

Most students who achieved a **Grade 7** or above answered a similar question well.

19.6 Translating graphs of functions

Key point

- The graph of $y = f(x)$ is transformed into the graph of $y = f(x) + a$ by $\begin{pmatrix} 0 \\ a \end{pmatrix}$

  The graph of $y = f(x)$ is transformed into the graph of $y = f(x + a)$ by $\begin{pmatrix} -a \\ 0 \end{pmatrix}$

△ Purposeful practice

Look at the table of values and graph of $y = f(x) = x^3$

x		−2	−1	0	1	2
$y = f(x) = x^3$		−8	−1	0	1	8

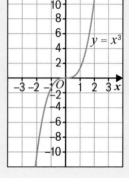

Copy and complete these tables of values and draw the graphs.

1 $y = f(x) + 1 = x^3 + 1$

x	−2	−1	0	1	2
x^3	−8	−1	0	1	8
$y = f(x) + 1 = x^3 + 1$					

2 $y = f(x) − 1 = x^3 − 1$

x	−2	−1	0	1	2
x^3	−8	−1	0	1	8
$y = f(x) − 1 = x^3 − 1$					

3 $y = f(x + 1) = (x + 1)^3$

x	−2	−1	0	1	2
x^3	−8	−1	0	1	8
$y = f(x + 1) = (x + 1)^3$					

4 $y = f(x − 1) = (x − 1)^3$

x	−2	−1	0	1	2
x^3	−8	−1	0	1	8
$y = f(x − 1) = (x − 1)^3$					

Reflect and reason

From **Q1** and **Q2**

how does adding 1 to $f(x)$ affect the y-values in the table and the graph?
how does subtracting 1 from $f(x)$ affect the y-values in the table and the graph?

From **Q3** and **Q4**

how does adding 1 to x shift the y-values in the table and the graph?
how does subtracting 1 from x shift the y-values and the graph?

257

1   The graph of $y = f(x)$ is shown on the grid.
    Sketch the graph of $y = f(x - 2)$

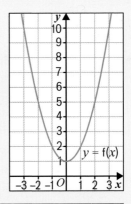

2   The graph of $y = f(x)$ is shown on the grid.
    The graph G is a translation of the graph of $y = f(x)$.
    Write down the equation of graph G.

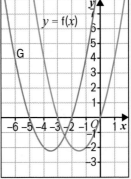

3   Here is the graph of $y = \cos x°$ for $-90 \leqslant x \leqslant 270$
    Sketch the graph of $y = \cos x° - 1$ for $-90 \leqslant x \leqslant 270$

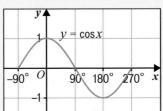

1   Here is the graph of $y = \sin x°$ for $-180 \leqslant x \leqslant 180$

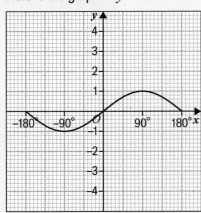

    Copy the grid and sketch the graph of $y = \sin x° + 2$ for $-180 \leqslant x \leqslant 180$ **(2 marks)**

    Adapted from 1MA1/1H, May 2018, Q18

Exam feedback   ResultsPlus

Most students who achieved a **Grade 7** or above answered a similar question well.

Key point

- The transformation that maps the graph $y = f(x)$ onto the graph $y = f(-x)$ is a reflection in the y-axis.
  The transformation that maps the graph $y = f(x)$ onto the graph $y = -f(x)$ is a reflection in the x-axis.

△ Purposeful practice 1

1 The diagram shows points A to D on a coordinate grid.
Copy and complete the table

Point	Coordinates of reflection in x-axis	Coordinates of reflection in y-axis
A(3, 2)		
B(−2, 3)		
C(1, −4)		
D(−4, −1)		

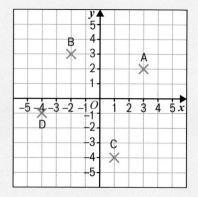

Reflect and reason

How does reflection in the x-axis change the coordinates of a point?

How does reflection in the y-axis change the coordinates of a point?

△ Purposeful practice 2

1 Here is a graph of $y = f(x) = (x - 1)^2$
Copy and complete this table of values and draw the graph of
$y = -f(x)$ and $y = -f(x) = -(x - 1)^2$

x			−2	−1	0	1	2
$y = f(x) = (x - 1)^2$			9	4	1	0	1
$y = -f(x) = -(x - 1)^2$							

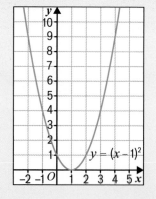

2 Copy and complete this table of values for $y = f(-x) = (-x - 1)^2$

x			−2	−1	0	1	2
$y = f(x) = (x - 1)^2$			9	4	1	0	1
$y = f(-x) = (-x - 1)^2$				0			9

3 Draw the graphs of $y = f(x) = (x - 1)^2$ and $y = f(-x) = (-x - 1)^2$ on the same coordinate grid.

Reflect and reason

What transformation maps $y = f(x)$ onto $y = -f(x)$?

What transformation maps $y = f(x)$ onto $y = f(-x)$?

1 The graph of $y = f(x)$ is shown on the grid.
   Copy the diagram and sketch

   a the graph of $y = f(-x)$

   b the graph of $y = -f(x)$

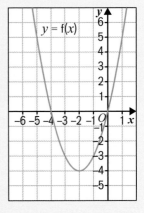

2 Here is the graph of $y = \cos x°$ for $-90 \leq x \leq 270$
   Sketch the graph of $y = -\cos x°$ for $-90 \leq x \leq 270$

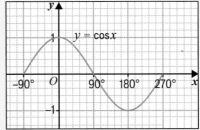

3 Here is the graph of $y = \sin x°$ for $-180 \leq x \leq 180$
   Sketch the graph of $y = \sin(-x)°$ for $-180 \leq x \leq 180$

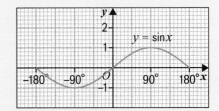

4 The graph of $y = f(x)$ is shown on the grid.

   a Copy the diagram and sketch the graph of
   $y = f(-x) + 3$

   b Find the coordinates of the image of the point
   $(-1, 2)$ after the transformation $y = f(-x) + 3$

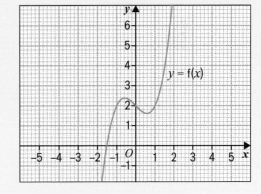

Exam practice

1 The graph of $y = f(x)$ is transformed to give the graph of $y = -f(x) + 2$
   The point A on the graph of $y = f(x)$ is mapped to the point P on the graph of
   $y = -f(x) + 2$
   The coordinates of the point A are $(4, 5)$.
   Find the coordinate of the point P.   **(2 marks)**

   Adapted from 1MA1/3H, Specimen Papers, Set 1, Q16

Mixed exercises E

Mixed problem-solving practice E

1 A, B and C are points on the circumference of a circle, centre O.
OCD is a straight line.
AD is the tangent at A to the circle.
Angle ADO = 25°
Work out the size of angle ABC.
Give a reason for each stage of your working.

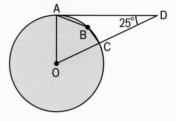

2 The vectors **a** and **b** are shown on the grid.
Work out **a** + **b** as a column vector.

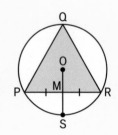

3 n is an integer.
Prove algebraically that the sum of $\frac{1}{2}n(n + 1)$ and $\frac{1}{2}(n + 2)(n + 9)$ is always a square number.

4 P, Q, R and S are points on the circumference of a circle, centre O.
PQR is an equilateral triangle.
OS bisects side PR at M.
Prove that OPS is an equilateral triangle.
Give reasons for each stage of your working.

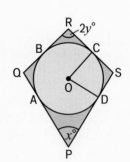

5 Chantal is asked to rationalise the denominator of $\frac{12}{2 - \sqrt{5}}$
Here is Chantal's working and answer.

$$\frac{12}{2 - \sqrt{5}} = \frac{12 \times (2 + \sqrt{5})}{(2 - \sqrt{5})(2 + \sqrt{5})}$$

$$= \frac{24 + 12\sqrt{5}}{4 - 2\sqrt{5} + 2\sqrt{5} + 5}$$

$$= \frac{24 + 12\sqrt{5}}{9}$$

$$= \frac{8 + 4\sqrt{5}}{3}$$

Chantal's answer is wrong. Explain why Chantal is wrong.

6 A, B, C and D are points on the circumference of a circle, centre O.
PAQ, QBR, RCS and SDP are tangents to the circle.
PQRS is a kite.
Angle APD = $x°$
Angle BRC = $2y°$
Find an expression in terms of x and y for the size, in degrees, of the angle COD.
Give your expression in its simplest form. Give reasons for your answer.

7 Make x the subject of the formula $\frac{1}{x} - \frac{1}{y} = 1$.

8 This is the graph of $y = f(x)$

The graph F is the reflection of $y = f(x)$

Write down an equation of graph F.

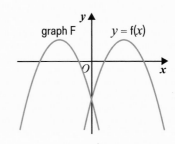

9 OAB is a triangle.

P is the midpoint of OA.

Q is the midpoint of OB.

$\overrightarrow{OP} = \mathbf{p}$

$\overrightarrow{OQ} = \mathbf{q}$

Show that AB is parallel to PQ.

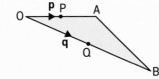

10 $2 - \dfrac{x + 1}{x - 2} - \dfrac{x - 4}{x + 2}$ can be written as a single fraction in the form $\dfrac{px + q}{x^2 - 4}$ where p and q are integers.

Work out the values of p and q.

11 Here is a sketch of the curve $y = -\sin(x + a)° + b, 0 \le x \le 360$

Find the values of a and b.

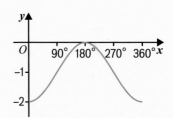

12 The diagram shows part of the graph of $y = x^2 - 3x + 4$

Calculate an estimate for the gradient of the graph at the point where $x = 3$

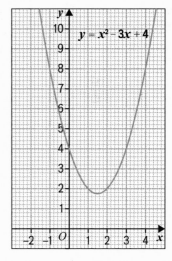

13 Triangles PQR and XYZ are mathematically similar.

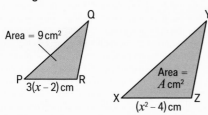

The base, PR, of triangle PQR has length $3(x - 2)$ cm.

The base, XZ, of triangle XYZ has length $(x^2 - 4)$ cm.

The area of triangle PQR is 9 cm^2

The area of triangle XYZ is A cm^2

Prove that $A = x^2 + 4x + 4$

14 For right-angled triangles, the adjacent side, a, is directly proportional to the hypotenuse, h.

$a = \sqrt{3}$ when $h = 2$

Calculate the value of h when $a = 7$.

Give your answer as a surd.

 ✦ **Exam practice**

15 f and g are functions such that

$f(x) = \dfrac{5}{x^2}$ and $g(x) = 10x^3$

  a Find f(–3)   **(1 mark)**

  b Find fg(1)   **(2 marks)**

Adapted from 1MA1/2H, June 2018, Q11

Exam feedback   **ResultsPlus**

Most students who achieved a **Grade 6** or above answered a similar question well.

✦ **Exam practice**

16 Make c the subject of the formula

$a = \dfrac{8(b + 3c)}{c}$ **(3 marks)**

Adapted from 1MA1/3H, June 2017, Q14b

Exam feedback   **ResultsPlus**

Most students who achieved a **Grade 7** or above answered a similar question well.

✦ **Exam practice**

17 The table shows a set of values for p and q.

q is inversely proportional to the square of p.

p	1	2	3	4
q	16	4	$1\frac{7}{9}$	1

  a Find an equation for q in terms of p.   **(2 marks)**

  b Find the positive value of p when $q = 25$ **(2 marks)**

Adapted from 1MA1/1H, June 2017, Q13

Exam feedback   **ResultsPlus**

Q17a: Most students who achieved a **Grade 7** or above answered a similar question well.

Q17b: Most students who achieved a **Grade 8** or above answered a similar question well.

18 A, B, C and D are four points on the circumference of a circle.
AEC and BED are straight lines.
Prove that triangle ABE and triangle DCE are similar.
You must give reasons for each stage of your working.

(3 marks)

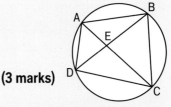

Adapted from 1MA1/2H, June 2017, Q15

Exam feedback

ResultsPlus

In a similar question, many students tried to prove the two triangles were congruent instead of similar.

19 y is inversely proportional to t^2.
When $t = 10, y = 3$
t is directly proportional to x^2.
When $x = 2, t = 20$
Find a formula for y in terms of x.
Give your answer in its simplest form.

(5 marks)

Adapted from 1MA1/1H, June 2018, Q14

Exam feedback

ResultsPlus

Most students who achieved a **Grade 8** or above answered a similar question well.

20 Prove algebraically that the straight line with equation $x - 2y = 15$ is a tangent to the circle with
equation $x^2 + y^2 = 45$ **(5 marks)**

Adapted from 1MA1/3H, November 2017, Q19

Exam feedback

ResultsPlus

In a similar question, some students rearranged the equation of the straight line to make either x or y
the subject. Those students who realised that they needed to solve the equations simultaneously then
substituted into the equation of the circle.

21 OMA, APB and OBN are straight lines.
BN = 3OB
M is the midpoint of OA.
$\overrightarrow{OA} = \mathbf{a}$, $\overrightarrow{OB} = \mathbf{b}$ and $\overrightarrow{BP} = k\overrightarrow{BA}$, where k is a scalar quantity.
Given that MPN is a straight line, find the value of k.

(5 marks)

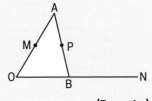

Adapted from 1MA1/3H, November 2017, Q21

Exam feedback

ResultsPlus

In a similar question, some students scored 1 mark for AB = $\mathbf{b} - \mathbf{a}$ or BA = $\mathbf{a} - \mathbf{b}$, but few were able to
make any further progress.

Answers

1 Number

1.1 Number problems and reasoning

Purposeful practice 1

1 2 ways   **2** 6 ways   **3** 24 ways   **4** 120 ways
5 60 ways   **6** 20 ways   **7** 5 ways   **8** 1 way

Purposeful practice 2

1 120   **2** 720   **3** 5040

Purposeful practice 3

1 a 900   **b** 450
2 720

Problem-solving practice

1 15   **2** 81   **3** 5   **4** 5 735 160
5 a 36   **b** 9
6 a 216   **b** 2 more dice

Exam practice

1 54 516 060   **2** 132

1.2 Place value and estimating

Purposeful practice 1

1 a 126 000   **b** 12 600   **c** 1260   **d** 12.6
  e 1.26   **f** 0.126   **g** 0.054 83   **h** 0.5483
  i 5.483   **j** 548.3   **k** 5483   **l** 54 830
2 a 463.68   **b** 463.68   **c** 463.68
3 a 20.48   **b** 20.48   **c** 20.48

Purposeful practice 2

1 6   **2** 7   **3** 6 or 7   **4** 7   **5** 6

Purposeful practice 3

1 a 100   **b** 100 000   **c** 40
  d 140   **e** 100 or 110   **f** 11
  g 11   **h** 0.25
2 a i underestimate   **ii** overestimate   **iii** difficult to tell
  b i underestimate   **ii** overestimate   **iii** difficult to tell

Problem-solving practice

1 0.3 to 0.7   **2** £300 to £315   **3** £75
4 2400 cm²   **5** Car B
6 a 19 250 cm²   **b** 0.1925 cm²   **c** 1.925 cm²
7 a Any answers where one number has been multiplied by a power of 10
   and the other number has been divided by the same power of 10.
   For example: $1790 \times 0.245 = 438.55$ or $17.9 \times 24.5 = 438.55$
  b Any answers where both numbers have been multiplied or divided by the
   same power of 10. For example $4970 \div 284 = 17.5$ or $49.7 \div 2.84 = 17.5$
8 a 20 kg to 21 kg
  b An underestimate. Both numbers in the estimate have been rounded
   down so the accurate answer is likely to be higher.

Exam practice

1 6

1.3 HCF and LCM

Purposeful practice 1

1 3×5 **2** $2 \times 3 \times 5$ **3** $2^2 \times 3 \times 5$
4 $2^2 \times 3 \times 5 \times 7$ **5** $2^2 \times 3^2 \times 5 \times 7$

Purposeful practice 2

1 Any two of 105, 126, 140, 180
2 Factors, multiple

Purposeful practice 3

1
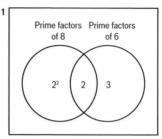
HCF = 2, LCM = 24

2
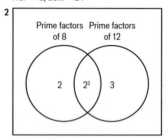
HCF = 4, LCM = 24

3
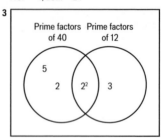
HCF = 4, LCM = 120

4
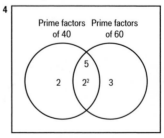
HCF = 20, LCM = 120

5
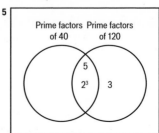
HCF = 40, LCM = 120

6

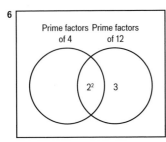

HCF = 4, LCM = 12

7

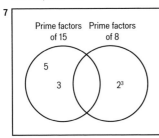

HCF = 1, LCM = 120

Purposeful practice 4

1 HCF = 1 LCM = 210	**2** HCF = 6 LCM = 12
3 HCF = 1 LCM = 330	**4** HCF = 50 LCM = 300
5 HCF = 24 LCM = 72	**6** HCF = 1 LCM = 600
7 HCF = 3 LCM = 45	**8** HCF = 2 LCM = 56

Problem-solving practice

1 a 6 is a factor because within the prime factors you can have 2×3.

  b 21 is not a factor of 1320 because 21 cannot be made by multiplying any of the prime factors of 1320.

2 24 and 30

3 Any pair of 2-digit numbers with no common factors (apart from 1), for example, 15 and 16

4 600 cm

5 $a = 540$ $b = 1$

Exam practice

1 9.42 am

2 a 390   **b** 45

1.4 Calculating with powers (indices)

Purposeful practice 1

1 3^4	**2** 3^6	**3** 3^8	**4** 3^{10}
5 3^8	**6** 3^6	**7** 3^4	**8** $3^0 = 1$

Purposeful practice 2

1 a 3^4 **b** 3^6 **c** 3^8 **d** 3^8 **e** 3^4

2 a 7^4 **b** 7^6 **c** $3^4 \times 7^1$ or $3^4 \times 7$

  d 7^7 **e** 7^7 **f** 7^{17}

  g 7^{12} **h** 7^{15} **i** 7^{12}

  j 7^8 **k** $6^2 \times 7^2$ **l** $6^{20} \times 7^7$

Problem-solving practice

1 3^6

2 a 5   **b** 9

3 3, 3

4 a 2^7 **b** 2^9 **c** 5^6

5 a $n = 10$ **b** $n = 10$

6 a 3^8 **b** 3^4

7 2^6

Exam practice

1 3^{12}

2 a $x = 5$ **b** $y = 5$

1.5 Zero, negative and fractional indices

Purposeful practice 1

1 5^4 **2** 5^3 **3** 5^2 **4** 5^1

5 5^0 **6** $5^{-1} = \dfrac{1}{5}$ **7** $5^{-2} = \dfrac{1}{5^2}$

Purposeful practice 2

1 a $\sqrt{7}$ **b** $\sqrt[3]{7}$ **c** $\sqrt[4]{7}$ **d** $\sqrt[5]{7}$ **e** $\dfrac{1}{\sqrt{7}}$ **f** $\dfrac{1}{\sqrt[3]{7}}$

2 a $6^{\frac{1}{2}}$ **b** $6^{\frac{1}{3}}$ **c** $6^{\frac{1}{4}}$ **d** $6^{-\frac{1}{2}}$ **e** $6^{-\frac{1}{3}}$ **f** $6^{-\frac{1}{4}}$

Purposeful practice 3

1 $6^{\frac{9}{2}} = \left(\sqrt{6}\right)^9$ **2** $6^{-\frac{3}{2}} = \dfrac{1}{\left(\sqrt{6}\right)^3}$ **3** $6^{\frac{3}{2}} = \left(\sqrt{6}\right)^3$

4 $6^{-\frac{9}{2}} = \dfrac{1}{\left(\sqrt{6}\right)^9}$ **5** $6^{\frac{3}{2}} = \left(\sqrt{6}\right)^3$ **6** $6^{-\frac{9}{2}} = \dfrac{1}{\left(\sqrt{6}\right)^9}$

7 $6^{\frac{9}{2}} = \left(\sqrt{6}\right)^9$ **8** $6^{-\frac{3}{2}} = \dfrac{1}{\left(\sqrt{6}\right)^3}$ **9** $6^{\frac{9}{2}} = \left(\sqrt{6}\right)^9$

10 $6^{-\frac{3}{2}} = \dfrac{1}{\left(\sqrt{6}\right)^3}$ **11** $6^{\frac{3}{2}} = \left(\sqrt{6}\right)^3$ **12** $6^{\frac{9}{2}} = \left(\sqrt{6}\right)^9$

Problem-solving practice

1 a $\dfrac{1}{2}$ **b** 125   **c** $\dfrac{1}{27}$ **d** $\dfrac{9}{4}$

2 a $\dfrac{5}{2}$ **b** $\dfrac{7}{2}$

3 $6^{\frac{1}{6}}$

4 1

5 a –3   **b** 0   **c** –2   **d** $-\dfrac{1}{2}$ **e** 0   **f** 0

6 a $x = -1.5$ **b** $x = -2$

7 $\dfrac{100}{9}$

8 a $16^{-\frac{3}{4}} \times 27^{\frac{2}{3}} = \dfrac{1}{\left(\sqrt[4]{16}\right)^3} \times \left(\sqrt[3]{27}\right)^2 = \dfrac{1}{2^3} \times 3^2 = \dfrac{1}{8} \times 9 = \dfrac{9}{8}$

  b She thought that $16^{-\frac{3}{4}} \times -16^{\frac{3}{4}}$

Exam practice

1 $x = \dfrac{1}{4}$

1.6 Powers of 10 and standard form

Purposeful practice 1

1 10^4	**2** 10^3	**3** 10^2
4 10 or 10^1	**5** 10^0	**6** 10^{-1}
7 10^{-2}	**8** 10^{-3}	**9** 10^{-4}
10 10^{-5}	**11** 10^{-6}	

Purposeful practice 2

1 a 6 300 000   **b** 630 000   **c** 63 000   **d** 63

  e 630   **f** 63   **g** 6.3   **h** 0.63

  i 0.063   **j** 0.0063   **k** 0.00063   **l** 0.000063

2 a 3.425×10^6 **b** 3.425×10^5

  c 3.425×10^4 **d** 3.425×10^3

  e 3.425×10^2 **f** 3.425×10^1

  g 3.425 or 3.425×10^0 **h** 3.425×10^{-1}

  i 3.425×10^{-2} **j** 3.425×10^{-3}

  k 3.425×10^4 **l** 3.425×10^5

  m 3.425×10^6 **n** 3.425×10^{-2}

  o 3.425×10^{-3} **p** 3.425×10^{-4}

  q 3.425×10^2 **r** 3.425×10

  s 3.425   **t** 3.425×10^3

  u 3.425×10^{-5}

Purposeful practice 3

1 6×10^8	**2** 6×10^{10}	**3** 6×10^5
4 6×10^2	**5** 6	**6** 6×10^{-12}
7 1.2×10^9	**8** 1.2×10^{-3}	**9** 1.2×10^{-11}
10 3×10^2	**11** 3×10^{-2}	**12** 3×10^{-12}

Problem-solving practice

1 Students' own answers, for example, two of 0.01, $\frac{1}{10^2}$ and 10^{-2}

2 -2×10^3, -6.9×10^{-5}, 8×10^3, 0.0016×10^8, 2.6×10^6, 28×10^5

3 1.8×10^{-2}

4 a 300   b 200

5 4.29×10^2 hours

6 $(2 \times 10^3) \boxed{\div} (5 \times 10^5) = \boxed{4} \times 10^{-3}$

7 6×10^{26}

8 8.0808×10^6

9 The indices are 3, 4 and 6 in any order

Exam practice

1 7.08×10^{-4} 2 2.5×10^{25}

1.7 Surds

Purposeful practice 1

1 $2\sqrt{2}$	2 $3\sqrt{2}$	3 $4\sqrt{2}$	4 $5\sqrt{2}$
5 $6\sqrt{2}$	6 $7\sqrt{2}$	7 $2\sqrt{3}$	8 $3\sqrt{3}$
9 $4\sqrt{3}$	10 $5\sqrt{3}$	11 $6\sqrt{3}$	12 $7\sqrt{3}$
13 $\sqrt{15}$	14 $\sqrt{21}$	15 $\sqrt{35}$	

Purposeful practice 2

1 $\frac{1}{2}$ 2 $\frac{\sqrt{3}}{2}$ 3 $\frac{\sqrt{3}}{4}$ 4 2   5 $\frac{2\sqrt{3}}{3}$ 6 $2\sqrt{2}$

Purposeful practice 3

1 $\frac{\sqrt{2}}{2}$ 2 $\frac{\sqrt{3}}{3}$ 3 $\frac{\sqrt{5}}{5}$

4 $\sqrt{2}$ 5 $\frac{3\sqrt{2}}{2}$ 6 $\frac{\sqrt{3}}{3}$

Problem-solving practice

1 $\sqrt{2} + \sqrt{15} + 7 + \frac{6\sqrt{5}}{5}$

2 a $k = 63$

3 a 9   b 4 and 3

4 a 4   b 108

5 8 square units

6 $6\sqrt{2}$

7 $a = 2\sqrt{2}$ $b = 20\sqrt{2}$ m

Exam practice

1 a $\frac{3\sqrt{5}}{5}$ b $\frac{2\sqrt{5}}{5}$ 2 $\frac{13\sqrt{3}}{6}$

2 Algebra

2.1 Algebraic indices

Purposeful practice 1

1 a $\frac{1}{x}$ b $\frac{1}{x^2}$ c $\frac{1}{x^3}$ d $\frac{2}{x^3}$

   e $\frac{7}{x^3}$ f $\frac{7}{2x^3}$ g $\frac{7}{2x^2}$

2 a $\sqrt{x}$ b $\frac{1}{\sqrt{x}}$ c $\sqrt[3]{x}$ d $\frac{1}{\sqrt[3]{x}}$

   e $\frac{1}{\sqrt[4]{x}}$ f $\sqrt{x}$ g $\frac{1}{\sqrt{x}}$ h $4\sqrt{x}$

   i $\frac{4}{\sqrt{x}}$

Purposeful practice 2

1 x^4	2 x^6	3 $21x^6$	4 $\frac{x^6}{21}$
5 x^4	6 x^{-6}	7 x^{-2}	8 $18x^{-2}$
9 x or x^1	10 $x^{\frac{5}{2}}$	11 x^2	12 x or x^1
13 1	14 3	15 $3x^3$	

Purposeful practice 3

1 x^{12}	2 x^{21}	3 $\frac{x^{-12}}{81}$	4 $\frac{x^{-12}}{16}$
5 $81x^2$	6 $3x^2$	7 $3x^2y^3$	

Problem-solving practice

1 **A** and **D**

2 a $\left(\frac{2a^2\boxed{s^4}}{\boxed{3}}\right)^3 = \frac{\boxed{8}a^6s^{12}}{27}$ b $\sqrt{9\boxed{p^2}t^4} = \boxed{3}p\boxed{t^2}$

   c $(\boxed{4}c^3k^2)^{\boxed{2}} = 16c^6k^{\boxed{4}}$

3 $9x^4 \boxed{\div} 3xy \boxed{\times} 2y^3 = 6x^3y^2$

4 a $4x^2$ b $64x^6$ c $64x^4$ d $8x^2$

5 a pq b $\frac{a}{p}$ c p^2 d $\frac{q}{9}$

6 $2^4 x^{\frac{1}{2}}$

7 $6x^{\frac{11}{2}}$

Exam practice

1 a a^6 b $4b^4c^6$ c $\frac{5de}{2}$

2.2 Expanding and factorising

Purposeful practice 1

1 $x^2 + 2x$	2 $5x^2 + 10x$	3 $5x^2 - 10x$
4 $5x^2 - 2x$	5 $2x - 5x^2$	6 $5x^2 - 2x$
7 $2y - 5xy$	8 $5xy + 2y$	9 $5xy - 2y$
10 $5xy - 2y^2$	11 $2y^2 - 5xy$	12 $2xy - 5x^2$
13 $5x^2 - 2xy$	14 $2xy + 5x^2$	15 $2y^2 + 5xy$

Purposeful practice 2

1 a $5x - 12$ b $5x$ c $x - 12$

   d $x - 2$ e $-x - 2y$ f $-x^2 - 2xy$

2 a $3(x + 2)$ b $3(2x + 5)$ c $6(2a + c)$

   d $d(3b + 1)$ e $6k(gh - 2)$ f $x^2(y + 2)$

   g $2y^2(x + a)$ h $3xy^2(2x - 3y)$ i $5b(1 + 10a)$

3 a $(f + 2)(f + 5)$ b $(f + 2)(f - 1)$ c $(p + 2)[2(p + 2) + 3]$

   d $2(p + 2)(p + 5)$ e $2(r + 2)(r - 1)$ f $2(r + 2s)(r + 2s - 3)$

   g $(t + 2)(t + 3)$ h $(t + 2)(t + 1)$

Problem-solving practice

1 $2(y + 6)(y + 8)$

2 $20x + 42$

3 5, 3

4 $(x + 3)^2$

5 a $c, d, 2c, 2d, d^2, 2d^2, cd, 2cd, cd^2, 2cd^2$

   b $2cd^2$

   c $4c^2d^2(2c + 3d^2 - 4cd^3)$

Exam practice

1 $3m(4 - 3m)$ 2 $5ab - 18ag - 8bg$

2.3 Equations

Purposeful practice 1

1 $x = 2$	2 $x = 3$	3 $x = \frac{3}{2}$	4 $x = -3$
5 $x = -8$	6 $x = 8$	7 $x = 1$	8 $x = \frac{1}{2}$

Purposeful practice 2

1 $x = 3$	2 $x = 0$	3 $x = -6$	4 $x = -6$
5 $x = 6$	6 $x = 30$	7 $x = 7\frac{1}{2}$	

Purposeful practice 3

1 $x = -18$	2 $x = -7\frac{1}{2}$	3 $x = 7$	4 $x = -5$
5 $x = -7\frac{1}{4}$	6 $x = -2\frac{3}{4}$	7 $x = 4$	8 $x = \frac{7}{18}$

Problem-solving practice

1 $26°$ 2 $270°$ 3 $\frac{9}{13}$

4 a $5(x - 23) = 2(x + 7)$ b The man is 43.

5 30

Exam practice

1 $3\frac{1}{7}$

2.4 Formulae

Purposeful practice 1

1 $b = \frac{a}{2}$ **2** $b = \frac{a}{3d}$ **3** $b = 3a$

4 $b = \frac{3a}{2}$ **5** $b = a + 3$ **6** $b = \frac{a+3}{2}$

7 $b = 2(a + 3)$ **8** $b = \frac{2(a+3)}{3}$

9 $b = \frac{2a+3}{2}$ or $b = a + \frac{3}{2}$ **10** $b = a + 3$

11 $b = \frac{2a}{3cd} + 3$ **12** $b = \sqrt{a}$ **13** $b = \sqrt{a-6}$

14 $b = \sqrt{\frac{a-6}{3}}$ **15** $b = \sqrt{a^2 - 9}$

Purposeful practice 2

1 a $u = 3$ **b** $u = 6$ **c** $u = 12$
2 a $a = 0$ **b** $a = -10$ **c** $a = 380$

Problem-solving practice

1 a 4 **b** Tetrahedron or triangular pyramid
2 $0.155\,\text{m}^3$
3 a area = $31.5\,\text{m}^2$ **b** $h = 8\,\text{m}$
  c i $b = -6\,\text{cm}$
    ii You cannot have a trapezium with a negative dimension.
4 Students' own answers, for example, $u - v = 10t$,
  $2(u - v) = 20t$, $2t = \frac{u-v}{5}$
5 $3.16\,\text{ms}^{-1}$
6 a $V = \frac{1}{3}\pi r^2 h$ **b** $h = \frac{3V}{\pi r^2}$ **c** 9.55 cm

Exam practice

1 $b = 3$

2.5 Linear sequences

Purposeful practice 1

1 a 18, 20 **b** $4\frac{3}{7}, 4\frac{6}{7}$ **c** 3.26, 3.54
  d 0, −4 **e** $\frac{3}{4}, \frac{3}{8}$ **f** −3, 1
  g −5, −4.5 **h** 8.5, 10 **i** 7, 15, 23
2 a 3, 5, 7, 9, 11 **b** 5, 7, 9, 11, 13 **c** 1, 3, 5, 7, 9
  d 4, 7, 10, 13, 16 **e** 6, 9, 12, 15, 18 **f** 2, 5, 8, 11, 14
  g 6, 11, 16, 21, 26 **h** 8, 13, 18, 23, 28 **i** 0, 1, 2, 3, 4
  j 8, 15, 22, 29, 36 **k** 10, 17, 24, 31, 38 **l** 6, 13, 20, 27, 34

Purposeful practice 2

1 n **2** $2n$ **3** $2n + 3$ **4** $2n + 4$
5 $2n + 5$ **6** $2n - 2$ **7** $2n - 0.5$ **8** $4n$
9 $4n + 3$ **10** $4n + 4$ **11** $4n + 5$ **12** $4n - 2$
13 $4n - 0.5$ **14** $7n$ **15** $7n + 3$ **16** $7n + 4$
17 $7n + 5$ **18** $7n - 2$ **19** $7n - 0.5$ **20** $-3n$
21 $-3n + 3$ **22** $-3n + 4$ **23** $-3n + 5$ **24** $-3n - 2$
25 $-3n - 0.5$

Problem-solving practice

1 a $6\frac{1}{2}, 7, 7\frac{1}{2}, 11$
  b Jamie is correct. For even number positions $\frac{n}{2}$ gives an integer so $\frac{n}{2} + 6$ also gives an integer; for odd number positions $\frac{n}{2}$ is not an integer and so $\frac{n}{2} + 6$ is not an integer.
2 Students' answers may vary, for example, the common difference in the sequence is 4. The sequence starts with an even number and so all the terms will be even. 81 is odd and can't be in the sequence.
3 The nth term rule is $3n + 7$
  81 would be the $\left(\frac{81-7}{3}\right) = \left(24\frac{2}{3}\right)$th term. n must be an integer, so 81 is not in the sequence.
  OR The two closest terms are the 24th = 79 and 25th = 82. Therefore 81 cannot be a term in the sequence.
4 1004 (168th term)
5 −501 (73rd term)
6 a $4n + 1$ **b** $4n - 4$ **c** $8n - 3$

Exam practice

1 a $3n$
  b The sequence is the 3 times table. $299 \div 3$ is not an integer so 299 is not in the 3 times table and is not a term in this sequence.
  c $3(n + 1)$ or $3n + 3$

2.6 Non-linear sequences

Purposeful practice 1

1 a $a = 1$ **b** $a = 1$ **c** $a = 1$ **d** $a = 2$
  e $a = 2$ **f** $a = 2$ **g** $a = 3$ **h** $a = 3$
  i $a = 3$ **j** $a = 4$ **k** $a = 4$ **l** $a = 10$
2 a $n^2 + n$ **b** $n^2 + 2n + 1$ **c** $n^2 + 5n - 2$
  d $2n^2 + 3n + 4$ **e** $2n^2 + n$ **f** $2n^2 + 2n + 2$
  g $3n^2 + 2n + 10$ **h** $3n^2 + 2n + 5$ **i** $3n^2 + 2n - 2$
  j $4n^2 + 7n + 2$ **k** $4n^2 + n - 5$ **l** $4n^2 + 3$

Purposeful practice 2

1 $n^2 + 3n + 2$ **2** $3n^2 + n - 4$ **3** $2n^2 + 3n + 1$
4 $5n^2 + 5n + 6$ **5** $n^2 + 6n + 10$ **6** $2n^2 + 2n + 4$

Problem-solving practice

1 $n^2 + 1$
2 a $2n^2$ **b** $2n - 2$ **c** $2n^2 + 2n - 2$
3 Ben has subtracted each term in the original sequence from the corresponding term in the n^2 sequence, instead of the other way around. Subtracting corresponding terms in the correct order would have given the sequence 2, 7, 12, 17, 22, so the nth term rule of the original sequence is $n^2 + 5n - 3$.
4 a $0.5n^2 + 0.5n$
  b The initial difference between terms is 2. The difference increases by 1 each time.
  c The triangular number sequence

Exam practice

1 $2n^2 + 4n - 1$

2.7 More expanding and factorising

Purposeful practice 1

1 $x^2 + 2x + 1$ **2** $x^2 + 3x + 2$ **3** $x^2 + 3x + 2$
4 $x^2 - 2x - 3$ **5** $x^2 + 2x - 3$ **6** $x^2 + 3x - 10$
7 $x^2 - 4x + 4$ **8** $x^2 - 9x + 18$ **9** $x^2 - 8x + 16$
10 $x^2 + 6x + 9$ **11** $x^2 - 2x + 1$ **12** $x^2 - 4x + 4$

Purposeful practice 2

1 a $(x + 1)(x + 1)$ **b** $(x + 2)(x + 3)$ **c** $(x + 1)(x - 2)$
  d $(x + 3)(x + 4)$ **e** $(x - 3)(x - 4)$ **f** $(x + 3)(x - 4)$
  g $(x - 5)(x + 4)$ **h** $(x + 7)(x + 10)$ **i** $(x - 1)(x - 1)$
  j $(x + 2)(x + 7)$ **k** $(x - 3)(x - 3)$ **l** $(x - 5)(x - 5)$
2 a $(x + 1)(x - 1)$ **b** $(p + 2)(p - 2)$ **c** $(c + 3)(c - 3)$
  d $(x + 10)(x - 10)$ **e** $(a + 6)(a - 6)$ **f** $(k + 13)(k - 13)$
  g $(10 + x)(10 - x)$ **h** $(5 + y)(5 - y)$ **i** $(2 + k)(2 - k)$
  j $(2x + 2)(2x - 2)$ or $4(x + 1)(x - 1)$
  k $(3x + 4)(3x - 4)$ **l** $(4 + 3x)(4 - 3x)$

Problem-solving practice

1 $x + 4$
2 $a = 6$ $b = 2$
3 a $x(x + 3) = x^2 + 6$ **b** $x = 2$
4 Aidan has worked out -6×-6 incorrectly. The answer should be $+36$ not -36.
5 $x^2 + 10x$
6 $x = 2$

Exam practice

1 $(x - 4)(x + 2)$

3 Interpreting and representing data

3.1 Statistical diagrams 1

Purposeful practice

1 a School A 350, School B 240   **b** School A

2 a School A 350, School B 320   **b** School A

3 School B

Problem-solving practice

1 It is not possible to tell how many matches either team won from the pie charts as the total number of matches played by each team is not known. Therefore, Jo's statement might not be correct.

2 Maisie won 8 more matches than Luke (50 compared to 42).

Exam practice

1 Becky is incorrect: she cannot tell as there is no information about the population size for this week or last week.

3.2 Time series

Purposeful practice

1 a 3.4 (million), 3.8, 4.2 so the numbers are increasing.

b Second quarter: 5 (million), 5.2, 5.4 so the numbers are increasing.
Third quarter: 5.2 (million), 5.4, 5.6 so the numbers are increasing.
Fourth quarter: 4.4 (million), 4.8, 5.2 so the numbers are increasing.

c The overall number of visitors is increasing each year.

d Each year the least number of visitors is in the first quarter, then it increases for the second and third quarters, and then decreases for the fourth quarter.

2 a 370 (thousand), 340, 320 so the numbers are decreasing.

b Second quarter: 350 (thousand), 320, 300 so the numbers are decreasing.
Third quarter: 380 (thousand), 350, 340 so the numbers are decreasing.
Fourth quarter: 420 (thousand), 410, 380 so the numbers are decreasing.

c The overall number of visitors is decreasing each year.

d Each year the number of visitors decreases from the first to the second quarter, with the lowest numbers for the year in the second quarter; the numbers then increase for the third quarter and then increase again for the fourth quarter.

Problem-solving practice

1 Mila has described the variation, not the trend. The overall trend is that the amount spent is increasing.

2 The number of hours students spend watching TV varies from term to term. The overall trend is that the number of hours watched remains similar.

Exam practice

1 Average visitors per day
$$= \frac{700 + 600 + 300 + 400 + 800 + 1300 + 1000}{7} = 728.57$$
This is less than 750, so the attraction did not meet the predicted number.

3.3 Scatter graphs

Purposeful practice

1 a 53 kg

b Positive correlation

c The greater the height of a student, the greater their weight.

2 a £9900 (approximately)

b Negative correlation

c The older the car, the lower its value.

Problem-solving practice

1 No, because there is no correlation, so there is no relationship between the height and test score of the students.

2

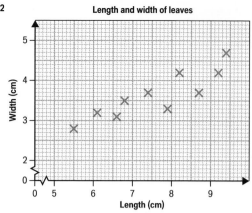

Length and width of leaves

Yes, because there is positive correlation, so the longer the leaves, the wider they are.

Exam practice

1 a 25.8 cm

b Positive correlation

c Yes, the positive correlation shows that the longer the length of a student's hand, the greater the length of their foot.

3.4 Line of best fit

Purposeful practice

1 158.5 cm (approximately)

2 a

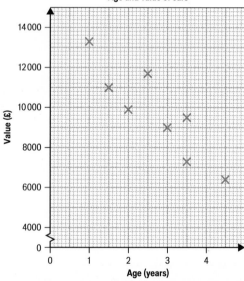

Age and value of cars

b Answers may vary. Check students' lines of best fit are reasonable.

c Students' own answers, depending on line of best fit drawn. Should fall in range £6000–8000

3 a

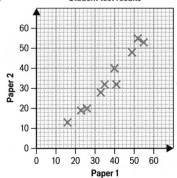

Student test results

b 24–28

Problem-solving practice

1 Using a line of best fit suggests a more accurate estimate will be higher (8 cm–8.5 cm)

Exam practice

1 25.2–25.6 cm

3.5 Averages and range

Purposeful practice

1 a 0.5 hours
  b 1.5 hours, 2.5 hours, 3.5 hours, 4.5 hours
  c 205 hours
  d 80 students
  e 2.5625 hours
2 a 840 cm
  b 60 plants
  c 14 cm
3 a 125 staff
  b 34.8 years

Problem-solving practice

1 a The range of the data is from 80 to 180 cm so the mean should be somewhere in this range, but 1856 cm is outside this range.
  b Error 1 – Paul has not used the midpoint of each class interval; he has used the lowest value.
  Error 2 – Paul has divided by 5 instead of the total of the frequency column.
  c $(90 \times 12) + (110 \times 17) + (130 \times 25) + (150 \times 19) + (170 \times 6) = 10\,070$, $10\,070 \text{ cm} \div 79 = 127.5 \text{ cm}$

Exam practice

a £3000
b Yes, because the outliers in the range $5000 < x \le 6000$ affect the mean.

3.6 Statistical diagrams 2

Purposeful practice

1 a

	Museum	Art Gallery	Theatre	Total
Male	29	7	19	55
Female	18	25	28	71
Total	47	32	47	126

b 25

2 a

	Apple	Banana	Orange	Total
Girls	27	13	6	46
Boys	18	10	11	39
Total	45	23	17	85

b 45

3 a 7
b

	Home	UK	Abroad	Total
Girls	5	2	7	14
Boys	6	5	5	16
Total	11	7	12	30

7

Problem-solving practice

1

	Walk	Car	Cycle	Total
Full-time	124	48	7	179
Part-time	106	26	35	167
Total	230	74	42	346

$\frac{106}{167}$

2

	$\frac{1}{2}$ litre bottles	1 litre bottles	2 litre bottles	Total
Saturday	9	16	19	44
Sunday	5	4	7	16
Total	14	20	26	60

$26 - 7 = 19$, so 19 2-litre bottles were sold on Saturday.
$60 - 16 = 44$, so 44 bottles in total were sold on Saturday.
So $44 - 9 - 19 = 16$, so 16 1-litre bottles were sold on Saturday.
$20 - 16 = 4$, so 4 1-litre bottles were sold on Sunday.
They sold the greatest number of 1 litre bottles on Saturday.

3 13

Exam practice

1 $\frac{11}{37}$

4 Fractions, ratio and percentages

4.1 Fractions

Purposeful practice 1

1 a $\frac{1}{2}$ **b** $\frac{1}{3}$ **c** $\frac{1}{4}$ **d** $\frac{1}{5}$
2 a 2 **b** 3 **c** 4 **d** 5
3 a 5 **b** $3\frac{1}{3}$ **c** $\frac{10}{13}$ **d** $\frac{10}{17}$
  e $8\frac{1}{3}$ **f** $6\frac{1}{4}$ **g** $6\frac{2}{33}$ **h** $1\frac{87}{113}$
4 a $3\frac{1}{2}$ **b** $2\frac{1}{3}$ **c** $1\frac{3}{4}$ **d** $1\frac{2}{5}$
5 a $\frac{6}{7}$ **b** $\frac{7}{16}$ **c** $\frac{9}{31}$ **d** $\frac{11}{49}$

Purposeful practice 2

1 a $3\frac{31}{35}$ **b** $3\frac{46}{63}$ **c** $3\frac{55}{63}$ **d** $4\frac{7}{36}$
2 a $1\frac{6}{35}$ **b** $1\frac{5}{28}$ **c** $1\frac{22}{63}$ **d** $\frac{17}{36}$
3 a $1\frac{13}{35}$ **b** $4\frac{1}{2}$ **c** $4\frac{4}{5}$ **d** $5\frac{5}{8}$
4 a $1\frac{1}{15}$ **b** $1\frac{2}{7}$ **c** $2\frac{5}{36}$ **d** $3\frac{9}{10}$

Problem-solving practice

1 $2\frac{2}{9}$ **2** Perimeter $= 12\frac{1}{14}$ m, Area $= 9\frac{1}{28}$ m²
3 7 strips **4** $1\frac{17}{20}$ m
5 3 tins. Total area for two coats is $14\frac{3}{10}$ m²
6 $\frac{5}{7}$ **7** $2\frac{1}{3}$ **8** $2\frac{9}{14}$

Exam practice

1 0.625
2 a $\frac{83}{15}$ or $5\frac{8}{15}$ **b** $3\frac{1}{4}$

4.2 Ratios

Purposeful practice 1

1 a $1 : 1.5$ **b** $1 : 2.5$ **c** $1 : 3.5$ **d** $1 : 0.75$
  e $1 : 1.25$ **f** $1 : 1.75$
2 a $\frac{2}{3} : 1$ **b** $\frac{2}{5} : 1$ **c** $\frac{2}{7} : 1$ **d** $\frac{4}{3} : 1$
  e $\frac{4}{5} : 1$ **f** $\frac{4}{7} : 1$
3 a $1 : 300$ **b** $1 : 200$ **c** $1 : 100$ **d** $1 : 40$
  e $1 : 12.5$ **f** $1 : \frac{70}{3}$ **g** $1 : 16$

Purposeful practice 2

1 a £80 : £160 **b** £60 : £180
  c £30 : £210 **d** £96 : £144
  e £100 : £140 **f** £64 : £176
2 a £60 : £120 : £180 **b** £45 : £135 : £180
  c £36 : £144 : £180 **d** £72 : £108 : £180
  e £60 : £90 : £210 **f** £80 : £60 : £220

3 a £16.67 : £33.33 : £50.00   **b** £12.50 : £37.50 : £50.00
   c £10.00 : £40.00 : £50.00   **d** £16.67 : £25.00 : £58.33
   e £5.56 : £16.67 : £77.78   **f** £33.33 : £22.22 : £44.44

Problem-solving practice

1 Ann 6, Bert 12, Callum 24

2 Doris 15, Ed 25, Frank 40

3 24 years old

4 No, Sandi needs 10 more grams of butter; she has enough of everything else.

5 22.5 cm

6 1 : 280 000

7 25 ml of white, 10 ml of green and 125 ml of blue

Exam practice

1 243 cm^2

4.3 Ratio and proportion

Purposeful practice 1

1 a 1 : 1.5, Q = 1.5P   **b** 1 : 2.5, Q = 2.5P
   c 1 : 0.75, Q = 0.75P   **d** 1 : 1.25, Q = 1.25P
   e 1 : 0.375, Q = 0.375P   **f** 1 : 0.625, Q = 0.625P

2 a $\frac{2}{3}$: 1, P = $\frac{2}{3}$ Q   **b** $\frac{2}{5}$: 1, P = $\frac{2}{5}$ Q
   c $\frac{4}{3}$: 1, P = $\frac{4}{3}$ Q   **d** $\frac{4}{5}$: 1, P = $\frac{4}{5}$ Q
   e $\frac{8}{3}$: 1, P = $\frac{8}{3}$ Q   **f** $\frac{8}{5}$: 1, P = $\frac{8}{5}$ Q

Purposeful practice 2

1 a R = 2D   **b** R = 3D   **c** R = 0.5D
   d R = 1.5D   **e** R = 0.25D

2 a Y = 3X, 30   **b** N = 2.5M, 25
   c T = 3.5S, 16   **d** V = 0.25W, 60.8

Problem-solving practice

1 5 : 6

2 a No   **b** Yes, Y = 6X   **c** No

3 688 km

4 £192.18

5 5 kg bag is better value, at £2.40 for 1 kg. 8 kg bag is £2.50 for 1 kg.

6 6.08 m

7 12 inches

Exam practice

1 Milk is better value for money in Australia. Students' own workings, for example, in England, 1 litre costs $(0.49 ÷ 0.568 × 1.76) = $1.52, compared to $1.44 in Australia.

4.4 Percentages

Purposeful practice 1

1 a 20%   **b** 50%   **c** 100%
   d 12.5%   **e** 25%   **f** 50%
   g 150%   **h** 200%   **i** 320%

2 a 25%   **b** 37.5%   **c** 87.5%
   d 5%   **e** 20%   **f** 90%
   g 80%   **h** 75%   **i** 98%

3 a 30% increase   **b** 6% decrease   **c** 20% increase
   d 7.5% decrease   **e** 300% increase   **f** 96% decrease

Purposeful practice 2

1 a £80   **b** £90   **c** £320   **d** £600

2 a £60   **b** £48   **c** £192   **d** £150

3 a £65   **b** £84   **c** £45   **d** £5500

Problem-solving practice

1 Bob by 0.8%   **2** 61.4% (1 d.p.)   **3** £250 000

4 £0   **5** 0.875   **6** £240

Exam practice

1 £400   **2** 8.8%   **3** £166 154

4.5 Fractions, decimals and percentages

Purposeful practice 1

1 0.3   **2** 0.6   **3** 0.16   **4** 0.8̇3̇
5 0.1̇   **6** 0.4̇   **7** 0.18̇   **8** 0.6̇3̇
9 0.1̇42857̇   **10** 0.4̇28571̇

Purposeful practice 2

1 a $\frac{7}{9}$ **b** $\frac{2}{9}$ **c** $\frac{8}{9}$ **d** $\frac{5}{9}$
   e $\frac{13}{99}$ **f** $\frac{31}{99}$ **g** $\frac{6}{11}$ **h** $\frac{5}{11}$
   i $\frac{41}{333}$ **j** $\frac{107}{333}$ **k** $\frac{44}{333}$ **l** $\frac{104}{333}$

2 a $\frac{11}{18}$ **b** $\frac{19}{30}$ **c** $\frac{23}{45}$ **d** $\frac{26}{45}$

Problem-solving practice

1 0.2̇6̇, 27%, $\frac{3}{11}$, $\frac{7}{25}$ **2** $\frac{3}{22}$ **3** 0.4

4 $2\frac{7}{22}$ **5** $1\frac{4}{33}$ **6** $1\frac{7}{11}$

7
$$x = 0.878\,787\,878\,7...$$
$$100x = 87.878\,787\,878\,7...$$
$$100x - x = 87$$
$$99x = 87$$
$$x = \frac{87}{99} = \frac{29}{33}$$

8 Sarah is correct. Ryan has not subtracted 6 from 65.

Exam practice

1
$$x = 0.218\,181\,818\,...$$
$$10x = 2.181\,818\,181\,8\,...$$
$$1000x = 218.181\,818\,181\,...$$
$$990x = 216$$
$$x = \frac{216}{990} = \frac{12}{55}$$

2
$$x = 0.136\,363\,636\,3\,...$$
$$10x = 1.363\,636\,363\,6\,...$$
$$1000x = 136.363\,636\,36\,...$$
$$990x = 135$$
$$x = \frac{135}{990} = \frac{3}{22}$$
$$y = 0.444\,444\,44\,...$$
$$10y = 4.444\,444\,4\,...$$
$$9y = 4$$
$$y = \frac{4}{9}$$
$$x \times y = \frac{3}{22} \times \frac{4}{9} = \frac{2}{33}$$

Mixed exercises A

Mixed problem-solving practice A

1 No, you must multiply them, not add.

2 190

3 8.30 am

4 No, because the information about how many matches each team played is not given in the question. It is only possible to say what proportion of matches they won.

5 22 cm

6 a $7n - 5$

   b No, solving $7n - 5 = 200$ doesn't give a whole number solution, so 200 is not in the sequence.

7 a 20 minutes and 15 seconds (or 20.25 minutes)

   b Yes, as the mean is affected by the 8 higher values in the class interval $40 < t < 60$

8 No, as $5.8 \times 10^7 \times 100 = 5.8 \times 10^9$, $1.427 \times 10^9 < 5.8 \times 10^9$

9 a £113.04

   b In Madrid the shirt costs £63.83, so it is £3.83 (or €4.40) cheaper in London.

10 Karen hasn't multiplied the first numerator by 5 and the second numerator by 3, so she has not replaced fractions with equivalent ones.

11 24

12 £234

13 $10x = 3.1515..., 1000x = 315.1515..., 990x = 312, x = \frac{312}{990}, x = \frac{52}{165}$

14 $2n^2 + n - 2$

Exam practice

15 Yes, as $\frac{80}{30} = 2\frac{1}{3}, \frac{90}{40} = 2\frac{1}{4}$

so the percentage decrease = $\dfrac{2\frac{1}{3} - 2\frac{1}{4}}{2\frac{1}{3}} \times 100 = 15.625\% < 20\%$

16 Yes, number of children = $108 \div 3 \times 4 = 144$,
number of people = $144 \div 2 \times 7 = 504$,
percentage of seats filled = $504 \div 800 \times 100 = 63\%$, which is more than 60%.

17 a 13 years   **b** Negative correlation

   c Yes, as the points for dogs that are heavier appear where there are lower life expectancies.

   d Answer in the range of 10.6–12.6 years.

18 a 0.2

   b $\sqrt{\frac{1.05}{1.1}} \times 100 = 97.70...\%$, which is less than 100%, so it will decrease by 2.30%.

19 $x = \frac{34}{11}$

20 a $(p + q)(p - q)$ **b** $24(x^2 + 3)$

21 $-\frac{7}{10}$

22 Kate has written $\sqrt{20}$ as $5\sqrt{2}$ instead of $2\sqrt{5}$

5 Angles and trigonometry

5.1 Angle properties of triangles and quadrilaterals

Purposeful practice 1

1 $x = 140°, y = 40°$ **2** $x = 60°, y = 40°$ **3** $x = 20°, y = 100°$

4 $x = 80°, y = 20°$ **5** $x = 130°$ **6** $x = 120°$

Purposeful practice 2

1 $x = 120°$ **2** $x = 30°$ **3** $x = 30°$

Problem-solving practice

1 a Mia included the angle at the same vertex as the exterior angle. She needs to add the angles at the other two vertices.

   b $x = 130°$

2 $x = 100°$ Angles within the equilateral triangle are 60°, so the larger angles within the isosceles triangle are $180° - 60° - 40° = 80°$ (angles on a straight line add to 180°). So $x = 180 - 80 = 100°$ (angles on a straight line add to 180°).

3 No.
Angle ACB = 43° (corresponding angles are equal).
Angle BAC = 43° (ABC is isosceles triangle).
Angle ABC = 94° (angles in a triangle add to 180°).
Therefore, quadrilateral is not a rectangle (at least one angle is not a right angle).

4 $x = 90°$. Students' reasoning may vary, for example,
Angle ACF = 135° (corresponding angles are equal).
Angle ACB = 45° (angles on a straight line add to 180°).
Angle ABC = 45° (ABC is isosceles triangle).
Therefore, $x = 90°$ (angles in a triangle add to 180°).

5 $y = 13°$. Students' reasoning may vary, for example
Angle DFE = 13° (angles on a straight line add to 180°).
Angle EDF = 13° (DEF is isosceles).
Therefore, angle $y = 13°$ (corresponding angles are equal).

Exam practice

1 Angle AFB = 40° (vertically opposite angles are equal)
Angle BAD = 65° (opposite angles of a parallelogram are equal)
Angle ABF = $180° - 40° - 65° = 75°$ (angles of a triangle add to 180°)

5.2 Interior angles of a polygon

Purposeful practice 1

1 156°   **2** 157.5°   **3** 158.8°   **4** 160°   **5** 161.1°

Purposeful practice 2

1 $x = 110°$ **2** $x = 120°$ **3** $x = 157°$

Purposeful practice 3

1 6   **2** 12   **3** 24

Problem-solving practice

1 Students' answers will vary, but should include a counter-example, for example, a regular heptagon has an interior angle of 128.57°.

2 No, a regular octagon has an interior angle of 135°.
Sum of interior angles = $(8 - 2) \times 180° = 1080°$.
In a regular octagon, angles are the same so each angle = $1080° \div 8 = 135°$.

3 Students' own answers. Any combination of three angles that add to 360°.

4 Angle FEA = 60°. Students' reasons may vary, for example, the hexagon is regular so AGH is an equilateral triangle with interior angles of 60°. Since FAE = 60° and AE = AF, angle AEF and angle AFE are both equal to $\frac{1}{2}(180° - 60°) = 60°$.

5 $x = 112°$

6 No, because the interior angles of a regular pentagon are all 108° and there is no combination of 108° that can sum to 360°, so there will always be a gap.

Exam practice

1 Angle BCD = 135°.
Students' own working, for example,
Let angle ABC be x. Therefore, angle BCD = 3x.
Sum of internal angles of a pentagon = $(5 - 2) \times 180° = 540°$.
So, $90° + 125° + 145° + 4x = 540°$.
Thus $4x = 180°$, so $x = 45°$.
Therefore, angle BCD = $3 \times 45° = 135°$.

5.3 Exterior angles of a polygon

Purposeful practice 1

1 d, f, o, l, m

Purposeful practice 2

1 $w = 80°, x = 70°, y = 90°, z = 100°$; $70 + 90 + 100 + 100 = 360°$

2 $a = 50°, b = 70°, c = 135°, d = 120°, e = 85°, f = 130°$
$50 + 70 + 45 + 60 + 85 + 50 = 360°$

3 $g = 36°, h = 80°, i = 104°, j = 110°, k = 110°, l = 58°$
$36 + 80 + 76 + 110 + 58 = 360°$

Purposeful practice 3

1 36°   **2** 32.7°   **3** 30°   **4** 27.7°

Problem-solving practice

1 Students' sketches of an equilateral triangle.
An equilateral triangle has exterior angles = $\frac{360°}{3} = 120°$. A 4-sided regular polygon (square) has exterior angles = 90°. As more sides get added, the angles get smaller, so the only regular polygon with obtuse exterior angles is an equilateral triangle.

2 $360° \div 72 = 5°$ so the shape would have 72 sides.

3 $y = 36°$ **4** 12 sides

5 16 sides   **6** $x = 144°$

Exam practice

1 Angle of equilateral triangle = 60°
Sum of interior angles of 15-sided polygon = $13 \times 180° = 2340°$
Interior angle of regular 15-sided polygon = 156°
Interior angle of polygon P = $360° - 60° - 156° = 144°$
Exterior angle of polygon P = $180° - 144° = 36°$
Number of sides of polygon P = $360° \div 36° = 10$

5.4 Pythagoras' theorem 1

Purposeful practice 1

1 a, d

Purposeful practice 2

1 5 cm   **2** 5.8 cm   **3** 7.2 cm   **4** 7.8 cm

Purposeful practice 3

1 Yes, $6^2 + 8^2 = 10^2$ **2** No, $6.1^2 + 8.1^2 \neq 10.1^2$

3 No, $5.9^2 + 7.9^2 \neq 9.9^2$

Problem-solving practice

1 0.2 m

2 £30 to buy 2 m² (or £17.11 to buy 1.14 m² if possible to buy the exact area required)

3 34.4 cm **4** 217.6 cm **5** 0.9 km (to 1 d.p.)

Exam practice

1 28.2 kg

5.5 Pythagoras' theorem 2

Purposeful practice 1

1 12 m **2** 5 m **3** 13 m
4 5.7 m **5** 7.3 m **6** 3.9 m

Purposeful practice 2

1 a $\sqrt{7}$ cm **b** 2.6 cm
2 a $\sqrt{45}$ cm $= 3\sqrt{5}$ cm **b** 6.7 cm
3 a $\sqrt{5}$ cm **b** 2.2 cm

Purposeful practice 3

1 2.4 cm **2** 2.1 cm **3** 3.9 cm

Problem-solving practice

1 12.6 m **2** 43.3 cm² **3** 5.4 m **4** 110.9 cm² **5** 0.6 m

Exam practice

1 CD² = 45 − 9 = 36, so CD = 6 cm
AE = 6 cm − 4 cm = 2 cm
AD = 3 cm + 1 cm = 4 cm
Area of triangle DEF =
$(6\,\text{cm} \times 4\,\text{cm}) - \frac{1}{2} \times 6\,\text{cm} \times 3\,\text{cm} - \frac{1}{2} \times 4\,\text{cm} \times 1\,\text{cm} - \frac{1}{2} \times 4\,\text{cm} \times 2\,\text{cm}$
= 9 cm²

5.6 Trigonometry 1

Purposeful practice 1

1 8 cm **2** 4.6 cm **3** 8.7 cm **4** 6.1 cm

Purposeful practice 2

1 2 cm **2** 2.3 cm **3** 2.9 cm **4** 3.5 cm

Purposeful practice 3

1 3.5 cm **2** 6.9 cm **3** 3.5 cm **4** 6.9 cm

Problem-solving practice

1 17.4 cm² **2** 2.2 m **3** 28.3 m **4** 6.60 cm **5** 8.7 km

Exam practice

1 19.2 cm

5.7 Trigonometry 2

Purposeful practice 1

1 48.6° **2** 41.4° **3** 53.1° **4** 59.0° **5** 36.9° **6** 53.1°

Purposeful practice 2

1 a $x = 63.4°$ **b** $y = 63.4°$
2 a $x = 5.7°$ **b** $y = 5.7°$

Problem-solving practice

1 $x = 70.5°$
2 Angle ACB = $\cos^{-1}\left(\frac{5}{12}\right) = 65.4°$,
so angle ABC = $180° - 40° - 65.4° = 74.6°$.
Triangle ABC has no equal angles and therefore is not isosceles.
3 60.9° **4** 123.7° **5** 41.8°, 66.4°, 71.8°

Exam practice

1 39.3°

---

6 Graphs

6.1 Linear graphs

Purposeful practice 1

1 a B, E, F, H, I **b** A, C, D, G
c A, B, G, H **d** A, C and D; B, E and F; H and I
2 B, A, E, D, C. (A and E are as steep as each other, so the order of those two can be swapped.)
3 A is $y = 2x + 4$, B is $y = 2x + 3$, C is $y = 2x$, D is $y = 2x - 1$

Purposeful practice 2

1 a 12 **b** 8 **c** 6 **d** 3
2 a (−6, 0) **b** (4, 0) **c** (−3, 0) **d** (2, 0)
3 a 4 **b** 4

Problem-solving practice

1 Peter is incorrect. B and C each have a gradient of 2, but A rearranges to $y = -2x + 8$ so it has gradient −2. D rearranges to $y = \frac{1}{2}x + 2$ so it has gradient $\frac{1}{2}$.
2 Only Rebecca is correct. It will cross the y-axis at (0, 4) so Sarah is wrong, and cross the x-axis at (2.5, 0) so Theresa is wrong.
3 Line A is $y = \frac{2}{3}x + 2$ and line B is $y = \frac{1}{2}x + \frac{3}{2}$
4 C $5x + 6y = 21$ (intercept 3.5), A $2y = 4x + 8$ (intercept 4), B $3y = 4x + 13$ (intercept $4\frac{1}{3}$), D $3y + 2x + 15 = 0$ (intercept −5)
5 a Students' answers will vary, so accept any equations where the coefficient of x in the first equation is half the coefficient of x in the second equation, for example, $y = 4x + 3$ and $2y = 8x + 4$
b Students' answers will vary, so accept any equations where the constant term in the first equation is half the constant term in the second equation, for example, $y = 2x + 3$ and $2y = 2x + 6$
c Any equations where the ratio of the coefficient of x to the constant term is the same for both equations, for example,
$y = x + 3$ and $2y = 3x + 9$.

Exam practice

1 The equation for L2 can be rearranged to give $y = 2x + \frac{1}{2}$, so the gradient of both lines is 2. Same gradient shows the lines are parallel.
2 A and D

6.2 More linear graphs

Purposeful practice 1

1 a 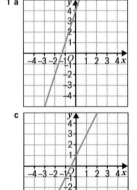 **b**
c **d**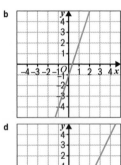

2 $y = 5x + 2$ = C; $y = 5x - 3$ = A; $y = 2 - 3x$ = D; $y = 4 - 3x$ = B

3 a 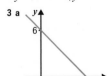 **b**

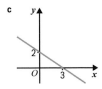
c

Purposeful practice 2

1 a (3, 14) **b** (3, 15) **c** (3, 9)
2 a (8, 8) **b** (8, 0) **c** (0, −4) and (8, −8)
  d (8, 4), (0, 8) and (12, 2) **e** (8, 0), (0, −4), (−8, −8) and (12, 2)
  f (0, −8) and (−8, −4)

Problem-solving practice

1 A has gradient of $(6 − 2) ÷ (5 − 1) = 1$
  B has gradient of $(4 − 2) ÷ (5 − 1) = \frac{1}{2}$
  C has gradient of $(−6 − 2) ÷ (5 − 1) = −2$
  B is the only graph with a gradient of $\frac{1}{2}$

2 a $y = 2x − 1$ **b** $y = \frac{1}{2}x + 3$ **c** $y = −3x + 12$
  d $y = 3x − 1$ **e** $y = −4x + 13$ **f** $y = −0.5x + 2.5$

3 a   **b** (4, 1)

4 $y = \frac{1}{2}x + \frac{5}{2}$

Exam practice

1 $y = 3x − 2$

6.3 Graphing rates of change

Purposeful practice 1

1 a 10 m/s **b** 1.5 seconds **c** At point D
  d Between A and B (in the first second); between C and D (2.5 to 3.5 seconds)
  e Slowing down and coming to rest

Purposeful practice 2

1 1600 km/h² **2** 200 km **3** 3600 km **4** 200 km

Problem-solving practice

1 a 10 minutes **b** 12 km **c** 0.0083 m/s² **d** 7.2 km
2 a 60 m/s **b** 5 m/s² **c** 3
  d Answers in the range 2750 m to 2800 m.

3
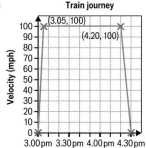

Distance $= \frac{1}{2}(1.5 + 1.25) × 100 = 137.5$ miles

Exam practice

1 a $\frac{20}{40} = 0.5$ m/s²

  b $\frac{1}{2}(50 + 30) × 40 + 80 × 50$
  $= 1600 + 4000 = 5600$ m
  $= 5.6$ km

6.4 Real-life graphs

Purposeful practice

1 a $18 **b** £16 or £17
  c i Allow between 1.8 and 1.9
   ii You receive $1.80 − $1.90 for each £1
2 a £110 **b** 8 hours
  c i £10 **ii** The cost to hire the hall, before time is taken into account. This could be called a 'standing charge'.
  d i £25 **ii** The cost per hour
3 a i 24°C **ii** The temperature of the room when the freezer was turned on
  b 6°C **c** 12 hours
  d i −3 **ii** That the freezer gets 3°C colder each hour

Problem-solving practice

1 a

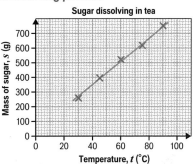

b 670 g (approx.) **c** 84°C (approx.)
d The gradient is about 8. This means 8 g more sugar will dissolve for every 1°C increase in temperature.
2 a Company A £1250; Company B £3500
  b Company A £200 (approx.); Company B £80 (approx). These are the costs per month.
  c At 12 months, Company A is cheaper.
  d At 2 years, Company B is cheaper.
  e They cost the same after approximately 19 months.

Exam practice

1 a −2
  b The rate at which the liquid flows from the container (2 litres per second)
  c The volume of liquid in the container at the beginning

6.5 Line segments

Purposeful practice 1

1 (2, 4) **2** (3, 5) **3** $\left(2\frac{1}{2}, 4\frac{1}{2}\right)$
4 (0, 5) **5** (4, 0) **6** $\left(−\frac{1}{2}, 4\frac{1}{2}\right)$
7 (−3, −1) **8** (−4, 0) **9** $\left(−3\frac{1}{2}, 4\frac{1}{2}\right)$
10 $\left(3\frac{1}{4}, −\frac{3}{4}\right)$ **11** $\left(−\frac{3}{4}, 4\frac{1}{4}\right)$ **12** $\left(−\frac{1}{4}, −\frac{1}{4}\right)$

Purposeful practice 2

1 Just A **2** B and C **3** $y = −\frac{1}{2}x + 5$ **4** $y = 2x − 5$

Problem-solving practice

1 $y = −7x + 6$
2 Perpendicular gradient should be −7, not 7.
  Tim needs to find midpoint of line segment and substitute its coordinates into equation $y = −7x + c$ (rather than coordinates of one end of segment, as he has done).
  Tim has substituted values incorrectly (substituted x-value for y and y-value for x).
3 a (2, 3), (4, 1) and (4, 3)
  b (4, 5), (6.5, 5), (5, 3) and (2.5, 3)
  c (3.25, 4), (5.25, 5), (5.75, 4), (3.75, 3)

4 Eliza is correct. The gradient of the line segment from $(-3, 2)$ to $(-1, 5)$ is $\frac{3}{2}$. The gradient of the line segment from $(-3, 2)$ to $(-2, 1\frac{1}{3})$ is $-\frac{2}{3}$. Therefore these line segments are perpendicular and $(-2, 1\frac{1}{3})$ could be the a vertex of the rectangle.

5 a $y = \frac{1}{2}x - \frac{1}{2}$ and $y = -2x + 12$

 b $(2, 3)$ and $(4, 4)$ or $(6, 0)$ and $(4, -1)$

 c 3.2 (1 d.p.)

Exam practice

1 $y = -x + 11$

6.6 Quadratic graphs

Purposeful practice

1 A and D are quadratic graphs

2 B and C are quadratic equations

3 Equation **i** is graph C; equation **ii** is graph A; equation **iii** is graph D; equation **iv** is graph B

4 a 1   **b** 2   **c** 0

Problem-solving practice

1 a $x = -0.7$ and 3.7   **b** $x = -0.8$ and 1.3   **c** $x = 3$

2 a i $x = -3$ and 2   **ii** $x = 1.4$ and -1.4 (approx)   **iii** $x = -4$ and 2

 b The graphs of $y = x^2 + x - 6$ and $y = 3x - 8$ never meet, so the equation cannot have any solutions.

Exam questions

1 It should be joined with a smooth curve

6.7 Cubic and reciprocal graphs

Purposeful practice

1 A and C are cubic graphs

2 a Cubic   **b** Quadratic   **c** Reciprocal   **d** Cubic

3 a 2   **b** 3   **c** 1   **d** 1

Problem-solving practice

1 a and **b**

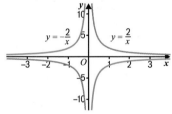

2 a $x = -2.9, -0.3, 1.2$ (approx)   **b** $x = -3, 0, 1$

3 a $a = 1, b = 2$ **b** $a = 2, b = 1$ **c** $a = -1, b = -2$ **d** $a = -1, b = \frac{1}{2}$

Exam questions

1 i C   **ii** D   **iii** F   **iv** E

6.8 More graphs

Purposeful practice 1

1 There is no relationship between the temperature and shoe sales.

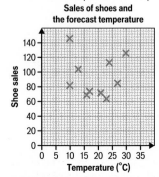

2 There is a positive correlation between temperature and visitors, which suggests that the higher the temperature forecast, the more visitors come to the theme park.

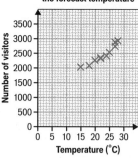

Purposeful practice 2

1 Only D will produce a circle.

2 a 2   **b** 4   **c** 8   **d** 10   **e** $\sqrt{7}$

3 Only A and B lie on the circle.

Problem-solving practice

1 a 2500   **b** 925 (approx)   **c** 16 minutes   **d** 7 minutes

2 i C   **ii** A   **iii** B

Exam questions

1

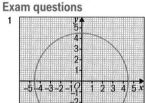

7 Area and volume

7.1 Perimeter and area

Purposeful practice 1

1 56 cm²   **2** 56 cm²   **3** 56 cm²

Purposeful practice 2

1 28.7 cm²   **2** 8.5 m²   **3** 60 cm²   **4** 60 cm²

Problem-solving practice

1 a $h = 7.5$ cm   **b** $a = 8$ cm   **c** $b = 8$ cm

2 a James:

 • forgot the $\frac{1}{2}$ from the formula

 • used the side length of 8 cm, not the perpendicular height of 5 cm

 • incorrectly worked out his calculation – he should have completed the calculation inside of the brackets first

 b The correct answer is $\frac{1}{2}(6 + 10) \times 5 = 40$ cm²

3 Area of A = 54 cm², $b = 21$ cm, $c = 4.5$ cm, $d = 5$ cm

Exam practice

1 Accept any triangle with area of 9 cm²

7.2 Units and accuracy

Purposeful practice 1

1 a 48 cm²   **b** 4800 mm²

2 a 17.5 cm²   **b** 1750 mm²

3 a 11.2 cm²   **b** 1120 mm²

Purposeful practice 2

1 a i $13.5\,\text{mm} \leqslant l \leqslant 16.5\,\text{mm}$ **ii** $135\,\text{cm} \leqslant l \leqslant 165\,\text{cm}$

 iii $1.35\,\text{m} \leqslant l \leqslant 1.65\,\text{m}$ **iv** $13.5\,\text{m} \leqslant l \leqslant 16.5\,\text{m}$

 b i $14.25\,\text{mm} \leqslant l \leqslant 15.75\,\text{mm}$ **ii** $142.5\,\text{cm} \leqslant l \leqslant 157.5\,\text{cm}$

 iii $1.425\,\text{m} \leqslant l \leqslant 1.575\,\text{m}$ **iv** $14.25\,\text{m} \leqslant l \leqslant 15.75\,\text{m}$

    c **i** 14.625 mm ⩽ l ⩽ 15.375 mm   **ii** 146.25 cm ⩽ l ⩽ 153.75 cm

      iii 1.4625 m ⩽ l ⩽ 1.5375 m   **iv** 14.625 m ⩽ l ⩽ 15.375 m

2 a 17.5 cm ⩽ l < 18.5 cm   **b** 179.5 mm ⩽ l < 180.5 mm

   c 1.795 m ⩽ l < 1.805 m   **d** 1.75 m ⩽ l < 1.85 m

   e 2.25 m ⩽ l < 2.35 m   **f** 2.295 m ⩽ l < 2.305 m

   g 1.95 km ⩽ l < 2.05 km   **h** 1.995 km ⩽ l < 2.005 km

Problem-solving practice

1 a Holly has the wrong answer for 0.8 × 0.8. The answer is 0.64 cm².

   b She might find it easier to find the area in mm² and then divide by 100 to give cm².

2 a h = 6 cm or 60 mm   **b** b = 40 mm or 4 cm

3 Adam, Charlie and Daisy

4 a Lower bound 4932.25 m², upper bound 5078.25 m²

   b Lower bound 4974.0075 m², upper bound 4988.5975 m²

5 No, because the actual measurements could be bigger than 4 m and 5 m, making the area more than 20 m². The upper bound is 4.5 × 5.5 = 24.75 m², which would require 25 carpet tiles.

Exam practice

1 4.5 cm ⩽ L < 5 cm

7.3 Prisms

Purposeful practice 1

1 222 cm²   **2** 420 cm²   **3** 247.2 cm²   **4** 216 cm²

Purposeful practice 2

1 Q1: 180 cm³   **Q2:** 360 cm³   **Q3:** 187.2 cm³   **Q4:** 144 cm³

2 Q1: 180 ml   **Q2:** 360 ml   **Q3:** 187.2 ml   **Q4:** 144 ml

Problem-solving practice

1 6 units   **2** 6.25 cm

3 Fifty 8 cm cubes have a surface area of 50 × 6 × 8² = 19 200 cm², so yes one container of paint is enough as 20 000 − 19 200 = 800 cm² of paint remaining.

4 Square base has sides of 5 cm, cuboid is 20 cm tall. Volume = 500 cm³

5 108 cm²

Exam practice

1 Volume of cuboid = 230 cm × 120 cm × 15 cm = 414 000 cm³ = 414 litres
414 litres ÷ 50 litres = 8.28, so the gardener needs 9 bags of compost. Therefore, it will cost £63, which is £3 more than £60.

7.4 Circles

Purposeful practice 1

1 a 56.5 cm   **b** 113.1 cm   **c** 22.0 mm

   d 44.0 mm   **e** 47.1 m   **f** 94.2 m

2 a 18π cm   **b** 36π cm   **c** 7π mm

   d 14π mm   **e** 15π m   **f** 30π m

Purposeful practice 2

1 a 254.5 cm²   **b** 1017.9 cm²   **c** 38.5 mm²

   d 153.9 mm²   **e** 176.7 m²   **f** 706.9 m²

2 a 81π cm²   **b** 324π cm²   **c** $\dfrac{49}{4}\pi$ mm²

   d 49π mm²   **e** $\dfrac{225}{4}\pi$ m²   **f** 225π m²

Problem-solving practice

1 50.3 cm   **2** 4 units

3 The father's wheel turns 2273 times, the daughter's 5305 times. The daughter's wheel turns 3032 more times.

4 32.93 m²   **5** Area = 9.42 cm²

Exam practice

1 x = 6.38

7.5 Sectors of circles

Purposeful practice 1

1 a 6.3 cm   **b** 8.0 cm   **c** 14.6 cm

2 a 11.3 cm   **b** 17.7 cm   **c** 40.6 cm

   d 54.6 cm   **e** 56.5 cm   **f** 43.9 cm

Purposeful practice 2

1 a 12.6 cm²   **b** 15.9 cm²   **c** 29.2 cm²

2 a 4π cm²   **b** $\dfrac{76\pi}{15}$ cm²   **c** $\dfrac{418}{45}\pi$ cm²

Problem-solving practice

1 a Graham:

   • missed out a 2 from his calculation, so the arc length should be 50.3 cm

   • used the wrong units

   • forgot to add on the two radii to give a perimeter

   b 102.7 mm

2 The 40° sector has an area of 50.3 m². The smaller sector has an area of 19.6 m². The shaded area is 30.6 m².

3 There are two ways to solve this. Students will need to work out the interior angles of the hexagon (120°). Then either:

   • find the area of one sector $\dfrac{120}{360} \times \pi \times 5^2$ = 26.18 cm² and multiply this by 6 to give 157.1 cm²

   or

   • realise they have six thirds of a circle – which is the same as two complete circles – and so calculate $2 \times \pi \times 5^2$ = 157.1 cm²

Exam practice

1 29.3 cm

7.6 Cylinders and spheres

Purposeful practice 1

1 628.3 cm³   **2** 785.4 cm³   **3** 7068.6 cm³

Purposeful practice 2

1 478 mm²   **2** 729 mm²   **3** 2790 mm²

Purposeful practice 3

1 a 2144.66 mm³   **b** 804.25 mm²

2 a 57.91 cm³   **b** 72.38 cm²

3 a 24.43 m³   **b** 40.72 cm²

Problem-solving practice

1 Volume of cylinder A = 3769.91 (1200π) cm³

   Volume of cylinder B = 30 159.29 (9600π) cm³

   The volume of cylinder B is 8 × larger than the volume of cylinder A. Maria might have realised this by looking at the formula, $\pi r^2 h$. When the r is doubled then the volume will be multiplied by 4, and then when the height is doubled this multiplies by a further 2, making the volume 8 times greater overall.

2 37 900 000 km²   **3** 161 cm³   **4** 3.23 cm

Exam practice

1 236 cm² (to 3 s.f.), students' working may vary. Volume of sphere is $\frac{4}{3}\pi r^3$, so volume of hemisphere is $\frac{2}{3}\pi r^3$.

   For P, $\frac{2}{3}\pi r^3 = \frac{250}{3}\pi$. r^3 = 125, so radius of P = 5 cm.

   Surface area of sphere = $4\pi r^2$, so area of curved surface of hemisphere = $2\pi r^2$.

   Area of flat surface of hemisphere = πr^2, so total surface area of a hemisphere = $3\pi r^2$.

   Surface area of P is $3\pi \times 5^2$ cm² = 236 cm² (to 3 s.f.)

7.7 Pyramids and cones

Purposeful practice 1

1 a 405 cm³   **b** 300 cm³   **c** 500 cm³

2 a 225π cm³   **b** 150π cm³   **c** 100π cm³

Purposeful practice 2

1 a 96π cm²   **b** 160π cm²   **c** 300π cm²

2 a 169.6 cm²   **b** 301.6 cm²   **c** 16.5 cm²

Problem-solving practice

1 The volume is 2 592 100 m³, so 2 592 100 stones were needed to fill this volume. Even with some smoothing needed on the sloping edges this answer would be fairly accurate.

2 2.7 cm

3 1 single ice cream has a volume of 208.69 cm³ so she can make 23 complete ice creams from a 5 litre container.

4 579.41 cm²

1 230 m (to nearest m)

8 Transformations and constructions

8.1 3D solids

Purposeful practice 1

1
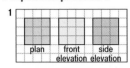

2 a
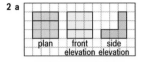

b
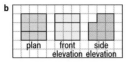

c
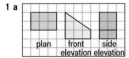

Purposeful practice 2

1 a
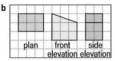

b
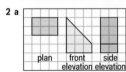

2 a
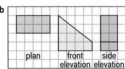

b
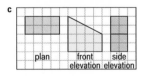

c

Problem-solving practice

1 a
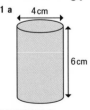
4 cm
6 cm

b Cylinder

2

Exam practice

1

front elevation   side elevation

8.2 Reflection and rotation

Purposeful practice 1

1 a Reflection in the y-axis or line $x = 0$

b Reflection in the line $y = 5$

c Reflection in the line $y = -2$

d Reflection in the line $x = -3$

Purposeful practice 2

1 a Rotation 90° clockwise about (0, 0)

b Rotation 90° clockwise about (0, −1)

c Rotation 90° clockwise about (−1, −1)

d Rotation 90° clockwise about (−2, −1)

Problem-solving practice

1 Sophie has stated the angle and direction correctly (90° anticlockwise) to score 1 mark. The centre of rotation is (−1, 0) not (0, 1). She needed to state that the transformation is a rotation for a third mark.

2 a–c
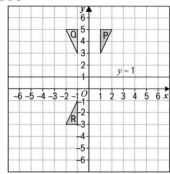

d Rotation 180° about (0, 1)

Exam practice

1 Rotation 180° about (−1, −1)

2 Rotation 90° clockwise about (0, 1)

8.3 Enlargement

Purposeful practice 1

1 B: $\frac{1}{2}$, C: 2, D: $-\frac{1}{2}$, E: −1, F: −2

Purposeful practice 2

1–4
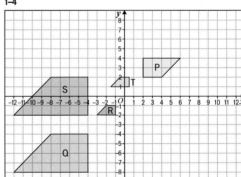

Problem-solving practice

1 a Olivia has given the scale factor from triangle Q to triangle P rather than from triangle P to triangle Q. The centre of enlargement is not (0, 0).

b An enlargement with scale factor $-\frac{1}{2}$, centre of enlargement (4, 2)

2
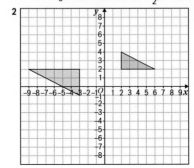

Exam practice

1

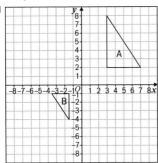

8.4 Translations and combinations of transformations

Purposeful practice 1

1–3

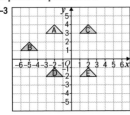

Purposeful practice 2

1, 2, 4, 5

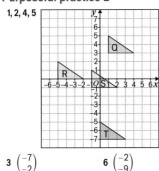

3 $\begin{pmatrix} -7 \\ -2 \end{pmatrix}$ **6** $\begin{pmatrix} -2 \\ -9 \end{pmatrix}$

Problem-solving practice

1 $\begin{pmatrix} -4 \\ 5 \end{pmatrix}$

2 Students' vectors that total $\begin{pmatrix} 9 \\ -4 \end{pmatrix}$, for example $\begin{pmatrix} 5 \\ -2 \end{pmatrix}$ and $\begin{pmatrix} 4 \\ -2 \end{pmatrix}$; $\begin{pmatrix} -1 \\ 1 \end{pmatrix}$ and $\begin{pmatrix} 10 \\ -5 \end{pmatrix}$

3 Translation by the vector $\begin{pmatrix} -7 \\ 2 \end{pmatrix}$

Exam practice

1 No, as triangles C and E are in different positions.

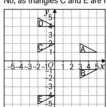

8.5 Bearings and scale drawings

Purposeful practice 1

1 a i 050°   **ii** 230°
  b i 070°   **ii** 250°
  c i 140°   **ii** 320°

2 a i 130°   **ii** 310°
  b i 100°   **ii** 280°
  c i 060°   **ii** 240°
3 a 080°   **b** 335°

Purposeful practice 2

1 a 210°   **b** 245°   **c** 315°
2 a 010°   **b** 045°   **c** 125°

Problem-solving practice

1 220°

2 054°

3 a Sam is incorrect as 110° is the bearing of B from A, not A from B.
  b Paul is incorrect as he has worked out the acute angle at B (anticlockwise angle from north), not the reflex angle (clockwise angle from north).

4

Exam practice

1 132°

8.6 Constructions 1

Purposeful practice

1 a

b

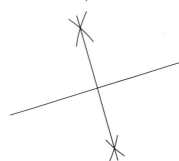

c

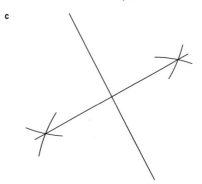

d

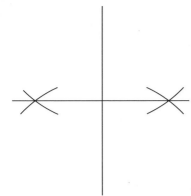

2 a

b

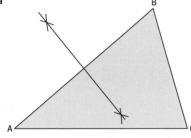

3

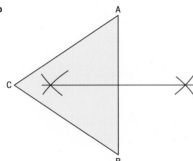

Problem-solving practice

1 a Jake has opened his compasses to less than half the length of the line, not more than half, so the arcs do not intersect.

   b Emily did not keep her compasses at the same distance when she moved the point to the other end of the line.

2 a

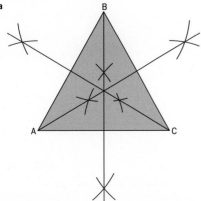

b All of the perpendicular bisectors intersect at the centre of the equilateral triangle.

c Students draw their own isosceles and scalene triangles and bisect each side. For example:

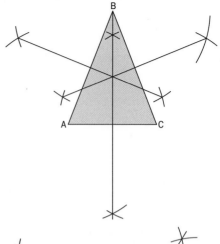

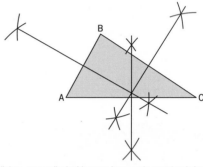

All three perpendicular bisectors intersect in any triangle but not necessarily in the centre of the triangle.

Exam practice

1

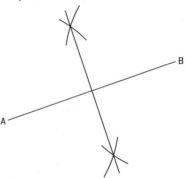

8.7 Constructions 2

Purposeful practice

1 a   **b**

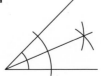 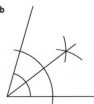

c

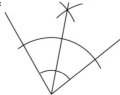

279

d

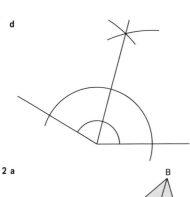

2 a

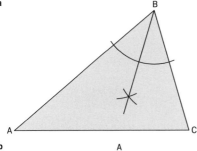

b

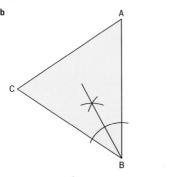

3

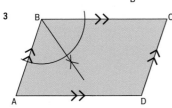

Problem-solving practice

1 George has drawn his arcs from the end of each arm of the angle. He should have first drawn an arc that crosses each arm of the angle from the vertex. Then he should have drawn arcs from where the first arc intersects each arm of the angle.

2

3

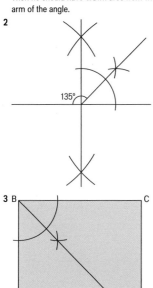

1

8.8 Loci

Purposeful practice

1 a–b

2 a–b

3 a–b

Problem-solving practice

1

2

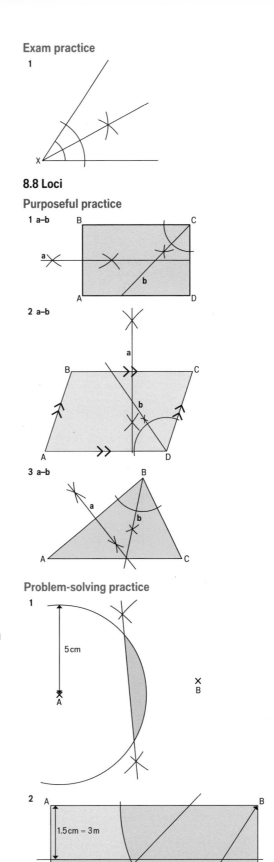

Exam practice

1

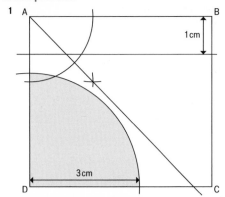

Mixed exercises B

Mixed problem-solving practice B

1 Sean used straight lines to join the points but should have used a smooth curve.

2 a I   **b** C   **c** D   **d** G

3 a $-\frac{1}{2}$

b The rate at which the water in the barrel is changing, in litres per second. The negative sign tells us that the barrel is emptying at the rate of $\frac{1}{2}$ litre per second.

c $L = 20$ represents the volume of water, in litres, in the barrel at the start.

4

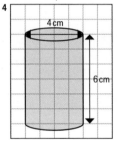

5 Area $= 5 \times 1.8 + \frac{1}{2} \times 0.8 \times (3 + 5) = 12.2\,\text{m}^2$

Cost = 20% off 13×28 = 20% off 364 = £291.20 < £300

Yes, Charlotte has enough money to buy all of the tiles she needs.

6 A rotation 90° clockwise about $(2, -2)$

7 Rearranging L_2 gives $3y = 12x - 7$, $y = 4x - \frac{7}{3}$, therefore the gradient of L_2 is 4. The gradient of L_1 is 4. As the gradients are equal the two lines are parallel.

8 $829\,\text{cm}^3$

9

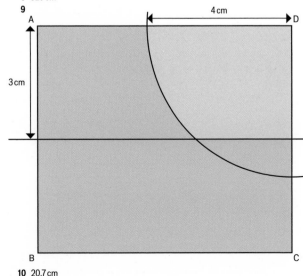

10 $20.7\,\text{cm}$

Exam practice

11 $y = \frac{1}{2}x - 2$

12

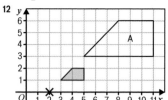

13 Angle sum $= (10 - 2) \times 180 = 1440$, angle ABC $= 1440 \div 10 = 144°$

14 $6.38\,\text{cm}$

15 Volume of sphere $= 4 \times 243\pi = 972\pi = \frac{4}{3}\pi r^3$

$$729 = r^3$$
$$r = 9\,\text{cm}$$

Surface area of S $= \frac{1}{4} \times 4\pi r^2 + \pi r^2 = \pi \times 9^2 + \pi \times 9^2 = 509\,\text{cm}^2$

9 Equations and inequalities

9.1 Solving quadratic equations 1

Purposeful practice 1

1 a $3^2 + 2 \times 3 = 9 + 6 = 15$ **b** $3^2 + 3 = 9 + 3 = 12$

   c $3^2 - 3 \times 3 = 9 - 9 = 0$

2 a $x = -3$ and $x = 2$ **b** $x = -3$ and $x = -2$

   c $x = 2$ and $x = 2$ (repeated root)

Purposeful practice 2

1 a $x = -3$ and $x = 2$ **b** $x = -2$ and $x = 3$

   c $x = -3$ and $x = -2$ **d** $x = 2$ and $x = 3$

2 a $x = -4$ and $x = -3$ **b** $x = -4$ and $x = 3$

   c $x = -3$ and $x = 4$ **d** $x = 3$ and $x = 4$

Problem-solving practice

1 a Salma has only found one solution, but a quadratic equation has two solutions. She needs to rearrange the equation to equal zero before solving it.

   b $x = -3$ or $x = 4$

2 $x = -3$ or $x = 5$ **3** $x = -1$ and $x = 1$

4 It factorises to $(x - 4)^2$, so its roots are $x = 4$ and $x = 4$ (repeated root).

5 a $y = x^2 - 6x + 9$ **b** $y = x^2 - 9$ **c** $y = x^2 + 6x + 9$

6 6 or −6

7 $x = -6$

8 $y = x^2 + 18x + 72$

9 There is a repeated root of $x = -5$. So the sketch cannot be correct because it shows two different roots.

Exam practice

1 $x = -5$, $x = 4$

9.2 Solving quadratic equations 2

Purposeful practice 1

1 a $x = -\frac{3}{2}$ and $x = 2$ **b** $x = -\frac{2}{3}$ and $x = 3$

   c $x = -2$ and $x = -\frac{3}{2}$ **d** $x = \frac{2}{3}$ and $x = 3$

2 a $x = -\frac{1}{2}$ and $x = 3$ **b** $x = \frac{1}{2}$ and $x = 3$

   c $x = 2$ and $x = -\frac{1}{2}$ **d** $x = -2$ and $x = -\frac{1}{2}$

Purposeful practice 2

1 a i $x = -3.58$ or $x = -0.42$ **ii** $x = -2.22$ or $x = -0.45$

   iii $x = -1.59$ or $x = -0.16$

   b i $x = -2.62$ or $x = -0.38$ **ii** $x = -4.79$ or $x = -0.21$

   iii $x = -6.85$ or $x = -0.15$

   c i $x = -4.30$ or $x = -0.70$ **ii** $x = -4$ or $x = -1$

   iii $x = -3.62$ or $x = -1.38$

   d i $x = -0.25$ or $x = 2.45$ **ii** $x = -0.55$ or $x = 0.82$

   iii $x = -1.25$ or $x = 2.92$

e i $x = -0.25$ (repeated)   **ii** $x = 0.6$ (repeated)

iii $x = -0.625$ (repeated)

Purposeful practice 3

1 a $x = -3 + \sqrt{2}$ or $x = -3 - \sqrt{2}$ **b** $x = 3 + \sqrt{2}$ or $x = 3 - \sqrt{2}$

c $x = 3 + \sqrt{10}$ or $x = 3 - \sqrt{10}$

2 a $x = 2 + \dfrac{\sqrt{6}}{2}$ or $x = 2 - \dfrac{\sqrt{6}}{2}$ **b** $x = -\dfrac{1}{2} + \dfrac{\sqrt{21}}{6}$ or $x = -\dfrac{1}{2} - \dfrac{\sqrt{21}}{6}$

c $x = \dfrac{9}{4} + \dfrac{\sqrt{113}}{4}$ or $x = \dfrac{9}{4} - \dfrac{\sqrt{113}}{4}$

Problem-solving practice

1 a Mark has forgotten the negative sign in front of the 3 at the beginning of the formula, and dropped the negative sign from the 4 in the equation.

His initial equation should be $x = \dfrac{-3 \pm \sqrt{3^2 - 4 \times 2 \times (-4)}}{2 \times 2}$

b $x = -2.35$ or $x = 0.85$

2 a i 73   **ii** -55 **iii** 0

b i A   **ii** C   **iii** B

3 All rearrange to the same quadratic, all with $x = -5$ or $x = -7$

4 a $1 + \dfrac{1}{x} = x$

$x + 1 = x^2$

$x^2 - x - 1 = 0$

b $x = -0.618$ or $x = 1.618$

Exam practice

1 $x = 2 \pm \sqrt{3}$

9.3 Completing the square

Purposeful practice

1 a $x^2 + 6x + 9$ **b** $x^2 - 6x + 9$ **c** $2x^2 + 12x + 18$

d $2x^2 - 12x + 18$ **e** $5x^2 + 30x + 45$ **f** $5x^2 - 30x + 45$

2 a $x^2 + 6x + 12$ **b** $x^2 + 6x + 5$ **c** $x^2 + 6x - 6$

d $x^2 - 6x + 12$ **e** $x^2 - 6x + 5$ **f** $x^2 - 6x - 6$

3 a $(x + 3)^2 + 3$ **b** $(x + 3)^2 + 1$ **c** $(x + 3)^2 + 6$

d $(x + 3)^2 - 10$ **e** $(x + 3)^2 - 20$ **f** $(x + 3)^2 - 100$

4 a $(x - 3)^2 + 3$ **b** $(x - 3)^2 - 21$ **c** $(x - 3)^2 - 9$

d $(x + 3)^2 + 3$ **e** $(x + 3)^2 - 21$ **f** $(x + 3)^2 - 9$

5 a $2(x + 3)^2 + 2$ **b** $2(x + 3)^2 - 10$ **c** $2(x + 3)^2 - 36$

d $3(x + 2)^2 + 9$ **e** $3(x + 2)^2 + 6$ **f** $3(x + 2)^2 - 30$

6 a $9(x + 1)^2 - 12$ **b** $9(x + 1)^2 - 9$ **c** $9(x + 1)^2 + 10$

d $16(x + 1)^2 - 12$ **e** $16(x + 1)^2 - 16$ **f** $16(x + 1)^2 + 48$

7 a $(x + 4)^2 + 1$ **b** $4\left(x - \dfrac{5}{2}\right)^2 - 10$ **c** $2\left(x + \dfrac{3}{2}\right)^2 - \dfrac{11}{2}$

d $(x + 2.5)^2 - 5.25$ **e** $(x + 0.5)^2 + 0.75$ **f** $10(x - 0.1)^2 + 0.9$

Problem-solving practice

1 a Jenny used the wrong number inside the bracket. This should be 4. The $-8x$ has been incorrectly included.

b $(x + 4)^2 + 34$

2 $x^2 + 4x + 10 = (x + 2)^2 + 6$, so square A has side $x + 2$ and rectangle B has area 6.

3 a $3x^2 + 12x + 7 = 3\left(\dfrac{x^2 + 4x + 7}{3}\right)$

$= 3\left[\dfrac{(x + 2)^2 - 5}{3}\right]$

$= 3(x + 2)^2 - 5$

b $3x^2 + 12x + 7 = 3(x^2 + 4x) + 7$

$= 3[(x + 2)^2 - 4] + 7$

$= 3(x + 2)^2 - 12 + 7$

$= 3(x + 2)^2 - 5$

4 a $3(x + 3)^2 - 6$

b $3(x + 3)^2 - 6 = 0$

$3(x + 3)^2 = 6$

$(x + 3)^2 = 2$

$x + 3 = \pm\sqrt{2}$

$x = -3 + \sqrt{2}$ or $x = -3 - \sqrt{2}$

5 a $(x + 3)^2 - 8$

b Substitution: $2y = x$, so $(2y + 3)^2 - 8 = 0$, giving $y = -0.086$ or -2.9

6 a $(x + 2)^2 + 6$

---

b Setting this to be zero would give $(x + 2)^2 = -6$, which is not possible because square numbers are never negative.

7 a $n^2 + n + 0.25 = (n + 0.5)^2$

(This is a perfect square.)

b $n^2 + n + 0.25 = n(n + 1) + 0.25$

c Part **a** gives $(2 + 0.5)^2 = 2.5^2 = 6.25$, and part **b** gives $2 \times 3 + 0.25 = 6.25$. As the answers are the same, Anna is correct.

d $(n + 0.5)^2 = n(n + 1) + 0.25$ so substituting $n = 5$ gives $5.5^2 = 5 \times 6 + 0.25 = 30.25$

Exam practice

1 $(x + 4)^2 - 21$

9.4 Solving simple simultaneous equations

Purposeful practice 1

1 a $x = 2, y = 8$ **b** $x = 4, y = 8$ **c** $x = 4, y = 12$

2 a $x = 1.5, y = 7$ **b** $x = 1, y = 8$ **c** $x = 3, y = 4$

Purposeful practice 2

1 a $x = 4, y = 2$ **b** $x = 12, y = -14$

c $x = 3, y = 15$ **d** $x = 2, y = 18$

2 a $x = 3, y = 4$ **b** $x = 3, y = 4$ **c** $x = 3, y = 4$

d $x = 2, y = 3$ **e** $x = 2, y = 3$ **f** $x = 2, y = 3$

3 a $x = 4, y = 2$ **b** $x = 2, y = 6$ **c** $x = \dfrac{1}{2}, y = -\dfrac{1}{4}$

4 a $x = 3, y = 1$ **b** $x = -2, y = 3$ **c** $x = \dfrac{1}{2}, y = -4$

Problem-solving practice

1 The numbers are 3.5 and 2.5

2 $x = 8$ and $y = 7$, giving an area of $144 \, \text{cm}^2$.

3 A cup of coffee costs £2.70 and a cake costs £1.89.

4 a 8p or £0.08   **b** 12p or £0.12

5 Cost per day is 5p; cost per unit is 2p.

6 Simultaneous equations are $2x + y = 12$ and $x - y = 3$, or $2x + y = 12$ and $y - x = 3$. The combinations are 3, 3, 6 ($x = 3, y = 6$) or 5, 5, 2 ($x = 5, y = 2$)

Exam practice

1 $x = 3, y = 4$

9.5 More simultaneous equations

Purposeful practice 1

1 a $x = 2, y = -1$ **b** $x = 2, y = -1$

2 a i ①$\times 7$ and ②$\times 3$ **b** $x = -3, y = 1$

ii ①$\times 3$ and ②$\times 4$

Purposeful practice 2

1 a $x = 4, y = 4$ **b** $x = 1, y = -3$ **c** $x = -7, y = 2$

2 a $x = 3, y = 1$ **b** $x = 5, y = -2$ **c** $x = \dfrac{1}{2}, y = 2$

Purposeful practice 3

1 $x = \dfrac{2}{3}, y = \dfrac{19}{8}$ **2** $x = \dfrac{3}{8}, y = \dfrac{1}{3}$ **3** $x = \dfrac{3}{2}, y = -\dfrac{1}{5}$

Problem-solving practice

1 One bag of sand is 20 kg, therefore 20 bags of sand can be carried.

2 Adult tickets cost £8.50, child tickets cost £5.50. Offer is £4 less.

3 a When $x = 4, y = 19$, so $19 = 4m + c$

When $x = 8, y = 31$, so $31 = 8m + c$

b Solving the equations gives $m = 3$ and $c = 7$, so equation of line is $y = 3x + 7$

c Yes, if $x = 6$ then $y = 3 \times 6 + 7 = 25$

4 40 sheep, 75 chickens

5 $y = 5x^2 + 11$

6 $x = 3, y = -2$

7 Shorts = £4.99 and t-shirts = £5.99

8 $(2, 1)$

Exam practice

1 $x = -2, y = 3$

9.6 Solving linear and quadratic simultaneous equations

Purposeful practice 1

1 a $x = -2, y = -2$ or $x = 3, y = 3$
 b $x = -3, y = 3$ or $x = 2, y = -2$
 c $x = -2, y = -4$ or $x = 3, y = 6$
 d $x = -3, y = 6$ or $x = 2, y = -4$
2 a $x = -3, y = -1$ or $x = -2, y = 0$
 b $x = -4, y = -6$ or $x = -3, y = -5$
 c $x = 1, y = 5$ or $x = 7, y = 23$
 d $x = -6, y = -20$ or $x = 5, y = 13$
3 a $x = -1.58, y = 1.42$ or $x = 1.58, y = 4.58$
 b $x = -2.16, y = 0.84$ or $x = 1.16, y = 4.16$
 c $x = -2.44, y = 2.56$ or $x = 1.44, y = 6.44$

Purposeful practice 2

1 a $x = -3, y = -10$ or $x = 0, y = -1$
 b $x = -3.56, y = -9.68$ or $x = 0.56, y = 2.68$
 c $x = -8, y = -13$ or $x = 0, y = 3$
 d $x = -10.12, y = -23.25$ or $x = -1.88, y = 6.75$
2 a $x = -2, y = -1$ or $x = 1, y = 2$
 b $x = -1, y = -2$ or $x = 2, y = 1$
 c $x = -2.2, y = -0.4$ or $x = -1, y = 2$
 d $x = 2.2, y = 0.4$ or $x = 1, y = -2$
3 a $x = 3, y = 18$ (repeated)
 b $x = 2, y = 15$ (repeated)
 c $x = -4, y = 23$ (repeated)

Problem-solving practice

1 $a = 3$
2 $x = -2.45, y = 7.55$ and $x = 2.45, y = 12.45$
3 480 m
4 a $(-5, 9)$ and $(1, 3)$ **b** distance = 8.49   **c** $(0, -1)$
5 $x = 3, y = 4$ and $x = -4, y = -3$
6 $a = 25$
7 $c = 0.75$

Exam practice

1 $x = 3, y = 5$ or $x = -5.4, y = 2.2$

9.7 Solving linear inequalities

Purposeful practice 1

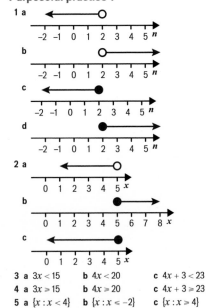

1 a

b

c

d

2 a

b

c

3 a $3x < 15$ **b** $4x < 20$ **c** $4x + 3 < 23$ **d** $4x - 1 < 19$
4 a $3x \geqslant 15$ **b** $4x \geqslant 20$ **c** $4x + 3 \geqslant 23$ **d** $4x - 1 \geqslant 19$
5 a $\{x : x < 4\}$ **b** $\{x : x \leqslant -2\}$ **c** $\{x : x \geqslant 4\}$ **d** $\{x : x < 8\}$

Purposeful practice 2

1 a $-2 > -5$ **b** $-4 < -1$ **c** $3 > -7$ **d** $2 < 6$
2 a $x > -5$ **b** $x < -1$ **c** $x > -7$ **d** $x < 6$
3 a $x < 3$ **b** $x \geqslant -7$ **c** $x < -4$ **d** $x \geqslant -4$

e $x \leqslant -5$ **f** $x \geqslant 4$ **g** $x \geqslant -6$ **h** $x < -6$
i $x < -3$ **j** $x > -7$ **k** $x \leqslant 7$ **l** $x \leqslant 4$

Problem-solving practice

1 A4, B1, C3, D2
2 a i $x < \dfrac{8}{3}$ **ii** $x \geqslant 1$
 b

(number line: filled circle at 1, open circle at 3, line between them; axis 0 1 2 3 4 5 x)

3 $x = 1, 2, 3, 4$
4 150 cm²
5 105 cm²
6 Students' inequality with solution set $\{x : x > -2\}$
7 Between the first and second line Esther should have subtracted 2 so the line ends in -24 not -20. Between the second and third lines she should have reversed the inequality sign. The final answer should be $x \leqslant 8$
8 The values of x^2 would be 16, 9, 4, 1, 0, 1, 4, 9, 16, so if $x^2 > 9$ then $x < -3$ or $x > 3$.

Exam practice

1 $x > 2$

10 Probability

10.1 Combined events

Purposeful practice 1

1 a H, T   **b** 1, 2, 3   **c** H1, H2, H3, T1, T2, T3
2 a H, T   **b** 1, 2, 3, 4, 5, 6
 c H1, H2, H3, H4, H5, H6, T1, T2, T3, T4, T5, T6
3 a 7, 8, 9   **b** 1, 2, 3, 4, 5, 6
 c 7, 1; 7, 2; 7, 3; 7, 4; 7, 5; 7, 6; 8, 1; 8, 2; 8, 3; 8, 4; 8, 5; 8, 6; 9, 1; 9, 2; 9, 3; 9, 4; 9, 5; 9, 6

Purposeful practice 2

1

		Four-sided spinner			
		1	**2**	**3**	**4**
	1	2	3	4	5
Three-sided spinner	**4**	5	6	7	8
	9	10	11	12	13

2 a $\dfrac{1}{12}$ **b** $\dfrac{7}{12}$ **c** $\dfrac{4}{12}$ or $\dfrac{1}{3}$
 d $\dfrac{5}{12}$ **e** $\dfrac{8}{12}$ or $\dfrac{2}{3}$

Problem-solving practice

1 $\dfrac{15}{36}$ or $\dfrac{5}{12}$ **2** $\dfrac{6}{36}$ or $\dfrac{1}{6}$ **3** $\dfrac{3}{6}$ or $\dfrac{1}{2}$
4 a 10   **b** $\dfrac{5}{60}$ or $\dfrac{1}{12}$
5 No, it is not fair. P(12 or more) = $\dfrac{17}{36}$ and P(less than 12) = $\dfrac{19}{36}$ therefore Kim is more likely to win.
6 Students' own answers, for example, cards should be organised into a set of 3 cards and a set of 5 cards to give 15 possible outcomes.

Exam practice

1 a $\dfrac{4}{40} = \dfrac{1}{10}$ **b** $\dfrac{11}{40}$

10.2 Mutually exclusive events

Purposeful practice 1

1 $\dfrac{1}{10}$ **2** $\dfrac{2}{10}$ or $\dfrac{1}{5}$ **3** $\dfrac{3}{10}$ **4** $\dfrac{4}{10}$ or $\dfrac{2}{5}$
5 $\dfrac{3}{10}$ **6** $\dfrac{4}{10}$ or $\dfrac{2}{5}$ **7** $\dfrac{5}{10}$ or $\dfrac{1}{2}$ **8** $\dfrac{6}{10}$ or $\dfrac{3}{5}$
9 $\dfrac{7}{10}$ **10** $\dfrac{9}{10}$ **11** $\dfrac{8}{10}$ or $\dfrac{4}{5}$ **12** $\dfrac{8}{10}$ or $\dfrac{4}{5}$
13 $\dfrac{7}{10}$ **14** $\dfrac{6}{10}$ or $\dfrac{3}{5}$ **15** $\dfrac{5}{10}$ or $\dfrac{1}{2}$ **16** $\dfrac{7}{10}$
17 $\dfrac{4}{10}$ or $\dfrac{2}{5}$ **18** $\dfrac{3}{10}$

Purposeful practice 2

1 0.4   **2** 0.05   **3** $\frac{1}{8}$ **4** 45%

Problem-solving practice

1 0.97   **2** > 90%   **3** 0.3   **4** 0.2

5 Students' own reasoning, for example, the probability of picking a black counter is $\frac{1}{12}$. This means that $\frac{1}{12}$ of the counters must be black. $\frac{1}{12}$ of 6 is $\frac{1}{2}$ and it is not possible to have $\frac{1}{2}$ a counter, so there cannot only be 6 counters in the bag.

6 a Black

  b There are half as many black as pink, so 6 black. There are $1\frac{1}{2}$ times as many white as pink, so 18 white. There are three times as many pink as green, so 4 green.

Exam practice

1 1 − 0.4 − 0.45 = 0.15.
P(blue) = 2 × P(green), so P(blue) = 0.1, P(green) = 0.05.
A probability of 0.4 represents 8 cubes, so 0.1 represents 2 cubes and 0.05 represents 1 cube. Therefore, there is 1 green cube.

10.3 Experimental probability

Purposeful practice 1

1 a 21   **b** 15   **c** 32   **d** 52

2 a

Score	1	2	3	4	5	6
Experimental probability	0.15	0.175	0.23	0.2	0.16	0.085

  b **i** 69   **ii** 48
      iii 70.5 so estimate is 70 or 71   **iv** 138

Purposeful practice 2

1 a $\frac{15}{33} = 0.45$ **b** $\frac{49}{110} = 0.45$

  c $\frac{12}{20} = 0.60$ **d** $\frac{76}{163} = 0.47$

Problem-solving practice

1 28   **2** 6 red, 8 blue, 2 green, 4 white

3 a i, iii, v, vi   **b** ii, iv

4 P(6) = 0.16, 0.16 × 120 = 19.2. Estimate 19.

5 a Students' answers will vary, for example, it is likely to be fair because for a fair five-sided spinner the expected number of each score in 80 spins is 16, and all the frequencies are close to this.
OR Students may calculate all experimental probabilities and compare them to the theoretical probability of 0.2 for each score.

  b Increase the number of trials

Exam practice

1 Min's results give the best estimate because she carried out the largest number of trials.

10.4 Independent events and tree diagrams

Purposeful practice

1 a

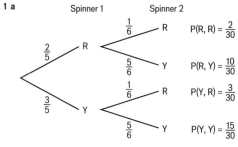

  b Yellow, yellow   **c** 5

2 a Spinner 1 P(R) = 0.4, Spinner 2 P(R) = 0.75

  b

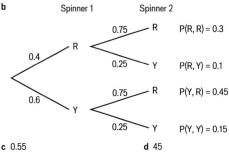

  c 0.55   **d** 45

Problem-solving practice

1 a i $\frac{3}{4}$ **ii** $\frac{3}{8}$

  b Students' answers will vary, for example, spinner 1 with P(B) = $\frac{1}{4}$ e.g. 4 sections, 1 blue and 3 green. Spinner 2 with P(B) = P(G) = $\frac{1}{2}$, so with equal number of green and blue sections.

2 14   **3** $\frac{1}{72}$

Exam practice

1 The probability for not white on the first spin should be 0.55 (not 0.65) On the second spin, P(white) should be 0.45 and P(not white) should be 0.55. Jake has written them the wrong way round.

10.5 Conditional probability

Purposeful practice 1

1

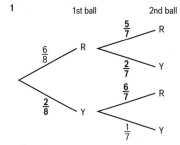

2 $\frac{2}{56} = \frac{1}{28}$

Purposeful practice 2

1 a

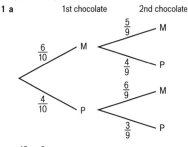

  b $\frac{48}{90} = \frac{8}{15}$

2 a

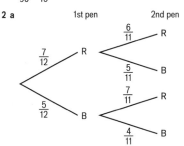

  b $\frac{112}{132} = \frac{28}{33}$

Problem-solving practice

1 One of:

the probabilities on the branches for the second sweet do not add to 1

she has changed the numerators and not the denominators for the second sweet

on the top pair, the probabilities should be $\frac{14}{27}$ and $\frac{13}{27}$

on the bottom pair, the probabilities should be $\frac{15}{27}$ and $\frac{12}{27}$

the probabilities for mints and toffees are the wrong way around

2 $\frac{210}{1320} = \frac{7}{44}$

3 a $\frac{40}{72} = \frac{5}{9}$

b If he has to take a third sock, it means he already has one black and one white. If he takes another sock it will be either black or white, so will make a pair with one of the ones he has already.

Exam practice

1 a

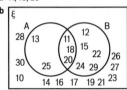

b 0.262

10.6 Venn diagrams and set notation

Purposeful practice

1 a 11, 18, 20

b

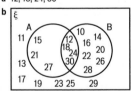

c i 11, 12, 13, 15, 18, 20, 22, 24, 25, 29

ii 10, 12, 14, 15, 16, 17, 19, 21, 22, 23, 24, 26, 27, 28, 29, 30

iii 12, 15, 22, 24, 29

iv 10, 14, 16, 17, 19, 21, 23, 26, 27, 28, 30

2 a 12, 18, 24, 30

b

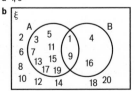

c i 10, 12, 14, 15, 16, 18, 20, 21, 22, 24, 26, 27, 28, 30

ii 10, 11, 13, 14, 16, 17, 19, 20, 22, 23, 25, 26, 28, 29

iii 10, 14, 16, 20, 22, 26, 28   **iv** 11, 13, 17, 19, 23, 25, 29

3 a 1, 9

b

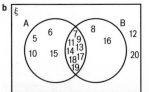

c i 1, 3, 4, 5, 7, 9, 11, 13, 15, 16, 17, 19

ii 2, 4, 6, 8, 10, 12, 14, 16, 18, 20

iii 4, 16   **iv** 2, 6, 8, 10, 12, 14, 18, 20

4 a 7, 9, 11, 13, 14, 17, 18, 19

b

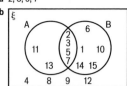

c i 5, 6, 7, 8, 9, 10, 11, 13, 14, 15, 16, 17, 18, 19

ii 8, 12, 16, 20   **iii** 8, 16   **iv** 12, 20

5 a 2, 3, 5, 7

b

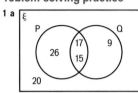

c i 1, 2, 3, 5, 6, 7, 10, 11, 13, 14, 15

ii 1, 4, 6, 8, 9, 10, 12, 14, 15

iii 1, 6, 10, 14, 15   **iv** 4, 8, 9, 12

Problem-solving practice

1 a

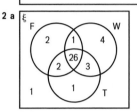

b $\frac{2}{5}$

2 a

b $\frac{32}{40} = \frac{4}{5}$

3 a $\frac{27}{29}$ **b** $\frac{14}{29}$ **c** $\frac{25}{29}$ **d** $\frac{2}{29}$

Exam practice

1 a

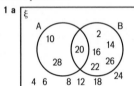

b $\frac{8}{14} = \frac{4}{7}$

11 Multiplicative reasoning

11.1 Growth and decay

Purposeful practice 1

1 a £52.50   **b** £55.13   **c** £57.88

d £81.44   **e** £85.52   **f** £132.66

2 a £55   **b** £60.50   **c** £66.55

d £129.69   **e** £142.66   **f** £336.37

Purposeful practice 2

1 a £47.50   **b** £45.13   **c** £42.87

d £29.94   **e** £28.44   **f** £17.92

2 a £59.87   **b** £56.88   **c** £35.85

Purposeful practice 3

1 15.5% increase   **2** 4.5% increase   **3** 1% decrease

Problem-solving practice

1 34.6%

2 £21 125.63 (or £21 133.68 using exact value of multiplier)

3 Put it in savings because that yields 10.25% interest overall not a 10% increase.

4 3.125%

5 a The first option is better, as on the fourth day you will get £84.38 from the first option or £0.08 from the second.

b The second option is better. On the 28th day you will get £0.08 from the first option but £1 342 177.28 from the second option.

c On the 12th day.

6 a 3249   **b** 77.2%   **c** 16 minutes

7 £802.82

Exam practice

1 £21 640.32

11.2 Compound measures

Purposeful practice 1

1 a 15 words per minute   **b** 8.3 words per minute
    c 120 words per minute

Purposeful practice 2

1 a 216 000 m/h   **b** 108 000 m/h   **c** 21 600 m/h   **d** 2160 m/h
2 a 216 km/h   **b** 108 km/h   **c** 21.6 km/h   **d** 2.16 km/h

Purposeful practice 3

1 a $-1/3 \, \text{m/s}^2$ **b** $-1/3 \, \text{m/s}^2$
2 a $-1.29 \, \text{m/s}^2$ **b** $-1.66 \, \text{m/s}^2$
3 a $-2.5 \, \text{m/s}^2$ **b** $-3.5 \, \text{m/s}^2$

Problem-solving practice

1 Jahidul – he writes at a rate of $\frac{60}{5} \times 140 = 1680$ words per hour compared to Angela's rate of 1570 words per hour.

2 4.17 seconds (3 s.f.)

3 No, using formula $s = ut + \frac{1}{2}at^2$:
Distance cheetah travels $= 0 + \frac{1}{2} \times 8.93 \times 11^2 = 540.3$ m (1 d.p.)
Distance gazelle travels $= 0 + \frac{1}{2} \times 4.2 \times 11^2 = 254.1$ m (1 d.p.)
Cheetah starts 300 m behind gazelle.
$(254.1 + 300) - 540.3 = 13.8$, so the gazelle will be 13.8 m ahead of the cheetah after 11 seconds.

4 Rowan: $a = \dfrac{v - u}{t} = \dfrac{3.5}{2.5} = 1.4 \, \text{m/s}^2$
Nurhad: $a = \dfrac{v - u}{t} = \dfrac{3.8}{3} = 1.2\dot{6} \, \text{m/s}^2$
So Rowan has the greater acceleration.

5 The cyclist will win in 4.19 s compared to the car's 4.63 s

6 £63

7 a Grant would finish first. Archie plants $5y$ flowers in 2 minutes, which is $150y$ in an hour. This is a slower rate than Grant.
   b 5 minutes and 36 seconds

Exam practice

1 For first 10 seconds: $u = p$, $v = 3p$, $t = 10$
Using $v = u + at$
$3p = p + 10a$
$\dfrac{2p}{10} = a$, or $a = \dfrac{p}{5}$
$s = 10p + \dfrac{1}{2} \times \dfrac{p}{5} \times 10^2$
$s = 20p$
For final 20 seconds: $u = 3p$, $a = 0$, $t = 20$
$s = ut + \dfrac{1}{2}at^2$
$s = 3p \times 20 = 60p$
Total distance $= 20p + 60p = 80p$

11.3 More compound measures

Purposeful practice 1

1 a $3 \, \text{N/cm}^2$ **b** $6 \, \text{N/cm}^2$ **c** $3 \, \text{N/cm}^2$
2 a $3 \, \text{g/cm}^3$ **b** $1.5 \, \text{g/cm}^3$ **c** $3 \, \text{g/cm}^3$

Purposeful practice 2

1 a 12 g   **b** 6 g   **c** 3 g
2 a 12 N   **b** 24 N   **c** 48 N
3 a $3 \, \text{cm}^3$ **b** $1.5 \, \text{cm}^3$ **c** $3 \, \text{cm}^3$
4 a $3 \, \text{cm}^2$ **b** $6 \, \text{cm}^2$ **c** $3 \, \text{cm}^2$

Problem-solving practice

1 16 100 cm³ of feathers.

2 1.006 g/ml

3 The second person exerts greater pressure.
First person:
Force $= (67 \times 9.8)$ N $= 656.6$ N
Area $= 2 \times (40 + 0.25) \, \text{cm}^2 = 80.5 \, \text{cm}^2$
Pressure $=$ Force $\div$ Area $= 8.16 \, \text{N/cm}^2$ (2 d.p.)

Second person:
Force $= (75 \times 9.8)$ N $= 735$ N
Area $= 2 \times (40 + 0.7) \, \text{cm}^2 = 81.4 \, \text{cm}^2$
Pressure $=$ Force $\div$ Area $= 9.03 \, \text{N/cm}^2$ (2 d.p.)

4 No, it has a density of 0.32 g/cm³.

5 Yes. The swimming pool only exerts 1.25 N/cm²

6 Yes, its density is 650 kg/m³, which is less than that of water.

Exam practice

1 0.71 grams per cm³

11.4 Ratio and proportion

Purposeful practice 1

1 a 16 patients   **b** 9 nurses   **c** 10 patients
   d 9 nurses   **e** 3 hours   **f** 12 nurses

Purposeful practice 2

1 a $y = 4x$ **b** $y = 12$ **c** $x = 0.75$
2 a $y = \dfrac{100}{x}$ **b** $y = 33\frac{1}{3}$ **c** $x = 33\frac{1}{3}$
3 a $y = 4.2x$ **b** $y = 12.6$ **c** $x = 0.71$ (to 2 d.p.)
4 a $y = \dfrac{420}{x}$ **b** $y = 140$ **c** $x = 140$

Problem-solving practice

1 10.9 hours
2 a 110   **b** 2m
3 £4212
4 5.625 hours
5 It will cost the same amount to hire 10 or 12 workers.
6 a 12 hours 10 minutes   **b** 6 hours 51 minutes (to the nearest minute)
7 4 hours

Exam practice

1 £37.20

12 Similarity and congruence

12.1 Congruence

Purposeful practice 1

1 SAS   **2** AAS   **3** RHS   **4** AAS   **5** SSS   **6** SAS

Purposeful practice 2

1 Triangles B and C are congruent to triangle A. B by SAS (as the missing angle in triangle A is 90°). C by RHS (as the missing angle in triangle A is 90°).

Problem-solving practice

1 a True, SSS
   b False, it can only be RHS if both hypotenuses are the same and one of the other sides is the same, but we are not told which side is which. It can only be SAS if the right angle is the included angle between the 6 cm and 8 cm sides for both triangles.
   c False, it can only be SAS if the 55° angle is the included angle between the 7 cm and 10 cm sides for both triangles.
   d False, the corresponding angles may all be equal but the sides may not be equal.
2 No, Tiff is incorrect because for triangle Y, the 100° angle is not the included angle between 4 cm and 7.5 cm.
3 Yes, using Pythagoras' theorem AC = 8 cm, so the triangles are congruent, RHS
4 Two angles and a corresponding side are equal, AAS, so triangle PQM and triangle RSM are congruent.

Exam practice

Angle AEB = Angle DEC (vertically opposite angles)
Angle ABE = Angle EDC (alternate angles are equal)
Angle BAE = Angle ECD (alternate angles are equal)
As DC = AB and the angles in each triangle are the same, triangle ABE is congruent to triangle DEC using the AAS condition.

12.2 Geometric proof and congruence

Purposeful practice

1 a Angle AEB = angle CED because vertically opposite angles are equal.
Angle BAE = angle CDE because alternate angles are equal.
AB = CD

  b AAS

2 a, b Pairs of corresponding sides from: AB with BC or CD, AD with BC or CD (accept BD with BD)

  c Yes, either because alternate angles are equal or opposite angles in a rhombus are equal (depending on answer to **Q2a** and **b**).

  d SAS

3 a AB = CD because opposite sides in a rectangle are equal.
AE = CE (or DE), BE = DE (or CE) because the diagonals of a rectangle are equal and intersect at their midpoints.

  b SSS

Problem-solving practice

1 Students' own proofs, for example, AB = BC as ABC is an equilateral triangle.
Both triangles have the common side BD and angle ADB = angle CDB = 90°.
AB is the hypotenuse of triangle ABD and BC is the hypotenuse of triangle BCD, therefore triangle ABD is congruent to triangle BCD by RHS.

2 Students' own proofs, for example, QR = PS as opposite sides of a parallelogram are equal.
Angle MQR = angle MSP because alternate angles are equal.
Angle QMR = angle PMS as vertically opposite angles are equal.
Therefore triangle PSM is congruent to triangle QRM by AAS.

3 AB = BC, AN = CM, AM = CN and both triangles have a common side AC, therefore SSS, so triangle AMC is congruent to triangle CNA.
Students' own proof, for example,
AB = BC and AM = $\frac{1}{2}$AB, CN = $\frac{1}{2}$BC, so AM = CN.
Angle MAC = angle NCA (base angles of isosceles triangle ABC).
AC is a common side in triangles AMC and CNA.
Therefore triangle AMC is congruent to triangle CNA by SAS.

4 Students' own proofs, for example,
AD = GD as ADG is an isosceles triangle.
AD is a side of the square ABCD, GD is a side of the square DEFG therefore these squares are congruent.
So, DE = DC as these are sides of congruent squares.
Angle ADC and angle GDE are angles in squares so they both equal 90°.
Therefore, angle ADE = 90° + angle CDE and angle GDC = 90° + angle CDE, so angle ADE = angle GDC.
Thus, triangle ADE is congruent to triangle GDC by SAS.

Exam practice

AX = YC, AD = CD because adjacent sides of a kite are equal and angle XAD = angle DCY because the base angles of an isosceles triangle are equal, therefore SAS, so triangle ADX is congruent to triangle CDY. Students' own proof, for example, AD = CD as a kite has two pairs of adjacent equal sides.
Angle DAX = angle DCY as these are base angles in the isosceles triangle ACD.
AX = CY, therefore triangle ADX is congruent to triangle CDY by SAS.

12.3 Similarity

Purposeful practice 1

1 a i $\frac{\text{length of B}}{\text{length of A}} = 2$ **ii** $\frac{\text{width of B}}{\text{width of A}} = 2$

  b Yes, the rectangles are similar as the ratios of corresponding sides are the same.

2 a i $\frac{\text{base of B}}{\text{base of A}} = 3$ **ii** $\frac{\text{height of B}}{\text{height of A}} = 3$

  b Yes, the triangles are similar as the ratios of corresponding sides are the same, and the included angles are equal.

3 **a** $3 \div 1.2 = 2.5$ and $4.25 \div 1.7 = 2.5$ so the parallelograms are similar.

  b $5 \div 3 = 1\frac{2}{3}$ and $4 \div 2 = 2$ so the triangles are not similar.

Purposeful practice 2

1 B $x = 6$, C $x = 5$, D $x = 11.25$

2 A $x = 0.8$, C $x = 3.6$, D $x = 17.1$

Problem-solving practice

1 Ben is not right because the corresponding angles in similar shapes are equal.

2 22.5 cm   **3** 3.33 cm

Exam practice

1 $58.5 \div 13 = 4.5$, $54 \div 12 = 4.5$ and $22.5 \div 5 = 4.5$. All ratios for corresponding sides are the same so the two triangles are mathematically similar.

12.4 More similarity

Purposeful practice 1

1 a Angle ECD = 30° (alternate angles are equal).
Angle CDE = 58° (alternate angles are equal).
Angle CED = 92° (vertically opposite angles are equal).

  b From **Q1a** all corresponding angles are equal, so triangles ABE and CDE are similar.

2 a Angle ABC = 80° (corresponding angles are equal)
Angle ACB = 60° (corresponding angles are equal)

  b Both triangles have a common angle of 40° and from **Q2a**, all corresponding angles are equal, so triangles ADE and ABC are similar.

Purposeful practice 2

1 a CED = 92° (vertically opposite angles are equal); EDC = 58° and DCE = 30° (alternate angles are equal). Therefore triangles ABE and DCE are similar (AAA).

  b 2.8 cm

2 a Angle DAE = angle BAC (common); angle ADE = angle ABC and angle AED = angle ACB (corresponding angles are equal). Therefore triangles ABC and ADE are similar (AAA).

  b 42 cm

Problem-solving practice

1 No. WX = 20 cm and XY = 10 cm, $30 \div 20 = 1.5$ and $20 \div 10 = 2$.
Corresponding sides are not in the same ratio, so rectangle ABCD and rectangle WXYZ are not mathematically similar.

2 4.5 cm

3 a AE = 19 cm

  b CD = 7 cm

Exam practice

1 Assuming that AE is parallel to BD, $9 \div 3 \times 2 = 6$, $x = 6$ cm
Assuming that the corresponding sides are EC and BC, $12 \div 2 \times 3 - 2 = 16$, $x = 16$ cm

12.5 Similarity in 3D solids

Purposeful practice 1

1

Question	Linear scale factor	Surface area of A	Surface area of B	Area scale factor	Volume of A	Volume of B	Volume scale factor
1	2	6 cm²	24 cm²	4	1 cm³	8 cm³	8
2	2	10 cm²	40 cm²	4	2 cm³	16 cm³	8
3	3	10 cm²	90 cm²	9	2 cm³	54 cm³	27
4	4	22 cm²	352 cm²	16	6 cm³	384 cm³	64

Purposeful practice 2

1

Linear scale factor	Area scale factor	Surface area of A	Surface area of B	Volume scale factor	Volume of A	Volume of B
2	4	52 cm²	208 cm²	8	24 cm³	192 cm³
3	9	52 cm²	468 cm²	27	24 cm³	648 cm³
5	25	52 cm²	1300 cm²	125	24 cm³	3000 cm³
7	49	52 cm²	2548 cm²	343	24 cm³	8232 cm³

Problem-solving practice

1 10 125 cm²   **2** 10 cm

3 a 320 cm³   **b** 72.5 cm²

4 55.6 cm²   **5** 1 : 9   **6** 160 cm³

Exam practice

1 9.16 cm

Mixed problem-solving practice C

1 **a** 0.15   **b** 60

2 Students' own answer, for example, $(x + 5)(x - 3) = 0$

3 $2\frac{3}{4}$ hours

4 Bank A: $8000 \times 1.028^3 = 8690.99$, so £690.99 interest
   Bank B: $8000 \times 1.04 \times 1.022^2 = 8690.11$, so £690.11 interest
   Sasha should choose bank A.

5 49.25 cm

6 No, Lauren is not correct. The triangles are mathematically similar but just because the angles are the same, it does not mean that the sides are the same length.

7 **a**

		Tom				
		1	1	1	4	5	6
Sasha	1	(1, 1)	(1, 1)	(1, 1)	(1, 4)	(1, 5)	(1, 6)
	2	(2, 1)	(2, 1)	(2, 1)	(2, 4)	(2, 5)	(2, 6)
	3	(3, 1)	(3, 1)	(3, 1)	(3, 4)	(3, 5)	(3, 6)
	4	(4, 1)	(4, 1)	(4, 1)	(4, 4)	(4, 5)	(4, 6)

  b No, as the probability that Tom will win is $\frac{11}{24}$, which is higher than the probability that Sasha will win, which is $\frac{9}{24}$

  c Tom 66 and Sasha 54

8 40 clips in a tub and 72 clips in a box.

9 **a** 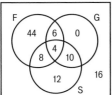   **b** $\frac{2}{17}$

10 **a** $5 < 2n - 7 < 12$ **b** $6 < n < 9.5$ **c** 7, 8 or 9

11 $3x^2 - 9x + 4 = 0$

12 **a** Kit has substituted $y = 4x + 3$ for x, instead of y. Kit should have written $x^2 + 3x = 4x + 3$

  b $x = 4$ and $y = 19$ or $x = -3$ and $y = -9$

13 0.3688

14 **a** 12.5 cm   **b** 168 cm^2

15 3.64

Exam practice

16 £14 550.73

17 A tea costs £1.60 and a coffee costs £2.80.

18 Ratio of the length of cone A to the length of cone B is $\sqrt[3]{64} : \sqrt[3]{27} = 4 : 3$
   Ratio of the area of cone A to the area of cone B is $4^2 : 3^2 = 16 : 9$
   $592 \div 16 \times 9 = 333$, therefore, the surface area of cone B = 333 cm^2

19 $P(\text{GB or BG}) = \frac{5}{9} \times \frac{4}{8} + \frac{4}{9} \times \frac{5}{8} = \frac{40}{72} = \frac{5}{9}$, students may draw a probability tree diagram to help.

20 Length upper bound = 14.25, length lower bound = 14.15
   Width upper bound = 17.05, width lower bound = 16.95
   Height upper bound = 22.75, height lower bound = 22.65
   Mass upper bound = 1982.5, mass lower bound = 1977.5
   Density upper bound = $\dfrac{1982.5}{14.15 \times 16.95 \times 22.65} = 0.364\,937\,798$
   Density lower bound = $\dfrac{1977.5}{14.25 \times 17.05 \times 22.75} = 0.357\,763\,345$
   Density = 0.36 g/cm^3 as the upper and lower bounds both round to 0.36 to 2 decimal places (or 2 significant figures)

21 **a** PS = QR as opposite sides of a parallelogram are equal,
   angle TQR = angle PSU as opposite angles of a parallelogram are equal and angle TRQ = angle SPU is given,
   so using ASA, triangle TRQ is congruent to triangle SPU.

  b TQ = SU as triangle TRQ is congruent to triangle SPU and TQ is parallel to SU, so TQUS is a parallelogram. Opposite sides of a parallelogram are parallel, so TS is parallel to QU.

13 More trigonometry

13.1 Accuracy

Purposeful practice 1

1 **a** 3.55 and 3.45, 3.45 and 3.35   **b** 3.55 and 3.45, 3.35 and 3.25
  c 3.45 and 3.35, 3.35 and 3.25

2 **a** 45.8°, 46.7°, 45.8°, 45°   **b** 45.8°, 46.7°, 46.7°, 47.5°
  c 46.7°, 45.8°, 45°, 45.9°

Purposeful practice 2

1 **a** 4.3 and 5.7   **b** 5.1 and 6.5   **c** 5.7 and 7.1

2 **a** 45° and 60.9°   **b** 52.1° and 65.6°   **c** 45° and 57.5°

Problem-solving practice

1 Students' own answer $\geqslant 16.5$ cm

2 The upper bound of the angle is 44.4° so it cannot be too steep.

3 0.35 m and 0.30 m

4 Simon is incorrect. The bounds when the side lengths are rounded to 1 decimal place are 72.4° and 74.8°, but when the side lengths are rounded to 1 significant figure the bounds are 75.9° and 67.7°, which is a wider range.

5 26.3 cm^2

Exam practice

1 $\sqrt{7.65^2 - 4.15^2} = 6.43$ cm to 2 d.p.

13.2 Graph of the sine function

Purposeful practice 1

1 0.7   2 −0.6

Purposeful practice 2

1 0.5   2 −0.5   3 0.5   4 0.0872
5 0.9962   6 −0.0872   7 −0.9962   8 0.0872

Purposeful practice 3

1 **a** 36.9°, 143.1°, 396.9° and 503.1° **b** 36.9°, 143.1°, 396.9° and 503.1°
  c 23.6°, 156.4°, 383.6° and 516.4°

2 **a** 0   **b** 0   **c** 0

Problem-solving practice

Students' own answers for **Q1–6** (multiple answers possible), for example:

1 30° and 210°, 170° and 190°

2 Hypotenuse length 3 cm and opposite side length 1.8 cm (any pair of lengths in the ratio 5 to 3)

3 431°, 425.5°, 474° any angles in the range ($424.1° < x < 475.9°$)

4 $-180° < x < 0°$ (any range of the form $(360n - 180)° < x < 360n°$)

5 $-30° < x < 30°$ and $330° < x < 390°$ (any ranges of the form $(180n - 30)° < x < (180n + 30)°$)

6 $0° < x < 53.1°$

7 A (90, 2)   B (180, −2)   C (270, 1)   D (540, −1)

8 1.75

9 (0, 0)

Exam practice

1 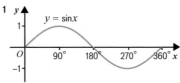

13.3 Graph of the cosine function

Purposeful practice 1

1 −0.83   2 0.43

Purposeful practice 2

1 0.87   2 −0.87   3 0.87   4 0.996
5 −0.0872   6 −0.996   7 0.0872   8 0.996

Purposeful practice 3

1 a 53.1°, 306.9° and 413.1° **b** 25.8°, 334.2° and 385.8°
  c 113.6°, 246.4° and 473.6°

2 a 1 **b** 1 **c** 1

Problem-solving practice

Students' own answers for **Q1–6** (multiple answers possible), for example:

1 30° and 210°, 45° and 225°

2 Hypotenuse length 4 cm and adjacent side length 2.4 cm.

3 325°, 386°, 390° (angles in the range 323.2° < x < 334.1° or 385.9° < x < 396.8°)

4 −270° < x < −90° (any range of the form $(360n − 270)°$ < x < $(360n − 90)°$)

5 60° < x < 120° (any ranges of the form $(180n + 60)°$ < x < $(180n + 120)°$)

6 36.87° < x < 90°

7 A (90, 1) B (180, 0) C (360, −1)

8 One

9 Four

10 Any line in the form $y = c$, where c is a constant and $c > 1$ or $c < −1$

11 Because the maximum value of cosine is 1.

Exam practice

1

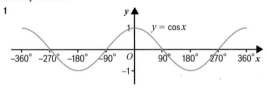

13.4 The tangent function

Purposeful practice 1

1 −1.3 **2** 0.7

Purposeful practice 2

1 0.5774 **2** 0.5774 **3** 0.5774 **4** 0.0875
5 −11.4301 **6** 0.0875 **7** −11.4301 **8** 0.0875

Purposeful practice 3

1 a 31.0°, 211.0° and 391.0° **b** 82.4°, 262.4° and 442.4°
  c 91.4°, 271.4° and 451.4°

2 a 1 **b** 1 **c** 1

Problem-solving practice

Students' own answers for **Q1–7** (multiple answers possible), for example:

1 30° and 150°

2 Adjacent side length 13 cm and opposite side length 18 cm (any pair of lengths in the ratio 13 to 18)

3 263°, 443°, 443.5° (angles in the range 262.9° < x < 263.6° or 442.9° < x < 443.6°)

4 −90° < x < 0° (any range of the form $(180n − 90)°$ < x < $180n°$)

5 −26.56° < x < 26.56° (any range of the form $(180n − 25.56)°$ < x < $(180n + 25.56)°$)

6 0° < x < 38.6° (any range of the form $180n°$ < x < $(180n + 38.6)°$)

7 a 90°, 270°, 450°, 630° (any angles of the form $(180n + 90)°$)

  b 1, −1, 1, −1 (corresponding to students' own answers to **Q7a**)

  c 0, 0, 0, 0

8 a four **b** four

9 Any equation describing an asymptote of the tan graph, for example, $x = 90$, (any line of the form $x = (180n + 90)°$)

Exam practice

1

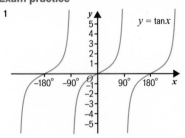

13.5 Calculating areas and the sine rule

Purposeful practice 1

1 12 cm² **2** 20.8 cm² **3** 24 cm²

Purposeful practice 2

1 a 2.13 cm **b** 2.03 cm **c** 9.40 cm
2 a 23.6° **b** 93.7° **c** 65.8°

Problem-solving practice

1 21.6 cm **2** 16.6 cm² **3** 9.2 cm

4 a 25 cm, 36.6 cm and 18.3 cm **b** 213.1 cm²

5 10 cm

Exam practice

1 Area of triangle = $\frac{1}{2} ab \sin$ C, so $\frac{1}{2}(x + 2)(x − 5)\left(\frac{\sqrt{3}}{2}\right) = 2\sqrt{3}$

$$\left(\frac{\sqrt{3}}{4}\right)(x^2 − 3x − 10) = 2\sqrt{3}$$
$$x^2 − 3x − 10 = 8$$
$$x^2 − 3x − 18 = 0$$
$$(x − 6)(x + 3) = 0$$
$$x = 6$$

13.6 The cosine rule and 2D trigonometric problems

Purposeful practice 1

1 1.61 cm **2** 2.05 cm **3** 5.70 cm

Purposeful practice 2

1 $x = 82.8°$ **2** $x = 90°$ **3** $x = 34.0°$ and $y = 44.4°$

Purposeful practice 3

1 5.87 cm **2** 5.73 cm **3** 5.23 cm

Problem-solving practice

1 No, the perimeter is 45.0 cm

2 Let angle at centre of unshaded sector be x.

  Using cosine rule: $\cos x = \dfrac{(8^2 + 8^2 − 10^2)}{(2 \times 8 \times 8)}$

  So, $x = \cos^{−1}\left(\dfrac{7}{32}\right) = 77.4°$ (1 d.p.)

  Therefore angle of shaded sector is $360° − 77.4° = 282.6°$.

  This is $\dfrac{(282.6 \times 100)}{360}$ percent of the circle i.e. 78.5%.

3 81.3 cm **4** 20.5 miles

Exam practice

1 $\dfrac{15}{\sin 103°} = \dfrac{BD}{\sin 27°}$

  $BD = \dfrac{15 \times \sin 27°}{\sin 103°} = 6.99$

  $AD^2 = 12^2 \times 6.99^2 − 2 \times 12 \times 6.99 \times \cos 74° = 146.62$

  $AD = 12.1$ cm (3 s.f.)

13.7 Solving problems in 3D

Purposeful practice 1

1 a 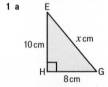 **b**

2 a $x = 12.8$ cm **b** $y = 13.7$ cm

Purposeful practice 2

1 $\theta = 51.3°$ **2** $\alpha = 21.3°$

Problem-solving practice

1 647.4 cm³ **2** 7.07 cm

3 No, the diagonal length of the pot is only 11.0 cm. **4** 60.9°

5 No, the diameter of the base is only 179 cm.

Exam practice

1 $\sin 34° = \dfrac{6.2}{AC}$

$AC = \dfrac{6.2}{\sin 34°} = 11.087\,40...$

$x = \tan{-1}\left(\dfrac{7.5}{11.087\,40}\right)$

$= 34.1°$

13.8 Transforming trigonometric graphs 1

Purposeful practice 1

1

x	$\sin(x)$	$-\sin(x)$	$\sin(-x)$
0°	0	0	0
45°	0.71	−0.71	−0.71
90°	1	−1	−1
135°	0.71	−0.71	−0.71
180°	0	0	0
270°	−1	1	1
360°	0	0	0

2

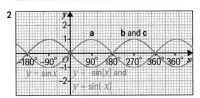

Purposeful practice 2

1

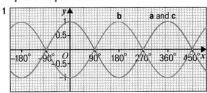

2

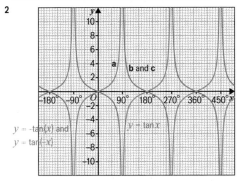

Problem-solving practice

1 180° and 360°   **2** $y = \sin x$

3 $y = \tan(-x)$ or $-\tan(x)$

4 Students' own transformations, for example, a reflection in the y-axis followed by a reflection in the x-axis.

5 $y = -\cos(x)$

6 $(-180, -1)$

Exam practice

1

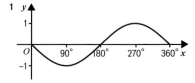

13.9 Transforming trigonometric graphs 2

Purposeful practice 1

1

x	$y = \sin(x)$	$y = \sin(x + 90)$	$y = \sin(x) + 90$
0°	0	1	90
90°	1	0	91
180°	0	−1	90
270°	−1	0	89
360°	0	1	90

2

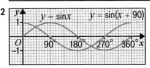

a The maximum and minimum values of both graphs are 1 and −1.
b $y = \sin x$: 0, 180°, 360°
$y = \sin(x + 90)$: 90°, 270°

Purposeful practice 2

1

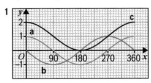

a i 1 and −1   **ii** 90° and 270°
b i 1 and −1   **ii** 180° and 360°
c i 2 and 0   **ii** 180°

2

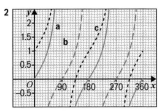

a 0, 180°, 360°   **b** 90°, 180°   **c** 135°, 315°

Problem-solving practice

1 A translation of $\begin{pmatrix} -90 \\ 0 \end{pmatrix}$

2

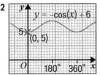

3 a $(87, 1)$ **b** $(93, 1)$ **c** $(90, 4)$ **d** $(90, -2)$

4 Students' own answer, for example, $(71.3°, 2.9)$ (multiple answers possible)

5 Students' own transformations, for example, translation of $\begin{pmatrix} 0 \\ 3 \end{pmatrix}$ (multiple answers possible)

6 $y = \tan(x - 5) + 6$

7 Students' own answers, for example, $y = \sin(-x) + 1$ (multiple answers possible)

Exam practice

1

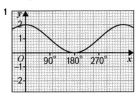

14 Further statistics

14.1 Sampling

Purposeful practice 1

1 a $\frac{50}{N}$ b $\frac{1}{10}$ c $\frac{50}{N} = \frac{1}{10}$ d 500

2 a $\frac{50}{N}$ b $\frac{1}{5}$ c $\frac{50}{N} = \frac{1}{5}$ d 250

3 a $\frac{50}{N}$ b $\frac{1}{4}$ c $\frac{50}{N} = \frac{1}{4}$ d 200

4 a $\frac{30}{N}$ b $\frac{1}{8}$ c $\frac{30}{N} = \frac{1}{8}$ d 240

Purposeful practice 2

1 400   2 250   3 280

Problem-solving practice

1 A is $N = 900$, B is $N = 1000$, C is $N = 540$, D is $N = 1680$

2 9000, the assumptions are that the mouse population has not changed between Saturday and Sunday, the chance of being captured is the same for all mice and the marks on the mice have not disappeared.

3 2000, the assumptions are that the rabbit population has not changed between Monday and Tuesday, the chance of being captured is the same for all rabbits and the tags on the rabbits have not come off.

4 a 80

   b The assumptions are that the frog population has not changed between the capture and recapture, the chance of being captured is the same for all frogs and the marks on the frogs have not come off.

5 Jonathan should not have added 10 and 20, he should have multiplied them to give 200 and then divided by 5 to give 40, instead of multiplying by 5.

Exam practice

1 a 400

   b If some of the tags had fallen off, then more than ten of the chickens which had originally been tagged may have been recaptured. This means that the estimate would be less than 400 as you would be dividing by a bigger number.

14.2 Cumulative frequency

Purposeful practice

1 b Estimate of median = 26

2 a

Cumulative frequency graph

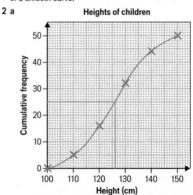

   b Estimate of median = 66

3 a

Cumulative frequency graph

b Estimate of median = 67

4 a

Cumulative frequency graph

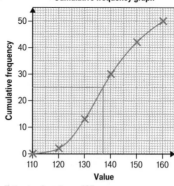

b Estimate of median = 137

5 a

Cumulative frequency graph

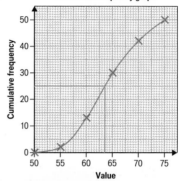

b Estimate of median = 63.5

Problem-solving practice

1 Ewan has plotted the points at the midpoints of the class intervals instead of the upper class boundaries and he has used a ruler to join the points instead of a smooth curve.

2 a

Heights of children

   b Louise has halved the cumulative frequency but not read the value of this median piece of data from the height axis. The median height is 126 cm.

   c The estimate of the median gives you an estimate for the middle value of the data. Here the median height is 126 cm. 50% of the children are shorter than 126 cm and 50% are taller than 126 cm.

3 a

Weights of apples   b 9 apples

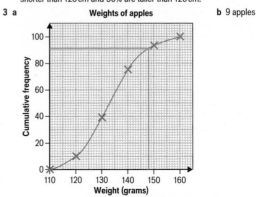

1 a

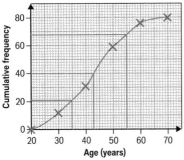

Ages of people

b 43 years old

c No, 68 − 21 = 47, 47 ÷ 80 × 100 = 58.75%

14.3 Box plots

Purposeful practice 1

1

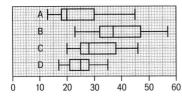

Exam scores in different schools

Purposeful practice 2

1 20 students   **2** 50 students   **3** 30 students   **4** 10 students

5 40 students   **6** 60 students   **7** 100 students   **8** 30 students

Problem-solving practice

1 The median is plotted incorrectly at 30 kg and not 32 kg. The box plot shows a maximum value of 52 kg, however this is the range of the data not the maximum value. The lightest weight is 5 kg and the range is 52 kg, so the maximum value should be 57 kg.

2 a i

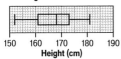

Heights of 80 students

ii Lower quartile = 161 cm, range = 29 cm

b 60 students

3 a

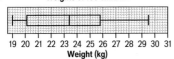

Weights of 100 children

b 75 children

Exam practice

1 a

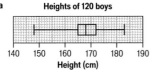

Heights of 120 boys

b 90 boys

14.4 Drawing histograms

Purposeful practice

1 a

Height, x (cm)	Frequency	Class width	Frequency density
$0 < x \leqslant 10$	5	10	$5 \div 10 = 0.5$
$10 < x \leqslant 15$	12	**5**	**2.4**
$15 < x \leqslant 30$	15	**15**	**1**
$30 < x \leqslant 50$	6	**20**	**0.3**

b

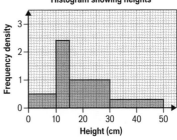

Histogram showing heights

c The area of each bar should match its frequency.

2 a 0.8, 2.8, 0.6, 0.35

b

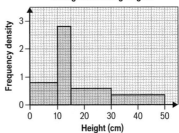

Histogram showing heights

c The area of each bar should match its frequency.

3 a

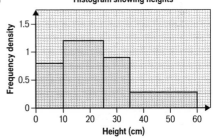

Histogram showing heights

b The area of each bar should match its frequency.

Problem-solving practice

1 Megan has drawn the bars to the height of the frequency, not the frequency density. The last bar is too wide; it is from 20 to 50 but should only be from 20 to 40.

2 Frequency densities are 4, 26, 34, 56 and 12.

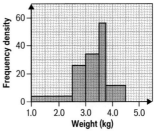

Weights of babies

3 a Frequency densities are 1, 4, 6.8, 4.8, 0.8.

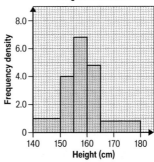

Heights of students

b The final bar would need to be extended to 190, and its height would decrease to show the new frequency density of the bar, which is 0.48.

Exam practice

1 Frequency densities are 0.5, 4, 8.2, 5.2 and 0.533.

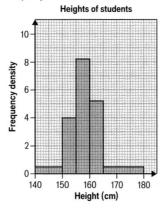

Heights of students

14.5 Interpreting histograms

Purposeful practice

1 a

Height, x (cm)	Frequency density	Class width	Frequency
$0 < x \leq 10$	0.7	10	$0.7 \times 10 = 7$
$10 < x \leq 15$	2.6	5	$2.6 \times 5 = 13$
$15 < x \leq 20$	3.2	5	$3.2 \times 5 = 16$
$20 < x \leq 40$	0.2	20	$0.2 \times 20 = 4$

b 40

2 a

Height, x (cm)	Frequency density	Class width	Frequency
$0 < x \leq 10$	0.6	10	6
$10 < x \leq 15$	2.8	5	14
$15 < x \leq 25$	1.5	10	15
$25 < x \leq 40$	0.4	15	6

b 35

3 a 47   **b** 6   **c** 53

Problem-solving practice

1 105 houses

2 a 8

b The data is grouped so we know that there are 16 people who took between 70 and 90 seconds, but we don't know if half of these took over 80 seconds, which is why 8 is an estimate.

Exam practice

1 7

14.6 Comparing and describing populations

Purposeful practice

1 a B   **b** B   **c** B, B

2 a A   **b** A   **c** higher, greater

3 a A   **b** B

c On average, students in class A are heavier and students in class B have a greater spread of weights.

4 On average, students in class B are taller and students in class A have a greater spread of heights.

5 On average, students in class C are taller and students in class D have a greater spread of heights.

6 On average, students in class E are taller and have a greater spread of heights.

Problem-solving practice

1 On average, Ben's potato plants yield a greater mass of potatoes than Jordan's and have a greater spread of weights.

Exam practice

1 a

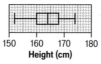

Heights of Year 11 girls

b On average, the Year 11 girls are taller and the Year 7 girls have a greater spread of heights.

15 Equations and graphs

15.1 Solving simultaneous equations graphically

Purposeful practice 1

1

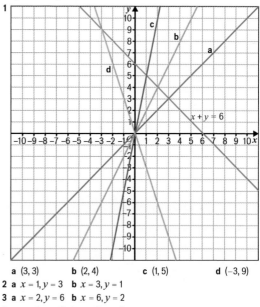

a (3, 3)   **b** (2, 4)   **c** (1, 5)   **d** (−3, 9)

2 a $x = 1, y = 3$ **b** $x = 3, y = 1$

3 a $x = 2, y = 6$ **b** $x = 6, y = 2$

4 a $x = 3, y = 9$ **b** $x = 9, y = 3$

Purposeful practice 2

1 $x = 1, y = 4$ **2** $x = 6, y = -1$ **3** $x = -1, y = -2$

Problem-solving practice

1 a $x = 1, y = 2$ and $x = -4, y = 7$ **b** $x = 1, y = 2$ and $x = 0, y = 3$

   c $x = 4, y = 3$ and $x = -4, y = -3$ **d** $x = 2, y = 1$ and $x = -1, y = -2$

2 After 10 months, each method would have cost a total of £150.

3 Roughly $x = 0.4, y = 1.4$ and $x = 4.6, y = 5.6$.

4 a 49p   **b** £2.93

5 James' graph intersection would give a negative y, which is not possible. The blue line is incorrect. James has drawn the line $x - 5y = 7$ instead of the line $x + 5y = 7$

Exam practice

1 a

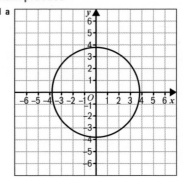

b Approximate answers $x = 2.5, y = 3$

   $x = -0.9, y = -3.8$

15.2 Representing inequalities graphically

Purposeful practice 1

1
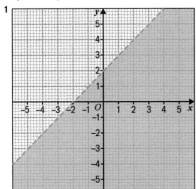

2
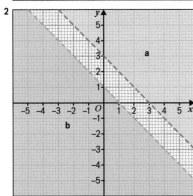

3
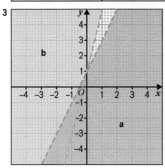

4 a No   **b** Yes

Purposeful practice 2

1 a $\{x : x < 5\}$ **b** $\{x : x < 6\}$ **c** $\{x : x < 4\}$
   d $\{x : x > 8\}$ **e** $\{x : x > 10\}$ **f** $\{x : x > 12\}$
2 a $\{x : -4 \leqslant x \leqslant 4\}$ **b** $\{x : -9 < x < 9\}$
   c $\{x : x < -16\} \cup \{x : x > 16\}$ **d** $\{x : x \leqslant -8\} \cup \{x : x \geqslant 8\}$
3 a $\{x : 3 \leqslant x \leqslant 8\}$ **b** $\{x : 4 \leqslant x \leqslant 6\}$

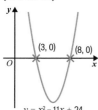
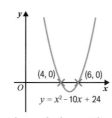

c $\{x : x \leqslant 2\} \cup \{x : x \geqslant 12\}$ **d** $\{x : x \leqslant 1\} \cup \{x : x \geqslant 24\}$

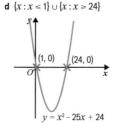

Problem-solving practice

1
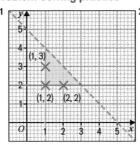

2
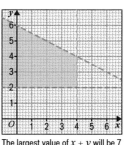

The largest value of $x + y$ will be 7 when $x = 3$ and $y = 4$

3 a $y \leqslant 2x + 6, x + y \leqslant 6, y \geqslant 4$ **b** $y \geqslant -1, y \leqslant 3 - x, y \leqslant 2x + 4$
   c $y \geqslant \dfrac{x}{2} - 4, x \geqslant 2, y \leqslant 6 - 2x$

4
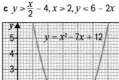
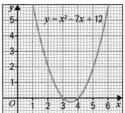

The graph is below the x-axis for $\{x : 3 < x < 4\}$

Exam practice

1 $y \leqslant 2x + 3$
$y \leqslant 4 - x$
$y \geqslant -1$

15.3 Graphs of quadratic functions

Purposeful practice 1

1 a $y = (x - 1)(x - 3)$; roots are $x = 1$ and $x = 3$
   b $y = (x - 1)(x + 1)$; roots are $x = 1$ and $x = -1$
   c $y = (x - 1)(x + 3)$; roots are $x = 1$ and $x = -3$
2 a $y = (4x - 1)(x - 1)$; $\left(\dfrac{1}{4}, 0\right)$ and $(1, 0)$
   b $y = (3x - 1)(3x + 4)$; $\left(\dfrac{1}{3}, 0\right)$ and $\left(-\dfrac{4}{3}, 0\right)$
   c $y = \left(\dfrac{1}{4}x - \dfrac{1}{2}\right)(x + 6)$; $(-6, 0)$ and $(2, 0)$
3 From **Q1**
   a $(x - 2)^2 - 1$ turning point $(2, -1)$ **b** $x^2 - 1$ turning point $(0, -1)$
   c $(x + 1)^2 - 4$ turning point $(-1, -4)$
   From **Q2**
   a $\left(2x - \dfrac{5}{4}\right)^2 - \dfrac{9}{16}$ turning point $\left(\dfrac{5}{8}, -\dfrac{9}{16}\right)$
   b $\left(3x + \dfrac{3}{2}\right)^2 - \dfrac{25}{4}$ turning point $\left(-\dfrac{1}{2}, -\dfrac{25}{4}\right)$
   c $y = \left(\dfrac{1}{2}x + 1\right)^2 - 4$ turning point $(-2, -4)$
4 From **Q1**

a
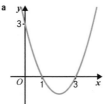

b
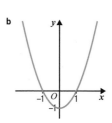

c
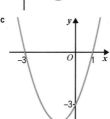

From **Q2**

a

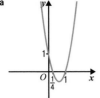

b

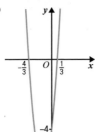

c

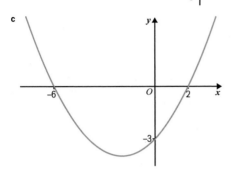

Purposeful practice 2

1 a completing the square: $y = 2(x + 1)^2 + 4$, so turning point is $(-1, 4)$

  b completing the square: $y = 3(x + 1)^2 + 4$, so turning point is $(-1, 4)$

  c completing the square: $y = 5(x + 1)^2 + 4$, so turning point is $(-1, 4)$

2 All three are minimums because the graphs will be $\cup$ shaped.

3 a $x = 3$ **b** $x = 3$

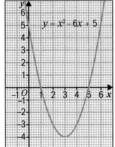

  c $x = 1$

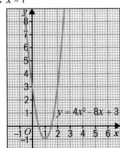

Problem-solving practice

1 a matches graph **ii** because it is $\cup$-shaped (x^2) and has roots at $(1, 0)$ and $(6, 0)$ since $y = (x - 1)(x - 6)$

  b matches graph **i** because it is an upside down $\cup$ $(-x^2)$ and has roots at $(-3, 0)$ and $(2, 0)$ since $y = (x + 3)(2 - x)$

  c matches graph **iv** because it is $\cup$-shaped (x^2) and has roots at $(-3, 0)$ and $(2, 0)$ since $y = (x + 3)(x - 2)$

  d matches graph **iii** because it is an upside down $\cup$ $(-x^2)$ and has roots at $(3, 0)$ and $(-2, 0)$ since $y = (x + 2)(3 - x)$

2 The graph is the wrong way up. The negative x^2 in the equation would give a $\cap$ shape.

The graph has roots at $x = -3$ and $x = 2$, but if these values of x are substituted into the equation, the corresponding y-values are not 0.

The equation would intersect the y-axis at $y = 4$, but the graph has an intersection at $y = -6$

3 $y = x^2 - 2x - 3$

Exam practice

1 a

x	−1	0	1	2	3	4	5
y	8	3	0	−1	0	3	8

  b

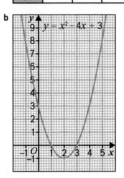

15.4 Solving quadratic equations graphically

Purposeful practice 1

1 a One repeated root   **b** Two roots

  c Two roots   **d** No real roots

2 a One repeated root   **b** No roots

  c Two roots   **d** Two roots

  e One repeated root   **f** No roots

3 Roughly $x = 0.3$ and $x = 3.7$

Purposeful practice 2

1 a The iterations are 1.63, 1.93, 2.05

  b The iterations are 4.47, 4.63, 4.68

2 a 3.72   **b** 2.65   **c** 1.14

Problem-solving practice

1 a is graph **iii**   **b** is graph **i**   **c** is graph **iv**   **d** is graph **ii**

  Solutions **a** $x = 0.5$ and $x = -0.7$ **b** $x = -2$ and $x = 1$

           c $x = -1$ and $x = 2$ **d** $x = 2$ (repeated)

2 a $x = 4 \pm \sqrt{14}$

  b The quadratic formula leads to $\sqrt{(-3)^2 - 16} = \sqrt{-7}$ so no real roots.

3 a 0.73   **b** $16x^2 + 2x - 10 = 0$

Exam practice

  a $2x^2 = 5 - x$ **b** $x_1 = 1.414213562 \dots$

     $x^2 = \dfrac{5 - x}{2}$ $x_2 = 1.338989626 \dots$

     $x = \sqrt{\dfrac{5 - x}{2}}$ $x_3 = 1.352961635 \dots$

15.5 Graphs of cubic functions

Purposeful practice 1

1 a, c and **d** are cubic equations.

2 a

x	−2	−1	0	1	2	3	4
$x^3 - 4x^2 + x + 2$	−24	−4	2	0	−4	−4	6

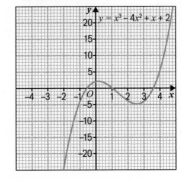

b

x	-4	-3	-2	-1	0	1	2
$x^3 + 4x^2 + x + 2$	-2	8	8	4	2	8	28

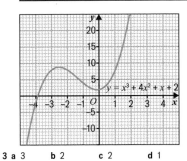

3 a 3   **b** 2   **c** 2   **d** 1   **e** 1

Purposeful practice 2

1 a 1, 2, 3   **b** 1, -2, 3
   c 1 (repeated) and 2   **d** 1 and 2 (repeated)

2 a graph ii   **b** graph iii   **c** graph iv   **d** graph i

Problem-solving practice

1

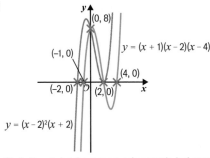

Similarities: students' own answers, for example, both cross the y-axis at y = 8; both have a root (2, 0).

Differences: students' own answers, for example $y = (x - 2)^2(x + 2)$ has two roots while $y = (x + 1)(x - 2)(x - 4)$ has three roots; $y = (x - 2)^2(x + 2)$ has a turning point in the second quadrant while $y = (x + 1)(x - 2)(x - 4)$ has a turning point in the fourth quadrant.

2 a $y = x^3 - 4x^2 + x + 6$ **b** $y = x^3 - 7x^2 + 16x - 12$
   c $y = 2x^3 - 7x^2 - 68x - 32$

3 a First error $-1 \times 2 \times -3 = -6$ should give $+6$
      Second error $(x - 1)(x + 2)(x - 3) = 0$ should give $x = 1$, and then -2 and then 3

b

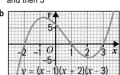

Exam practice

1 a

x	-3	-2	-1	0	1	2	3
y	-18	-2	2	0	-2	2	18

b

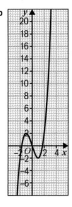

---

16 Circle theorems

16.1 Radii and chords

Purposeful practice 1

1 OPQ, OPR, OEF

2 $a = 40°$ $b = 100°$ $c = 30°$ $d = 60°$
   $e = 60°$ $f = 80°$ $g = 48°$

Purposeful practice 2

1 6 cm   **2** 16 cm   **3** 5 cm   **4** 12 cm

Problem-solving practice

1 $3\sqrt{7}$ cm

2 OA = OB (radii)
OBA = $32°$ (base angles in an isosceles triangle are equal)
AOB = $116°$ (the angles in a triangle add to $180°$)
$m = 64°$ (angles on a straight line add to $180°$)

3 For N to be the midpoint, ORN must be a right-angled triangle and RN must be 8 cm. Using Pythagoras, assuming it is a right-angled triangle, RN = $\sqrt{13^2 - 11^2}$ = 6.9 cm (1 d.p.). This is not 8 cm, so N is not the midpoint.

4 OQP = $20°$ (angles on a straight line add to $180°$)
OQ = OP = 7 cm (radii)
Distance between midpoint of PQ and Q = $7\cos 20°$ = 6.5778...
PQ = $2 \times 6.5778...$ = 13.2 cm (1 d.p.)

Exam practice

1 OBA = $40°$ (angles on a straight line add to $180°$)
OB = OA = 5 cm (radii)
$\left(\frac{1}{2}AB\right)$ = $5\cos 40°$ = 3.8302...cm
AB = $2 \times 3.8302...$cm = 7.7 cm (1 d.p.)

16.2 Tangents

Purposeful practice 1

1 Yes   **2** Yes   **3** No

Purposeful practice 2

1 a $a = 64°, b = 26°$ **b** $c = 120°$ **c** $d = 46°$
2 a $a = 30°, b = 75°$ **b** $c = 40°, d = 140°$ **c** $e = 38° f = 19°$

Problem-solving practice

1 Triangle OMN is right-angled (the angle between a tangent and the radius is $90°$)
ON^2 = $10^2 + 24^2$ (Pythagoras' theorem)
ON^2 = 676
ON = 26 cm

2 OBC = $90°$ (the angle between a tangent and the radius is $90°$)
BOC = $52°$ (the angles in a triangle add to $180°$)
BOA = $128°$ (the angles on a straight line add to $180°$)
OB = OA (radii)
$x = (180° - 128°) \div 2 = 26°$ (the angles in a triangle add to $180°$ and the base angles of an isosceles triangle are equal)

3 ORP = $32°$ (angles on a straight line add to $180°$)
OPR = $90°$ (the angle between a tangent and the radius is $90°$)
POR = $58°$ (the angles in a triangle add to $180°$)
QOP = $122°$ (the angles on a straight line add to $180°$)
$x = (180° - 122°) \div 2 = 29°$ (the angles in a triangle add to $180°$ and the base angles of an isosceles triangle are equal)
$y = 180 - (90 + 29) = 61°$ (the angles on a straight line add to $180°$)

4 ABO = $90°$ (the angle between a tangent and the radius is $90°$)
Sin OAB = $\frac{4}{8} = \frac{1}{2}$ (opposite over hypotenuse for a right-angled triangle)
OAB = $30°$ (known fact that sin $30° = \frac{1}{2}$)

Exam practice

1 Angle OBC = $90°$ as OB is a radius of the circle and the angle between the tangent and a radius is $90°$.
Angle BOC = $(90 - x)°$ because angles in a triangle add to $180°$.
Angle AOB = $(90 + x)°$ because angles on a straight line add to $180°$.
Angle OAB = $(180 - (90 + x))° \div 2 = \frac{(90 - x)}{2} = \left(45 - \frac{x}{2}\right)°$ as triangle AOB is an isosceles triangle.

16.3 Angles in circles 1

Purposeful practice 1

1 $a = 50°$ **2** $b = 140°$ **3** $c = 43°$

4 $d = 112°$ **5** $e = 121°$ **6** $f = 264°$

Purposeful practice 2

1 $a = 90°$ **2** $b = 45°$ **3** $c = 29°, d = 48°$

4 $e = 51°$ **5** $f = 50°, g = 65°$

Problem-solving practice

1 $a = 118°$ (the angle at the centre of a circle is twice the angle at the circumference)

AOC = 124° (the angles at a point add to 360°)

$b = 62°$ (the angle at the centre of a circle is twice the angle at the circumference)

2 QOR = 30° (the angle at the centre of a circle is twice the angle at the circumference)

$x = 15°$ (the angle at the centre of a circle is twice the angle at the circumference)

3 OYZ = 90° and OWZ = 90° (the angle between a tangent and the radius is 90°)

WOY = 96° (the angles in a quadrilateral add to 360°)

$x = 48°$ (the angle at the centre of a circle is twice the angle at the circumference)

4 FGH = $\frac{n}{2}$ (the angle at the centre of a circle is twice the angle at the circumference)

$m = 180 - \frac{n}{2}$ (the angles on a straight line add to 180°)

$\frac{n}{2} = 180 - m$

$n = 2(180 - m)$ or $n = 360 - 2m$

Exam practice

1 Students' own proof, for example,

let angle OYZ be labelled a.

Angle OZY = a (base angles in an isosceles triangle are equal)

Angle YOZ = $180° - 2a$ (angles in a triangle add to 180°)

Angle XOZ = $2a$ (angles on a straight line add to 180°)

Angle OZX = $\frac{(180° - 2a)}{2} = 90° - a$ (angles in a triangle add to 180° and base angles of an isosceles triangle are equal)

Angle XZY = Angle OZY + Angle OZX = $a + (90° - a) = 90°$

16.4 Angles in circles 2

Purposeful practice 1

1 $a = 41°$ **2** $b = 37°, c = 37°$ **3** $d = 83°, e = 28°$

Purposeful practice 2

1 $a = 88°$ **2** $b = 85°, c = 82°$ **3** $d = 88°, e = 89°$

Purposeful practice 3

1 $a = 75°$ **2** $b = 72°, c = 78°$ **3** $d = 126°$

Problem-solving practice

1 $x = 43°$ (alternate segment theorem)

BAC = 43° (angles subtended by the same arc are equal)

$y = 137°$ (angles on a straight line add to 180°)

2 $a = 38°$ (the angle on a semicircle is 90°)

$b = 52°$ (angles subtended by the same arc are equal)

$c = 128°$ (opposite angles in a cyclic quadrilateral add to 180°)

3 Yes. Angle ADC = 50° (angles on a straight line add to 180°)

So, angle ABE = 50° (angles subtended by the same arc are equal)

Therefore, angle BAD = 50° (angles in a triangle add to 180°).

Angle BAD = angle ADC, so AB and CD are parallel (alternate angles are equal for parallel lines)

4 Students own reasoning, for example,

Angle ADC + $x + y = 180°$ (angles on a straight line add to 180°)

Angle ADC = $180° - z$ (opposite angles in a quadrilateral add to 180°)

Therefore, $180° - z + x + y = 180°$

So, $z = x + y$

Exam practice

1 Angle BDF + angle BDO = 90° (the angle between the radius and the tangent is 90°)

So, angle BDF = $90 - x$.

Angle BCD = angle BDF (alternate segment theorem)

Therefore, angle BCD = $90 - x$.

16.5 Applying circle theorems

Purposeful practice 1

1 a 2   **b** -0.5

2 a $-\frac{1}{3}$ **b** 3

Purposeful practice 2

1 $y = \frac{2}{3}x + \frac{13}{3}$ **2** $y = -\frac{2}{3}x - \frac{13}{3}$

Problem-solving practice

1 a $y = -\frac{3}{4}x + \frac{25}{4}$ **b** $y = -\frac{4}{3}x + \frac{25}{3}$

2 $(0, -\frac{10}{3})$

3 $(\frac{34}{3}, 0)$

4 T $= (0, \frac{41}{5})$, R $= (\frac{41}{4}, 0)$

$\frac{1681}{40} = 42\frac{1}{40}$ units^2

5 P $= (-10, 0)$, Q $= (0, 5)$

PQ $= 5\sqrt{5}$

Exam practice

1 $y = -\sqrt{3x} + 2\sqrt{3}$

Mixed exercises D

Mixed problem-solving practice D

1 a i B   **ii** E   **iii** C   **iv** H   **v** I   **vi** F

b A: $y = -\sin x$ or $y = \sin(-x)$ D: $y = -(x + 2)^2(x - 2)$

G: $y = -\tan x$ or $y = \tan(-x)$

2 a 169.5 cm

b No, Jane may not be correct as the minimum height could be less than 160 cm since the graph is not completed to show the data for the shortest 4 students.

c 14 students have a height greater than 175 cm. 25% of 60 = 15 and 14 is less than 15, so less than 25% of the students have a height greater than 175 cm.

3 a $a = 5$ and $b = 3$ **b** (5, 3)

4 35.4°

5 3.60 m

6 a

Time, m (minutes)	Frequency
$0 < m \leqslant 10$	35
$10 < m \leqslant 15$	47
$15 < m \leqslant 20$	59
$20 < m \leqslant 30$	18
$30 < m \leqslant 50$	2

b 10.6 (1 d.p.)

7 $x < 1, y \geqslant -x - 4$ and $y \leqslant 2x + 2$

8 a and **b**

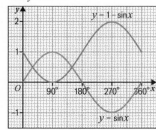

9 (3, −11)

Exam practice

10 a 11 kg

b

Weight of leopards

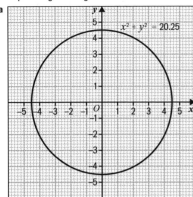

Weight (kg)

c Yes, Tom is correct as the median cougar weight is 58 kg and the median leopard weight is 55 kg.

11 a

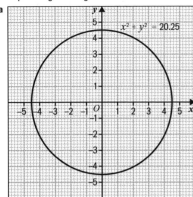

$x^2 + y^2 = 20.25$

b Approx $x = 1.7$ and $y = -4.2$ or $x = -1.1$ and $y = 4.4$

12 $x < -3, x > \frac{1}{2}$

13 a $2^3 + 2 = 10$, $3^3 + 3 = 30$, 17 is between 10 and 30 so the equation $x^3 + x = 17$ has a solution between 2 and 3

b $x^3 + x = 17$, so $x^3 = 17 - x$ and therefore $x = \sqrt[3]{17 - x}$

c $x = 2.44$ (2 d.p.)

14 $MN^2 = AC^2 = x^2 + x^2 - 2 \times x \times x \times \cos 45°$ (cosine rule on triangle ABC)

$= 2x^2 - 2x^2 \times \frac{\sqrt{2}}{2}$

$= x^2(2 - \sqrt{2})$

$\cos MBN = \frac{5^2 + 5^2 - x^2(2 - \sqrt{2})}{2 \times 5 \times 5} = 1 - \frac{x^2(2 - \sqrt{2})}{50}$

(cosine on triangle MBN)

17 More algebra

17.1 Rearranging formula

Purposeful practice 1

1 $k = \frac{5bct}{2a}$

2 $k = 5bt - 2a$

3 $k = \frac{5bt - 2a}{2}$

4 $k = \sqrt{\frac{5bt}{2a}}$

5 $k = \sqrt{5bt - 2a}$

6 $k = \sqrt{\frac{5bt - 2a}{3}}$

7 $k = t - \frac{2a}{5b}$

8 $k = 4\left(t - \frac{2a}{5b}\right)$

9 $k = \sqrt{t - \frac{2a}{5b}}$

10 $k = \sqrt[3]{t - \frac{2a}{5b}}$

11 $k = \left(\frac{t}{2a}\right)^2$

12 $k = \left(\frac{5t}{2a}\right)^2$

13 $k = \left(\frac{5bct}{2a}\right)^2$

14 $k = \left(t - \frac{2a}{5b}\right)^2$

15 $k = \left(t - \frac{2a}{5b}\right)^3$

16 $k = t^2 - \frac{2a}{5b}$

17 $k = (5bt)^2 - 2a$

18 $k = \frac{(5bt)^2 - 2a}{7}$

Purposeful practice 2

1 $a = \frac{3}{1 - b}$

2 $a = \frac{3}{4 - b}$

3 $a = \frac{3}{4 - 6b}$

4 $a = \frac{3 + c}{4 - 6b}$

5 $a = \frac{3b + c}{4 - 6b}$

6 $a = \frac{3b + c}{4 - 6b}$

7 $a = \frac{3b + c}{4 - 6b}$

8 $a = \frac{bc}{c - b}$

9 $a = \frac{2bc}{c - b}$

Problem-solving practice

1 $h = \sqrt{\frac{p - a}{a}} = \sqrt{\frac{p}{a} - \frac{\cancel{a}}{\cancel{a}}} = \sqrt{\frac{p}{a} - 1}$

2 a $h = \frac{6}{\pi}$　　**b** $r = \sqrt{\frac{210}{\pi}}$

3
$a^2 = b^2 + c^2 - 2bc \cos \theta$

$a^2 + 2bc \cos \theta = b^2 + c^2 - \cancel{2bc \cos \theta} + \cancel{2bc \cos \theta}$

$2bc \cos \theta + \cancel{a^2} - \cancel{a^2} = b^2 + c^2 - a^2$

$\frac{2bc \cos \theta}{2bc} = \frac{b^2 + c^2 - a^2}{2bc}$

$\cos \theta = \frac{b^2 + c^2 - a^2}{2bc}$

4 $h = \frac{A - 2\pi r^2}{2\pi r}$　　**5** $g = \frac{3}{h^2 - 1}$

6 John should multiply by $\frac{-1}{-1}$

7 Hannah has incorrectly expanded the bracket on the third line. It should say $xV + x = V$.

On the fourth line the right-hand side should be $V - xV$ not $V + xV$.

Exam practice

1 $t = \sqrt{3k^2 + 1}$

17.2 Algebraic fractions

Purposeful practice 1

1 $\frac{5x}{6}$

2 $\frac{11x}{4}$

3 $\frac{15x - 2}{6}$

4 $\frac{5x - 4}{2}$

5 $\frac{x}{2}$

6 $\frac{13x}{6}$

7 $\frac{5x + 4}{6}$

8 $\frac{5x - 8}{6}$

9 $\frac{-7x + 16}{6}$

10 $\frac{-3x + 10}{4}$

11 $\frac{5}{6x}$

12 $\frac{16}{9x}$

13 $\frac{2}{9x}$

14 $\frac{-14}{9x}$

15 $\frac{28}{15x}$

Purposeful practice 2

1 $\frac{xy}{6}$

2 $\frac{x^2}{6}$

3 $\frac{3x^2}{2}$

4 $\frac{9x^2}{10}$

5 $\frac{9xy^2}{10}$

6 $\frac{3xy^2}{2}$

7 $\frac{3x}{2y^3}$

8 $\frac{3}{2x\,4y^3}$

9 $\frac{3(y + 6)}{2x\,4y^5}$

10 $\frac{9(y + 6)}{2x\,5y^6}$

11 $\frac{27x\,2}{y^3}$

12 $\frac{y}{x}$

13 $\frac{x}{y}$

14 $\frac{3}{2}$

15 $\frac{9x}{2}$

16 $\frac{3x}{20}$

17 $\frac{20}{3x}$

18 $\frac{10x}{3(x + 5)}$

Problem-solving practice

1 $T = \frac{600x - 3000}{x(x - 10)}$

2 $\frac{4x + 3}{2} + \frac{x + 2}{4} = \frac{9x + 8}{4}$

3 a $\frac{20y}{x}$　　**b** $\frac{2x}{3y^2}$

4 a $\frac{7}{2x} + \frac{5}{3x} = \frac{31}{6x}$　　**b** $\frac{2x + 2}{3} - \frac{x - 5}{4} = \frac{5x + 23}{12}$

c $\frac{25x^2}{7y^3} \div \frac{10x^2}{21y^4} = \frac{15y}{2}$

Exam practice

1 $\frac{3x + 10}{10}$　　**2** $\frac{y^5x^2}{9}$

17.3 Simplifying algebraic fractions

Purposeful practice 1

1 3

2 $3(x - 6)$

3 $\frac{3}{x - 6}$

4 $3x$

5 $3x$

6 $x - 2$

7 $\frac{x + 3}{x - 2}$

8 $\frac{x + 4}{x - 2}$

9 $\frac{x - 4}{x + 4}$

Purposeful practice 2

1 $\frac{x + 1}{x + 4}$

2 $\frac{x + 3}{x + 2}$

3 $\frac{x + 3}{x - 1}$

4 $\frac{x + 1}{x + 5}$

5 $\frac{x + 3}{x + 4}$

6 $\frac{x - 1}{x + 1}$

7 $\frac{x - 1}{x + 3}$

8 $\frac{x + 3}{x - 2}$

9 $\frac{x - 1}{x - 2}$

10 $\frac{2(x - 2)}{x + 1}$

11 $\frac{x + 1}{x + 3}$

12 $\frac{2(x + 2)}{x - 5}$

13 $\frac{2x - 1}{2x + 1}$

14 $\frac{3x + 2}{x - 5}$

15 $\frac{5x + 2}{x - 4}$

Problem-solving practice

1 $x - y$; 12

2 $\dfrac{6x^2 + 10x + 4}{4x^2 - 2x - 6}$

$= \dfrac{3x^2 + 5x + 2}{2x^2 - x - 3}$

$= \dfrac{(3x + 2)(x + 1)}{(2x - 3)(x + 1)}$

$= \dfrac{3x + 2}{2x - 3}$

3 Students' own answers, for example,

$\dfrac{x^2 + 7x + 12}{x^2 + 2x - 8} = \dfrac{(x + 4)(x + 3)}{(x + 4)(x - 2)} = \dfrac{x + 3}{x - 2}$

4 $\dfrac{x^2 - 5x - 14}{x^2 - 49} = \dfrac{(x - 7)(x + 2)}{(x - 7)(x + 7)} = \dfrac{(x + 2)}{(x + 7)}$ **5** -2

6 a $\dfrac{x - 5}{x + 1}$ **b** $\dfrac{3}{x + 6}$ **7** $3 - x$

8 $= \dfrac{(9 - x^2)(x^2 - 3x - 10)(2x^2 + 14x + 24)}{(14x + 42)(x^2 - 2x - 15)(x + 4)}$

$= \dfrac{(3 - x)(3 + x)(x + 2)(x - 5)2(x + 4)(x + 3)}{14(x + 3)(x - 5)(x + 3)(x + 4)}$

$= \dfrac{(3 - x)(x + 2)}{7}$

Exam practice

1 $\dfrac{5x + 1}{3x - 2}$

17.4 More algebraic fractions

Purposeful practice 1

1 $\dfrac{10x + 7}{6}$ **2** $\dfrac{3}{2x}$ **3** $\dfrac{2x + 1}{2x\,2}$ **4** $\dfrac{(2x - 1)}{(x + 2)(x - 4)}$

5 $\dfrac{3x - 24}{(x + 2)(x - 4)}$ **6** $\dfrac{-1}{3x - 12}$ or $\dfrac{-1}{3x - 4}$ or $\dfrac{1}{12 - 3x}$ or $\dfrac{1}{3(4 - x)}$

7 $\dfrac{9x - 4}{4x}$ **8** $\dfrac{2x + 9}{(x + 4)(x + 1)}$ **9** $\dfrac{9x - 19}{(x + 4)(x - 3)(x + 1)}$

10 $\dfrac{3x + 13}{(x + 2)(x + 3)}$ **11** $\dfrac{x - 13}{(2x - 1)(x + 2)(x - 3)}$

12 $\dfrac{5x + 7}{(x + 1)(x - 1)(x + 3)}$

Purposeful practice 2

1 $\dfrac{x + 2}{x - 3}$ **2** $\dfrac{(x + 2)(x + 1)}{2(x - 3)}$ **3** $\dfrac{4(x + 2)}{5(x - 3)}$

4 $\dfrac{6}{x + 1}$ **5** $(x + 4)(x - 3)$ **6** $\dfrac{(2x - 3)(x - 4)}{(x - 5)(3x + 1)}$

Problem-solving practice

1 a $\dfrac{12x + 12}{x(x + 2)}$ **b** $\dfrac{42x - 78}{3x - 6}$

2 a $\dfrac{x + 1}{x + 4}$ **b** $\dfrac{1}{4}$

3 a $\dfrac{2x + 3}{(2x + 4)(x - 8)}$ **b** $\dfrac{2x + 3}{(x - 1)(x + 3)(x + 4)}$

4 $\dfrac{1}{x^2 - 25} + \dfrac{2}{x + 5} = \dfrac{2x - 9}{x^2 - 25}$

5 $x + 1$ and $x - 1$

6 $\dfrac{1}{3(x - 3)} + \dfrac{1}{(x - 3)(x + 6)}$

$= \dfrac{1}{3(x - 3)} \times \dfrac{x + 6}{x + 6} + \dfrac{1}{(x - 3)(x + 6)} \times \dfrac{3}{3}$

$= \dfrac{x + 6}{3(x - 3)(x + 6)} + \dfrac{3}{3(x - 3)(x + 6)}$

$= \dfrac{x + 9}{3(x - 3)(x + 6)}$

$A = 9, B = 3$

Exam practice

1 $\dfrac{x + 10}{x(x - 5)}$

17.5 Surds

Purposeful practice 1

1 $3(\sqrt{2} + 2)$ **2** $2(\sqrt{3} + 3)$ **3** $6(\sqrt{2} + 1)$

4 $6(\sqrt{2} + 1)$ **5** $2(2\sqrt{3} + 3\sqrt{2})$ **6** $2(2\sqrt{6} + 3\sqrt{2})$

Purposeful practice 2

1 $4\sqrt{3} + 8$ **2** $\sqrt{6} + 2\sqrt{2}$ **3** $\sqrt{6} - 8\sqrt{2}$

4 $6\sqrt{2} - 4$ **5** $30\sqrt{2} - 20$ **6** $30\sqrt{2} - 80$

7 $7 + 4\sqrt{3}$ **8** $79 + 20\sqrt{3}$ **9** $31 + 10\sqrt{6}$

10 40 **11** $292 - 160\sqrt{3}$ **12** -92

Purposeful practice 3

1 $\dfrac{1 + \sqrt{3}}{2}$ **2** $\dfrac{\sqrt{3} - 1}{2}$ **3** $\sqrt{2} - 1$

4 $\dfrac{4 + \sqrt{2}}{14}$ **5** $\dfrac{2 + \sqrt{2}}{4}$ **6** $\dfrac{6 + 3\sqrt{2}}{2}$

7 $\dfrac{6 + 5\sqrt{2}}{14}$ **8** $\dfrac{4 + 3\sqrt{2}}{4}$ **9** $3 - 2\sqrt{2}$

Problem-solving practice

1 a $8\sqrt{2}$ **b** $\dfrac{(-25\sqrt{2})}{2} + 2\sqrt{5}$

2 $16 + 17\sqrt{2}$

3 $8 + 5\sqrt{2}$

4 a $-1 - \sqrt{6}, -1 + \sqrt{6}$ **b** $\dfrac{2 + \sqrt{13}}{3}, \dfrac{2 - \sqrt{13}}{3}$

5 $\dfrac{4 + 3\sqrt{2}}{2}$

6 a $\dfrac{3 + \sqrt{3}}{3}$

7 a In the third line Andrew has multiplied $\sqrt{2} \times \sqrt{3}$ to give $\sqrt{5}$. It should be $\sqrt{6}$. In the fourth line he has cancelled the 2s. We can only cancel if all the terms in the numerator and the denominator have a common factor.

b $\dfrac{2 - \sqrt{2} - 2\sqrt{3} + \sqrt{6}}{2}$

Exam practice

1 $\dfrac{23 + 17\sqrt{2}}{49}$

17.6 Solving algebraic fraction equations

Purposeful practice 1

1 $x = 4$ **2** $x = \dfrac{3}{4}$ **3** $x = \dfrac{3}{4}$

4 $x = 11$ **5** $x = \dfrac{3}{10}$ **6** $x = 2$

7 $x = -3$ **8** $x = 3$ **9** $x = \dfrac{-11}{3}$

Purposeful practice 2

1 a $x = 5, x = -5$ **b** $x = 2\sqrt{2}, x = -2\sqrt{2}$

   c $x = 7, x = -7$ **d** $x = 4, x = -4$

2 a $x = 3.85, x = -2.85$

   b $x = 3.46, x = -2.46$ **c** $x = 4.39, x = -2.39$ **d** $x = 4.13, x = -3.63$

   e $x = 5.50, x = -6.00$ **f** $x = 4.90, x = -4.90$ **g** $x = -0.87, x = 6.87$

   h $x = 0.00, x = 9.00$ **i** $x = -19.00$

Problem-solving practice

1 2, 3

2 a $\dfrac{x}{3} + \dfrac{3x}{4} = 26$ **b** 24

3 $R_1 = 3000$ Ohms, $R_2 = 6000$ Ohms

4 a 0.5, 8

   b If $x = 0.5$ the $5\,\text{cm}^2$ rectangle would have a side of $-2.5\,\text{cm}$, which is impossible.

5 a 2nd line: Edmund has made an error expanding $-2(x + 1)$. It should be $-2x - 2$

   Final Line: He has added 5 to both sides but he should have subtracted 5 from both sides.

   b $x = 0$ or $\dfrac{1}{2}$

6 $x = +\sqrt{3}, -\sqrt{3}$

Exam practice

1 $x = \frac{1}{41}$

17.7 Functions

Purposeful practice 1

1 a 0 **b** 12 **c** 12 **d** 0.75 **e** $\frac{4}{9}$ **f** 8.16

2 a 4 **b** 3.4 **c** −12 **d** 3.3 **e** $\frac{73}{21}$

f $-\frac{489}{35} = -13.97$ (2 d.p.)

Purposeful practice 2

1 32 **2** 86 **3** 32 **4** 30 **5** 132 **6** 240
7 20 **8** 6 **9** 132 **10** −5 **11** −23 **12** −5

Purposeful practice 3

1 $f^{-1}(x) = \frac{x}{3}$ **2** $f^{-1}(x) = \frac{x-2}{3}$ **3** $f^{-1}(x) = 3(x-2)$

4 $f^{-1}(x) = \frac{3(x-2)}{5}$ **5** $f^{-1}(x) = 3x - 2$ **6** $f^{-1}(x) = \frac{3x-2}{4}$

7 $f^{-1}(x) = \frac{x}{4} - 3$ **8** $f^{-1}(x) = \frac{\frac{x}{4} - 3}{5} = \frac{x}{20} - \frac{3}{5}$

9 $f^{-1}(x) = \frac{\frac{7x}{4} - 3}{5} = \frac{7x}{20} - \frac{3}{5}$

Problem-solving practice

1 a i $\frac{2}{2x+3}$ **ii** $\frac{2}{3-x}$ **iii** $\frac{3x+11}{x+3}$

b $x = -3$ would mean that the denominator would be 0. Dividing by zero is undefined.

2 a $d^{-1}(x) = \frac{x+4}{5}$ **b** $x = 1$ **3** B, D

4 a −5, 4 **b** −4, 10 **5** −31.5

6 $a = -1 + \sqrt{6}, a = -1 - \sqrt{6}$ **7** −1, −7

8 95 **9** $a = 4, b = 3$

Exam practice

1 $a = 2, b = 14$

17.8 Proof

Purposeful practice 1

1 Students' own answers, for example, $\frac{3}{4} \times \frac{8}{3} = \frac{24}{12} = 2$

2 The answer will be the same, zero, when the numbers in the calculation are both the same.

3 Any number between −1 and 1, for example, $\left(\frac{1}{2}\right)^2 < \frac{1}{2}$

4 Students' own answers, for example, $3^2 + 4^2$ or $6^2 + 7^2$

Purposeful practice 2

1 Any number squared is positive or zero. When you add 4 to a positive number or zero, the answer will always be positive.

2 a 2

b When a is a non-zero integer, $2a$ is a multiple of 2 and so is an even number.

3 $m + n$ is **even**. $2(m + n)$ is **even** because **it is a multiple of 2**.

4 $2(2mn + n + m)$ is **even** because **it is a multiple of 2**.

Adding 1 to the previous expression will therefore be **odd** because **any number which is 1 more than a multiple of 2 is odd**.

5 $2n$ is a multiple of 2, and so is an even number. An even number plus an odd number (3) is always odd.

6 a Students' own answers, for example, $n, n + 1, n + 2$

b $(2n + 1) + (2n + 3) + (2n + 5) = 6n + 9 = (6n + 8) + 1$

$6n + 8$ can be written as $2(3n + 4)$ so is even. Adding 1 to it will make the result odd.

7 In any two consecutive numbers, one number will be even and one will be odd. The even number can be written as $2n$, where n is an integer.

Let us call the odd number m.

Therefore the product will be $2nm$, which is a multiple of 2.

So, the product of any two consecutive numbers is even.

Problem-solving practice

1 a 5 **b** The answer is still 5.

c $\frac{x + (x + 1) + 9}{2} - x = \frac{2x + 10}{2} - x$
$= (x + 5) - x$
$= 5$

2 a 2 is the 5th term in the sequence.

b Students' own answers, for example, $3^2 + 1 = 10$

c Students' own answers, for example, $3^3 + 4^3 = 91$

d Students' own answers, for example, $(-2)^3 = -8$ and $-8 < -2$. Any negative integer

3 $(2m)^2 + (2m + 2)^2 = 4m^2 + (4m^2 + 8m + 4)$
$= 8m^2 + 8m + 4$
$= 4(2m^2 + 2m + 1)$

$2m^2 + 2m + 1$ is an integer, so $4(2m^2 + 2m + 1)$ is a multiple of 4 and therefore in the 4 times table.

4 $4n^2 + 4n + 1 = 4(n^2 + n) + 1$

$n^2 + n$ is an integer, therefore $4(n^2 + n)$ is even. Adding 1 to an even number will always give an odd number.

5 $x^2 + (x + 1)^2 = x^2 + (x^2 + 2x + 1) = 2x^2 + 2x + 1 = 2(x^2 + x) + 1$

$(x^2 + x)$ is an integer, so $2(x^2 + x)$ is even. Therefore $2(x^2 + x) + 1$ will always be odd.

6 $A = 1$

7 $3x - a = 15$
$3x = 15 + a$
$x = \frac{15}{3} + \frac{a}{3}$
$x = 5 + \frac{a}{3}$

For x to be an integer $\frac{a}{3}$ must be an integer. For $\frac{a}{3}$ to be an integer a must be divisible exactly by 3 and so is in the 3 times table.

8 Height and length of base of large triangle = x, so its area is $\frac{1}{2} \times x \times x = \frac{x^2}{2}$

Height and length of base of small triangle = $\frac{x}{2}$, so its area is $\frac{1}{2} \times \frac{x}{2} \times \frac{x}{2} = \frac{x^2}{8}$

So, the area of the shape which is left is $= \frac{x^2}{2} - \frac{x^2}{8}$
$= \frac{4x^2}{8} - \frac{x^2}{8}$
$= \frac{3x^2}{8}$

9 $(2n - 2)^2 - (4n - 4)(n - 2) = (4n^2 - 8n + 4) - (4n^2 - 12n + 8) = 4n - 4$
$= 4(n - 1)$

Since n is an integer, $(n - 1)$ is also an integer and therefore $4(n - 1)$ is a multiple of 4.

Exam practice

1 $a^2 - b^2$ is the difference between two square numbers.

$a^2 - b^2 = (a + b)(a - b)$

$a + b$ is the sum of the two numbers. $a - b$ is the difference between the numbers. Therefore the sum of the two numbers multiplied by the difference between the two numbers will always be equal to the difference between the square of the numbers.

18 Vectors and geometric proof

18.1 Vectors and vector notation

Purposeful practice 1

1 a (8, 8) **b** (2, 8) **c** (8, 0) **d** (2, 0)
  e (9, 7) **f** (9, 8) **g** (5, 8) **h** (9, 4)

2 a $\begin{pmatrix} 3 \\ 4 \end{pmatrix}$ **b** $\begin{pmatrix} 3 \\ 4 \end{pmatrix}$ **c** $\begin{pmatrix} -3 \\ -4 \end{pmatrix}$ **d** $\begin{pmatrix} -2 \\ -6 \end{pmatrix}$ **e** $\begin{pmatrix} -5 \\ -3 \end{pmatrix}$ **f** $\begin{pmatrix} -6 \\ -2 \end{pmatrix}$

Purposeful practice 2

1 5 **2** 5 **3** 5 **4** 10 **5** 10 **6** $\sqrt{73}$
7 $\sqrt{68}$ **8** $\sqrt{65}$ **9** 8 **10** $\sqrt{65}$ **11** $\sqrt{68}$ **12** $\sqrt{68}$

Problem-solving practice

1 a $\begin{pmatrix} 4 \\ -3 \end{pmatrix}$ **b** 12 **c** A right-angled triangle

2 a $\begin{pmatrix} -2 \\ -7 \end{pmatrix}$ **b** (15, 13)

3 Students' own answers, for example, $\binom{2}{9}$

4 (3, 15) or (3, −9)

5 Students' own answers, for example, $\binom{7}{24}$

Exam practice

1
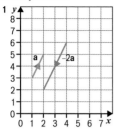

18.2 Vector arithmetic

Purposeful practice 1

1 a $\binom{4}{6}$ **b** $\binom{6}{9}$ **c** $\binom{1}{1.5}$ **d** $\binom{-2}{-3}$ **e** $\binom{-4}{-6}$

f $\binom{0}{-6}$ **g** $\binom{0}{-9}$ **h** $\binom{0}{9}$ **i** $\binom{0}{3}$ **j** $\binom{1}{-2}$

2 a
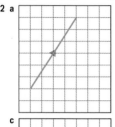
b
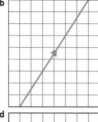

c
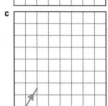
d
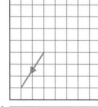

e
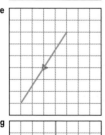
f
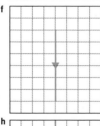

g
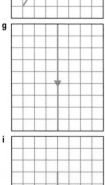
h

i
j
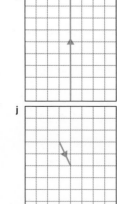

Purposeful practice 2

1 a
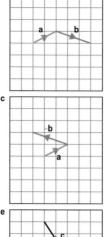
b
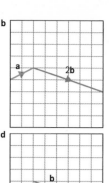

c
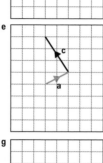
d
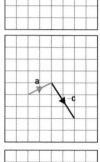

e
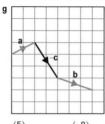
f
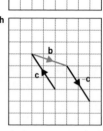

g
h
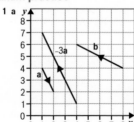

2 a $\binom{5}{0}$ **b** $\binom{8}{-1}$ **c** $\binom{-1}{2}$ **d** $\binom{1}{-2}$

e $\binom{0}{4}$ **f** $\binom{4}{-2}$ **g** $\binom{7}{-3}$ **h** $\binom{3}{-1}$

3 Students' own answers, for example, $\binom{4}{-3}$

4 $\binom{-4}{3}$

Problem-solving practice

1 a $\binom{6}{10}$ **b** $\binom{9}{15}$ and $\binom{3}{5}$

2 $\mathbf{a} = \mathbf{b}$

3 $\overrightarrow{SQ}$ is parallel to $\overrightarrow{TP}$. $\overrightarrow{SQ} = \mathbf{b} - \mathbf{a}$ and $\overrightarrow{TP} = \mathbf{a} + \mathbf{b} - \mathbf{a} - \mathbf{a} = \mathbf{b} - \mathbf{a}$

4 17.66

5 Students' own answers, for example, $\binom{2}{-12}$

Exam practice

1 a
b $\binom{-11}{4}$

18.3 More vector arithmetic

Purposeful practice 1

1 $\mathbf{b} + \mathbf{a}$ **2** $-\mathbf{b}$ **3** $-\mathbf{a}$ **4** $-\mathbf{a} - \mathbf{b}$ **5** $-\mathbf{a} - \mathbf{b}$

6 $\frac{1}{2}(-\mathbf{a} - \mathbf{b})$ **7** $\frac{1}{2}(\mathbf{a} - \mathbf{b})$ **8** $\frac{1}{2}(\mathbf{a} - \mathbf{b})$ **9** $\frac{1}{2}(\mathbf{b} - \mathbf{a})$

Purposeful practice 2

1 $\mathbf{h}$ **2** $\mathbf{k}$ **3** $\mathbf{h} + \mathbf{k}$ **4** $-\mathbf{k} - \mathbf{h}$ **5** $\mathbf{k} - \mathbf{h}$

Problem-solving practice

1 $\overrightarrow{AD} = 3\mathbf{b}$

$\overrightarrow{AD} = \mathbf{a} + \mathbf{b} + \mathbf{c}$

$3\mathbf{b} = \mathbf{a} + \mathbf{b} + \mathbf{c}$

$2\mathbf{b} = \mathbf{a} + \mathbf{c}$

$\mathbf{b} = \frac{1}{2}(\mathbf{a} + \mathbf{c})$

2 a $\frac{1}{2}(\mathbf{a} + \mathbf{b})$ **b** Yes, sides are 13, 9.19 and 9.19.

3 $\overrightarrow{JK} = \mathbf{b} + \mathbf{a}$

$\overrightarrow{IL} = \mathbf{a} + \mathbf{b} + \mathbf{a} + \mathbf{b}$

$= 2(\mathbf{a} + \mathbf{b})$

$\overrightarrow{IL} = 2\overrightarrow{JK}$, therefore parallel

Exam practice

1 a $\overrightarrow{QR} = 2\mathbf{a} + 5\mathbf{b}$ **b** $\overrightarrow{PR} = -2\mathbf{a} + 5\mathbf{b}$

18.4 Parallel vectors and collinear points

Purposeful practice 1

1 a $\begin{pmatrix} 3 \\ 4 \end{pmatrix}$ **b** $\begin{pmatrix} 4 \\ 5 \end{pmatrix}$ **c** $\begin{pmatrix} 3 \\ 5 \end{pmatrix}$ **d** $\begin{pmatrix} 4 \\ 4 \end{pmatrix}$ **e** $\begin{pmatrix} 1 \\ 0 \end{pmatrix}$

2 a $\begin{pmatrix} 6 \\ 10 \end{pmatrix}$ **b** $\overrightarrow{OY}$ because they both pass through the origin and are parallel.

Purposeful practice 2

1 a $\begin{pmatrix} 4 \\ 8 \end{pmatrix}$ **b** $\begin{pmatrix} 4 \\ 8 \end{pmatrix}$ **c** $\begin{pmatrix} 3 \\ 7 \end{pmatrix}$ **d** $\begin{pmatrix} 2 \\ 4 \end{pmatrix}$ **e** $\begin{pmatrix} 3 \\ 5 \end{pmatrix}$ **f** $\begin{pmatrix} 2 \\ 6 \end{pmatrix}$

2 a $\begin{pmatrix} 2 \\ 4 \end{pmatrix}$ **b** $\begin{pmatrix} 2 \\ 4 \end{pmatrix}$ **c** $\begin{pmatrix} 2 \\ 4 \end{pmatrix}$ **d** $\begin{pmatrix} 1 \\ 1 \end{pmatrix}$ **e** $\begin{pmatrix} 1 \\ 1 \end{pmatrix}$ **f** $\begin{pmatrix} 1 \\ 3 \end{pmatrix}$

3 a Yes **b** Yes **c** No **d** No **e** No **f** Yes

4 Yes **a** and **d**. No **b**, **c**, **e** and **f**.

5 a, **b** and **d**

Problem-solving practice

1 a Yes, LM is parallel to KL and they both go through point L.

  b $(-12, 14.5)$

2 $g = 60$ $h = 2$

3 Students' own answers, for example, $\begin{pmatrix} 1.25 \\ -1.5 \end{pmatrix}$

4 a Yes, because it will be a scalar multiple of **a**.

  b Yes, because it will be a scalar multiple of **b**.

  c Yes, because it will be a scalar multiple of **a**.

5 $x = 4$

6 Two possible student answers: $(4, 4)$ with the vector $\overrightarrow{PR} = \begin{pmatrix} 1 \\ 4 \end{pmatrix}$ and

  the vector $\overrightarrow{RQ} = \begin{pmatrix} 1 \\ 4 \end{pmatrix}$

  Or R $(6, 12)$ with $\overrightarrow{PQ} = \begin{pmatrix} 2 \\ 8 \end{pmatrix}$ and $\overrightarrow{QR} = \begin{pmatrix} 1 \\ 4 \end{pmatrix}$ meaning $\overrightarrow{PQ}$ is a scalar multiple and so is parallel.

7 a 10   **b** Multiple answers possible, for example, **a** = 11, **b** = 22

Exam practice

1 $\mathbf{a} + \mathbf{b} = \begin{pmatrix} 2 \\ 5 \end{pmatrix}$

  $3(\mathbf{a} + \mathbf{b}) = \begin{pmatrix} 6 \\ 15 \end{pmatrix}$

18.5 Solving geometric problems

Purposeful practice 1

1 a $\begin{pmatrix} 5 \\ 5 \end{pmatrix}$ **b** $\begin{pmatrix} 15 \\ 15 \end{pmatrix}$ **c** $\begin{pmatrix} -15 \\ -15 \end{pmatrix}$

2 a $\begin{pmatrix} 12 \\ 12 \end{pmatrix}$ **b** $\begin{pmatrix} 8 \\ 8 \end{pmatrix}$ **c** $\begin{pmatrix} -8 \\ -8 \end{pmatrix}$

Purposeful practice 2

1 $\mathbf{c}$ **2** $\mathbf{a} + \mathbf{b} + \mathbf{c}$ **3** $\mathbf{a} + \mathbf{c}$ **4** $\mathbf{a}$

5 $-\mathbf{a}$ **6** $-3\mathbf{a}$ **7** $-4\mathbf{a}$ **8** $\mathbf{c} - 4\mathbf{a}$

9 $\mathbf{b} + \mathbf{c} - 4\mathbf{a}$ **10** $\mathbf{b} + \mathbf{c} - 3\mathbf{a}$

Problem-solving practice

1 $\frac{2}{5}\mathbf{b} - 3\mathbf{a}$

2 a $\overrightarrow{AD} = \frac{5}{2}\mathbf{a} + 15\mathbf{b}$ **b** $(-28.5, 75.5)$

3 a $8\mathbf{a} - 3\mathbf{b}$ **b** 109.56

Exam practice

1 $\overrightarrow{MP} = -\frac{1}{2}\mathbf{b} + \mathbf{a} + k\mathbf{b} = \mathbf{a} + (k - \frac{1}{2})\mathbf{b}$

  $\overrightarrow{PN} = (1 - k)\mathbf{b} + 2\mathbf{a}$

  Comparing $\overrightarrow{MP}$ and $\overrightarrow{PN}$

  $2\overrightarrow{MP} = \overrightarrow{PN}$

  $2(k - \frac{1}{2}) = 1 - k$

  $2k - 1 = 1 - k$

  $3k = 2$

  $k = \frac{2}{3}$

19 Proportion and graphs

19.1 Direct proportion

Purposeful practice 1

1 $y \propto x$ y is directly proportional to x $y = kx$

  $x \propto y$ x is directly proportional to y $x = ky$

  $a \propto b$ a is directly proportional to b $a = kb$

  $b \propto a$ b is directly proportional to a $b = ka$

Purposeful practice 2

1 $y = 2x$ **2** $y = \frac{1}{2}x$ **3** $y = -\frac{1}{2}x$ **4** $y = -2x$

5 $a = 0.6b, a = \frac{6}{10}b$ or $a = \frac{3}{5}b$

6 $a = -0.6, a = -\frac{6}{10}b$ or $a = -\frac{3}{5}b$

7 $a = 0.6, a = \frac{6}{10}b$ or $a = \frac{3}{5}b$ **8** $a = 1.6b, a = \frac{10}{6}b$ or $a = \frac{5}{3}b$

9 $p = 0.3125q$ or $p = \frac{5}{16}q$ **10** $p = \frac{5}{74}q$

11 $h = \frac{1}{6}d$ **12** $h = \frac{5}{6}d$

Problem-solving practice

1 $m = 9.6$

2

x	-5	-2	0	7
y	7.5	3	0	-10.5

3 $r = -0.78z$ **4** £11.60 **5** $y = 28$

6 $\frac{t}{m} = \frac{2.66}{0.7} = \frac{3.42}{0.9} = \frac{6.08}{1.6} = 3.8$

  So $t = 3.8\,m$, which means t is directly proportional to m.

Exam practice

1 $s = 6$

19.2 More direct proportion

Purposeful practice 1

1 $y = \frac{1}{2}x^2$ **2** $y = \frac{1}{8}x^3$ **3** $y = 4\sqrt{x}$ **4** $y = -5a^2$

5 $y = -5a^3$ **6** $y = -5\sqrt{a}$ **7** $f = 0.09375g^2$ or $f = \frac{3}{32}g^2$

8 $f = 0.0234375g^3$ or $f = \frac{3}{128}g^3$ **9** $f = 0.75\sqrt{g}$ **10** $w = \frac{1}{9}t^2$

11 $w = \frac{1}{27}t^3$ **12** $w = \frac{1}{\sqrt{3}}\sqrt{t}$

Purposeful practice 2

1 $y = 0$ **2** $y = 0$ **3** $y = 0$

Problem-solving practice

1 $d = 10t^2$ **2** $V = 4.16r^3$ **3** $C = 36\sqrt{A}$

4 a 372 m   **b** 161 seconds

5 £27   **6** $y = 1\frac{4}{5}$ or $y = 1.8$

7 4.47 m   **8** 400 J   **9** $y = 56$

Exam practice

1 $y = \frac{8}{9}$

19.3 Inverse proportion

Purposeful practice 1

1 a 400   **b** −400   **c** 4000   **d** −4000
2 a 16 000   **b** 16 000   **c** 1 600 000   **d** 1 600 000
3 a 640 000   **b** −640 000   **c** 640 000 000   **d** −640 000 000
4 a $20\sqrt{10}$ **b** $-20\sqrt{10}$ **c** 200   **d** −200

Purposeful practice 2

1 a 0.4   **b** −0.4   **c** 0.04   **d** −0.04
2 a 0.016   **b** 0.016   **c** 0.000 16   **d** 0.000 16
3 a 0.000 64   **b** −0.000 64   **c** 0.000 000 64   **d** −0.000 000 64
4 a 2   **b** −2   **c** $0.2\sqrt{10}$ **d** $-0.2\sqrt{10}$

Problem-solving practice

1 $x = 2$ **2** $x = \dfrac{4}{9}$
3 a $y = \dfrac{5}{\sqrt{x}}$ **b** $y = \dfrac{5}{8}$ **c** $x = \dfrac{25}{49}$

Exam practice

1 a Graph D   **b** Graph C   **c** Graph B   **d** Graph A
2 $y = \dfrac{9}{x^2}$

19.4 Exponential functions

Purposeful practice 1

1 a

x	−5	−2	−1	0	1	2
y	0.031 25	0.25	0.5	1	2	4

b

x	−5	−2	−1	0	1	2
y	0.004 11...	0.111...	0.333...	1	3	9

c

x	−5	−2	−1	0	1	2
y	0.000 976...	0.0625	0.25	1	4	16

2 a

x	−2	−1	0	1	2	5
y	4	2	1	0.5	0.25	0.031 25

b

x	−2	−1	0	1	2	5
y	9	3	1	0.333...	0.111...	0.004 11...

c

x	−2	−1	0	1	2	5
y	16	4	1	0.25	0.0625	0.000 976...

Purposeful practice 2

1 a   **b**

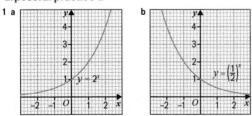

2 a In the graph of $y = 2^x$, y doubles every time x increases by 1.

b In the graph of $y = \left(\dfrac{1}{2}\right)^x$, y halves every time x increases by 1.

3 a, c

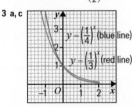

$y = \left(\dfrac{1}{4}\right)^x$ (blue line)

$y = \left(\dfrac{1}{3}\right)^x$ (red line)

b y values decrease fastest in the graph of $\left(\dfrac{1}{3}\right)^x$

Problem-solving practice

1 a 25 years   **b** $\dfrac{1}{8}$

2 a

Time, t (minutes)	0	1	2	3	4	5
Number of cells, n	1	2	4	8	16	32

b The number of cells is $n = 2^t$, which is an exponential function, and the number of cells is growing.

3 a In each match one player wins and one loses, so half the players lose and leave each round.

b

Round, x	1	2	3	4	5
Number of players, y	$32 = 32\left(\dfrac{1}{2}\right)^0$	$16 = 32\left(\dfrac{1}{2}\right)^1$	$8 = 32\left(\dfrac{1}{2}\right)^2$	$4 = 32\left(\dfrac{1}{2}\right)^3$	$2 = 32\left(\dfrac{1}{2}\right)^4$

The numbers are halving each time so the exponential function is of the form $y = ka^{x-1}$.
When $x = 1$, $y = 32$, so $y = ka^0 = 32$, and $k = 32$

c At the end of round 5 (after the match is played), there will only be one player. So 5 rounds are needed.

4 One of:
For exponential growth the price has to be multiplied by the same number every year, and the graph does not show this (with an example, between 2000 and 2005 the price was multiplied by 1.1 and between 2005 and 2010 the price was multiplied by 1.55 to 2 d.p.).

The graph is not the same shape as an exponential curve – it is not rising steeply enough and 2018 shows a reduction in chocolate price from 2017.

Exam practice

1 $(0, 1)$

19.5 Non-linear graphs

Purposeful practice 1

1 The speed gradually decreases as the time increases.

2

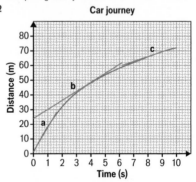

Car journey

3 a 16.7 m/s (accept between 15 and 18)
b 6.1 m/s (accept between 5 and 8)
c 3.3 ms (accept between 2 and 5)
4 a 12 m/s (accept between 11 and 13)
b 8.25 m/s (accept between 7 and 9.5)

Purposeful practice 2

1 Car A: distance travelled is 92 m.
Car B: distance travelled is 230 m.

Problem-solving practice

1 Between 17 and 21 m/s
2 Fred has not drawn the tangent. A tangent does not have to go through zero. It should touch the graph only once and not intersect the graph. He has found the average speed in the first 4 seconds instead.
3 Gradient = −3

Exam practice

1 a 540 m (accept 520–560)
b The estimate is an underestimate as the strips do not include all the area under the graph.

19.6 Translating graphs of functions

Purposeful practice

1

x	-2	-1	0	1	2
x^3	-8	-1	0	1	8
$y = f(x) + 1 = x^3 + 1$	-7	0	1	2	9

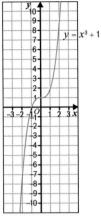

2

x	-2	-1	0	1	2
x^3	-8	-1	0	1	8
$y = f(x) - 1 = x^3 - 1$	-9	-2	-1	0	7

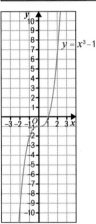

3

x	-2	-1	0	1	2
x^3	-8	-1	0	1	8
$y = f(x + 1) = (x + 1)^3$	-1	0	1	8	27

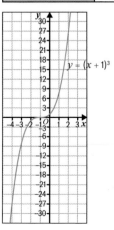

4

x	-2	-1	0	1	2
x^3	-8	-1	0	1	8
$y = f(x - 1) = (x - 1)^3$	-27	-8	-1	0	1

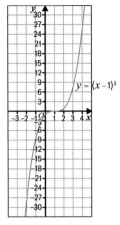

Problem-solving practice

1

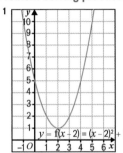

2 $y = (x + 2)^2 + 3(x + 2)$

3

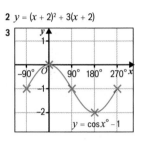

Exam practice

1

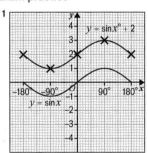

19.7 Reflecting and stretching graphs of functions

Purposeful practice 1

1

Point	Coordinates of reflection in x-axis	Coordinates of reflection in y-axis
A(3, 2)	(3, −2)	(−3, 2)
B(−2, 3)	(−2, −3)	(2, 3)
C(1, −4)	(1, 4)	(−1, −4)
D(−4, −1)	(−4, 1)	(4, −1)

Purposeful practice 2

1

x	-2	-1	0	1	2
$y = f(x) = (x - 1)^2$	9	4	1	0	1
$y = -f(x) = -(x - 1)^2$	-9	-4	-1	0	-1

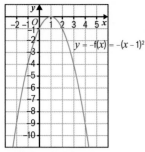

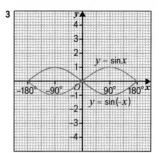

x		-2	-1	0	1	2
$y = f(x) = (x - 1)^2$		9	4	1	0	1
$y = f(-x) = (-x - 1)^2$		1	0	1	4	9

3

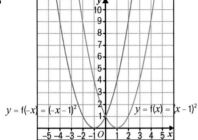

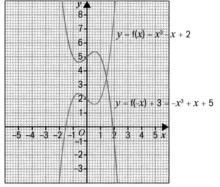

b $(1, 5)$

Problem-solving practice

Exam practice

1 P is $(4, -3)$

1 a

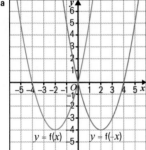

Mixed exercises E

Mixed problem-solving practice E

1 Angle OAD = $90°$ because the angle between a tangent and the radius is $90°$.

Angle AOC = $65°$ because the angle sum of a triangle is $180°$.

The reflex angle AOC = $295°$ because the angle sum at a point is $360°$.

Angle ABC = 147.5 because the angle at the centre of a circle is twice the angle at the circumference when subtended by the same arc.

2 $\begin{pmatrix} 3 \\ -1 \end{pmatrix}$

3 $\frac{1}{2}n(n + 1) + \frac{1}{2}(n + 2)(n + 9) = \frac{1}{2}(n^2 + n) + \frac{1}{2}(n^2 + 11n + 18)$

$= \frac{1}{2}(2n^2 + 12n + 18)$

$= n^2 + 6n + 9 = (n + 3)^2$

$(n + 3)^2$ is a square number so the sum of $\frac{1}{2}n(n + 1)$ and $\frac{1}{2}(n + 2)(n + 9)$ is always a square number.

b

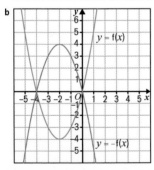

4 OP = OS = OR as they are the radii, so triangles POR and OPS are isosceles. Angle POR = $120°$ as it is double angle PQR (the angle at the centre of a circle is twice the angle at the circumference). Angle POS = half of $120°$ because OS bisects side PR, so angle POS = $60°$. Triangle OPS is isosceles so angle
OPS = angle OSR = $60°$. Therefore, triangle OPS is equilateral.

5 Chantal should have written -5 not $+5$ on the denominator in the second line of working as $-\sqrt{5} \times +\sqrt{5} = -5$ not $+5$

6 ROP bisects angle ORS and angle OPS because it is the line of symmetry of the kite.

So, angle OPS = $\frac{x}{2}°$ and angle ORS = $y°$.

Angle PDO and angle RGO are $90°$ because the angle between the radius and the tangent is $90°$.

Therefore, angle POD = $(180 - 90 - \frac{x}{2})° = (90 - \frac{x}{2})°$ and angle ROC = $(180 - 90 - y)° = (90 - y)°$ as angles in a triangle add to $180°$.

So, angle COD = $180° - (90 - \frac{x}{2})° - (90 - y)° = (\frac{x}{2} + y)°$ since angles in a straight line add to $180°$.

2

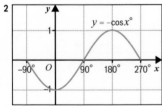

7 $x = \dfrac{y}{y+1}$

8 $y = f(-x)$

9 $\overrightarrow{AB} = -2\mathbf{p} + 2\mathbf{q}$

$\overrightarrow{PQ} = -\mathbf{p} + \mathbf{q}$

$\overrightarrow{AB} = 2\overrightarrow{PQ}$ so AB is parallel to PQ.

10 $p = 3$ and $q = -18$

11 $a = 90$, $b = -1$

12 3

13 Length scale factor $= \dfrac{x^2 - 4}{3(x - 2)} = \dfrac{(x+2)(x-2)}{3(x-2)} = \dfrac{x+2}{3}$

Area scale factor $= \dfrac{(x+2)^2}{3^2}$

$A = 9 \times \dfrac{(x+2)^2}{9} = (x+2)^2 = x^2 + 4x + 4$

14 $\dfrac{14\sqrt{3}}{3}$

Exam practice

15 a $\dfrac{5}{9}$ **b** $\dfrac{1}{20}$ or 0.05

16 $c = \dfrac{8b}{a - 24}$

17 a $q = \dfrac{16}{p^2}$ **b** $\dfrac{4}{5}$

18 Students identify two correct pairs of equal angles with correct reasons, for example, angle BAE = angle CDE because angles in the same segment are equal, and angle AEB = DEC because vertically opposite angles are equal. Therefore, the three pairs of angles are equal ABE = DCE, BEA = CED, EAB = EDC, as the angles in a triangle total $180°$. So triangle ABE and triangle DCE are similar.

19 $y = \dfrac{12}{x^4}$

20 Substitute $x = 2y + 15$ into $x^2 + y^2 = 45$ to give $(2y + 15)^2 + y^2 = 45$

$4y^2 + 60y + 225 + y^2 = 45$

$5y^2 + 60y + 180 = 0$

$5(y + 6)^2 = 0$

There is only one solution of $y = -6$ and $x = 3$, so the straight line with equation $x - 2y = 15$ is a tangent to the circle with equation $x^2 + y^2 = 45$

21 $\overrightarrow{BA} = \mathbf{a} - \mathbf{b}$, $\overrightarrow{BP} = k(\mathbf{a} - \mathbf{b})$, $\overrightarrow{MN} = -\dfrac{1}{2}\mathbf{a} + 4\mathbf{b}$,

$\overrightarrow{PN} = -k(\mathbf{a} - \mathbf{b}) + 3\mathbf{b} = (-k)\mathbf{a} + (k + 3)\mathbf{b}$

PN is a line segment of MN so yPN = MN for some number y

$y[(-k)\mathbf{a} + (k + 3)\mathbf{b}] = -\dfrac{1}{2}\mathbf{a} + 4\mathbf{b}$

Equating coefficients of $\mathbf{a}$ gives $-yk = -\dfrac{1}{2}$, therefore $ky = \dfrac{1}{2}$

Equating coefficients of $\mathbf{b}$ gives $(k + 3)y = 4$ or $ky + 3y = 4$

So, $\dfrac{1}{2} + 3y = 4$ and therefore $y = \dfrac{7}{6}$

$ky = \dfrac{1}{2}$ so $k = \dfrac{1}{2} \div \dfrac{7}{6} = \dfrac{3}{7}$

Index

O

opposite angles 213
opposite direction, vectors 239
opposite side of triangles 65, 175
outcomes 133, 137, 141
output sequences 23

P

parabolas 79, 201
parallel lines 159
parallel movement 105
parallel sides 85
parallel vectors 239, 243–244
parallelogram law 241
percentages 47–50, 145–146
perfect squares 123
perimeter 85–86, 91
perpendicular bisectors 109, 113, 207
perpendicular lines 77
perpendicular planes 179
Peterson capture-recapture method 185
pie charts 29
place values 3–4
planes 179
plans 99
plotting equations 197
points of intersection 197
polygons 57–60
populations
    comparing 195–196
    describing 195–196
    estimating size 185
position vectors 243
positive gradients 73
possibility space diagrams 133
powers
    of 10 11–12
    algebra 15–16, 221
    cubic function 205
    number 7–8, 11–12
    see also indices
pressure 149
prime factors 5–6
prisms 89–90
probability 133–144
    combined events 133–134
    conditional 141–142
    dependent events 141–142
    experimental 137–138
    independent events 139–140
    mutually exclusive events 135–136
    set notation 143–144
    tree diagrams 139–140
    Venn diagrams 143–144
proof 155–156, 235–246
proportion 45–46, 151–152, 185,
    247–260
pyramids 97–98
Pythagoras' theorem 61–64

Q

quadratic equations 79, 119–122,
    129–130, 203–204, 231
quadratic formulae 121
quadratic functions 119, 201–202
quadratic graphs 79–80
quadratic sequences 25
quadrilaterals 55–56, 213
quartiles 189

R

radii 95–98, 207–209, 215
radius of circles 83, 91–94, 169–174
range 37–38, 189, 195
rates of change 73–74, 147
ratios 43–46, 151–152
    comparing 43
    proportion 45–46
    right-angled triangles 65
    similar shapes 157
    unit ratios 43
    vector problems 245
real-life graphs 75–76
rearranging equations 231
rearranging formulae 221–222
reasoning 1–2, 145–152
recapture sample size 185
reciprocal functions 81
reciprocal graphs 81–82
reciprocal number 41
reciprocal of tangent 215
recurring decimals 49
reflections 101–102, 181, 259–260
regular polygons 59
representation of data 29–40
resultant vector 105, 241
right angle/hypotenuse/side (RHS)
    triangles 153, 155
right-angled triangles 61–68
roots
    algebraic formulae 221
    cubic function 205
    proportion 249
    quadratic 119, 201–204
    simplification 13
    see also cube root; square root
rotations 101–102, 181
rounding numbers 3, 87
rulers, constructions 109

S

sample space diagrams 133
sampling 185–186
SAS triangles *see* side/angle/side
    triangles
scalars 239
scale drawings 107–108
scale factor 103, 161
scatter graphs 33–36, 83
second differences 25
sectors 93–94
segments
    angles in 213
    line segments 77–78
semicircles 211
sequences 23–26

set notation 131, 143–144, 199
sets 135
shapes, similarity 157, 159
side/angle/side (SAS) triangles 153–156
side elevation 99
side/side/side (SSS) triangles 153–156
sides
    area calculation 175
    congruent triangles 153–156
    cosine rule 177
    enlargement 103
    similar shapes 157–160
similarity 157–162
simplification
    algebra 225–226, 231
    roots 13
simultaneous equations 125–130,
    197–198
sine functions 169–170
sine ratios 65
sine rule, areas 175–176
solid lines 199
solids 89, 99–100, 161–162
solution sets 199
speed 147, 255
spheres 95–96
spread measure 195
square roots 3, 13, 249
squaring brackets 27
SSS triangles *see* side/side/side
    triangles
standard form 11–12
statistical diagrams 29–30, 39–40
statistics 185–196
straight-line graphs 69–73
stretching graphs 259–260
subject of formula 21, 221
substitution 125, 233
subtraction, equations 125–128
surds 13–14, 229–230
surface area 89, 95–98
surface of plane 179
symmetry 201

T

tables 37–40, 187–194
tangent function 173–174
tangent ratio 65
tangents 209–210, 213–216, 255
terms
    algebraic formulae 221
    cubic function 81
    linear sequences 23
    quadratic equations 79
time, compound measures 147
time series graphs 31–32
transformations 99–114, 181–184,
    257–260
translations 105–106, 183, 257–258
trapezia 85
tree diagrams 139–140
triangle laws 239